Biography of the Great Indians

Biography of the Great Indians

Part- I

Parameshwar Hegde

Neha Publishers & Distributors

Delhi- 110002

Neha Publishers & Distributors

4832/24, Prahlad Lane, S- 207

Ansari Road, Daryaganj, New Delhi - 110002

Tel. : 011- 43570976, 23278261

Email- nehapubdistributors@gmail.com

First Edition, **2013**

ISBN: 978-93-80318-25-7 (Set)

978-93-80318-26-4 (Vol 1)

978-93-80318-27-1 (Vol 2)

Price: ₹ 1695/-

Laser Typesetting by: Tamalika Computers, Delhi

Printed at: Nagri Printers, Delhi

PRINTED IN INDIA

Published by Neha Publishers & Distributors, Delhi- 110002

Contents

Preface

A biography is telling the story of someone's life. This is a relatively old genre. of literary writing, the beginnings of which can be dated back to the Egyptian civilization. The artisans and writers of that age would write glorious tales of their pharaohs that were inscribed on the stone. And through the ages this has become an important literary form with immense educative value. Today, biographies of great personalities are not just written in books, but are also made in television series, as well as film.

The biographies of great men and women have been written and rewritten not only to glorify their great deeds, but also to provide great inspirational tales of achievement, sacrifice, courage, commitment and all those exemplary qualities that made them as farmed as they are. And India is a country that has produced innumerable-countless- men and women who have served great purposes and are written about in the history books.

The list as mentioned is beyond count, yet there are some of them who are placed on bookshelves and regarded as precious gems of Indian history. Some of them belong to the age when India was ruled by the kings and few queens who managed to gain the throne. And these vastly read biographies include those of the rulers themselves, as well as certain personalities who added to the value of that particular rule.

To ago a little further behind into the history of India, there are works written on the lifetime of Gods and Goddesses, literally putting them to the level of the human being, as if they had led a glorious life on earth. Well, this does bring onw question to the fore- are the Gods abd Godesses who are worshipped actually glorious human beings who did tread upon earth at one point ? Leaving that aside one can read the biographies of Lord Shiva, Lord Krishna, Allah, Jesus Christ, Guru Nanak and all other names and forms worshipped.

One question that people usually ask is why should one read biographies ? Well, the fact is that all those who have been penned about have achieved and magnanimous amount having made a difference not only to the contemporary society of their time, but for generations to come.

They have been ordinary people who have done extraordinary deeds, all in the name of humanity. And they all did so selflessly. They only knew one thing-they are here with a mission and for purpose. And they considered their prime duty to do some for the human race.

— Parameshwar Hegde

M.Sc.,M.A.

1

Mahatma Gandhi

The Gandhi is belong to the Bania Caste. Uttamchand Gandhi was the Grand father of M.K. Gandhi who was the man of principle.

Uttamchand Gandhi married a second time, having lost his first wife. He had four sons by his first wife and two by his second wife. The fifth of these brothers was Karamachand Gandhi. father of M.K. Gandhi (M.K. gandhi was born on Oct.2-1869).

Karamchand Gandhi (Kaba Gandhi) was for some time prime minister in Rajkot and then in Bikaner.

Kaba Gandhi married four times in succession having lost his wife each time by death. He had two daughters by his first and seccond marriages. His last wife Putalibai, born him a daughter and three sons, M.K. Gandhiji being the youngest.

Karamchand Gandhi was a lover of his clan, truthful, brave, and genious but he was short tempered. To a certain extent, he might have been given to carnal pleasures. Karamchand Gandhi never had ambition to accumulate riches and left his children very property.

M.K. Gandhi's mother Putalibai had a strong common sense. She was well informed about all matters of state and ladies of the court thought highly of her intelligence.

M.K. Gandhi passed his childhood in Porbandar.

Childhood and Child Marriage

When Karamchand Gandhi left Porbandar for Rajkot, M.K. Gandhi was seven years old boy. in Rajkot M.K. Gandhi was put into a primary school. He had been studied there about 5 years.

Here Gandhiji have been a medicore student. Then Gandhiji joined suburban school and thence to the high school. He was very shy and avoided all company. His books and his lessons were his sole companions. Literally Gandhiji was backward because he could not talk to anybody. He was even afraid lest any one should poke fun at him. Gandhiji had number of experiences in his childhood.

Once the Educational Inspector Mr. Giles had come on a visit of inspection. He had set the students to write some words. (Spelling execrise) One of the word was 'Kettle'. Gandhiji spelt it wrongly. His teacher tried to prompt him. with the point of his boot. But Gandhiji would not be prompted. Teacher wanted him to copy the spelling from his neighbour's slate. But Gandhiji never wanted to learn the art of copying.

Betrothal

Betrothal is a preliminary promise on the part of the parents, of the boy and the girl, to join them in the marriage, and it is not inviolable. it is the arrangement (agreement) purely between the parents and the children have no concern with it.

Gandhiji was betrothed thrice without his knowledge. He

was told that two girls were chosen for him had died in turn.

Gandhiji had two brothers. The first was already married. Parents were thinking about the marriage of second son. After that they were thinking about M.K.Gandhiji.

Marriage among Hindus is not simple matter. The parents of the bride and the bridegroom often being themselves to ruin over it. They waste their substance, and their time also.

Months are taken up over the preparations in making cloths and ornaments and in preparing budgets for dinners. Women used to sing themselves hoarse.

During the time of M.K. Gandhiji's marriage, his father was wounded in some incidence. But he put on a brave face, inspite of his injuries, he look full part in the wedding. The Marriage ceremony was ended with a grand success. M.K.G. performed his saptapadi and Kansar program happily.

Gandhiji and his elder brother, unwittingly hurled themeselves into the ocean of life. Kasturbai became his life partner.

The Twist in Life

As everybody experinces, Gandhiji found a little twist after his marriage. His severities were all based on love. He wanted to make his wife an ideal wife. His ambition was to make her live a pure life learn what he learnt, and identify her life and thought with his thoughts.

Kasturbai was illiterate by nature she was simple independent. She was not impatient of her ignorance.

As Gandhiji has written in his autobiography, he was passionately fond of his wife, Kasturbai. Gandhiji was willing to teach his wife, but lustful love left him no time. Another thing to be noticed was, he had to teach her against her will.

Gandhiji never dared to meet his wife infront of elders. Even at school he used to think about her. Their subsequent meeting was ever haunting him. Separation was unbearable. Gandhiji used keep his wife awake till late in the night with his idle talk.

According to Gandhiji "God ultimately saves him whose motive is pure."

In those days Hindu society had number of customs, apart from child marriages. Parents never used to allow young couples to stay long together.

During the first five years of Gandhiji's marriage life, they could not have lived together longer than an aggregate period of three years. They would hardly had spent six months together, when three would be a call to, Kasturbai from her parents.

At the age of 18 Gandhiji went to England; this meant a long and healthy spell of separation. When Gandhiji returnes from England, he heardly stayed with his wife not longer than six months.

Gandhiji as a Student

Gandhiji was not regarded as a dunce at the high school. He always enjoyed the affection of his teachers. Gandhiji never had a bad certificate of progress or character.

In those days, scholarships were not open to all, but reserved for the best boys amongest those coming from the Sorath division of Kathiawad.

Gandhiji had not any high regard for his ability. He used to be astonished whenever he won prizes and scholarships.

Once Gandhiji had received corporal punishment. He did not so much mind the punishment. As the fact that it was considerd his desert. He wept piteously. He was popular among boys, as he was a disciplinarian. Gandhiji never liked gymnastics. He requested Mr. Gimi (his teacher) to exempt him from gymnastics.

Once Gandhiji was convicted of lying. That deeply pained him. In the circumstance he had cried in deep anguish. He understood that, a man truth must also be a man of care. Afterwards he was always careful in school premises.

Gandhiji used to think that bad handwriting should be regarded as sign of imperfect education. He warned the Youngsters that, good handwriting is a necessary part of good education.

In Sanskrit language Gandhiji used to do very hard work. He worked in this subject with full care.

Gandhiji's friends used to talk themselves that, Persian is a very easy subject to learn. The word 'easiness' tempted him.

The name of teacher in which Gandhiji remembered in his life time was Krishnashankar Pandya. He taught Sanskrit to Gandhiji to his level best.

Gandhiji in his autobiography says that, in many occasions he was coward. He used to be haunted by the fear of thieves, ghosts and serpents. He did not dare to sit out of the doors at night. Darkness was a terror for him. It was almost imposible for him to sleep in entire darkness. He could not bear to sleep without a light in his room.

The great poet Narmad who wrote following stanza influenced Gandhiji very much.

Behold the mighty Englishman,

He rules the Indian small

Because Being a meat-eater

He is five cubits tall.

The poet very much influenced Gandhiji. He was thinking meat-eating was good, it would make him strong and daring.

One day Gandhiji was thinking about his first experiment of eating meat.

The Gandhiji's were Vaishnavas. His parents were particularly staunch Vaishnavas. In those days Jainism was very strong at Gujrat. The opposition to an abhorrence of meat-eating that existed in Gujrat among Jains and the Vaishnavas. This was the situation where Gandhiji was born and bred.

Gandhiji many times thought how to become dare and strong! what would be the solution ? He wanted to be strong and also his contrymen.

He was thinking about reformation. "The freedom movement" this word already had entered in Gandhiji's mind.

In his student life (for few days...) Gandhiji was fond of smoking. He and his relative were fond of smoking. They did not saw any goodness in smoking.

They were getting pleasure in emitting clouds of smoke from their mouths.

When Gandhiji and his few friends decideed to take poison in order to commit suicide.

Later they realized that it was not as easy to commit suicide as to contemplate it.

When Gandhiji, was grown up, he never desired to smoke and always regarded the habit of smoking as barbarous dirty and harmful.

Gandhiji decided to write out the confession, and submit it to his father, and to ask his forgiveness.

Then he wrote all the things on a slip of paper and handed it to his father. In the paper slip Gandhiji had confessed all his guilt. In the note he had asked adepuate punishment for his guilt.

Because of Gandhiji's clean confession, his father did not became angry. His confession made his father absolutely safe about him and increased his affection, beyond the measure.

Father's Death

When Gandhiji was sixteen years old his father was bed-ridden. He was suffering from a fistula. Gandhiji was nursing his father, with all type of service. Every day night he used to do massage his father's legs.

Gandhiji, never neglected the service to his father, when his father was feeling well he used to go evening walk.

Gandhiji's father was getting worse everyday. Ayurvedic Physcians had tried all their ointments, Hakims their plasters. An English surgeon had also used his skill. He was getting weaker and weaker. One day at mindnight it was about 11 p.m. Gandhiji's father's health become too worse, and he was passed away. Full family was under sorrow.

Gandhiji in his autobiography says that, "I Should have been massaging him and he would have died in my arms."

The Tour For England

In 1887 Gandhiji had passed his matriculation. His parents wanted him to pursue his studies at college after the matriculation. There was a college in Bhavnagar as well as in Bombay, since the former was cheaper Gandhiji decided to go there and join the samaldas college. He went there but he found himself entirely at sea. For him Everything was difficult.

Mavji Dave was a shrewd and learnt Brahman, and he was an old friend and an adviser to Gandhiji's family. He gave certain suggestions to Gandhiji regarding his further studies.

He told to Gandhiji, "The times are changed. And none of you can expect to succeed to your father's gadi without having had a proper education". Gandhiji realised the situation, and he got ready to start of for Porbandar. In those days there was no railway. It was a 5 day's bullock cart journey. Gandhiji took the permission of his uncle and he met Mr. Lely, in Porbandar.

Gandhiji had to take an oath that he would not touch wine, woman and meat. After this oath his mother gave him permission to go to England.

With the blessings of his elders Gandhiji started for Bombay. It was his first Journey from Rajcot to Bombay, leaving his wife with a baby of a few months.

Some People told that in June and July Indian Ocean becomes rough.

So Gandhiji stood for some time in Bombay. Gandhiji sailed at last from Bombay on the 4th of September. He did not felt any kind of sea sickness, but as the days passed, he became fidgety.

He felt shy even in speaking to the steward. In the ship while travelling. Gandhiji never took meals at table. He had his meals in his cabin. Gandhiji was astonished when he reached England. His inner voice told him that he had to finish three years in England.

The Faith in Vegetarianism

Gandhiji's faith in vegetariansim grew on him day to day. (It was in England).

He had studied thoroughly. Howard William's book, "The Ethics of diet." Gandhiji also studied, Dr. Anna Kingford's. The perfect way in diet. He knew well that all philosophers and prophets, from Pythagoras and Jesus down to those of the present age were vegetarians.

Dr. Allinson's writings on health, made Gandhiji to understand about the importance of vegetarianism.

Gandhiji always used to think about the oath in which he had given to his mother, infront of elders.

Gandhiji had number of friends in England. Among them a very few were close to Gandhiji. He had different experiences when he stood for some time in hotel Victoria.

Gandhiji was always to think that, he had not to spend his life time in England. He used to say himself, "What was the use of learning elocution ?"

Way of Living in London

Gandhiji developed vegetarianism, and also some other good habits, like meditation....etc in London. He used quite more time in correcting hair style. His hair was not soft. Everyday he used more time to keep the hair in a particular style.

Gandhiji had decided to take dancing lesson. He took 6 lessons in three weeks But it was beyond him to achieve anything like rhythmic motion. He could not follow the piano and hence found it impossible to keep time. Gandhiji's ambitions grew like the family of the recluse. He had invested some money in order to learn violin.

Gandhiji in his autobiography says that his experiments in dancing and a like marked a stage of indulgence in his life. He had kept strict watch over on his way of living. He decided to reduce his experises by half. This was because his accounts showed numerous items spent on fares.

Gandhiji had always taken conveyance whenever he went anywhere, and had to find extra time for walks. He had developed the habit of long walking which kept him practically free from illness throughout his stay in England and gave him a fairly strong body.

One of his friends in England suggested him to learn latin, which is an essential language to learn. He added latin is very much needed to learn and understand Law.

Later Gandhiji had acquired a taste for latin. Later Gandhiji Prepared to attend London Matriculation. The way of Gandhiji's life changed and his heart was more truthful, and his soul was full of joy. Gandhiji searched within him self the necessity for changes, both internal and external.

The Committee of The Vegetarian Society

In London Gandhiji was elected to the executive committee of the vegetarian society.

He never used to open his mouth in the committee. One of the members of the committee, Dr. Oldfield said to him. "You talk to me quite all right but why is it that you never open your lips at a committee meeting ? you are a drone.

The president of the vegetarian Society was Mr. Hills. He was a Puritan. The existence of the society depended practically on his financial assistance.

Dr. Allinson of vegetarian fame was a member of the Committee. Members of the Society used to think that, the vegetarian Society had for objects not only but also moral reform.

Gandhiji did not had more confidence to speak infront of

crowd. His last effort to make a public speech in England was on the eve of his departure for home. In the function Gandhiji invited his vegetarian friends for the dinner.

Gandhiji had hasitating nature whenvever he had to face strange audiences.

The Student in England

When Gandhiji was in England he found very less amount of Indian Students. It was a practice with them to affect the bachelor, even though they might be married. School or College students in England were all bachelors, studies being regarded as incompatible with married life.

Indian youths in England felt ashamed to confess that they were married. There was also another reason for dissembling namely that, in the event of the fact being known it would be inpossible for the young men to go about or flirt with the young girls of the family in which they lived. The flirting was more or less innocent.

The Indian youths on arrival in England indulge in these relations, which was quite natural to English youths. Gandhiji's cowardice was on a par with his reserve.

Once a girl took Gandhiji to the lovely hills round ventor. She was very cute and chattering away all the while. Gandhiji responded to her chatter, sometimes whispered 'yes' or 'no' or at the most, "Yes how beautiful"!

The girl was flying like bird, whilst Gandhiji was wondering, when he should get back home. At last they reached the top of the hill. How to get down again, was the question. At last Gandhiji reached the bottom, with all difficulties.

Many times Gandhiji felt himself that, God wanted to rid

him of the canker of untruth. Towards the end of his second year in England, Gandhiji came acoss two Theosophists brothers. They talked to him about Gita.

They were reading, Sir Arnold's translation, "The song celestial", They told Gandhiji to read the original one (Gita).

The brothers also recomonded Gandhiji to read "The light of Asia" Which was written by Sir Edwin Arnold.

During the mean while Gandhiji met, a good christian from Manchester in a vegetarian boarding house. He talked with Gandhiji about Christianity. Gandhiji narrated to him about his Rajkot recollections. The man who met Gandhiji was like a saint. He told that, drinking wine and eating meat are sins.

Though Gandhiji acquired a nodding acquaintance with Hinduism and other religions of the world,-he knew well that, it would not be enough to save him in his trials. He discovered the futility of mere religious knowledge in England.

Mother's Death

When Gandhiji was returned to his country, his elder brother, came to dock to receive him. Gandhiji was pining to see his mother. He did not knew that she was no more in the flesh to receive him back into her bosom.

His brother told him the sad news. Gandhiji did not give himself up to any wild expression of grief. Most of his cherished hopes were shattered. Gandhiji's grief was ever greater then over his father's death. The bad news was none the less a severe shock to Gandhiji. But he must not dwell upon it. So he tried to forget the incidence. Begining of New Life in India

When Gandhiji returned to India his elder brother had built high hopes on him. The desire for wealth and name and fame was great in him. He had a big heart and generous to a fault. This combined with his simple nature had attrected to him many friends.

He had assumed that Gandhiji should have a swinging practice and had in that expectation allowed the household expenses to become top heavy. Gandhiji had planned reform in the education of children. The necessity for food reform was obvious. tea and coffee had found their place in the house. Expenses went up. Every day new things were added.

Gandhiji's friends advised him to go to Bombay for some time, inorder to gain experience of the High Court.

Gandhiji went to Bombay and began a household with a cook. The cook was a Brahman. Gandhiji never treated him as his servent. As Gandhiji says in his biography, the cook was not good in cooking He would pour water over himself but never wash. His dhoti was dirty also his sacred thread.

In the beginning Gandhiji's expenditure was more, so he was planning to return to his native place. The study of Indian law was a tedious business, Expenses were mounting up every month. Even he had no courage to conduct any case.

In his first case Gandhiji charged rupees 30 Only, As he says in autobiography he got chance to Cross examine the plaintiffs witnesses. But unfortunately he could not able to conduct his first case. He felt though the whole court was looking at him.

Later Gandhiji was thinking to do a teacher job. He attended the interview also, but he was regretfully refused, Then Gandhiji returned to Rajkot.

Practice in Rajkot

With certain disappointment Gandhiji left Bombay, and returned to Rajkot. There he setup his own office.

Drafting applications and memorials made him to earn about 300 Rs per, month. His elder brother had been secretary and adviser to the late Ranasaheb of Porbandar he use to give number of advices to Gandhiji. Once he said, "You do not know Kathiawad, you yet know the world." Gandhiji never refused or neglected his elder brother's suggestions. He kept his self-respect promptly.

Once Gandhiji was insulted by an officer. He made Gandhiji to go out from his office. Gandhiji was no doubt at fault in having gone to that officer. But his impatience and overbearing anger were out of all proportion to his mistake.

Gandhiji began to learn something of the petty politics of the country, Kathiawad being a conglomeration of small states, naturally had it's rich crop of politicals. this atmosphere, for Gandhiji, appeared to be poisonous, and how to remain un scathed was a perpetual problem for him.

He was depressed a little bit; his brother was also observed it. If he wanted to a job, he had to free from the atmosphere of intrigue. But without intrigue a ministership or judgeship was out of the question. In the meanwhile Meman firm had wrote a letter to Gandhiji's brother. It was as follows.

"We have business at South Africa. Ours is a big firm and we have a big case, there in the court.

It has been going on for a long time, we have engaged the services of the best Vakils and barristers. If you sent your brother there, he would be useful to us and also to himself."

Gandhiji's elder brother discussed the matter, with him, he was tempted by the opportunity. Gandhiji felt that it was a tempting opportunity. He got ready to go to South Africa.

The Attraction of South Africa

When Gandhiji was ready to go to South Africa, he was not so much tense, as in the case of London. His mother was no more. This time Gandhiji had to leave his wife and newborn baby. Gandhiji was not ready to travel as deck passenger.

In April 1893 Gandhiji set forth to South Africa. After thirteen days, the boat reached, the port Lamu. The next port was Mombasa and then Zanzibar. As the ship was landing for a week, Gandhiji, wandered in the town and had a good time.

Gandhiji came on contact with the christian Indians living in Durban. After eight days he left Durban. A first class seat was booked for him. It was usual there to pay five shillings extra, if one needed a bedding. It was winter and winter in the higher regions in South Africa will be severely cold. Gandhiji began to think about his duty.

As Gandhiji says in his biography, "Pretoria Station in 1893 was quite different from what it was in 1914. The travellers were few." South African tour was unforgettable in Gandhiji's life as explained in his biography.

The First Voyage With Family

As Gandhiji felt, a Hindu wife regards implicit obedience to her husband, as the highest religion. A Hindu husband regards himself as lord and master of his wife, who must ever dance attendance upon him.

As Gandhiji marked, on account of child marriages amongest middle-class Hindus the husband will be literate whilst the wife remains practically unlettered. (100 years back).

Gandhiji became a teacher a for his wife. He was very

much interested in arranging the dress of his wife and children. According to his wife weared Parsi sari and the children Parsi coat and trousers. Gandhiji and his family observed a storm, during their voyage. it was on 18th December. No passengers are allowed to land at any of the South Africn ports. The Durban had become the scence of an unequal duel. On the Christmas day, with all other passengers, Gandhiji and his family have also celebrated !.

Gandhiji With Gokhale

From the very first day of Gandhiji with Gokhle made him completly at home. Gokhale treated him as though he were his younger brother. Same time Gokhale was also deeply impressed by the habits of Gandhiji. The habits like personal cleanliness perservance, and regularity and would often overwhelm him with praise. Gokhale never kept any thing private from Gandhiji. He introduced him to all the important people came to him.

Gokhale never wasted a minute. His private relations and friendships were all for public good. All his talks and reference only to the good of the country and were absolutely free from any trace of untruth or insincerity. Indians poverty and subjection were matters of constant and intense concern to him. Various People sough to interest him in different things. He used to give same reply to every body.

He used to say "You do the thing yourself. Let me do my own work, what I want is freedom for my country. After that is won we can think of other things. Today that one thing is enough to engage all my time and energy". Gokhale's reverence for Ranade was great. Ranade's authority was final in every matter and he would cite it every step. The anniversary of Ranade's death occcurred during Gandhiji's Stay with Gokhale.

Gokhale compared incidentally Ranade, Telang and Mandlik.

Gokhale eulogized Telang's charming style and Mandilk's greatness as a reformer. In those days Gokhale used to have a horse-carriage. Gandhiji did not knew the circumstances that had made horsecarriage a necessity for him.

Gandhiji had great regard for Gokhale that, he never strove with him. Once Gandhiji had asked Gokhale about terrible sacrifice offered to Kali in the name of religion.

Gandhiji had asked the question.

"Who would regard killing of animals as religion ?"

Gokhale had answered, "All places are equally good for us. The people are like a flock of sheep, following where leaders lead them. It is no business of us."

Gandhiji could not swallow this. He thought that, if the sheep had speech, they would tell a diffrent tale. The terrible sacrifice offered to Kali in the name of religion. Enhanced Gandhiji's desire to know Bengali life.

Gandhiji had read and heard a good deal about the Brahmo Samaj. He knew about Pratapchandra Mazumdar also. Gandhiji understood the distinction between sadharan Brahmo samaj and Adi Brahmo Samaj.

Having seen enough of the Brahmo samaj it was impossible to be satisfied without seeing Swami Vivekanand. So, with great interest Gandhiji went to Belur Math. But at that time swamiji was at his Culcatta house, lying ill and could not be seen.

Then Gandhiji ascertained the place of residence of sister Nivedita and met her in a Chowringhee mansion. Gandhiji used to divide his day between seeing the leading people in Culcatta and studying the religious and public institutions of the City.

Gandhiji's stay under the roof of Gokhale made his work

in Culcatta very easy, and brought him in to touch with the foremost Bengali families and was the biginning of his intimate contact with Bengal. When Gandhiji returned from Burma he took leave of Gokhale.

The Unbroken Third Class Tours

In travelling third class Gandhiji mostly preferred the ordinary to the mail trains, as he knew that the latter were more crowed and the fares in them higher. The third class compartments were practically as dirty and the closet arrangements as bed.

The indifference of the railway authorities to the comforts of the third class passengers combined with the dirty and in considerate habits of the passengers themselves, makes third class travelling a trial for a passenger of cleanly ways.

These unpleasant habits commonly include throwing of rubbish on the floor of the compartment smoking at all hours and in all places. Betel and tobacco chewing, converting the whole carriage into a spittoon. In 1918-19 Gandhiji's health was upset As he says in biography, this illness had unfortunately compelled him practically to give up the third class travelling.

Gokhale's Advice

Gokhale was very much anxious that Gandhiji should settle down in Bombay. In those days the public work was meant by congress work. Gandhiji liked Gokhle's advice, but he was not confident of success as a barrister. The unpleasant memories of past failure were yet with him. His well wisher Kevalram Dave told him that, "winning or losing is no concern of yours, You will simply try your best," Gandhiji had got maximum experience in South Africa.

Gandhiji had decided to start work first at Rajkot. Kevalram Mavji Dave who had induced Gandhiji to go to England was there, and he started, Gandhiji straightway with three briefs.

Two of them were, appeals before the Judicial Assistant to political agent in Kathiawad, and one was an original case in Jamnagar. After some day's Gandhiji won the case and got some confidence. This inspired a hope in him that he might not fail in Bombay.

One of Gandhiji's friend had wired like this, "I should put in an application for the camp to be some other station because of the plague at Veraval. But Gandhiji had no fear about plague. He managed his friend's wishes.

Growing Simplicity in Gandhiji's Life

Knowingly or unknowingly Gandhiji had developed simplicity. With the growing simplicity of Gandhiji's life his dislike for medicines also steadily increased.

While practising in Durban Gandhiji suffered for some time from debility and rheumatic inflammation. Dr. P.J. Mehta who had came to see Gandhiji gave him the treatment, and he got well.

Gandhiji was bound by a vow (giving up all the milks. The vow of course meant the giving up all the milks, he had the vow that giving up mother cow and mother buffalo).

However Gandhiji decided to take goat's milk, when he started taking mother goat's milkk. The spirit of his vow destroyed. A variety of incidents in Gandhiji life have conspired to bring him in close contact with people of many creeds, and many communities. He had feelings of equal respect on strangers, countrymen and foreigners.

When Gandhiji was practising in Durban his office clerks often stayed with him, and there were among them Hindus and Christians. Some time Gandhiji used to think that, the wife was the object of her husband's lust born to do her husband's behest rather than a helpmate, a comrade and a partner in the husband's joys and sorrows.

Gandhiji in his autobiography says like this, (about his wife, Kasturbai). "Willingly or unwillingly, consciously she has considered herself blessed in following in her husband's footsteps."

There was a wide difference between Gandhiji and his wife but she never expressed any kind of bad feeling. They had a life of contentment happiness and progress. Kasturbai herself does not knew whether she has any ideals, independently of her husband.

The Untouchables

Some of the Classes which render us the greatest social service, but which we Hindus have chosen to regard as 'Untouchables' were relegated to remote quarters of a town or a village, called in Gujarati dhedvado, the name itself had a bad odour. Gandhiji never liked Untouchability.

The word coolie in India means only a porter or hired workman, but as Gandhiji says, in South Africa it had contemptuous connotation, It means what a pariah or an untouchable means to us, and the quarters assigned to the coolies were known as coolie locations.

The criminal negligence of the Municipality and the ignorance of the Indian, settlers conspired to render the location thoroughly insanitary, This was the condition in India.

Gandhiji speaks about the feeling of untouchability in

Johannesburg,-in his biography. He also talks about the black plague in Africa. The black plague enhanced Gandhiji's influence with the poor Indians and increased his business and his responsibility.

The Serious Illness of Kasturbai

Kasturbai, about three time narrowly escaped from death, through serious illness. The curse were due to household remedies.

First time during her illness satyagraha was going On. At that time she had frequent haemorrhage. A medical friend of Gandhiji, adviced him, for a surgical operation. Kasturbai was extremely emaciated, and the doctor had to perform, the operation without chloroform.

The operation was successful, but Kasturbai had to suffer much pain. However she went through it with wonderful bravery.

The doctor and his wife who nursed Kasturbai were all in good attention. This incident happend in Durban. When doctor gave Gandhiji to leave to go to Johannesburg he went difficultily.

In a few days, Gandhiji received a letter to the effect that, Kasturbai was in worse condition, and too weak to sit up in bed, and had once become unconscious.

Then Gandhiji took the train for Durban. The doctor said like this.

"I had already given Mrs. Gandhiji beef. tea when I telephoned to you."

Gandhiji became upset and told.

'Now, doctor I call this a fraud.'

Doctor answered like this; "No question of fraud in

prescribing medicine or diet for a patient. Infact we doctors consider it a virtue to deceive patients or their relatives if thereby we can save our patients.

the doctor was a good man and he was the personal friend of Gandhiji. Doctor and his wife had laid Gandhiji under debt of gratitude.

Kasturbai needed no cheering up. On the contrary she comforted her husband, saying "Nothing will happen to me Don't worry." After few days Kasturbai recovered slowly.

The Dieting Habit

According to Gandhiji the people who make light of dietetic restrictions and fasting are as much in error as those who stake their all on them. Gandhiji experience taught him that, for those whose minds are working towards self-restraint, Dietetic restrictions and fasting are very helpful.

Gandhiji gave up milk and cereals and started on the experiment of a fruit diet. In the experiment of fasting Mr. Kallenbach also joined Gandhiji. Having been born in a vaishnava family Gandhiji was not new for 'Ekadashi.' (In india.)

Gandhiji was experimenting about the total fasting that is allowing himself only water. When Gandhiji Started this experiment on himself, the Hindu month of Shravan and the Islamic month of Ramzan happened to coincide.

Mr. Kallenbach was also joined Gandhiji. The other members who joined with them were also from satyagrahi families. The result of the experiment was interesting. All were convinced of the value of fasting and a splended esprit de corps grew up among them. The famous verse from the second chapter of the Bhagavadgita is worth nothing. "For a man who is fasting his senses outwardly, the sense-objects disappear Leaving the yearning behind; but when He has seen the Highest Even the yearning disappears.'

Fasting and similar discipline is one of the means to the end of self-restraint; but it is not all if physical fasting is not accompanied by mental fasting it is bound to end in hypocrisy and disaster. When Gandhiji was fasting many number of friends had also followed him, and learnt the technique of self-restraint.

The Culture of The Heart-Training

As the farm grew, it was found necessary to make some provision for the education of it's boys and girls. There were among these Hindu, Musalman, Parsi and Christian boys and some Hindu girls.

Gandhiji thought that, there is no need of special teachers for them. At that time the qualified Indian teachers were scarce.

(The explanation refers to the place which was 21 K.M. away from Johannes burg.)

All the young people had not with Gandhiji because they had been brought up in different conditions and environments. they did not belong to the same religion.

Gandhiji gave importance to the culture of the heart training. Gandhiji was willing to teach every one of the youngsters some useful manual vocation.

In the training school. Gandhiji thought to teach about carpentry, cooking etc., Literary training was a more difficult matter. Gandhiji provided three periods for the literary training. Hindi, Tamil, Gujarati, Urdu... Were used to taught in the Classes.

The Tamil boys were all born in South Africa, So they

knew very little about Tamil, they did not know script at all.

The Tamilians who did not knew English came to Gandhiji. The youngsters did not knew, writing English. But Gandhiji thought that he had very little to teach them.

The Spiritual training of the boys was a much more difficult matter, than, their physical and mental training. Some boys were bad and unruly. Gandhiji had to show them good directions.

Gandhiji was thinking if good children are taught together with bad ones and thrown in to their company they will lose nothing. The experiment was conducted under the watchfull care of their parents and guardians.

Gandhiji realized that, the education and training was very difficult, task. However Gandhiji and his friends like, Mr. Kallenbach, were able to maintain the students.

The Satyagraha Ashram

The Satyagraha Ashram was founded on 25th of may 1915. The question of untouchability was always rising in Gandhiji's mind.

Once his vaishnava friend had asked him the question, "where is the untouchable who will satisfy your condition?" Gandhiji decided to found the Ashram at Ahmedabad. Gandhiji hired, sit. Jivanlal Desai's bungalow, for the purpose of Ashram. The aim of the ashram was, the devotion to truth and for the search of truth. For the conduct of the Ashram a code of rules and observances was very much needed.

One day a letter came to Gandhiji saying, "A humble and honest untouchable family is desirous of joining your Ashram will you accept them ?"

Gandhiji was perturbed. He had never expected that an untouchable family. (The letter had came from Amritlal Thakkar.)

Gandhiji wrote a letter to Amritlal Thakkar, That he had no objection to accept that family. But Gandhiji had to face number of problems in accepting that family.

Fasting

After giving up milk and cereals Gandhiji started on the fruit diet. He commenced fasting as a means of self retraint. In this Mr. Kallenbach also joined him. Gandhiji had been used to fasting now and again, but for purely health reasons.

Having been born in Vaishnava family and of mother who was given to keeping all sorts of vows, Gandhiji had observed., the Ekadashi and other fasts, but in doing so, he had merely copied his mother and sought to please his parents. In that time Gandhiji did not understand nor did he belived in the efficacy of fasting.

When Gandhiji began his experiment on fasting, Hindu month Shravan and Islam month Ramzan happen to coincided. During that month Gandhiji had persuaded the Islam youngsters, to observe the Ramzan fast.

He decided that the Hindu and the Parsi youngsters did not copy the Musalman ones in every detail. The Musalman youngsters had to wait for their breakfast until sunset where as the others did not do so. The result of these experiments was that all were convinced of the value of fasting, and splended esprit de corps grew up among all.

The Illness

Gandhiji used to take, groundnut butter and lemons. He

knew well that, eating more butter was injureous to health. But Gandhiji was taking more. This caused dysentery. Firstly Gandhiji did not took more care about his health. He Continued his work in the Ashram. He scarcely used to take medicine. The next day, Gandhiji had to Omit all the food he had taken in the morning. Gandhiji had to go to Nadiad, He walked with great difficulty to Sabarmati station, a distance of only ten furlongs.

Sir, Vallabhai also joined him. But Gandhiji had never shown any type of expression of pain. They reached nadiad at about ten 'O' clock The Hindu Anathashram was few furlongs away.

Gandhiji's health was too worse at the movement, Dysentery was began. Gandhiji had been trying hydropathy which gave him some relief, but it was hard job to, build up the body. Doctors gave different Suggestions to Gandhiji. But he had to withstand the pain, because of uncertain illness. One night, Gandhiji had to face too much pain because of his ill health.

The Kheda Campaign

The Kheda campaign was launched While the deadly war in Europe was still going on. At that time the viceroy had invited various leaders to a war conference in Delhi.

Gandhiji had also been urged to attend the conference. He had already referred to the cordial relations between Lord Chelmsford, the Viceroy and himself.

In response to the invitation Gandhiji went to Delhi. He had, however objections to taking part in the conference, the principle one being the exclusion from it of leaders like the Ali Brothers. They were then in jail. Gandhiji had met them only once or twice.

Gandhiji was seeking the friendship of good Musalmans,

and was eager to understand the Musalman mind, Through contact with their purest and most patriotic representatives. Gandhiji therefore never needed any pressure to go with them wherever they took him, in order to get into intimate touch with them.

Gandhiji had realized early enough in South Africa that there was no genuine friendship between the Hindus and Musalmans. Gandhiji never missed a single opportunity to remove obstacles in the way of unity. It was not in his nature to placate any one by adulation or at the cost of self respect. For Gandhiji argument was not new. The Viceroy was very keen on his supporting the resolution about recruiting. Many Indian leaders congratulated Gandhiji. the one word (Hindustani), that Gandhiji uttered at the conference had considerable significance. It was impossible for him to forget either the conference or the resolution, he supported.

Later Gandhiji expressed his regret for the exclusion from the conference, of leaders like Lokamanya Tilak and The Ali Brothers and stated the people's minimum political demands and also the demands of the muslims on account of the situation created by the war.

Himalyan Miscalculation

Almost immediately after the Ahmedabad meeting, Gandhiji went to Nadiad. Let us try to understand what the Himalayan Miscalculation was.

Before one can be fit for the practice of civildis-obedience. One must have rendered a willing and respectful obedience to the state laws. For the most laws out of fear of penalty not involve in moral principle. For instance, an honest respectable man will not suddenly take to stealing, whether there is a law against stealing or not.

According to Gandhiji "A satyagrahi obeys the laws of society intelligently and of his own free will. Because he considers it to be his sacred duty to do so. It is only when a person has obeyed the laws of society, that he is in a position to judge as to which particular rules are good and just and which unjest and iniquitous.

Only then does the right accrue to him of the civil dis obedience of certain laws in well defined circumstances.

The Fateful Evening

The day was Friday 30 January 1948 the time about 5 'O' clock in the evening. Emerging with is companions Gandhiji stepped briskly in to a cold winter evening and hurried to his place of prayer, where the usual crowd of devotees awaited him.

The darkness was slowly stepping. Godse a girm faced man stood up few feet away from Gandhiji without any hesitation he fired four shots at point blanks range.

Gandhiji, was mortally wounded.

Within another hour the tragic news was sent speeding through out India and around the world. Every one wept unashemedly little children, grown-up men and women, rich and poor, those in high places and the humble folk in their huts and hovels.

In the death of Gandhiji each human being seemed to experience a death of part of himself. If we elect to walk along the Gandhian way and be equal to his great heritage, will we, can we, realise that, instead of worshipping him as a God, we should study the Mahatma as a man and follow him as a leader?

2

Bhagat Singh

Family History

Sardar Arjun Singh of Banga village, which was in Layalpur district of Punjab Province, was anti-British. He was a farmer of a good standing, and a respected figure of the village.

Sardar Kishan Singh was the son of Arjun Singh. On 27th September 1907 a son was born to Mrs, Vidyawati the wife of Sardar Kishan Singh. Sardar Arjun Singh celebrated the birth of his grandson with the members of his family, relatives, and village folk.

Then, India was suffering the brutal British rule. The natives were fighting within themselves. Sardar Arjun Singh's son's were leading the revolt against British.

Arjun Singh's second son Ajit Singh was the main force of the militant activity. He had set up a society named, Bharat Mata, his younger brother Swaran Singh was it's publicity manager. He had toured the villages to fan the fire of the revolt.

One of the freedom movement was leading by the Congress. It was prominent in Bengal. The second movement was prevalent in punjab. (Now it is in Pakistan).

The Bengal movement was using the tactics of demonstrations, protest marches, boycott of British goods and adoption of swadeshi. British administration arrested Ajit Singh. The responsibility of the family fell on Kishan Singh's shoulders.

But he too was on the hit list of the authorities. So the family adviced him to flee to Nepal.

Sardar Kishan Singh tried to escape to Nepal with two other activists namely Nand Kishore Mehta and Sufi Amba Prasad. But they could evade the British police. The three were arrested and sent to jail. The youngest brother Sardar Swaran Singh had already been nabbed. that is how the three brothers were in jail when the baby arrived in the family.

Although Sardar Arjun Singh was not overtly in active militant politics yet it was no secret that he passively despised, British and approved to the activities of his sons.

The new born, later to be named Bhagat Singh brought some luck to the harassed family. His father and two uncles were released from the prisons on bail. Sardar Kishan Singh and Sardar Swaran Singh had been in Lahore Central Jail. They came home to join celebrations.

Ajit Singh was too dangerous for British to be allowed to run loose. So Kishan Singh wrote a letter to his brother advising him to escape. Ajit Singh slipped away to germany Via Iran, Turkey and Austria.

The Youngest Sardar Swaran Singh was rearrested shortly after his release. He was put to hard labour and tortured. The ill treatment and poor diet led to his falling victim T.B. After release from the prision on health grounds, the family saw him die slowly on the sick bed.

Ajit Singh's wife Harnam Kaur was forced to live like widow as her husband stayed away from her to evade, the British police. Mean-while the Congress was spreading it's influence fast and emerging as the biggest challenge to the British rulers.

The Childhood

Sardar Arjun Singh's wife jai Kaur was sure that her new born grand child was a lucky mascot as his arrival was followed by the release of her three sons from the prisons. She had decided to call the baby, Bhagat. Her daughter-in-law also liked the name.

The Six year old elder brother of Bhagat never ceased squealing in delight at the sight of his baby brother. The baby's full name became "Bhagat Singh". The little Bhagat Singh started growing up in the family that was suffering the British brutalities. Often the hatred was laced with seething anger.

The talks of the family members would invariably come around to the slavery of the country, freedom politics. Patriotic fervour was the only painkiller they had such atmosphere was bound to influence the growing Bhagat. He had seen his youngest uncle, die slowly before his eyes. The daring deeds of his another uncle Ajit Singh amazed the child.

The child wished to meet Ajit Singh. But he never did. "Bhagat Singh' from his childhood itself, imbibed the Anti-British feelings.

Bhagat would often wife the tears of the aunt Harnam Kaur and console her. He used to say, "Don't grieve aunt dear. Pray for my becoming youngman fast. I will wage a war against the British and bring back uncle Ajit to you". The aunt would hold him tighter and weep over whelmed. Many times Bhagat heard the sobs and the cries of his sorrowing aunts.

The boy was coming up with growing hatred for British rulers. His aunts adored Bhagat. They found great solace in fondling cuddling him.

Planting Guns

It was sowing and planting time. Kishan Singh was going to his fields to supervise the planting. The five year old Bhagat arrived on the scene to grab his father's finger. He too wanted to go to the fields. On the way they were joined by an old friend, Nand Kishore Mehta.

They walked on foot discussing the political situation. Along walked Bhagat thinking of his own little affairs. In the field the kid let go of his father's finger and ran off. He was stumbing picking himself up and then running again towards the far corner of the field. The field workers watched in amusement. Father looked indulgently at his son's prank. Then workers got busy in their work.

After some times Kishan Singh looked into the direction of his son had fled. He was looking hard as if puzzled. Nand Kishore automatically followed his gaze. Bhagat was bent on his knees, performing some task in dead seriousness. lost to the world.

Bhagat had ignored the surroundings. He was too busy planting small sticks of some dry grass stalks. Kishan Singh and Nand Kishore watched in amusement. The kid was working very feverishly in great excitement.

Nand Kishore asked, What are you doing son ?" Bhagat answered seriously, "I am planting guns". "Guns ! what for ?

Kishan Singh asked. Bhagat said, "to fight the British. They keep my uncle away. I must drive the white men away."

The two elders stared at each other. They realised that the kid was not as innocent as they had assumed. They took the kid home luring him with more promises.

Bhagat Singh's Education

Kishan Singh and his friend believed that, Bhagat already had the die of his future. In due course Bhagat Singh started going to the primary school of the village along with his brother jagat Singh. Bhagat was bright in the studies. The teachers also recognised it whatever he missed in the class, he could easily make it up by fast study at home or outside. His mind was wanderer. His heart was never in the class. He loved clouds, trees and streams.

Bhagat loved his brother, and confided things of his heart to him. Sadly Jagath died at the age of only eleven. Bhagat felt very lonely. Even god was not fair to his family, he would feel.

Inspite of all the bunking of classes Bhagat passed exams with no-problem. Sardar Kishan Singh shifted to Navakot town with his family. He had some landed property there. Over the years Kishan Singh's family had grown sizably.

So Kishan Singh was now extra careful about gettnig involved in active politics. Too much was at stake. He must stay out of jail for the sake of more then a dozen dependents namely old parents wife, eight children and two helpless wives of his brother's.

Sardar Arjun Singh and Kishan Singh preferred to enroll Bhagat Singh in D.A.V. School. Khalsa educational institutions were run by lackeys of the British.

The teaching staff accordingly was also of the mindset, slavish to the colonial rulers and their culture. It was not acceptable at all to the family of freedom fighters. In contrast D.A.V. Institutions were fiercely nationalistic and stood for the freedom of the motherland. The seeds of the freedom sown Bhagat by his family found rising ground in D.A.V. School. His feelings for nationalism and opposition to the British rule were intensifying.

Punjabi farmers realised that the whitamen were never true to their word. They founded an organisation called "Gadar Party" and started Gadar movement in 1914-15. They revealed to the locals how British were cheating them. Their bitter experience naturally made them openly hostile to the Englishmen.

Gadar Party people had contacts with Kishan Singh when his family lived in Banga.

Martyr Sarabha had become hero and inspiration of Bhagat Singh. He would always keep a pocket size photograph of Sarabha in his left pocket , of the shirt close to his heart.

While doing chores he always hummed the patriotic songs Sarabha used to sing. He used to tell his mother. "Ma ! He is the one who in my guru, my brother and my comrade".

Rawlett Act and Jalianwala Bagh Massacre

The British government passed a cunning law called, "Rawlett Act." The law was aimed at crushing the freedom movements and allied activities. Civil rights of Indians were drastically curtailed.

The law gave the police authorities sweeping powers to arrest any one and put in jail on mere suspicion. Whole country was fell in anger. Protest marches, demonstrations rocked the country. The police firings and lathi charges have considerably increased.

British tried to drive a wedge between Hindus and Muslims. But the attempt was failed. On a protest march in Delhi the police opened fire, some protesters were killed and some others were injured.

It triggered the condemnation of the British rule. The cities were put under curfew and prohibitory orders on 13th April 1919 on Baisakhi day, the people gathered in "Jalianwala Bagh" of Amritsar to celebrate the festival as every year. The festivities were on. Maximum number of children and women were gathered.

Some people erected a stage and started making speeches condemning the Rawlett Act, and the police brutalities against innocent people. The British authorities were waiting for an opportunity to teach lesson to the natives.

General 'O' Dyer arrived on the scene with hundreds of soldiers. Jalianwala Bagh was a big high walled compound with only one narrow exit. The exit was sealed by a machine gunmanned by soldiers.

General 'O' Dyer ordered the firing on the Baisakhi mob.

Hundreds of guns boomed. The bullets rained on the crowd. Thousand plus men, women, children were killed.

The news shocked the nation and the world. The entire nation mourned the death of the hundreds of innocents. Yonug Bhagat Singh's heart bleed for the victims. 12 year old Bhagat was too sensitive to just silently weep.

Amritsar was only 20 miles off labore. He slipped of his home and reached Amristar dodging police pickets and curfew regulations. The young boy managed to reach Jalianwala Bagh. He saw the blood socked soil. Bhagat had taken along a bottle, which he filled with that soil. For him it was a sacred soil. Evading the police cheek points. Bhagat was able to reach his home safety, His mother and sister were looking for him greatly worried when he did not show up all day, long after departing without telling anything to any one.

"Where have you been all day long ? Bhagat's Mother asked. Bhagat showed the bottle with soil and said, "look here it will explain my absence. I will Keep it as a cherished momento. I would always remind me of my duty to take revenge on the evil British".

He respectfully placed the bottle on the top of his bookshelp. His mother and sister stared at him in awe. They could see a glorious freedom fighter taking shape in their Bhagat.

Later, Bhagat Singh was drawing closer to the Congress. He Started attending the meeting held by the party and listened to the speeches of Congress leaders.

The Boycott of British Goods

Bhagat Singh was drawing closer to the Congress and he had begun to feel great respect for Gandhiji, mainly because, he was leading battle against the British. In 1920 Gandhiji launched 'Non-co-operation Movement to force the colonial rulers to accede to the demand of freedom of the Indians.

Sardar Kishan Singh's family was already using Khadi. For Bhagat Singh it was the opportunity he had been praying for. He quit school as 9th class student and jumped into the freedom battle. He had organised a band of boys who would go around the localities collecting the British goods.

They would pile up the goods, mostly cloth from England and set them on fire. It exhilarated Bhagat. In shouting anti-colonial slogans his zeal was obvious to all.

In Feb.1922 Gandhiii launched civil Disobedience Movement

which was fiercer verson of Non-co-operation Movement. But it was to be strictly non-violent, he made it clear. The frustarted people joined the movement in big way. With in no time the movement became a storm.

Just two days hence the movement turned violent. At a place named Chauri-Chaura near Gorakhpur some over-excited agitators burnt down a police post with an inspector and 21 constable shut inside. It was a gruesome act.

Bhagat Singh got admission in the National College of Labore. The atmosphere there was what he had drempt of. The air was charged the fierce patriotism and opposition to the colonial rule in India. The teachers and the lectures were nationalistic.

Most of the students were budding revolutionaries. Bhagat Singh met all the like minded youngmen here who later became his associates in his freedom crusade. The prominent among them were.

Yeshpal, Bhagwati Charan, Sukhdev, Ram Kishan, Tirath Ram, Jhanda Singh etc. Most of the students there were not for the diplomas. The main aim as to prepare themselves to do or die for the country or prove good political workers. The freedom politics was the only craze of the college. No one cared about fashion.

The students wore, ordinary dresses. Bhagat took the prize for being careless about his dress. He would sometimes reach the college in his lungi or in torn clothes. He did have his pockets bulging with revolutionary literature.

The National College had a great library called 'Dwarakadas Library' that had a goodly collection of books related to revolutions and revolutionaries freedom battles and the freedom heroes. It was the most favourite haunt of Bhagat Singh.

The revolution politics was becoming the main diet of Bhagat Singh's thoughts and activities. Before reaching home he would attend revolutionary meetings with friends at their private dense. Late arrival at home was his routine.

One day Bhagat's father told him that, "study, seriously or quit. If you don't want to study stay, home and do some useful work Don't waste my money." Bitter exchanges between the father and the son became order of the day.

Bhagat continued his wayward behaviour. He was too taken up with the liberation of the country to take notice of other matters.

The Broken Engagement

Bhagat was too taken up with the liberation of the country to take notice of other matters. Meanwhile Bhagat's grand mother suggested the age old formula. Get the youngmen married and let bride break in the wild colt in Bhagat.

The grand old lady's idea was good. The rest of the family passed it unanimously. At last, the family members find the suitable girl for Bhagat. A Sargodha girl was selected by the family.

Bhagat was informed of his engagement to a girl through a letter written by his father. In his reply to the father's letter Bhagat made it clear that he would not marry and that his only bride could martyrdom for the country.

Bhagat's father overruled his son's play. Some more argumentative letters were exchanged. At last Bhagat Singh felt cornered. In sheer despiration he fled from home and college to escape from the marital trap.

He was in contact with a well known revolutionary named, Shachindranath Sanyali, Bhagat Singh went straight to Kanpur, that had become the new home of Bengali revolutionaries.

The Revolutionary Activities

Bhagat Singh kept participating in the revolutionary activities planned by militant organisation named "Hindustan, Republican Association', which was infact formed by merging a Bengali revolutionary group. Bhagat Singh went to Pratapgarh fair with some of his comrades to distribute printed revolutionary hand bills.

The police was keeping an eye on the crowds. The youth distributing objectionable material were spotted by the police. The police concverged on Bhagat Singh and his friends. Bhagat played a clever ruse to distruct the attention of the police men, and ran with his companions. The police went in chase of them while running, Bhagat turned back and fired his revolver in the air with a warning.

The policemen stopped and did not continue the chase. Bhagat Singh and his companions were able to escape. But Bhagat Singh's presence in Kanpur become a risky affair. The police had seen his face. Then, Bhagat Singh went to serve in national primary school of Shadipur.

The school was also a product the movements against the British rule. The freedom people had controlled over the school. Bhagat Singh was to be the head master. As a teacher Bhagat Singh worked diligently. He was doing his duty in all seriousness. In short time, the school made all round improvement.

Meanwhile another bright young revolutionary Chandra Shekhar Azad had come in contact, with 'Hindustan Republican Association' and had Joined it. All the members of the association. discussed the political situation and the need to reorganise the party. Meanwhile the family of Bhagat Singh was frantically looking for him. Keeping in consideration the mindset of the youngman ads were published in the revolutionary newspapers.

Later, Bhagat Singh's where abouts were obtained from Vidyarthi Then two of the family members proceeded to Shadipur to meet Bhagat. When Bhagat saw them coming he fled from the school the family members returned unsuccessful. Then information was passed on the Bhagat, that his grandmother was seriously ill and she wished to see him. Vidyarthi advised him to go home for the sake of the old lady.

Bhagat went home to the delight of the family members. The grand mother was really ill. It was no ruse. She brighten up at the sight of her dearest grandson. Bhagat was also emotionally moved. In a couple of weeks the old lady recovered. Bhagat Singh stayed home honouring the wish of his grandma. But his soul was restless. His body and mind were itching for action. Whenever he saw protests marching by shouting anti-British slogans his body would tremble with excitement.

An Agitation to Reformation

The Gurudwaras were protected by the colonial administration. The Gurudwaras used to collect crores of rupees through the daily offerings of the devotees which was being spent on private luxuries. The Gurudwaras were being treated as private properties, by their priests, who were mostly British proteges. They were protected and supported by the colonial administration. To make the agitation fiercer Akalis decided to shift their head quarter from Nankana Sahib to jaiton. It worried the British. They wanted to put a fanner in the Akali works.

The task of according reception to this band was given to Sardar Kishan Singh. But he passed on the responsibility to Bhagat Singh. Bhagat Singh accepted the challege.

Bhagat Singh arrived in the village. He met people and asked them to send food and all other things required to honour Akalies to his house quietly. The people were with him. The Akali band arrived as the Akali slogans rant the air the people came out of their homes to give a rousing reception to the band.

Akalis stayed in Banga Village for three days. A meeting was organised. Bhagat Singh gave the first speech of his life. He condemned the foreign rule and called upon the people to fight for the liberation of the country and socialism. He was lustily cheered. The success of Bhagat Singh was a slap on the face of Dilbagh Singh. To settle scores he got a warant issued against Bhagat on trumped up charges.

To evade the arrest Bhagat slipped away to delhi where he found a job with daily 'Veer Arjun' on the strength of his stint with Pratap of Kanpur. He used the earlier pen name, 'Balawant Singh'. Then Kanpur are a got flooded with Ganga water thousands were rendered homeless. Bhagat Singh suspended all his revolutionary activities. Meanwhile the warrant against him got cancelled. He decided to return to labore. Back on his home ground he gathered up his friends and like minded people. With the co-operation of his comrades Bhagat Singh founded Young India Forum which became popular in short time. The country was in throes of communal riots.

The central Assembly elections were on. Sardar Kishan Singh was fighting the election on congress ticket. He was being opposed by Lala Lajapat Rai, who was from newly formed party Independent Congress.

Bhagat Singh managed the election campaign of his father. Meanwhile Young India Forum was going from strength to strength. A number of well known revolutionaries were swelling it's ranks. It opened up branches in other parts of the country.

The forum was dead set against the British. The forum decide to celebrate Kartar Singh Sarabha's day of hanging as 'Martyr Day'.

In an open ground a huge portrait of Sarabha was displayed. A white sheet of Khaddar was drapped over it. The patriotic feelings of the crowd surging skyhigh. The news unsettled the British authorities. Young India Forum was becoming a thorn in their flesh.

The Nabbed Revolutionaries

In 1925, a government treasury being transported by the train was looted. The revolutionaries decamped with the loot and escaped into nearly jungles. The authorities hit back with a prompt police and C.I.D. Action.

The Nabbed Revolutionaries were put on trail. What the nabbed revolutionaries revealed in no way showed that Bhagat Singh was also involved in the crime. The police was not convinced. It thought that Bhagat Singh had some connection to it. Bhagat Singh himself suspected that, the police was up to some trick against him.

Once he got down from the train at Amritsar Railway station. He had some uncanny feeling that he was under police watch. He had a pistol in his pocket. Out of the station, he entered a narrow lane. He saw a policeman follow him. He dogged the policeman and entered into the house of a lawyer, whom he knew. He found the lawyer pursuing some files. Bhagat Singh sat down on a chair. Bhagat opened his pistol and pur it on the table infront of the lawyer. The lawyer took the hint and dropped the weapon in his table drawer.

He got up and said "Follow me Bhagat". The lawyer took him to his inner room and left him in the care of a servant. The lawyer began to pace ground outside his gate. Meanwhile Bhagat washed himself and took meals offered by the servant. Outside, lawyer misguided the policeman.

There was the office of 'Keerti' a revolutionary magazine. The policeman searched the office hoping to find. Bhagat Singh who infact was sleeping comfortably in the lawyer's house. At night when the coast was clear Bhagat Singh took leave of the lawyer.

He took train to Labore. As he was going to his house on a tonga the police swooped in. He was taken to the police station in hand cuffs. The news of the arrest of his son, shocked Kishan Singh. He ran around to get Bhagat released.

The police had arrested Bhagat Singh in 'Dussehra Bomb'case. It was a false implication of an innocent youngman. In fact the Lucknow, Police inspector who was investigating 'the Kakori Train Robbery' case had arrived in Labore to take remand of Bhagat Singh.

Bhagat Singh stood his ground braving the police torture, and everything the officers threw at him. The police was getting desperate. The effort of kishen Singh to save his son was creating added pressure. When Bhagat Singh was produced before the magistrate he declared that he was innocent. The police had no evidence of his involvement, in the cases he was arrested for. At last Bhagat Singh was released.

Bhagat as a Dairyman

Bhagat Singh understood the compulsions of the new situations. He could imagine what his father must have gone through to raise the money for his bail. He could not fail his father.

Kishan Singh raised some more money and got a dairy started for Bhagat to run. Bhagat applied al his energies and mind to make his dairy a success. He had become a complete dairyman. The dairy prospered. In the begining Bhagat had just one helper. Bhagat worked day and night, feeding, tending buffaloes, cleaning the shed, washing and milking. Later he had to employ more helping hands. He had become a complete dairyman.

The case dragged on in the court at last in 1928 the case against Bhagat Singh was with drawn and the charges dropped. He became a free man. Later on he lost his interest in dairy business, and paid little attention to it. The dairy started incurring losses. For Bhagat dairy became a writing workshop. sitting there he would write articles, for news papers, and magazines. At young India Forum's meeting, the slides were shown by magic lantern and related sagas of the heroes were revealed to the viewers.

Revolutionary comrades would walk into the dairy to discuss plans and programmes. After 'Kakori Train Robery' the police had cracked down hard on the members of Hindustan Republican Association. Most of it's members were in the police custody. Bhagat Singh and a companion went to Kanpur to pick up the threads. The organisation was in Shambles. Bhagat Singh returned to Labore with a definite agenda to recive the revolutionary organisation on a big scale to launch a final challenge to the alien rulers and their stooges.

The H.S.R.A

A grand convention of the free revolutionaries was called at old fort, ruins of Delhi, to discuss the future strategies. Meanwhile the name of the organisation was changed. It was called, "Hindustan Socialist Republican Army". The new name clearly indicated it's political leanings. In the absentia, Chandra

Shekhar Azad was appointed "The commander-in-chief of the H.S.R. Army, Unanimously.

Some important decisions taken by H.S.R.A. were as follow.

* To bomb Simon Commission.

* To set up bomb manufacturing units.

* Train youth in bomb manufacturing.

* Procure arms.

* Loot Govt. treasuries for finance.

Somehow the C.I.D. got wind of the convention. The police was stationed at all exit points to nab the revolutionaries, who had taken part in the convention. All the delegates were able to dodge the police in various disguises. Bhagat Singh escaped in guise of a Sadhu. Bhagat Singh went to Kanpur to meet the commander to apprise him of the decisions taken by the conventions of the revolutionaries most of which, Chandra Shekhar Azad already knew.

The new clean shaven took of Bhagat gave Azad an idea. Bhagat Singh had very fair complexion who could pass as an European. And he had a penchant for wearing English hat. Rajguru was with Bhagat Singh so they were three. According to the plan the three went to the house of a rich merchant, Seth Dilsukh raid at 11 PM.

Bhagat wore hat safari shirt and shorts. He looked like an Angrez sahib. Azad was in body guard uniform. Rajguru guised like a Hindustani Babu. The frightened chowkidar was asked to inform his master that the P.A. to Lukhnow Governor had come to see him, on official business. Seth was checking account books he was too stunned to speak. He bent down to salute them, and led them in mumbling something.

Azad who was in uniform cut said, "Sethji an urgent matter necessitated sahib's visit. Sahib is the P.A. to Governor Bahadur with his is a government auditor. Seth got Bhagat and Rajguru seated. Muneed ran to bring refreshments. Bhagat Singh arrogantly took a sip of sherbet and a bite of biscuit. Dilsukh Rai watched in increasing anxiety.

Bhagat said "we won the war but it cost heavy. England is under heavy debt, so the Queen of England ordered, to collect funds from all rich people here". Rajguru flipped some papers and said, "Sir, sethji paid all his taxes. He had never defaulted, only due from his is Rs. 25,000 in war fund. Seth almost choked. Bhagat Singh added.

"It is war help from you to the Queen. You will be glad to know that, the government has decided to give you the title of 'Rai Bahadur' for your service. Then, seth spoke to his Muneed, "Muneemji don't stand here like a fool. Get the money and pay up. Before the P.A.Party departed with cash seth reminded them of the title. Seth Dilsukh Rai said to Muneem, God never does wrong. He knows who deserves the name "Rai Bahadur'. Just then a police party trooped in to the surprise of seth.

Then the police officer told about the militants, and how did the cheated the Dilsukh Rai. Dilsukh Rai was stunned to speak.

The Anti-Simon Commission Activity

In February 1928, the simon Commission landed in India. It was met with black flags and, "Simon go back" slogans. Mean while Bhagat Singh went to Lahore to prepare Young India Fortum for opposition to Simon Commission. Azad went to Delhi to plan and execute a bomb attack on the Viceroy, Lord Irwin. The attack was carried on the train that was taking the Viceroy to

Mathura at a spot near Faridabad. But the viceroy escaped unhurt. The Simon Commission was a great fraud played on the people of India by the colonial rulers. Entire country was up in arms against it.

The supposed aim of the commission was to review the administrative reforms and suggest ways to transfer more powers to the Indians. The government of England had promised that the proposed commission would consist of half of it's members of Indian origin. Bur when the commission was constituted and announced the Indian leaders found to their shock that all the seven mambers of the commission were Englishmen and it was to be headed by a lawyer called Lord simon. It was clear that the commission would naturally suggest nothing that would improve the situation of the natives. Indian gave a call to the countrymen to boycott the commission.

Simon Commission was to arrive in Labore on 17th October 1928. In Labore Bhagat Singh was in the forefront of organising anti-Simon commission rally. He had rallied the youth forum activists to prepare for a grand show. All the parties were cooperating with the Forum activities to put up a united front.

Every corner of the road was manned by activists of the forum, through which the commission was to pass. The commission was to arrive by train. Lalaji led the huge protest march surrounded by Bhagat Singh and his comrades to the railway station.

The Police commissioner Scott and his deputy sanders were there to keep away the protesters to save the commission from big embarrasment at all costs. Scott saw that to make way for the commission he will have to push back Lalaji and his young brigade. A human wall of rallists was behind them. It was no easy to step back. A narrow way was created but not enough to let the commission car through. Lalaji and the young activists were holding ground.

ASP Sanders came forward and asked the policemen to push back Lalaji's brigade. It didn't work. Frustrated and angry sanders moved hitting the protesters with is baton.

The policemen also rained lathis. The way was still bloked. Bhagat Singh and his comrades were determined to hold ground. Lalaji announced, "In protest against the brutality of the police this protest rally is being postponed". Lala Lajpat Rai fell ill. The doctors diagnosed internal injuries due to the lathi blow by Sanders. The injuries were fatally hurt. Lala Lajpat Rai succumbed to the injuries on 17th November 1928.

Entire country felt outraged and was grief stricken. Lakhs of people joined his funeral procession sobbing to the cremation ground.

The Protest Against the British

The colonial rulers had inflicted wound on the very soul of India. For the soldiers of Hindustan Socialist Republican Army it was an insult, they will not be able to live with, when especially, one of it's stars Sardar Bhagat Singh was involved in it. Only a befitting revenge could redeem their pride.

On 10th December 1928 a meeting was arranged in Labore. Bhagat Singh thundered, "Entire country is outraged at the distardly act of the British police, which resulted in the death of the one of our most respected leaders. This murder of Lalaji has to be avenged to teach the white men a lesson". Many revolutionaries, including Azad volunteered for the mission of revenge.

Bhagat Singh made it clear that he will be in the group for the mission. At last the mission to kill the police commissioner

Scott was entrusted to Bhagat, Azad, Rajguru and Jaigopal.

The job of scouting the routine of scott was given to Jaigopal. He spied on the movements of Scott for seven days and reported his daily routine to the mission group. Based on his report the assassination plan was finalised on 15th December 1928. On the 19th December Jaigopal reached the office of the Ministry of Home.

As the officer came towards the gate, on his motor cycle, Jaigopal gave prearranged singal. Bhagat and Rajguru rushed towards the gate from nearby spot where they had been lying in wait. Rajguru shot the officer in the neck at the gate. The officer fell down with a cry with his bike skidding arround. Bhagat pumped in bullets in the officer's head.

The assassinated officer infact was ASP sanders, not commissioner Scott. But it made no big difference. Sanders was as much guilty for the death of Lalaji as commissioner scott.

The Escape Technique

After the assasination of A.S.P. Sanders the revolutionary group went different ways. Bhagat Singh shaved of his beared, and got the hair cut at the room of an old friend. He borrowed pants and a hat from him. The friend knew all about the plot.

The friend learnt that he had only 200 rupees on him. He gave 100 rupees to Bhagat Singh. It was decided to seek the help of, Durga Bhabi, herself a revolutionary and the wife of a respected soldier of the army. The revolutionary spirit in Durga Bhabi prevailed and she was ready to accept any challenge. Her lahore house was infact a safe house for the revolutionaries on the run. A call fellow in overcoat arrived in the house of Durga Bhabi. She looked carefully and recognised Bhagat and the servant as Rajguru.

It was decided that they would leave Lahore for Calcutta by morning Calcutta mail. Durga Bhabi had one thousand rupees, which her husband had given her for emergencies. They reached the railway station posing as an Anglo-Indian couple. Rajguru carried their luggage and some files to creat an impression that the Anglo-Indian was some high ranking government official. The police didn't suspect and they got away. Chandra Shekhar Azad and his comrades had boarded the same train in the guise of Pandas of Mathura. Azad was the guise of Panda Guru.

It was a perfect Panda party. A Panda guru going to Mathura with his disciples. The police had no reason to suspect them. The assassins successfully gave a slip to the police dragnet. A 40 hour train journey took Bhagat Singh and company to Howrah Railway station of Calcutta.

In Howrah all of them were received by Bhagwati Charan Vohra and his sister Sushila. They had been informed by wife. During his stay at Calcutta, the Congress session was also held under, the chairmanship of Pt. Motilal Nehru. Bhagat Singh attended the meeting in the guise of a Bengali.

The congress meet throughly disappointed Bhagat. He felt that Congress was back tracking on the issue of total freedom. His conclusion was that only armed challenge to the British can send them packing to their homeland. A well known revolutionary leader Pratulla Chandra Ganguly was mightily impressed with Bhagat. He approved of Bhagat's plans and ideas. He even lent Bhagat his pistol as a token of aprreciation.

Bhagat Singh had drawn a 'Bomb Plan' he was getting restless to implement it. Finally itching for action he left Calcutta to join hands with Azad. In Calcutta Bhagat had befriended a man named Jatindranath who was an expert in Bomb making. To put his expertise to good use. Bhagat hired two houses at Agra.

Azad had reached there to join his forces.

In one of the houses bomb manufacturing unit was set up. In the other house a workship was opened to teach the young men of H.S.R.A., the art of making gun powder and bombs.

This second house was also used for meetings of the organisations, to discuss different plans and next comming programmes.

The Draconian Bills

In the year 1929, the British Government was looking to pass, Draconian bills in the assembly. The first was public safety bill and the second was Industrial Disputes Bill. The aim of public safety was to outlaw any opposition to the government. The Bill was aimed at crushing the spirit of the youth. Who were raising against the British under various leftist outfits.

The law was to give wide raging powers to the police to arrest any one and put him in the prison without fair trial. The bill if enacted could severely curtail civil rights. The Industrial Disputes Bill was designed to take away basic rights of the Industrial labour to run them into utter slaves. The Industrialists who were British stooges were to benifit by this bill. They could become slave drivers and earn the colonial rulers money through various taxes. This bill had another aim; it was to make trade union leaders important.

Bhagat Singh was agitated over these barbaric bills. In their Agra house meeting he voiced his concerns on these bills, and revealed his action plan against them. He had already discussed his plan with Prafulla Ganguly and won his hearted approval. In the meeting Bhagat said, "There is no place for justice in British imperialism. They want to strangle, plunder and kill the subjects especially the youth". "We can't give in meekly". It was clear that Bhagat had some plans.

He revealed his action plan. A couple of revolutionaries would throw bombs and hand bills in the assembly, when he bills would be being passed. After the bomb throwing the revolutionaries would get arrested. It would draw the attention of the entire nation.

Chandra Shekhar Azad liked the idea, but he was against getting arrested. But Bhagat had a different outlook. He was against the escape plan. For milions of youth of India Bhagat Singh had become a sacred figure. His name was echoed, in every city, town and village of India. Bhagat Singh was becoming a big inspiration and the motivating force. The growing popularity of Bhagat Singh was becoming an irritant for the Congress leaders.

Pandit Jawaharlal Nehru admits in his biography, "Bhagat Singh become a symbol. the killing of sanders was soon forgotton but the symbol remained. In a few months every village and town of punjab and most of the North India echoed with his name. Many songs were being written about him.

The Resolution on Assembly Bombing

The revolutionary meeting was concluded, after the resolution on, 'Assembly Bombing.' Azad left Delhi still feel very bad about the plan. He knew that Bhagat would be changed for the murder of Sardars once fell into the police hands. But Bhagat was hell-bent on walking into their hands deliberately. That did not make sense for Azad.

Bhagat wanted to build up on the popularity he had earned by killing sanders to make his martyrdom do the maximum damage to the British rule. Bhagat Singh travelled to Delhi to oversee the preparations for the final act being made by his friend Jaidev Kapoor, who was staying in Delhi to do all the ground work. With the help of an independent member of the central Assembly, Jaidev had managed to secure two passes for the entry into the assembly house.

To test the usefulness of those 'Visitor Passes' Azad and Bhagat one day went to the Assembly house in disguise. Using them, they were able to, go, into the house and come out without facing any problem All was set now.

The H.S.R.A. Made an emergency plan to bomb the motor car of the Viceroy, while it would be on it's way to the Assembly Houses for the Holi feast. The revolutionary youth chosen for the mission hid themselves in the roadside bush with bombs. In fact, the Viceroy had gone fishing on impulse in the morning. He reached, the Assembly Hall late using another route. Then, all the attention of the revolutionaries reverted to the original plan, 'Assembly Bombing'.

On 6th April 1929, the notorious bills were introduced in the central Assembly. The Congress members fiercely opposed the bills and voted them down. The British and their stooge members were furious. The speaker, an Englishman was red faced. Lord Simon was shaking his head.

The Viceroy Announced that the his bills would be passed into acts by special power of veto vested in him The formal declaration to that effect was to be made formally in the Assembly Hall on the 8th April 1929. 8th April 1929 was to be the fateful day. The Assembly session began on 8th April. Bhagat Singh and dutt were already in seats in the visitors gallery. They were in blue shirts and khaki pants. The members who were stooges of the British began to speak.

Thay pleaded the importance of the bills allowed to become

acts to enable the authorities to deal with communist militants, who were destroying the country and the British empire. The speaker rose to announce the bills have been passed into Acts by the special power of the Viceroy of India. That was the moment the revolutionaries waited for.

Bhagat Singh threw one bomb towards the empty benches. There was a deafening explosion Thick smoke was filling the hall. The assembly was too stunned to react immediately. There were some shouts and cries.

Then another bomb exploded. At the same moment some hand bills sailed down through smoke. Bhagat Singh drew out his revolver and fired two blanks in the air. Lord Simon was acting like a scared rat trying to hide behind the speaker's desk.

Many sought refuge in the galleries while others divided into toilets. When the smoke cleared the Assembly hall appeared empty. Up there in the gallery standing by the front railing Bhagat Singh and dutt were raising slogans "Inquilab Zindabad" and "Down with Colonialism".

The Police officers who entered, stood frozen in confusion, not exactly knowing what the two youth were upto. To allay their fears Bhagat Singh calmly put down his weapon on the bench, he was sitting upon with Dutt. The officers looked relived.

Bhagat Singh and Dutt refused to give any statements to the police. Thay insisted that they would speak only in the court, of law at the time of the trial.

The Trials and Verdict

On 7th May 1929, the trial began in the court of Additional Magistrate Mr. Pool. Lawyer Asaf Ali was representing the revolutionaries. The hearing began on 4th June 1929. The prosecuttion put forward it's case and paraded it's witnesses.

In the lawyer court Bhagat Singh was asked to define the revolution. He said, "There is no imperative place for bloody battles in revolution, not for any personal revenge." The revolution is not bombs and guns culture. By revolution we mean to change the system which is based on injustice.

The producers and labourers are basic units of economic system. The exploiters rob them of their fruits of labour and human rights. Bhagat ended the statement with the words of this altar of sacrifice we are determine to burn our young lives for. incense. For our great objective no sacrifice in big enough. We shall patiently wait for the culmination of the revolution."

The above statement greatly aroused the passions of the countrymen. Bhagat Singh became the nation's centre of attraction. The hearing ended on 10th June 1929. On 12th June the session judge sentenced Bhagat Singh and Batukeshwar Dutt to life imprisonment in the, "Assembly bombing' case. The appeal was heard in Labore High Court before the Justice Ford and Justice Edison. Here Bhagat Singh made an important statement.

"My Lord."

We are no barristers or scholars of English language. Nor have we any high educational degrees.

My Lord in these circumstances it would have been expected of the learned Session Judge to measure the extent of our crime by the result or to see it from the physiological angle with the help of our statement.

The first fact is that the bombs thrown by us in the assembly caused no physical or phychological damage to anyone. My lord we think that we have been misunderstood. We came to your court, not to big for pardon, or for lighter sentence but to clear our position. We want not to be subjected to improper treatment and no wrong assumptions be made about us. The question of the punishment is secondary. The judges upheld the verdict of the Session Judge on 13th January 1930.

Bhagat Singh and Dutt were kept Maionwali Jail. In the last week of June they were transferred to the Bostral Jail of Labore. Bhagat Singh and Batukeshwar Dutt were brought to the court on stretchers as they were too weak to walk. due to the hunger strike. Their condition shocked the countrymen. On 13th September 1929 one of the close friends of Bhagat Singh Yatindranath das passed away impovershed by the hunger strike. The authorities had tried to force feed the hunger strikers.

The death of the under trial meant trouble for the rulers. The people were losing the patience and getting in rebellious mood. The Jail committee speeded up it's work and submitted it's report. Bhagat conveyed to the authorities that he was ready to break his hunger strike provided all the strikers do it simultaneously. The authorities agreed.

On 5th October, 1929 Bhagat Singh broke his fast with his comrades by accepting dalroti after 114 days of the hunger strike.

During the hearing of Sanders shooting case Bhagat Singh and his friend created a lot of problems for the officials. They would loudly sing patriotic songs and recite challenging verses disrupting the proceedings.

On 5th May, 1930 the tribunal sat for it's first hearing. Some how Bhagat Singh and his friends allowed to be taken to the tribunal court. They began to play their old game of singing songs and shouting slogans to thwart the proceedings. The two British judges would watch it seething in anger. But the Indian Judge Aga Haider would watch the seen. calmly. The two judges further got antagonised, when they were told the meaning of the slogans, and the verses Bhagat Singh and company was shouting and singing. Of course they were blatantly offen-sive to the English ears.

One day a messenger of the tribunal arrived and he read out the case. It was so arranged because the tribunal knew that the accused won't come to it's court to hear the verdict. It was a 68 pages verdict. In first point it was mentioned as follows. Death by hanging to Bhagat Singh. Sukhdev and Rajguru. By 8th October 1930 most of the people of Labore and the rest of the country learnt about the verdict. Waves of the anger were sweeping through. Students union called for a strike. The schools and colleges closed down.

All over the country there were rallies, protest meetings and strikes held against the punishment. By December 1930 it became clear that the rulers will hang Bhagat Singh come what may. A peace pact was worked out between Lord Irwin and Mahatma Gandhi. he was certain that the pact won't satisfy the people. Bhagat Singh said, "The hanging must take place at a time when the people are emotionally at Boiling point and their attention is riveted on us".

During the trial, Chandra Shekhar Azad made some daring plans to resuce Bhagat Singh and Dutt from the jail. Bhagat Singh refused to co-operate.

1931, 23rd March

The morning of 23rd March 1931 arrived The sky was covered with blood red clouds. The jalior of the Labore Central Jail was a worried man. He liked and respected Bhagat Singh immensely. And it was his last day. He served Bhagat Singh rasgullas, as he had demanded. Bagat are with relish.

The doors of all the cells were ordered to be kept shut on that day. Havaldar Sardar Chatursingh was the chief warden of the jail. At 3 p.m. he was informed that the condemned were to be hanged in the evening. The necessary arrangements were orderd to be made. Chatur was a very religious and God fearing man. Recital of Guru Vani was his daily ritual. The door suddenly opened out there were jail authorities in their bright uniforms. Their Chief said, "Sardarji, the orders have come to hang you please get ready."

Bhagat was reading a book. He raised his left hand and said, "wait a revolutionary is meeting another revolutionary". The authorities stood frozen. Bhagat Singh read some more lines and toosed the book high towards ceiling. He got up and spoke, "Let us go".

Bhagat Singh was as carefree as if he were going for a walk in the park. Bhagat said, "Don't handcuff us and don't cover our faces with black hoods". His request was granted. Bhagat walked out of his cell flanked by officers.

Rajguru and Sukhdev also emerged out of their cells in similar fashion. They saw one another and impulsive embracing took place. Then Rajguru held Bhagat's left hand and Sukhdev grabbed the right hand.

They walked in that way singing a patriotic verse. The authorities walked in their front, back and on flanks. The Deputy Commissioner turned red. All three mounted the stairs and stood before the hanging nooses. Bhagat Singh in the middle and the other two on his sides. The three raised the slogan "Inquilab Zindabad-Colonialism Murdabad". Bhagat Singh said to the hangman.

"Set the ropes right".

The hangman adjusted the nooses with his shivering hands. Then he pulled the levers in one go. The foot planks swung down. The three revolutionary sons of India became martyrs.

3

Jawaharlal Nehru

The Family History

Jawaharlal Nehru's family hailed from the beautiful valley of Kashmir. They were Kashmiri Pandits. His father's name was Motilal. Motilal had to struggle all through childhood as his father had died very young, at the age of only thirty-four. He and his two elder brothers were hard working children, determined to succeed in life.

Motilal Nehru decided to follow in his brother's footsteps, and studied law. He was headstrong and strong-willed. He also belived that everything should be done perfectly. And with his good personality, confidence and sheer brilliance, it was just a matter of time when he became well-known and prosperous.

Motilal liked the English way of living. He dressed like an Englishman and could speak several languages fluently. He lived in great style, and loved good food and good company. He was a good host to his company immensely. Motilal married Swarup Rani, a beautiful Kashmiri Brahmin girl, and on 14th of November,

1889, she gave birth to a baby boy.

"Swarup, this child is more precious to me than all the jewels in the world", said Motilal when he beheld his son for the first time. "Let's call him Jawahar, meaning a jewel".

"One day when he grows up he will truly be like a Jewel," said his doting mother. In 1896, when Motilal's elder brother Bansidhar went to Europe for six months. he left his son Sridhar with them. Motilal admitted both the boys to St. Mary's Convent. After Sridhar left, Jawaharlal was children from that school.

Jawaharlal had two sisters but they both were born after many years of Jawaharlal's birth and thus, he had been somewhat of a lonely child in a large house full of uncles, aunts, cousins farolder than him. Although he admired and respected his father. Jawaharlal became closer to his mother because of Motilal's sudden moods of anger and also, in Jawaharlal's younger days Motilal had been an extremely busy man always surrounded by his friends and clients. In those days, Motilal did not have any interest in Politics but, even as a boy, Jawaharlal observed sadly how the English and the Eurasians were treating Indians with contempt regarding them as third class citizens. In spite of this, Jawaharlal, however, did not have any harted towards any particular Englishman or Eurasian.

The Childhood

Young Jawaharlal would listen with rapt attention to the tales of the Ramayan and the Mahabharat which his mother told him. He often used to accompany his mother for a dip in the Holy Ganges. There were many temples in the holy cities of Allahabad and Benaras. Young Jawahar would often go up there with his mother for prayers. All this left a deep impression on his mind.

Being a lonely child, with sisters much younger than he was, he would often pester his father's clerks for stories. He specially loved to hear the tales from the Arabian Nights. The Nehrus lived in the chowk of Allahabad. This was an old and crowded part of the city.

"I think it's about time we moved to a better area," said Motilal to his wife one day. "My practice is doing well and now we can afford a better house".

"Yes", replied Swarup, "With growing children, we need more space". "Civil Lines where all the Europeans live, would be good", said Motilal.

Soon, in 1900, when Jawaharlal was ten years old, the Nehrus shifted to a spacious bungalow in the civil Lines. It had sprawling lawns, Several rooms, and a swimming pool.

"Let us call our new home 'Anand Bhawan' the abode of happiness", said Motilal.

Jawaharlal's parents were wealthy and well respected. There was nothing he lacked. He had everything a child of his age could want-imported toys bought by his doting father during his trips to Europe, beautiful clothes, plenty of books and a lot of attention from loving aunts and uncles. As a result, Jawaharlal had a happy childhood.

One day Jawaharlal went to his father's study where he often worked till late in the night. He saw some pans lying on his desk. "This is my father's favourite pen." he said to himself, picking it up. 'I don't think he will be angry if I take it.;' quickly put it away in his pocket and walked away. A little later, when Motilal sat down to work he looked around for his favourite pen. "Jawaharlal, have you seen my pen", he called it, so I took it".

"How dare you take my pen without asking"? asked Motilal,

losing his temper. He gave Jawaharlal a sound thrashing. It was not because Motilal could not afford to buy another pen. It was to teach young Jawaharlal the sense of right and wrong.

Motilal wanted to spare no expenses as far as his son's education was concerned. "I am looking for a good tutor for young Jawahar who could stay over at our houses and teach him". said Motilal to Annie Besant one day.

"I know a very good teacher, Ferdinand T. Brooks", replied Annie. "He will be a good influence on him". Ferdiand's father was Irish and his mother was french. He instilled in Jawaharlal a great love for reading. "Remember, Jawaharlal, reading maketh a man", he would often say.

Jawaharlal read all the books he could lay his hands on-Lewis Carroll's Alice in Wonderland, Rudyard Kipling's Jungle Book and Kim, Scott, Dickens Mark Twain and Sherlock Holmes. And Jerome K. Jerome's Three men in a boat was a particular favourite with him. Ferdinand also got young Jawaharlal interested in science. "Let's make our own laboratory and conduct experiments", said the tutor. Both Jawaharlal and his tutor spent long and interesting hours in their laboratory doing elemantary experiments in Chemistry and Physics.

Ferdinand was a theosophist. A thesophist tries to gain knowledge of God through prayers and meditation. He held weekly meetings in his room which were attended by well-known people from all over. The discussions on death, rebirth and religion greatly fascinated the young boy.

One day he went to Motilal and said. "Father, I wish to join the Theosophical Society". Motilal burst into laughter. "Very well, son", he said. "You have my permission. Swarup Rani was worried. She did not like the thought of her son's head being filled by strange ideas.

"Don't worry", said Motilal reassuringly. "Jawahar is just thirteen. It is just a passing phase. If we let our child grow and think for himself, it will broaden his horizon". So at thirteen Jawahar joined the Theosophical convention at Benaras where he met Colonel Olcott. But Motilal's prediction proved right. Jawahar lost interest in Theosophy soon after Brooks left.

However, the love for reading which Brooks instilled in him remained with him all his life. He loved reading al the newspapers he could lay his hands on. He read about the Bore Wars and about the Japanese victories against Russia. In his own childish ways he began to ponder over British rule and India's freedom.

In May 1905, when he was fifteen, Jawaharlal was admitted to Harrow one of the famous schools in England, where he studies for only two years and, in the beginning of October 1907, he entered the Trinity College at Cambridge and took his Degree in Science in 1910.

From 1907 onwards for several years, India had been full of unrest and trouble. For the first time, since the Revolt of 1857, India was showing fight and not submitting tamely to Brtish rule. Great freedom-fighters like Bal Gandadhar Tilak and Aurobindo Ghosh had woken up the people of India inspiring them to fight for the Country's freedom far afar in England also decided that, soon after his education in England, he too would fight for Indian's freedom. WIth this belief in mind, he chose to study for law, in England, after his Science Degree, instead of studying for the Indian Civil Service (ICS) since he did not want to serve the British Government in India as one of it's obedient ICS officers.

Education

In 1905, when Jawaharlal was fifteen, he left for England

with his parents and his sister. It was the beginning of a new life and new opportunities for the young lad.

There, Jawaharlal Nehru was admitted to the famous Harrow Public School in England. He was an outsider there- homesick and lonely. He, somehow could not quite mix around with the English boys; He found them a bit immature. In one of his letters to his father he wrote that he found his class mates a little childish and that they could speak of nothing but sports. His interest were wider than an average English School boy, and was better read than any one of them. Jawahar was a keen student interested in his studies as well as in sports. "May God bless him", said Swarup Rani. "I feel so proud of our son".

Even as a School boy, Politics seemed to interest him moore than anything else. When the general elections were held in England in 1905 he was more aware of the candidates and their victories and defeats than his English class mates. When their teacher asked them questions about the elections. Jawaharlal knew more answers than anybody else in the class.

He also began to take a lot of interest in the news from India during this time. The struggle to free India from the British rule had begun. Indian freedom fighters like Lala Lajpat Rai and Bal Gangadhar Tilak who were fighting for our country, filled him with awe. He was very excited about the Swadeshi Movement which had begun in India. This movement called upon the people of India to boycott all foreign clothes and other foreign goods.

The British news papers did not write much about the happenings in India. So he wrote a letter to his father, asking for a local news paper which would inform him about all that was happening in India.

In October 1907, he joined Trinity college, Cambridge. He happily took up natural Sciences, Chemistry, Geology and Botany.

He had more freedom at Cambridge than at harrow. He grew mentally as a person. He attended lectures by world personalities like George Bernard Shaw, and could discuss writers like Nietzche, Lowes, Dickinson, and Walter Pater with equal ease. He spent three pleasant and rewarding years at Cambridge.

During a visit to Ireland in 1910, Jawaharlal developed a great interest in the Sinn Fein Movement which was like the extremists movement in India. The extremists in India did not want to beg for the country's freedom. they wanted to snatch it away because that was their birthright. In the same manner the sinn Fein Movement in Ireland was fighting for their rights against England.

Jawaharlal was slowly becoming influenced by the political thoughts of Bal Gangadhar Tilak who was extremist. There was an association called Majalis in Cambridge, where Indian students met to discuss their ideas, thoughts and opinions on matters which affected their country. Bipin Chandra Pal, Lajpat Rai and Gopal Krishna Gokhale gave speeches at Majalis. While studying at Cambridge, Jawaharlal travelled a lot during his vocations. Once he had gone to Norway with his friends. He accidentally slipped into a freezing waterfall. Had not one of his English friends rescued him, he would have certainly died.

In 1909 when Motilal went abroad, father and son went to Berlin and saw Count Zepplin arrive in his new airplane. They went to Paris, in France, where they saw Count D Lambert flyover the Eiffel Tower. All this travelling broadened his education.

Jawaharlal was twenty when he passed out of Cambridge with a second class honours." "How about a career with the Civil Services for our son", mused Motilal.

"But that would mean he will have to spend another two years in England", said Swarup Rani. "The age limit for the ICS exams is twenty-two to Twenty four years and Jawaharlal is only twenty now".

"Yes, he has been away from us for years now", said Motilal fondly. "Perhaps it is best that he should be near us now". "Yes", said Swarup Rani. "Being in the ICS would mean being posted to far-off places. Though hell be in India, well see little of him. let's give up the idea of making our son work for the ICS". "I'll advise him to study law and give the Bar examination instead", said Motilal. "He can come back and Practice with me".

The First World War

The Years from 1914 to 1918 kept the English people busy fighting the Germans who had declared the first World War. Many Indians, during this war, were happy whenever the Germans scored a victory against the English. It was not because they ermans. They did not. It was just liked the Germans. They did not. It was just that the English rule in India had become so cruel that the defeats they suffered in the first World War made many Indians happy.

As the war was coming to an end, political life in India grew again. Bal Gangadhar Tilak had come out of jail and he started, along with Mrs. Besant, Home Rule Leagues. Jawaharlal admired Mrs. Besant and joined the League started by her. From then on, the annual sessions of Congress became more exciting and even the Moslem League became friendly with the Congress. With the arrest of Mrs. Besant, a lot of tension got into Indian politics and the Home Rule Movement became even more strong. The movement attracted not only the old Extremists who had been hiding since 1907 but large numbers of newcomers from the Middle and other Moderate leaders joining the Home Rule league. Some months later, however, most of the Moderates resigned from the league but. Motilal stayed on amd became the president of the League's Allahabad Branch. Very soon, Motilal decided to take more active interest in the struggle for India's freedom ; even though Motilal was prepared to become a non-Moderate, the Extremists did not impress him since he did not like their language and methods. He left that he could take active part in the struggle for freedom only after a peace agreement was made between the Muslims and the Hindus.

The outward change in Motilal, which started at the time of Mrs. Besant's arrest, grew further, step by step, and the tragic events in the Punjab in 1919, finally led him to leave his old Moderate colleagues behind and he decided to join the new Movement started by Gandhiji.

Jawaharlal's first meeting with Gandhiji was in 1916, at the time of the Lucknow Congress. Gandhiji was admired by everyone for his heroic deeds in South Africa but, he refused to take part in Congress or National Politics and was totally active, instead, with the problems of South African Indians.

Jawahar And Politics

"From tomorrow, Jawahar, you shall start your career as my junior in the Allahabad High Court", said Motilal, a few days after he returned as a qualified barrister from England. "Very well, father", replied Jawaharlal. But after a few months, when the newness had worn of, Jawahar was bored of the same old dull court routine. Politics began to interest him more than his work.

The Indian leaders were divided into Moderates and Extremists. The Moderates were co-operating with the British, while the Extremists, led by Tilak, were calling for stronger action. The Indian National Congress was a Moderate group. Jawaharlal joined the Congress the very year he returned from England. In

1912, Jawaharlal attended the Congress Session in Bankinpore. When he returned to Allahabad, his father, Motilal, asked him, So how did the Congress Session go ?

"I was quite disappointed with all the members who had come to attend the meeting, father", replied Jawaharlal. "They were all dressed like Englishmen in morning coats and shirt tails, and spoke only English. They had nothing to do with the common man of India".

Meanwhile, the First World War broke out in 1914, India did not want to take part but was dragged into it by the British. Political activities in India were again renewed. Tilak's long sentence in jail was over. He, along with Mrs. Annie Besant, started the Home Rule League to demand the Freedom of the Country. All this while, though Jawaharlal was helping his father in his practice, his mind elsewhere. He was fast losing interest in his legal Practice.

"It's about time Jawaharlal got married", said Motilal one day, looking quite worried. "A family of his own would perhaps make him more interested in his legal works, so that he can provide well for his wife and children".

"Mr. Kaul's daughter, Kamala, would be an ideal march for our son". Said Swarup Rani, indulgently. "She is a Kashmiri Brahmin and is well educated. Her father has a well established business in Delhi. She is also beautiful and accomplished". So in February, 1916, on Basant Panchami day which heralds the on coming of spring, Jawaharlal Nehru married Kamala Kaul. A year later in November, 1917, a daughter was born to them. They named her India Priyadarshni.

'Even my new family life with my wife and dear daughter cannot keep me away from my chosen path', thought Nehru. "If I want, I can earn well and lead a happy and a luxurious life as a lawyer. But that is not what I want. I want to serve my nation and lead it no freedom".

At this point in his life, Jawaharlal Nehru could have strayed away from Politics into a happy family life. But he did not. In 1916, he met Mohandas Karamchand Gandhi at the Lucknow Congress. Gandhi had returned from South Africa in 1915 after a long struggle. The coloured people there were being oppressed by the whites. Gandhi fought this oppression with his new weapon Satyagraha. "So what do you think of Gandhi ?" asked Motilal, when Jawaharlal returned from Lucknow.

"I am confused by his political ideas, but am deeply impressed by his sheer personality. He is short, thin, soft-spoken and polite. But we should not be taken in by his looks because he seems determined. and hard as nails. I was completely bowled over by him", replied Jawahar.

Motilal and Jawaharlal were slowly influencing each other by their political ideas. Motilal, being an old, legal man, was always a Moderate. But now constant arguments with Jawaharlal were slowly turning him into a Nationalist. Father and son were prepared to sacrifice everything for the nation. Motilal knew that it was just a matter of time when his dear son would be put behind bars for his politi cal activities against the British Rule. Quietly, without the knowledge of anybody in his family, he started sleeping on the hard floor. He wanted to know how Jawaharlal would feel he would have to sleep on the floor during his imprisonment.

The Satyagraha

The end of the First World War found India in a state of high hopes in the Indian people industrialisation had spread and the capitalist class had grown in wealth and power. They became even more greedy to add to their wealth. The middle-class Indians and even the peasants were poor as ever and had been hoping that great political changes would bring a measure of freedom and open new ways to them for growth. It was not to be, however. The British passed the Rowlatt Bills which gave powers to arrest anyone they wished to put in jail. Indians were shocked and the British feared that there would soon be a revolt throughout India and this fearled them to declare that the Rowlatt Bills will be in force for only 3 years. And yet, in all the 3 years these Bills were in force, not one person was arrested !

Gandhiji had passed through a serious illness early in 1919 and he wrote to the Viceroy, from his sick bed, begging him not to pass the rowlatt Bills but, his request was ignored. Gandhiji decided to act and took the leadership in his first All-India Agitation. He formed Satyagraha Sabha the members of which pledged to disobey the Rowlett Act, if it was applied to them as well as other cruel laws as the British may pass from time to time.

Jawaharlal was full of enthusiasm and wanted to join the Satyagraha Sabha immediately. Motilal did not think nuch of people going to jail as a result of Satyagraha Sabha and it's programmes and Jawaharlal was upset that his father would not permit him to be a part of this programme. Motilal knew his son was unhappy and invited Gandhiji to Allahabad. Gandhiji agreed with Motilal and Jawaharlal was requested not to take any part in the Satyagrah Sabha, for the time being. Some tragic events took place soon after, they changed even Motilal's mind.

Satyagraha Day, All-India, hartals and complete Bandh, firing by the police and military at Delhi and Amritsar killing many people, mobviolence in Amritsar and Ahmedabad, the massacre of Jallianwala bagh, the long horror and shame of military law in the Punjab. As soon as the military law in the Punjab was withdraw people poured into the areas affected by massfiring, offering their services for relief work or enquiry work. The relief work was largely directed by Pandit Madan Mohan Malaviya and Swami Shraddananda. The enquiry part was mainly under Motilal and Deshbandhu Das. Most of the evidence relating to Jallianwala Bagh and a terrible lane where people were made to crawl on their bellies which later appeared in the Congress Inquiry Report was taken down by das and Jawaharlal.

During Christmas 1919, Motilal presided over Amritsar Congress which was the first Gandhi Congress. Bal Gangadhar Tilak too was present and everyone looked to Gandhiji for leadership. The cry Mahatma Gandhi ki jai was everywhere throughout India.

In the autumn of 1920 a special session of Congress met at Calcutta to consider what steps should be taken to prevent the British from their cruel, brutal acts of violence like the one they committed on helpless, unarmed crowd of innocent people at Jallianwala Bagh and, in this meeting at Calcutta, Gandhiji's proposal of non-co-operation, using totally non-violent means, was seriously considered by the delegates. Leaders like Lala Lajpat Rai and Deshbandhu Das were of the opinion that non-co-operation may not succeed; they also thought that people all over India may not all respond to the call of non--co-operation. At that time, those who opposed non-co-operation did not fully realize how persuasive, how convincing Gandhiji could be in getting the entire country of millions to respond to his call of non-co-operation !

Motilal Nehru was only one, among the senior leaders, to support Gandhiji's call for non-co-operation, It was no easy matter for him to do so. Apart from the struggle for his country's freedom, there was also a question of what he had to give up in his personal life. Like the luxuries he had become accustomed to, his comfortable social life and his profession which had been bringing him a great deal of money. However, in the end sensing a form of effective action in Gandhiji's proposal of non-co-operation his reason, his strong sense of self-respect and his pride led him step by step to join, whole heartedly. Gandhiji's non-co-operation movement.

The Imprisonment

The year 1921 was a year when thousands of Congressmen and those who admired Gandhiji, Jawaharlal and other leaders went to prison, most of them even voluntarily ! 1921 saw a mixture of partiotism, politics, religion ; behind all this, there was agrarian trouble too since the farmers and the peasants began demanding better living conditions for themeselves; and in big cities, a rising working-class labour movement, Yet, because of Gandhiji's policy of peaceful methods, no Englishman was hated personally. It was the English rule that the peopele did not want the Englishmen.

"Go to the villages !" was the slogan for Congressmen in 1921 and many of them, including Jawaharlal, went to the villages and held meetings with large crowds of peasants and farmers.

Right through the year 1921, Congressmen were being arrested but, there were no mass arrests. Towards the end of 1921, the Prince of Wales was coming to India. The Congress announced a boycott of all functions in connection with the Prince's visitr so, wherever he went, he was met by hartals and totaly empty streets. Early in December, a few days before the Prince came to Allahabad, mass arrests began and later, Motilal and his son Jawaharlal were arrested, the first imprisonment for both of them in their struggle for a Free-India. Mass arrests continued, especially in the United Provinces and in Bengal. All the prominent Congress leaders and workers were arrested and many who liked the Congress leaders, too, Young boys and girls jumped into Police vans, refusing to come out and the vans began carrying hundreds of more people to the jail than the number actually mentioned in the arrest warrants !

The jail officers did not know how to cope with this strange situations and, finally, the British were forced to release all the prisoners, detaining only a few prominent leaders. But, surprisingly, Gandhiji, the leader of the whole struggle was himself not arrested since the British feared that the Indian Army and the Police, which they controlled, may rebel if Gandhiji was touched.

Suddenly, early in February 1922, Jawaharlal heard in the prison that Gandhiji had stopped the non-co-operation movement, this was because of what had happened near the village of Chauri Chaura were a mob of village people angered by police action against them, set fire to the Police station with half a dozen or so Policemen in it. Jawaharlal and others in prison were greatly disappointed at the sudden stoppage of non-co-operation but, from within prison walls, they could do nothing.

After many months of strain and worry, the British government breathed easily again ; a few weeks later, they arrested Gandhiji too and sent him to jail for a long time.

The non-co-operation movement and non-violence were two methods very dear to Gandhiji. He had immense faith that these alone can make India free. But, after the Chauri Chaura tragedy and with most prominent leaders in jail, more acts of violence may be committed by other Indians too, when provoked by the British, as they were by the British police in Chauri Chaura. Such acts of violence by Indians, Gandhiji feared, would be crushed by the British in a bloody manner establishing a rule of terror. Gandhiji, however, started the non-co-operation movement again, later in 1930 and 1932, which were well organised and greatly successful because, by then, the Congress leaders and workers well-trained in the principles of non-co-operation and non-violence.

Jawaharlal was released, from his first imprisonmemt, after 6 months. Motilal who was in the same jail was, however, not released along with his son and Jawaharlal left the jail with a sad heart.

Soon after he came out of jail, Jawaharlal rushed to Ahmedabad to meet Gandhiji. but, Gandhiji was then in Sabarmati Jail by then. Jawaharlal met him there and was even present at Gandhiji's trial. He later returned to Allahabad, feeling unhappy and lonely outside the prison when so many of his friends were inside it. He found, that the Congress Organization was not working well and began setting it right. Later, he interested himself in the boycott of foreign cloth. Almost all cloth merchants in Allahabad had pledged that they would never import foreign cloth and had even formed an association for this purpose. The rules of this association for this purpose. The rules of this association made it clear that any merchant found guilty of importing or purchasing foreign cloth would be punished with a fine. Jawaharlal found that a few cloth merchants had broken their promises and were importing foreign cloth. Jawaharlal and his friends began to picket these shops and the merchants, scared, paid their fines and pledged themselves again not to import or purchase foreign cloth. Soon after Jawaharlal was arrested, for the second time, for 'threatening' the cloth merchants to pay fines ! So, after being out of jail for only 6 weeks, he went back for another year and nine months. This time, to Lucknow District Jail. He was released on January 31, 1923.

Nehru and Different Communities

As Jawaharlal was recovering in 1923 from the typhoid fever, understanding and friendship between the Hindu and Muslim communities were becoming weak, in North India, especially. In larger cities brutal and cruel clashes broke up between after a while and start again for some reason sensitive to both Hindus and Muslims. For instance, cow-sacrifice at Bakr-Id day would anger the Hindus, Another cause for clashes would be when Hindu and Muslim festivals took place at the same time, festivals like Moharam and Ram Lila. Fortunately, due to difference in the two calenders. Moharam and Ram Lila come together only once in 30 years.

But now in 1923, a new complaint came from the Muslims that the sounding of gongs and ringing of bells at evening worship time in Hindu temples disturbed the evening prayers in their Mosques. It is tragic that religious emotions do not let people to sit together and find a solution to their problems in peaceful ways. Especially when a third party tries to make one religious group dislike and distrust another religious group; from the 1920s, this third party making trouble between the Hindus and the Muslims was the British Government itself.

Long ago, at the time of this non-co-operation movement or, even earlier, Gandhiji had a method to bring peace between the Hindus and the Muslims. His belief was that the Hindus, as the majority community should be generous enough to meet all the demands and requests of the minority Muslim community. He wanted to win the Muslims over with love and generosity; he did not want to bargain with them. There were many Muslims in the Congress; their numbers were large and included many able men because the best known and most popular Muslims leades were in Congress ; mamny of these Congress Muslims formed a group for themeselves called the Natonalist Muslim Party and they trie to bring peace between communal Hindu and Muslim leaders; they did succeed, to begin with but, many of the communal leaders were upper middle-class and there were no men powerful enough to earn the respect and support of the masses; they were only worried about their professions and their own businesses and had no contact with the masses; as a result, gradually, the group called, the Nationalist Muslim party vanished, sadly.

The 'Nationalist Muslim Party' disappeared only as a group but, the individual Congress Muslims who had formed the group orginally still continued as prominent Congress leaders. During the middle twenties, many attempts were made to settle the communal problem by mutual talks and discussions. Unity Conferences, as they were called. The most famous conference was the one held by M.Mohamed Ali, the Congress president for 1924, at Delhi, under the shadow of Gandhiji's 21 day fast, There were many sincere and well-meaning people at the conference and they tried hard to come to an agreement. Some pious and good decisions were made but, the basic problem did not go away. Added to this, the Sikhs in the Punjab started making loud communal demands of their own. In some provinces agrarian trouble between the rich Hindu Zamindars (Landlord) and the poor Muslim tenants turned into rich communal riots and sind between the rich Hindu moneylendors and the poor Muslim borrowers. The Delhi Unity Conference of 1924 was barely over when a Hindu-Muslim riot broke up in Jawaharlal's home-town of Allahabad although, by the time he rushed to Allahabad from Delhi, the rioting was over but, later, there was a lot of ill-will between the Hindus and Muslims in Allahabad.

Back to Europe

Jawaharlal, going back to Europe after 13 years, to a Europe which had seen war revolution which had brought tremendous change. The old world he had known had died in the blood and horror of war and a new world awaited him. He expected to remain in Europe for 6 to 7 months or, at least until the end of

1926 but, actually, his stay extended to a year and 9 months. He returned to India towards the end of 1927 after travelling a little in France, England and else where. Although his wife was not wholly recovered she was for better and that relieved him of some worry on her behalf.

Soon after his return to India, he plunged back into Indian politics full of energy a restful holiday in Europe.

Soon after arrival in Madras, via Colombo, Jawaharlal was caught in a buzzle of Political activity at the Congress Session then being held in Madras. He presented the working committee with a bunch of proposals on Independence. Dangers of war, association with the League against Imperialism and so on. To his surprise, the working committee accepted every proposal of Jawaharlal's unanimously, without debate. Mrs. Besant, in particular, supported the Independence resolution. This whole hearted support made him happy but yet, he had an uncomfortable feeling that his proposals were either not understood property or were distorted to mean something else.

Before the leaders dispersed from Madras, news reached them of the death of Hakim Ajmal Khan at Delhi. The Hakim was well respected both by Hindus and Muslims and he had done a great deal to bring them together successfully. In Hindu-Muslim matters, his advice was final word to Gandhiji and the Hakim was well respected by other leaders like Motilal.

Jawaharlal noticed that, in his long absence in Europe, Indians throughout the country had regained thair patriotism and their faith in Gandhiji and he was delighted to see that the unity which had been present during the non-co-operation years of 1920/21 was back again in Indian's hearts. And thus. 1928, the year of Jawaharlal's return to India was politically, a full year. The Trade Union Movement had grown greatly with the Girni

Kamgari Union and G.I.P. Railway Union, both of Bombay, having become the strongest and most advanced of unions; the peasantry was also not quiet ; the bardoli Satyagraha on behalf of the Gujarat peasantry, led by Sardar Vallabhai Patel, was a huge successsince it praved way for the well-being of peasants all over India; another noticeable change in the india of 1928 was the growth of Youth Movement throughout the country; thus, there was a positive awakening of patriotism throughout the country.

From a purely political point of view, the year became famous for the boycott of the Simon Commission a boycot which was total and completely successful with crowds of Indians jeering "Simon, go back" wherever the Commission went ! The boycott was followed by an all parties conference which had no difficulty in settling the main principles of a constitution for a free India of a democratic, parliamentary variety which almost anyone could have drawn up; the main difficulty and, in fact, the only difficulty, came from the communal or minorities issue and, since representatives from all the Extreme communal oganisations were in the conference, an agreement became very difficult. It was a repetition of old unsuccessful Unity Conferences. finally, as a last step, a committee was formed with Motilal Nehru as Chairman, called the Nehru Committtee and it was asked to draft a constitution, making a full report on the communal issue, the report itself to be called as the Nehru Report. This committee's efforts were about to be successful but the Hindu-Sikh-Muslim triangle existing win the Punjab, looked upon the Nehru Report with fear and mistrust and, thus, all the efforts with fear and mistrust and , thus, all the efforts of the Nehru committee became useless.

The all parties conference met at Lucknow to consider the Nehru Report which put many of the members in difficulty since many of them did not want to come in the way of a communal settlement, if that was possible and yet, thay were not prepared to give up the question of independence.

The delegates at the all parties conference begged that the question be left open so that each party could have liberty of action, the Congress sticking to independence and the Moderates to Dominion status. Jawaharlal was then asked by the Independence group-and this was a large group-to make a statement to the conference on the group's behalf. dissociating themeselves from everything that came in the way of independence. He made it very clear that he would not come in the way of communal settlement. This, on Jawaharlal's part, was at best a negative gesture. A positive side soon came along since, on that very day, the "Independence for India" League was formed.

Gandhiji took no part in the all party conference or Nehru committee meetings. He was, infact, not even in Lucknow when these meeting were held.

Meanwhile, the Simon Commission was moving about India and was being shouted at "simon, go back!" wherever the commission went. As the commission passed through from city to city, occasionally there were minor trouble between the police and shouting demonstrators, but, a terrible happened as the commission passed through Labore which rocked the whole of India with anger, grief and a sense of shame.

The anti-Simon Commission demonstration in Labore was led by Lala Lajpat Rai and, as he stood by the roadside infront of the thousands of demonstrators, he was assaulted and beaten on the chest by a lathi by a young English Police officer; there had been no attempt on the part of the crowd and certainly none by Lalaji, to indulge in any method of violence. This unprovoked, brutal assult on one of the oldest and most respected leaders of

India sent wave after wave of shock and horror throughout India; not only Lalaji but many of his companions too were severelly beaten by the brutal British police; Lalaji was not only an old man but he had been suffering from heart disease for a long time and hence, when he died a few weeks later, every Indian belived firmly that it was the brutal attack on his chest which had hastened his death. Lalaji's own reaction to the whole incident was one shame nor for his personal injury or for the loss of his personal dignity but at the loss of dignity of the entire Indian people and the contempt in which the British treated the Indians.

The Freedom Fight

The First World War ended in 1919. Britain, which was part of the Allied Forces, was victorious. India had participated in this war with the British, and the Indian soldiers had fought bravely. The Indians had expected to be treated generously and fairly by the British. Instead, the British passed the Rowlett Act which gave them the power to arrest political agitators without a trial. This Act shocked both the Moderates and the Extremists in India.

Gandhiji started the Satyagraha Sabha to disobey this Act. He urged the nation to disobey the Act without causing any harm to any person or property. Jawaharlal joined this movement with enthusiasm. The Non-Co-operation movement swept the entire nation. It involved the 'triple boycott'- the boycott of foreign cloth, the boycott of law courts and legislatures and the boycott of schools and colleges.

Jawaharlal was deeply impressed by Gandhiji's thoughts and plan of action. He was feeling increasingly torn between his family duties and his duty to his nation.

'I cannot concentrate on my practice anymore', thought

Jawaharlal one day, 'I have a bigger mission in life, I shall give up my flourishing law practice, smoking eating non-vegetarian food and my aristocratic ways of life. I shall read the Gita every day and draw strength from it'.

The whole Nehru family was influenced by Jawaharlal"s change in lifestyle. They all switched over to wearing Khadi clothes and simple living. The large retinue of servants was reduced, and elaborate meals gave way to simple fare, Imported goods were collected and burnt in bonfires.

Motilal started a newspaper called The Independent with Jawaharlal as one of the directors. It was to serve the people of India by giving them correct information about the national movement. But Motilal and Jawaharlal had very little time to devote to it because of their hectic political activities. And so it had to be closed down after a short span of three years. In 1938, Jawaharlal became the chairman of the board of the National Herald.

In 1921, both Jawaharlal and Motilal were arrested. This was just the beginning of a series of imprisonments which kept Jawaharlal away from his family. It also gave him the opportunity for thinking, and a time to read and write. It was during this time that he began his now famous letters to his daughter, young Indira.

"My heart and soul is with my country's struggle for freedom, but I have some duty to wards my own family", said Jawaharlal to his father one day. "Kamala is stricken with tuberculosis and is getting weakr by the day. What should I do, father?"

"Why don't you take her for treatement to Switzerland ? Suggested Motilal, "with care and rest she should get better."

So in March, 1926, Jawaharlal Nehru left for Switzerland

with his wife and daughter, for kamala's treatement in a sanatorium. He could return to India in December, 1927.

On his return to India, the agitation against the Simon Commission gave a new directions to the Congress. The British beat up and fired at the peacefully demonstrating crowds, while participating in one such big demonstration in Lucknow, Jawahar received severe head injuries from the raining blows. Lala Lajpat Rai who recveived severe blows on his chest, died. The humiliated nation was in an angry mood.

It was the year 1929. The Congress President was yet to be elected. Someone strong was required who would steer the party to it's goal. If Gandhi refuses, I want you to take over as party president, said Motilal to Jawaharlal. "You will be a symbol of youth, and can lead the party to greater heights."

"No, father, I do not have the politician's flair for forming groups and parties", he said modestly. However, when Gandhi refused, he had no choice.

"For want of any other person, and in a spirit of resignation, I accept the post of president of the Congress", said Nehru in his address to the All India Congress Committee in Lucknow. He was not happy that he had reached the highest office of his Party in this manner.

"What the father is unable to accomplish, the son achieves", quoted Motilal in anemotional farewell speech as the outgoing Party President.

The youth of the nation was in a jubilant mood. Jawaharlal represented a shot of fresh blood. He would give a new direction to the Indian freedom struggle and, perhaps, even lead the country too independence.

On 31st December, 1929, at the stroke of midnight, at the

Congress Session in Labore on the banks of the Ravi river, India's tri-coloured flag was unfurled.

Jawaharlal Nehru in his president address demanded complete independenc. Though Gandhi was to remain the guidling force. The burden now largely fell on Nehru's shoulders. He had to lead India to greater heights.

The Prison Experience

Jawaharlal had been out of prisons of Naini, Barielly and Dehra Dun for exactly 5 months and 13 days and, on 12th February 1934, he was arrested once again and this was the 7th time that this great leader had to suffer a life a loneliness in jail. Until the 16th February, 1934, he had been kept in Calcutta and then sent to Alipore jail nearby, sentenced to two years.

This time, however, Jawaharlal was in a happy mood; during the five and a half months that he was free before being sent to Alipore, he had set many of his family matters right; his sister Krishna had got married during this time; he had made proper arrangements for his daughter Indira's education; his mother's health had improved; he had written a series of articles to newspapers which were liked by the people ; the letters that Jawaharlal and Gandhiji had written to each other during this period, when published later, became famous and are famous even now. His wife Kamala's health had become worse and this was the only matter which made him sad.

The climate at Alipore did not suit Jawaharlal's health and they were kind enough to transfer him, on 7th May, 1934, to the pleasant, hill-side jail of Dehra Dun. Towards the end of July, Kamala's illness became serious and, on 11th August, 1934, Jawaharlal was released temporarily, for only 11 day to be with her and on the 11th day, 23rd August, 1934, he was taken, this time to Naini jail. By this time, Jawaharlal had spent some 6 months in jail and still had a year and a half remaining in the 2 year jail sentence. He was told he would be released immediately so that he could be with his sick wife if he promised not to take part in politics for the remaining one had a half years. Jawaharlal refused.

Early in October, he was again taken to see her briefly and as he was about to leave her to return to jail, she whispered "What is this about your giving a promise to the British Government? Don't give it ! very soon later, her condition became so serious that she was sent to Bhowali in the hislls and, on the day before she was to leave for Bhowali, he was taken to her to bid her good-bye. 3 weeks later, Jawaharlal was taken from Naini to Almora jail which is nearer to Bhowali and in, treatement while Jawaharlal was still in Almora jail. On 4th September, 1935, Jawaharlal was released, five and a half months earlier, since Kamala had become very seriously ill in Switzerland, Jawaharlal flew to her side. On February 28, 1936, the poor, long suffering lady passed away.

Thus it was that, from 1936 until the end of the second World War in 1945, eminent leaders of India like Gandhiji, Jawaharlal, Sardar Vallabhai Patel were being dragged into and out of jails, many number of times but, the Indian people refused to surrender their self-respect, their love and worship of their beloved Mathrubhoomi (Motherland). No matter how much the heartless British rules tortured herassed the Indians and finally, in March 1946, a special team of eminent people arrived from London to decide the manner in which Independence should be given.

India became independent on August 15, 1947; although the entire country was jubilant, India, no longer, was one whole country; a portion of it had been sliced away to create a second Independent Country-Pakistan.

When the clock struck the magic hour of midnight on August 14/15, 1947, Pandit Jawaharlal Nehru, the first Prime Minister of "Free" India, rose to make a speech-a speech that lingers, to this day, in the Indian peoples' ears and minds.

"Long years ago we made a tryst with destiny and now the time comes when we shall redeem our pledge, not wholly or, in full measure, but very substantially. "At the stroke of the midnight hour, whe the world sleeps, India will awake to life and Freedom". Panditji served India, as Prime Minister untill his death on May 27, 1964, at the age of 76.

During his 18 years in office, he worked tirelessly and toured the country extensively. He created a special place for India, in the Map of the World-Until then, no one in the world had known much about India, since India had been suppressed, for centuries, by foreign domination. All that changed like magic, under Jawaharlal's leadership due to his charming ways and the courtesy with which he treated friends and enemies, alike.

Panditji gave special importance to Scientific Research and, as a result, National Physical Laboratory, National Chemical Laboratory, Central Electro-Chemical Research Institute and ever so many similar research institutions were established.

The Round Table Conferences

The First Round Table Conference was held in 1931, in London. This was boycotted by Gandhi. Soon, a second Round Table Conference was called. Meanwhile, Motilal's health had deteriorated. Eminent doctors were consulted, but they could not save him. on the 6th of February he passed away.

Both Jawaharlal and Gandhi were devastated. Jawaharlal lost his best friend, Philosopher and guide, He had shared a unique relationship with his father based on mutual love, respect and understanding. Gandhi said quite rightly that Motilal's love for India was derived from his love for Jawaharlal.

From 31st December, 1931 to September 1935, Jawaharlal had spent 1170 days in jail. In June, 1934, he began writing his autobiography in the Dehra Dun jail. This was completed in 1935 while he was in jail in Almora.

Meanwhile, his beloved wife, Kamala had a relapse and passed away in a Swiss sanatorium in 1936. She had borne her illness bravely without complaining. She had spent the greater part of her life away from her husband, who would either be in jail for his political activities, or, when out of jail, busy with his goal of achieving independence for the nation. She had whole heartedly taken part in the Indian struggle for freedom, and had shown great organising abilities, She had led women in the agitation for freedom, and in spite of her frail health, she had even courted arrest, she was a true wife to Nehru.

With Kamala suddenly gone, Jawaharlal felt lonely. His daughter, Indira. was also away studying in Oxford, and his parents were dead. Life seemed dull and isolated. Nehru found solace in reading and writing.

In September, 1939, the Second World War broke out. When Japan struck Pearl Harbour in 1941, the war seemed fat away. But when it occupied Malaya and Singapore and forced the British forces to withdraw from Burma, India became an important war base. By 1942 the 'Quit India Movement' was started. All efforts to pacify the Indians failed.

Nehru played a vital role in getting India her freedom. In February, 1947, the British Government announced that it would transfer political power to the Indian Government elected for and by the people of India, latest by June 1948.

On 22nd March, 1947, Lord Mountbatten arrived as the Viceroy, and he held talks with all the political leaders on various problems. He shared a particularty warm relationship with Nehru. In London the Indian Independence Bill was passed by both the houses of Parliament.

On 14th August, 1947, at the hour of midnight, Nehru made a speech which since then has become famous. It began like this; "At the stroke of the midnight hour when the world sleeps, India will awake to life and Freedom", Jawaharlal Nehru was sworn in as the Prime Minister of Free India.

The Planning Commission

The planning commission was set up in the year 1950, to make plans for the development of industries and agriculture. They were a great success in India and resulted in the Green Revolution which made India self-sufficient in food. It also industrialised the Nation.

Nehru also wanted friendly relations with the neighbouring countries. India signed Friendship Treaties in 1949 with Bhutan, Sikkim, Burma and Afghanistan.

However, China continually disputed it's borderline with India in the North-East, Nehru tried to solve the problem in a diplomatic way. So he was stunned when the Chinese army attacked India in 1962. The Indian armed forces were not very well prepared and Jawaharlal took it upon himself as his failing.

The Chinese attack was the saddest chapter of Nehru's life many say that this was also the beginning of his decline. It took a big toll on his health. He felt betraved. After the war was over, he hotold the people of India. "we must think of the Chinese attack as a blessing in disguise. We should make an effort to make our country progress so that we can have a strong military force and no one can dare attack us again.

Though Jawaharlal Nehru was so involved in politics, he always had time for children. His deep love for them is well known. He often said, "I like being with children and talking to them and, even more, playing with them. For a moment I forget that I'am terribly old and that it was a long time ago since I was a child". Children called him Chacha (Uncle) Nehru out of love and respect. He spent a lot of time playing with his two grandsons, Rajiv and Sanjay and their friends. He also had a great love for animals, and kept several pets all his life. The 14th of November, Nehru's birthday is still celebrated as children's Day all over the country. During the long and lonely days in prison, when he was fighting for the freedom of India, Nehru wrote three books, Glimpses of World History, An Autobiography and the Discovery of India.

Glimpses of World History contains 176 letters which he wrote to his young daughter Indira, from jail, between 26th March, 1930 to 9th August 1933, Through these detailed letters, Nehru traces the history of the world. Till today his book is widely appreciated and parts of it are used in textbooks which are used by many schools. In his book an Autobiography Nehru describes himself as 'English by education, Muslim bu culture, and Hindu by birth. It tells about his innermost thoughts and proves that he was a true Indian.

The Discovery of India is the story of our past and present. It is the story of our culture and civilisation. In a moving passage in the book, Nehru writes, "we are all citizens of a great Country, and are proud of the land of our birth, of our people, our culture and traditions. That pride should not be for the past to which we want to cling. It must never allow us to forget out many weaknesses and we should always try to get rid of them".

It is said that there has not been a better book about the cultural unity of India.

Jawaharlal remained very conscious of physical fitness all his life, right up to the end. He had developed this habit by observing his father who was conscious of exercising daily. Often, Gandhi and Nehru used to have their intensive discussions during their morning walks. Even at the age of seventy four, he would get up the crack of down to exercise.

After a simple breakfast of fruits and porridge, he would meet all the people who wished to see him. He often entertained formal and informal guests at breakfast, lunch and dinner in which he was always accompanied by his daughter, Indira. He was a brilliant conversationalist and would amuse his guests with humorous and witty stories. He was an attentive listener and a good correspondent, and would attempt to reply to each and every letter be received especially from children.

Once a group of children from Japan wrote to him and asked him to send them an elephant. He propmptly sent them a beautiful elephant on behalf of the children of India. The elephant travelled all the way by sea. from Mysore to Japan. When it reached from Mysore to Japan, when it reached Tokyo from thousands of children came to see it. Many of them had never seen an elephant before. It made him very happy to think that this gift from India had given so much joy to so many children of Japan, and made them think about our country.

The Last Days

In January, 1964, Nehru suffered from high blood pressure and was adviced complete rest. He recovered after spending a comfortable day reading books. On 26th January, the Republic Day of India, he sat through the entire three hour parade without feeling tired. After the Bombay session of AICC, on 15th May Jawaharlal went for a three-day holiday to Dehra Dun. He even went for a picnic with his family. He returned to Delhi on 26th May.

"I am feeling uneasy this morning", said Jawaharlal to his daughter, Indira. Indira rushed to summon all the doctors. The team of doctors did all they could but Nehru slowly started sinking. By two O' clock he was no more. It was the 27th of May, 1964. The entire nation was plunged in sorrow.

Even in death his thoughts were with India. In his will be said; "I am making this request that a handful of my ashes he thrown into the Ganga. at Allahabad, to be carried to the great ocean that washes India's shores, as a mark of my respect for my country. The rest of my ashes should be carried high up into the air in an aeroplane, and scattered from that height over the fields where the farmers of Indian soil.

4

Bal Gangadhar Tilak

Childhood

On 23rd July Gangadhar Pant's wife gave birth to a son, to the delight of Gangadhar Pant. The parent fondly started calling the child, Bal Gangadhar. At that time after a lot of bloodshed British were able to crush the Indians. While Bal Gangadhar was bawling for his milk the countrymen were crying in despair at the failure of the first freedom attempt.

Bal Gangadhar grew up adding years to his life in such atmosphere of dejection and frustration. The father, Gangadhar Pant was a nationalist to the core and his heart bled for his slaving country. The failure of 1857 uprising had deeply hurt him.

He found consolation in telling hid child about the state of the country, the miserable conditions and brutal repression of the natives by the colonial British. Bal Gangadhar was getting some symbolic picture in his childish mind of fairy tale variety like Indians being troubled by a horrible white sorcerer. In this way Bal Gangadhar grew up to the school going age. Gangadhar Pant got him admitted to the school. To the amazement of the other kids he would reveal to them that their country was not free.

Someone would ask, "What do you mean not free ?"

"We are slaves, white English men are our masters."

"who told you about it?" "My father tells me everything"

Bal Gangadhar had become popular among the kids for being source of strange informations. He had many friends besides having fans who thought he was the best informed kid in the whole world. For the kids 'whole world' was Slightly bigger than Ratnagiri area.

After shouting and crying the kids would return home. On the way the war against the whitemen would be a forgotten thing, and their own childish quarrels would take over. Enthused by the attention little Bal would proudly declare that he will grew up to drive the whitemen out of the country. He had many half-backed plans in the furnace of his kid brain.

One of them was acquiring mind beggining occult powers to undo the whitemen's spell over Indian soldiers. For kids it was as fascianting as a fairy tale. Many kids volunteered to be his future soldiers.

One evening Bal Gangadhar returned home to find his father in grim mood. The boy sensed that something new had happened. His father called the boy to him and upsetting news. Son I have been transferred to Pune. Our days here are over. We shall have to shift to that place.

The boy protested. He said, "But my school is here how can I come to Poona ?"

"Child, you will come with me, because your mother will also be accompanying me" The father spoke and assured.

"Don't worry about school. In Poona you will go to a bigger and better school.

Bal Gangadhar was panicky, said, "I Won't come to Poona".

The Head Master, Gangadhar Pant said to his stunned Son, "Dear Child, no one will be here to look after you and cook food for you since your mother would be with me, As far as friends are concerned you will make friends at Poona, new friends. You shouldn't worry on that score."

Thus, forced by the situation Bal Gangadhar had to go to Poona. A boy who had invested so much thought in his earlier place was bound to face adjustment problems. After sometime his mind settled in the new environment.

The memories of the old place and the friends began to fade away as new friends came into his life. Soon he was feeling at home and hopeful again. Then suddenly a tragedy struck which traumatised Bal Gangadhar.

His Mother passed away. Time is a great healer. The boy also accepted the life without mother and moved on. An aunt had walked into the family and taken charge of the household. Father, aunt and sisters provided the needed comfort.

The boys of Poona School were far more cleaver than the boys of the earlier school. They knew about the British rule in India. Discussing whitemen problem with new friends was more exciting and educative. Most of the boys disliked the foreign rule.

The Orthodox Tradition

The Child Marriages were order of the day during that period, a tradition in Orthodox families that could not be broken. The children were too young to understand the implications of the childhood marriages. They were just helpless before the orthodox traditionalist elders. The Child Marriage was infact not an ancient custom. It started when the foreign invaders flooded the country, especially the Muslim invaders, who followed no rule or code.

One of their prize targets were women or girls of beautiful type who they used to take forcibly. So on pretty or young face was safe during the period. But Strangely those invaders life married women alone as it was a grave sin according to Islamic tenets. So to save the honour of their daughters, the Hindu parents started marrying their daughters in the childhood.

Being legally married the girl child was relatively safe from abduction and dishonour. But it became a tradition and the people continued the practice even when it's usefulness was over, That is one of the tragedies of Indians, of being blindly slavish to customs.

When Bal Gangadhar was 15 years of age he was forced to marry a girl child named Tapi of a nearby village. The alliance was arranged by the elders. At that time his father, Gangadhar Pant was sick and was bedridden,.

In the case of Bal Gangadhar and Tapi the marriage was merely Some function in which they found themselves strangely the centre of all the activities and the attention of the relatives. It was an exciting experience to see all the women in finery and precious jewelry. Menfolk were also dressed in their best. Tapi was helped by aunts to get bedecked like a princess. She could not understand the reason, but enjoyed it any way.

When marriage was completed. The four carriers carried the palki away to grooms home. Tapi liked the house. The house was freshly white washed and decorated with flowers and leaves. The floors had flowery designs. The women of the house looked excited and the fawned over Tapi was being treated like a special guest. An adult woman had accompanied Tapi from their home as per the custom. She had travelled in the some palki as tapi.

At the new house she kept hovering around, all the time which made her feel at home. By now Bal Gangadhar was getting some ideas that he had been married although he could not understand the full importance of it.

Tapi and Bal felt happy whenever they were together. Bal liked the innocent moon like face of Tapi. The girl saw the pile of books in the room of Bal. She felt very ashamed that she could not read or write.

Bal and Tapi

Bal and Tapi liked each other but did not talk much. They did not know what to say to each other, or talk about what? The only meaningful talk was Tapi asked about the books, if they were really for the reading of Bal, and could he really read?

Tapi admitted that she was totally alien to reading and writing. During that period girls were rarely sent to school. Most of the people held the view that, education was not for the girls and they should confine themeselves to cooking, cleaning, kntting and making the husbands happy.

Tapi busied herself in playing with her friends or doing household chores. She forgot her promise made to Bal that she would learn to read and write. Besides she was afraid that if asked her mother to send her to the school all the women laugh at her.

Once women folk were talking about Tapi and her future. Tapi happened to be listening to their talk. The women were saying that in some years. Tapi would be a young lady and Bal Gangadhar would come to take her away.

Now Tapi was in panic. How would she face Bal Gangadhar without having learnt to read and write? Now the promise given to Bal loomed large. Tapi told her mother about it. The mother listened to her daughter's problem seriously.

She did not want her Tapi to loose face before her husband. She made up her mind that if son-ion-law wanted, it shall be done. Arrangements were made for Tapi to learn the letters. Meanwhile Bal Gangadhar was getting politically educated. Now he was understanding the British colonial rule over Indian more clearly.

He could practically feel the sting of being a slave of the foreign rulers, and how the whitemen were exploiting the natives. His friends also understood that sooner or later, they would have to wage the Battle of Freedom.

The maturing minds of the boys realised that guns and the soldiers were not the only weapons in the British arsenal. There were many factors in the play. The Englishmen were well educated. That was their real power. They could plan things and knew how to run the administration. Before Englishmen. Hindustanis looked horribly inefficient incompetent and bereft of ideas, And the Englishmen suffered from no social evils like untouchability, castism, widow burning, child marriages etc.

As Bal grew up natural instincts of the basic kind also began to influence his mind. Now he remembered more about the girl who had followed him around the fire, seven times like a pet.

A wish to meet her would haunt him. This desire became stronger whenever he saw women and young girls going about merrily chatting and giggling. Strangely he would remember Tapi before going to sleep and often saw her in his dreams as a grown. up girl.

The Dark Bands

Bal's father Gangadhar Pant had been sick and bedridden. The Marriage itself was a sick man's wish.

Bal's Satisfactory progress towards the adulthood gave immense relief to the sick man. The son was studying diligently and becoming politically wise. Gangadhar Pant knew that his end was near. But now he was satisfied that he would leave behind the son, who would probably make his name live longer. When Bal Gangadhar was still in his teens, his father breathed his last.

Father's death was a shock even though it was not totally unexpected. Bal broke down and wept bitterly. The caretaker aunt and the sisters wailed and remained inconsolable for weeks. The family had no adult male to take charge and bear the burden of the household. The neighbours and relatives converged on the family to commiserate.

Tapi and her family also come to share the grief. Tapi's dream of walking into her husband's house as an educated lady was cut short. She had begun to read and write. last time she entered into that house there was laughter in the air and it was festively decorated.

This time the mood was just the opposite. Smell of death hung in the air. There were gloomy and grief stricken faces all around. The women had their eyes red from weeping continuously. The sisters of Bal Gangadhar were in bad shape. There were dark bands around their eyes. Every now and then. they would break down and bitterly weep. Tapi was deeply saddened to see Bal Gangadhar who looked a picture of grief.

The caretaker aunt requested to the father of Tapi to leave the bride behind to live with them although merely 11 years old she reasoned that the family was too grief stricken that needed some one to cheer it up and Bal Gangadhar was a broken boy who badly needed some one around to kindle hope in him to bring him back to normal life. Bal's sisters also wanted Tapi to stay with them.

The father of the bride had to yield after all since the marriage his daughter belonged to the Pant family, for all practical purposes. And the bereaved family badly needed her as he could see their meserable state. It was a very defficult transition for Tapi to change over from a care free hop-scotching girl to nurse maid of the family suffering from deep grief.

She was only 11 year old. The Situation would rob her of her entire teenage life. Now she was supposed to act like a mature woman and prove to be a soothing balm to heal wounds of the family left behind by the death of Gangadhar Pant. Bal gradually made it back to normal state and got busy in his school books.

The College Education

Bal Gangadhar passed Matriculation Examination. For further studies he joined Deccan College of Poona, that had a great reputation for education with famous names on it's teaching staff which included Mr. Wordsworth, Mr. Khapre and prof. Shute among others. Father's death had played havoc with the psyche of young Bal Gangadhar. He was not as sharp as before in his studies As a result he failed in the first year exam of the college.

The friends and the family members tried to console Bal Gangadhar. He was thinking on some other lines. He had realised that the college education, was a different thing. It required more concentration and interaction with fellow students. He took a decision to leave the domestic environment which was proving a back-draft in his educational progress. He wanted to live in totally academic atmosphere. So he moved in to live with one of his close friends Agarkar.

The new environment proved very educative for Bal Gangadhar. It galvanised him nito action education wise and he became a youngman full of energy and verve. He debated with his friends on all Political, Social and Economic matters.

He was a fierce debater and expressed his opinions holding back nothing. His friend Agarkar thought on the same lines as Bal Gangadhar. On all the subjects their views were identical. They talked hours on the foreign rule in India. The economic plight of the countrymen all night, although they were merely students in the final year of graduation now.

Both were uncertain about what they were going to do after graduation. Both of them passed the B.A. Exams. Bal Gangadhar took adminission in M.A.Course but he found the course uninteresting. The friends talked about it. They came to the conclusion that since working for the freedom of the country was their final aim a law degree would come handy.

Somewhere along the line Bal Gangadhar added Tilak Surname instead of 'Pant' as his father used to be known by. Bal Gangadhar Tilak and Agarkar both joined Deccan college for L.L.B. Course.

They pursued the course seriously and continued their dialogue. Agarkar analysed that what the country needed was a massive education programme. Only education could lead to a situation where, the Indian society could be free of poverty ignorance and the foreign rule.

Bal Gangadhar agreed with Agarkar. The education was to be on the modern lines fit for the new times that could enable Indians to deal with the Englishmen. That was the period when the education was very modern, and it was producing a large number of meaningfully educated people, were inspiring the awekening of the Indian classes. The educated people knew what was needed to uplift the country and it's people.

Bal Gangadhar Tilak studied the working of the Christian Missions and the systems of their education. That was the positive aspect of the Missions but their real aim was influencing natives and converting them to Christianity. Bal Gangadhar Tilak and Agarkar came to the conclusion that Indians themeselves set up educational missions to produce the educated people to lead the people to freedom and prosperity.

Tilak had the mission of his life cut out for him. He would spread the light of the education in India to drive away. the darkness of blind faiths, ignorance, illiteracy, and thereby slavery.

Education would help people broaden the horizons of their minds which would solve many of the problems, the Indians faced due to narrow mindedness.

Bal Gangadhar in Home

For his education and future planning Bal Gangadhar Tilak had stayed away from home for almost six years which he had spent living with Agarkar.

In 1879 one evening Bal Gangadhar reached home and knocked at the door. In answer to his knock the door opened to reveal the figure of a young lady. The face looked vaguely familiar. Then, sudden realisation dawned on him that the young lady was his wife Tapi, she had grown up into a beauty in his absence. Bal Gangadhar dumbly stared at her and then opened his mouth to stammer.

"Oh ! You really !"

By now Tapi had also guessed who the visitor was. Her face turned red and legs felt like jelly. She could not stand the gaze of her husband who himself was tongue tied. She ran inside. The aunt and the sisters appeared at the door.

The aunt was overjoyed to see Bal Gangadhar. The sisters quailed in delight. Bal moved forward and touched the feet of the aunt; With tears of joy in her eyes she blessed Bal Gangadhar. Then he hugged his sisters. After getting Bal seated the aunt called out "Daughter-in -law ! come here and see who has come home.

Tapi felt panicky. Her hands were trembling. To gain time she put on an act of being busy in the kitchen. Her heart had never beat faster.

Somehow she controlled herself and put the end of her saree "Pallu" over her head in such a way that, it screened most of her face like a veil. After putting the glass on a side table she bent down to touch her husband's feet.

Bal Gangadhar Watched her greatly amused. He laughed at her veil to the utter embarrassment of Tapi. The aunt said toTapi "Tapi, we don't belive in orthodox practices like veils in our family. We always treated you as a daughter. Our Bal Gangadhar Tilak is an educated young man. Remove that veil and talk to him like a normal wife."

Tapi obediently sat beside Tilak after removing veil off her face. Aunt smiled at her approvingly and go up to retire to the kitchen on some excuse. Tilak suddenly turned to Tapi and spoke "Tapi ! what happened to your promise of learning to read and write?"

Answer came from a sister, "Brother, She is always learning to read and write. In fact now she writes letters to her parents. We were suspecting that she had been writing to you as well."

Tapi wished the sister. Tilak looked pleased. He wanted to make sure about it, "I hope that is no joke. Is it true, Tapi that you been learning ?" Tapi nodded her head shyly.

Tilak said, "Then I am really proud of you. Look my education in complete and I have decided what I am going to do with my life. I will dedicate my life to the society and the cause of the country.

The spread of the education is my primary goal. I hope Tapi you will stand by me. Your effort to learn and write on your own proves that you will understand me."

When the sisters found the talks taking a very serious and personal turn, they thought it prudent to leave the couple alone. They departed from there on some pretext.

Tapi now found tongue to say, "I will always stand by you in whatever is your venture. I am sorry that, I could not properly get educated due to the situations you know. I am trying to make up for that."

Tilak realised that Tapi had become mature young lady.

Tilak revealed his plan "I will be undertaking a mission to educate our people. Our people need it badly. Illiteracy and ignorance are the root causes of our problems. I shall a school to begin with."

"That will be good" Tapi said.

Later the aunt and Tilak talked about usual family things. She told in detail whatever had happened in his absence. Tilak hold her that the mate with whom he had lived was a wonderful cook and that kept him in good health. The aunt was relieved to know that because she had been worrying that Bal could be suffering the horrible hotel food.

"The New English School"

On 1st January 1880 'The New English School' Planned by Bal Gangadhar Tilak, Agarkar and Chiploonkar was formally opened.

The opening made a big news which attracted the well known educationists M.B.N. Joshi and V.S. Apte, to join the venture. With in three months the school has 500 students on it's rools.

The modern teaching methods adopted by the school, impressed everyone and the positive results showed very soon. The school earned fame fast. More and More parents wanted to send their children, the school run by Tilak and company. The success of the school proved a great inspiration to Tilak and he worked harder.

Just setting up one School was not the aim of Tilak. It was just a model. The message of the necessity to spread the education was required to be passed around. So he organised meetings, seminars and get togethers to give the message. He would exhort, "We must understand that education is the holy key to the solution of our problems. Only an educated India can fight of social evils it suffers from and the foreign rulers who are trampling upon our freedom and pride.

Education will make people wise enough to understand what is happening around them, how, the evil practices are eating away our society from within how ignorance is keeping them tied to the yoke of grinding poverty and economic exploitation is leading them to ulter ruin. The exploitative landed upper castes in collusion with foreign power are improvershing us."

Tilak had a very analytical mind. He was different from others who wanted to free the country but their outlook was shallow and the understanding of the problems superficial some of them wanted the country gain freedom through strikers, demonstrations and slogan shouting, others though in terms of guns and bombs. Tilak knew that Indians could not gain Independence unless, ignorance and illiteracy did not go away. If Englishmen left some others would walk in to take their place. An uneducated society did not know it's duty, rights and it's own power.

On the academic front his friends were doing a fine job of teaching. The school was making a name for itself and the success of the school was also earning fame for Bal Gangadhar Tilak. His views were being taken seriously by the people who mattered. Even British authorities and education experts were all praise for the efforts of Tilak.

Ironically Tilak had learnt the spirit of selfless services sacrifice and dedication from a particulars sect called "Jesuits" a Christian branch, that was well known for it's work in the field of social upliftment and service to people. Jesuits had done several experiments and had earned the respect and the admiration of the local people.

Tilak's Magazines

Bal Gangadhar Tilak had started two Magazines in Marathi and English, named "Maratha" and Kesari respectively, with the help of his old friends, Later he could not devote enough time to them due to his involvement in Deccan Education Society and the new English School project although he kept writing articles for the two magazines. The articles written by him used to be the main attractions of the periodicals.

After disassociating himself from the Deccan Education Society, Bal Gangadhar Tilak devoted his full time to the magazines in a professional manner.

Through his magazines he continued to campaign for education. He called upon armies of youth to work like missionaries all over the country to awaken the masses to the importance of education. To his chagrin, Tilak found that finding selfless volunteers was no easy task. Selfishness volunteers was no easy task. Selfishness prevailed in the society.

Once Tilak had the opportunity to meet the famed Swami Vivekananda in a train to Poona. Later he stayed Tilak's Poona home for a few days. He also revealed to Tilak that finding dedicated and selfless workers in India was an impossibility.

Infact, Hindustani's were good only at shriking work and quarrelling among themselves. Tilak had the the taste of that quarrelsome nature of his countrymen in Deccan Education Society. During those ten years he had not been able to give enough time to the family.

He only paid hurried veseis to his home. The family never got quality time from him. Some children born to Tapi were the only testimonials of his flying visits. Tapi's stout shoulders carried the entire burden of running the family. She soldiered on without any complaints.

Return to Home

For neglecting his family Tilak some times felt ashamed of himself. He had come home again. The children ran to their father. The family sat together. There was no betterness on the face of Tilak of his breakaway from the Deccan Education Society. Infact the looked cheerful and very satisfied, with the mark he was making through his magazines. A new determination had lighted up his face. The aunt was sick and bedridden in the next room. Tilak got up and went to that room to see the aunt. At his sight the old woman's face brightened up.

She said in weak voice. "My son come back home ? We have been dying to see you." After touching her feet Tilak enquired, "What is ailing you aunt ?"

The aunt groaned, she said, "It is nothing serious. The usual old age niggles. Some pains here and there always. The worst of all diseases is the old age, you know, And how are you?"

"Fine Kaki. I am devoting all time to the magazines. Now the whitemen know my power". Tilak informed.

The aunt said "I know. You are born to do great things son. We have so much hopes pinned in you" the old lady smiled.

Tilak's wife was overwhelmed she spoke with quivering lips. "I am avowed to stand by you. Serving husband without asking anything in return is the duty of a Hindustani wife. so we have been taught. Doing my bit gives me great pride."

Then Tilak took her hands in his and signed, "You are my real strength. I always feel quilty for the fact that I gave you so little. The missions I have undertaken Will Keep me mostly away in future also, you shall have to bear with me. I am afraid you will be burdened with more sacrifices. I hope you understand."

Satyabhama replied. "I will do whatever for your sake taking it as my solemn duty. Please don't say those kind of things."

Only an Indian woman could show such spirit of sacrifice and self denial. Tilak looked at his wife with wondrous admiration. When every Indian home had such selfless characters, then why it is not resulting in positive results, he wondered ?

The fact was that Indians were rotting at the bottom of the backwardness. One need not go far to seek the reason. Most of the men in Indian society were selfish, lazy and corrupt.

Thay were using the noble qualities of the Indian women for their own selfish ends. The and result was that those noble qualities wrought only self destruction and strengthened the hands of evil forces.

While departing. Bal Gangadhar Tilak looked at his two surviving kids quietly. He knew that he would not be able to spare enough time to help them grow in normal way.

The Social Unrest

The Indian society was groaning under social evils, caste systems, blind faths, horrendous customs and many many more woes.

The British were well set and they now knew the weakness of the Indian. They knew that, social evils had hollowed the Indian society and every Indian was in a trap of self doubts. Being an Indian meant no self respect and no confidence.

On the one hand Englishmen were introducing social reforms to look good and on the other hand large numbers of Christian Missionaries were being inducted to spread western culture thought and religion. This resulted in Indian reformists divided in two camps.

One camp was follower of English and the western way of life. They were asking people to adopt English language and western culture. The other camp opposed it. Their running battle was harming the interests of the people, and creating confusions in the native minds.

The warring camps were too busy in pulling the rug from under each other's feet to care for the political independence of India. That suited the Englishmen fine.

Meanwhile the reformist Rajaram Mohan Roy came on the

scene. He was close to the Englishmen. It helped him get some major reform laws passed. The prominent law being the one that banned sati custom. Rajaram Mohan Roy founded an organisation, called Prathana Samaj, to serve as a vehicle for his brand of reforms campaigns. The organisation spread fast all over India. It's objective was to remould, Indian society on western cultural format.

Then Swami Dayanand Saraswati emerged on the scene, who was opposed westernisation. He preached ancient vedic culture of India with a new modern interpretation which was different from what the orthodox brahmin clergy had been preaching for centuries.

Being home based and close to the hearts of Indians, Swami Dayanand's reformist movement under the banner of 'Arya Samaj' caught the imagination of the masses. It became very popular all over the country. It opposed those forces who were advocating adoption of western life style.

Mean-while, In Maharashtra Jotiba Phule founded "Satya Shodhak Samaj which also gained popularity. It was against the expolitation, by Brahmin cast of the Hindu society by loading it with reprehensible blind faiths, evil customs, and orthodoxy through, misinterpretation of scriptures. So, the various hues of reform movements were dividing the Hindu society instead of becoming one unified force of concerted reforms.

That was further confusing the people. It does not mean that the people leading reforms were villains. They were all good and noble intentioned people. Hindu society was a plethora of castes, sub castes, sects and a sea of local beliefs. Hence the evils were also of different hues, shades, and kinds. The people were ignorant and illiterate which confounded the situation. They were unable to use commonsense to realise which reform applied to them at the grassroot level.

There was economic dimension to the evils issue. Landlord class Zamindars and fiefs were colluding with priest class to keep the people chained to the evil practices which reduced them into sitting duck state for economic exploitation.

These situations deeply hurt Bal Gangadhar Tilak. There was complete silence on the political front barring a few revolutionary acts of revenge.

The British had succeeded in keeping the public attention diverted on the reforms. The foreign rulers were sitting pretty. No one was there to challenge them politically.

The administration could concentrate on dealing with the revolutionaries. Moves were a foot to declare them terrorists. It was a cunning and sinister move. Tilak decided to make noises to fell the Britishers that they could not fool everyone.

Tilak used Marathi periodical "Maratha" to give a clarion call to the people to rise against the alien rule. The politically minded people woke up form the state of inaction. Those who were up from the state of infaction. Those who were engaged in the social reforms works also realised that political battle for the liberation of the country was also a vital aspect of reforms. Thus political activities got initiated.

Tilak was realised that he had to take careful step as there was no well organised political party to take cover under.

The Political Activities

Congress Party came into existence in 1885. It was the beginning of the organised political movements, in post 1857 India. All those who were politically conscious flocked to the party. Bal Gangadhar Tilak was no exception. The party was formed by an Englishman named Sir, A.O. Hume. In the beginning

Congress Party was supposed to be a stage on which the Indians could raise their voice and address. the complaints to the British government.

The real aim was to provide the native politicians a permanent fortum where they could let off their pent up feelings to prevent the Anti-Government sentiments build up. Ostensibly it was a bridge between the people and the government.

Whatever the initial aims Bal Gangadhar Tilak realised that the party had all the potential to Struggle of India. From the very childhood, Tilak was ded-set against the foreign rule. There was no chance of his agreeing to become a political stooge of the British. But Congress Party was just right thing to give training to politicians and cadres. Indians were merely novices, in the matters of politics.

They badly needed a school which could teach them to become a viable political force. The congress Party was the best thing to happen to the long suffering natives of India. And it was also a fact that a political party could force social reforms in a more effective way.

Congress Party was also a place where Bal Gangadhar Tilak could meet other political and reformist leaders of the country exchange views, update one another and draw inspiration from one another, The discussions would prove greatly educative. Englishmen often complained that Indians were not patient and were easily excitable which was proving a hurdle in the way of solving the problems of the people.

A peaceful atmosphere was ruquired to find the solutions of the masses. To a great extent that was true. But it was also true that where there was injustice there can not be any peace. The people are bound to rise in anger. To suppress the uprisings the British were using brute force of police and the administration.

It was making the British government unpopular.

Bal Gangadhar Tilak lost no opportunity to condemn the British for their injustice and the cruel attitude berdering arrogance. Tilak himself was no toterant person. He was like that by nature. He was never able to hide his feelings. That is what made him an outspoken person to be nicknamed Mr. Blunt.

Because of that impatient nature he often offended his friends and he tried to control the organisations he was connected with to dictate terms. In the case of Deccan Education Society the same thing happened. But Tilak continued his crusade regardless. He might have earned the scorn of his colleagues but in the public eye he gained more and more esteem and popularity inspite of the controversies.

Tilak took part in Bombay session of the Congress Party after joining it where he came in contact with Gopal Krishna Gokhale. Lala Lajpat Rai and Vipin Chandrapal at much letter stage Mohan Das Karamchand Gandhi. Gokhale became his mentor. The growing influence of the hot heads in the Congress Party was metter of worry for the British.

Tilak as a Minister

In 1892, Bal Gangadhar Tilak was elected to a post one of the three ministers of Bombay, Provincial Political Conference. which enabled him to voice the people's demands as their representative in the Congress Party.

Tilak was a true friend of the common man and understood his plight. He opposed The Indian feudal classes who were economically explotiting the poor of India in collaboration with the foreign rulers who were following anti-labour policies to ruin the people qat the bottom.

As a Minister Tilak sharply critized the excise policy of the government under which more and more liquor shops were being opened in the towns and the rural areas. It earned the government more taxes. Easy availability of the liquor was turning the poor into drunkards and ruining their lives. The poor drank to forget their miseries and problems.

In the Congress Session for the following year he raised the demand for permanent land reforms. For Congressmen it was a new kind of reform that no one had thought of before. There were several reformists in the Congress. But their reforms were limited to social evils and education. They had not shown any concern for economic, agricultural and Industrial reforms.

Bal Gangadhar Tilak had realised that reforms in these fields were as essential as social reforms. The British were sucking the blood of the Indian masses with the help of industrialists traders, Rajas, Nawabs and Zamindars. The farmers and the labourers were getting reduced be the beasts of burden.

The main purpose of the Englishmen to be in India was profits. They came to India in the guise of East India company, a trading outfit. Later they managed to seize power and conspired to turn whole of India into a market for the industrial products of England.

When they had landed in India there were no large industries. It was a land of small scale industries cottage endeavours, craftsmen and artisans. The British deliberately followed, policies which led to the destruction of demestic industrial efforts to make room for industril products of England. All those people engaged in small scale cottage craft became jobless. To make a living they turned into agricultural labourers. Agricultural lands were controlled by Zamindars who paid starvation wages. Entire families worked in fields including, women and children.

Bal Gangadhar Tiilak proposed that through land reform laws the lands must go to the tillers. The gains of the agricultural produce should go to those who actually worked in the fields instead of to the Zamindars, who just sat in their havelis and pocketed all the gains. This demand angered the British. Because Zamindars were their favoured people who were acting as posts, and pillars of the british Empire.

The masses had begun to see in Tilak their real well wisher and possible deliverer. It made him hugely popular among the people. This positive response from the people enthused Tilak and his tone became more aggressive and sharper.

The young progressive generation was coming closer to the heart of Bal Gangadhar Tilak. He was cleaverly lighting the flame of the desire for independence among the youth. An atmosphere was building up where the start of the Independence Struggle against the British was becoming imminent. The hard work done by Congress leaders like Tilak was bearing fruit.

Tilak's Political Idea

Congress was a collection of leaders of some different shades. Meanwhile some revolutionary groups and organisations had mushroomed in different parts of the country.

The Congress was not connected to such militant outfits. The majority group in the Congress did not approve of the violent acts of revolutionaries. Infact, it considered them terrorists. Whenever thay were caught by police and the law meted out serve punishments to them, the Congress would not react. It remained silent and unconocerned.

Bal Gangadhar Tilak was not in that majority group, and did not fully support the neutral stance of the part in such matters.

The majority group thought that it was foolish to challenge the British foran armed combat as Indians had no arms and resources or training to do that. The violent acts of the revolutionaries was giving the government an excuse to enact repressive laws, the majority felt. There was big truth in it. Tilak also realised it. He advised the revolutionaries to act with restraint.

Tilak encouraged the revolutionary minded youth to join the Congress to turn it it into a fierce political force. The opponent leaders charged Tilak with being in league with militants and acting as their mole in Congress.

Supporters of Tilak hit back in harsh language. Bal Gangadhar Tilak demanded that Congress be made a open stage for people from where any one could air his opinion and demands.

The President of the Session, Bannerji felt that the matter was getting out of hand and there was a danger of Tilak supporters invading the Session. So he sent a message to Tilak asking him to hold the rally of his supporters somewhere else and leave the Congress alone. It resulted in riots and physical fights. Division in the Congress became imminent.

The "Ganesh Poojan"

Bal Gangadhar Tilak was an innovative person a man of ideas. He thought of introducing religious functions in Maharashtra on the lines of Durgapuja of Bengal, and Ramlila in North Indiia.

The functions were to be used for political mass awakening. He began it with 'Shivaji Festival' which was organised to be celebrated all over the province of Maharashtra.. Many political leaders laughed at his attempt. For some it was a poor joke. But Tilak did not give up. He persisted with his plans braving the criticism. He knew the working of the minds of the masses and was certain that the people would flock to his festivals.

Lord ganesha was most revered diety in Maharashtra, popularity known as Ganapati Bappà. Hence he launched, "Ganesh Poojan" festival.As he had anticipated huge. crowds flocked to the venues. His workers spread political message to the crowds and his periodical Kesari publicized the festivals to make them mass events.

Shivaji has been most popular soldierking and the greatest hero figure Marathi Circles. He had successfully challenged the Mogul rulers of Delhi Agra. It had a kind of symbolic importance. The British were in the process of shifting their capital from Calcutta to Delhi. It is a fact that. Shivaji's name stirs every Marathi heart. His birthday began to be celebrated as "shivaji Ramemb-rance Day", with great pomp and show.

It also became hugely popular. Another feather in the cap of Tilak. His political campaign received a big impetus through these mass participated festival. The air of these festivals used to be loaded with politics of British rule baiting.

The women would sing songs detailing the misdeeds of the white rulers and how they were dishonouring their sacred land through tyranny and injustice.

The songs would exhort youth to rise and crush the foreign rule. The manhood of the men folk. would be invoked to rise against the British.

However noble it's cause may be, the use of religion for political purposes was unjustified, many people said. The supporters of Tilak would counter it by asking Unjustified ?" Is British rule over India anyway justified ?"

Bal Gangadhar Tilak had one other strong reason for the festivals to justify.

Hinduism was a different religion from the others. It was

a way of life. Everything vital for life the literature, culture, music, dance, drama, arts, festivals, physical education and even medicine systems sprang from it. Thus Hindus had a mindset to accept things on religions format only and that included politics.

Another fact was that Hindus mostly worshipped alone. Every home had it's own private temple. They did not congregate like Muslims or Christians for prayers.

The only way to bring Hindus together was through festivals. The increasing popularity of Bal Gangadhar Tilak worried the rulers. Something needed to be done before he could become too big to handle.

An Englishman journalist worte In these festivals religious songs are sung dramas are played inwhich quotes from the hindu mythology are used to forment hatred against the aliens.

A very derogatory term "Malechch" used for the Europeans and Muslims. The aim of the festivals is to find excuses to use violence against muslims and the police, which results in court trials. Then the trials are used to deliver fiery speeches to incite the people. With the beginning of these festivals Tilak's area of influence widens and becomes stronger.

In his rebuttal Bal Gangadhar Tilak appealed to the Muslim brethren not to believe in what the whitemen were writing in the English papers. It was a trick of the British to drive a wedge between Hindus and Muslims, to perpetuate their evil rule. He invited Muslims to take part in Ganapati and Shivaji festivals.

Shivaji was not against Islam, he was merely fighting against Moghul rulers of Delhi, who were as cruel and arrogant as the British rulers.

The real fight was between the rulers and the poor masses. Most of the Muslims understood the trick being played by the foreign rulers. As a result Shivaji festival became popular in Bengal, where Muslims lived in sizable numbers.

British Administration During the Famines

In the last quarter of the 19th century India suffered 18 famines. The people of India had a bitter experince of cruelty and callous attitude of British administration, during these famines.

The government did nothing to help the affected people. Infact treated the famines as deserving punishment to Indians from the heavens. The officials never made any attempt to build up emergency food stocks even when the famines loomed on the horizon.

The administrators would put on an act that there was no famine. The reports and the requests for help would find place in the waste paper baskets. When the famine would stare in the face and denials became impossible they would put on act B. They would refuse to accept the death figures ad the extent of the loss of property and the live stock.

A wide spread famine hit Maharashtra in 1896. But the Viceroy of India and the England's Minister for India reported to the Government that there was no famine in India and that no relief fund was required.

In 1876, a 'Famine relief code' was worked out in India by the British government itself According to it when the farmers lost 69% of their harvests through natural calamities their land revenue was to be waived or it's payment deferred. But the code was never implemented.

This time the callous attitude of the rulers crossed all limits. While people were dying hunger the Viceroy of India had set out on a pleasure tour of the princely States to enjoy the lavish hospitality of the Rajas, Nawabs and Maharajas. All the higher-ups royally wined, dined and danced instead of providing relief to the people.

It greatly infuriated Tilak. He exposed shameless behaviour of the rulers, in the magazines. He organised groups of volunteers and sent them to the famine affected areas to collect the statistical figures of the devastation caused.

In his "Maratha" Paper Tilak printed full text of the "Famine relief code." In the accompanying article he wrote how the foreign rulers, ignoring rules and laws.

How could people pay the revenue, when they have no money or foodgrains to feed themeselves ? Should they sell their homes and themselves ? there is a limit of tolerance, he wrote.

Tilak campaigned fiercely against the rulers. He was sure that faced with life and death, situation the people would rise in protest against the administration. Here Tilak was in for a shock. The people did not respond to his call. It was not tolerance but extreme cowardice. They were dying of injustice but were too scared to rise in protest.

The British were laughing at Tilak. Now they knew that they could harass Tilak. The volunteers of tilak, who were out surveying the famine damage were arrested and put in jails.

Tilak challenged, "My volunteers were helping the famine affected and were merely telling the facts to the people. Helping the suffering people is no Crime. If it is then I am also to be blamed."

In defence of his volunteers Tilak organised public meetings and launched a scathing attack on the administration. He got an encouraging response. The people attended his meetings in large numbers. The trials began. When a close associate of Tilak professor Paranjpe was produced in the court, thousands of people besieged the court premises shouting slogans hailing Tilak.

The Judge asked Tilak to calm his supporters. He appealed to the crowd to be paceful and the people stopped shouting slogans. Prof. Paranjpe was acquitted of all charges and other trials were postponed.

Then, Plague epidemic struck Poona areas. There was no effective remedy for the epidemic at that time. It spread fast. The administration was helpless. The situation aggravated and horror scenes could be winessed every where. So many people were dying that the funeral places and burial grounds were becoming crowded. There were not enough people to carry the dead bodies off. The towns and the villages were becoming deserted. The administration did little to help the people. It took them even to admit that there was the epidemic indeed.

An, Epidemic Ordinance, was issued on 4th Feb 1897. This law gave the authorities unlimited powers. The police could enter any house, evacuate the inmates and search any house, and place. The sick persons were carried off to the hospitals like luggage items. The family members would be herded off to the so called safe places. In the process the policemen were getting opportunities to misbehave with the women of young age.

The chief of the Plague Committee Mr. Rand was a notorious character of sadistic nature. He was an India baiter. Abusing, insulting and outraging natives gave him immense pleasure. The volunteers of Tilak were keeping a close watch on the misdeeds of that particular officer.

Bal Gangadhar Tilak wrote in his newspaper, "It is a very shameful act on the part of the queen of England. But, the Government ignored the comment. The officer, Rand contonued his drama of torment and outrage. People had run out of patience.

Some infuriated youth killed the culprit officer Rand and his white Deputy.

The Revenge of the Administration

The killing of officer Rand was shocker for the administration and the British government. It was a grim warning to the government that Indians won't be taking things lying down any more.

The portents were grim. The murder was daringly executed. The authorities blamed the press for inciting people against the administration.

Among the publications Tilak's "Maratha" and "Kesari" had played the leading role in fanning harted against the government and the officials. Thus, Tilak was on the top of the administration's hit-list.

Exactly one month after the murder of Rand and his deputy, Bal Gangadhar Tilak was arrested for treason.

The charge against him was that through his writings and speeches he was creating anarchy, where the law and the order had become impossible to maintain. It was a blantant case of implication of a citizen by the authorities on trumped up charges.

At first people were shocked. Gradually the shock turned into anger. The charge of treason was very serious. It could create problems for friends and relatives of Tilak. Many of them broke links with Tilak, for fear of getting implicated. Others just felt silent. Even issuing statement in defence of Tilak had become a dangerous exercise.

Throughout the country meetings were held to express public support to Tilak in addition to demonstrations against his illegal arrest.

A group of prominent legal exports tried to secure bail for Bal Gangadhar Tilak. Bowing to the intense public pressure Judge Badruddin Tayyabji orderd the release of Tilak on bail.

But the administration was determined not to let Tilak take advantage of his release by making Political gain out of it. The instant trial was arranged by appointment of nine member Jury of six Europeans and three Indians.

Bal Gangadhar Tilak was led to the prison of serve his sentence for speaking out the truth.

The End of Tilak's Jail Term

The year of 1914 came and progressed towards the end of Tilak's jail term. He pulled himself out of the world of books nd waited for his release. He wished to be with his children as soon as possible.

The 400 books he received in Jail to study were sent to his home at Poona. At long last he was released from Jail on 8th June 1914. Tilak came back home to the delight of his family and associates.

Only after a few days with the family, Tilak again started issuing statements, attacking the alien rulers fiercely. If the authorities had hoped that the Jail term would demoralise Tilak or soften him up.

Bal Gangadhar Tilak was no jelly. The administration wilted. A large police force was deployed outside Tilak's house. Everyone who came to see Tilak was checked.

The government employees and students were not allowed in. It was administrations dirty trick to freeze the political activity of Tilak. It furiated Tilak.

Then, on 4rth August 1914 first world war broke out in Europe. Britain Jumped into the fray. England's problem could prove Indian's gain, he argued, Tilak made moves to sir a political storm to trouble the colonial rulers of India.

In 1916 Lucknow Congress Session, Tilak was again brought back on the centre stage of the party affairs. Both the groups came together to become a united force.

Tilak convinced the softline leaders that his "Home Rule" idea was not a militacy act. It was just a demand for right of Indians, to rule over themeselves a self rule.

The leaders agreed with him in principle but they were still reluctant to join. Tilak's campaign whole heartedly. Thay had reservations. So Tilak decided to go it alone.

In league with his associates and followers the hard liners organised a massive session at Poona, in which he put forward demand for "Home Rule" for the country. He called for a movement to achieve that goal.

Tilak group formally established "Home Rule" league with the aim to win the right of self rule under British Empire through constitutional, means and to prepare public opinion in its favour. Although Tilak was the founder of the organisation yet he held no chair in it.

Joseph Baptista was it's nominated president. N. Chintamani Dr. B.C. Munje, G.S. Khaparde, R.P. Kardikar and D.V. Belvi held other important posts.

Gandhiji expressed his unreserved support to "Home Rule" idea of Tilak. As a result it became a Congress Programme.

Tilak explained, through "Home Rule" we can take charge of the governance of our own country. British Empite will be there in the background unobtrusively for the time. It will be a step towards full freedom. The idea is that in my own country I must get the rights what an Englishmen has got in England." He made it clear that the demand for "Home Rule" is not rebellion against the British empitre. but just internal readjustement of the power sharing.

Gandhiji declared that demand for "home Rule" was a timely step and a neccessity to solve the problems of the people and entire Congress Party threw it's weight behind the "Home Rule."

British rulers were out pleased. They felt uneasy and wanted the "Home Rule." movement to fail. Any success for Tilak was bad news for them.

The movement grew stronger and stronger. The masses rose up to stand by Bal Gangadhar Tilak. He had again become a threat to the government.

The London Tour

Bal Gangadhar Tilak went to London in the later half of 1918. He wanted to explain "Home Rule" demand to the English Public. His other objective was to sue London Times reporter valentines. for writing scurrilous reports against him to vilify him when the reporter had visited India. Tilak lost case and was asked to pay expenses to the reporter. Instead of losing face Tilak became more popular having greater mass following. The people collected a purse of 3 lac rupees to help Tilak cover the case expenses.

Tilak extended his stay in Britain to 13 Months during which he met leaders, scholars and common folk. When Tilak returned to India the situation at home was not good.

Gandhiji had postponed non co-operation movement due to

violent incident. The people were demoralised. Meanwhile the British parliament passed Reforms Bill. There were some differences in the Congress over this Bill. Some wanted to accept it white others were in favour of it's rejection.

The Last Day's

Tilak looked very old and weak during the year 1919. He was not keeping well. Bal Gangadhar Tilak had a long talk with Gandhiji and handed him the baton of the leadership of the freedom struggle of India.

Tilak felt feverish two days before his 64th birthday. He stayed in bed. On the night of 2nd August 1920 Tilak felt pain in his chest and at 12-40 a.m. he breathed his last.

5

Jagjivan Ram

Jagjivan Ram's early life was one of poverty and hardship. His father, Sant Shobi Ram, had to struggle hard to make ends meet. He was born in the village of Maurasia in Bihar in 1864. An uncle of his was in military service in the Punjab. While young he lived with his uncle and acquired a working knowledge of the English language and the rudiments of an education.

Shobi Ram was a person of character, given to hard work. Out of his meagre earnings he saved a little regularly and married, while still in his teens a girl by name Basanti Devi. She was a fit wife to the hard working Shobi Ram, herself hardworking and a thrifty housewife. Ar first they had no house of their own. Basanti Devi's elder sister was living in the village Chandwa of the then Shahabad district in Bihar. (Two districts have been carved out of Shahabad; Chandwa is now in Bhojpur District.) The young Sant Shobi Ram purchased some land in Chandwa and built a house of his own.

It was in Chandwa that Jagjivan was born on April 5, 1908. His childhood days were the usual childhood days of many of his class. On vasant Panchami day in 1914, Jagjivan was put to primary school, dressed in a silken kurta and orange coloured dhoti, and velvet cap. By his time the financial status of the family had become a little better. Sant Shobi Ram was in a position to help needy persons with loans for which he charged no interest and he won the respect of the people in the village. He was deeply religious and people flocked to him for solace and advice.

The primary school to which Jagjivan went functioned in the veranda of the house of the teacher, Kapil Muni Tiwari. The teacher was a Brahmin but he observed no untouchability. He served as a good guide to young Jagjivan for many years. Jagjivan was a regular student, go home for lunch which he took with plenty of butter, He was partial to butter. He would come back, missing no class.

There was no strict untouchability observed in the village generally though there was as yet no community dining On the Holi festival sweets were served after the religious ceremony and all the families exchanged sweets. Community singing was also commom and devotional songs were joined in by caste and noncaste people.

Jagjivan's father was somewhat of a saintly character; many people assembled at his house to attend his pujas. He was know also for his enthusiasm for an Indian form of improvised cricket. He encouraged his son in sports, the cricket, kabaddi and chika. The boys of the age of Jagjivan used to come to Jagjivan's house every morning to pay their respects to his father. He tried to impress on these boys the value of character-he emphasised that the means were as important as ends, truthfulness and piety. He held that deceit was another name for cowardice. He, by his example, exhorted people to do hard work and no prayers.

But he died a few months after Jagjivan joined school. Jagjivan as well as his elder brother Sant Lal and the mother of the boys attended on Sant Shobi Ram's last illness. A large number of persons in the village and surrounding places who knew Shobi Ram attended the funeral. For some reason Jagjivan was called upon to perform the last rites.

Apart from the two sons Shobi Ram left three daughters; the eldest was 17 years older than Jagjivan and the been married even before he was born the other two girls were married when Jagjivan was a small boy.

After completing primary school Jagjivan joined the Aggarwal school at Arrah in 1920. Many children from his and other neighbouring village went to that school. Jagjivan soon distinguished himself by his aptitude in learning English and other subjects.

He had discovered the Ramayana through his father and it was particularly dear to him all his years. Every sunday he would assemble some of the villagers round him and sing verses from the Ramayana. Soon he was reading Prem Sagar and Sukh Sagar to his friends. There were many other religious books that he read thus.

But his reading was not confined to religious writings alone; while at school he had read Chandrakanta a famous novel of those days. Reading magazines also wasa habit which he formed early; among the magazines he read were the Bharat Mitra, Venkatesh Samachar, Saraswati. He used to borrow these magazines from the postman on his rounds, often keeping them for a day before they were delivered to the subscribers. It was thus that he read Mahatma Gandhi's Navjivan and Tarun Bharat while still at school.

In his class he stood second in English and not far behind in many subjects. Tulsidas, Kabir and Rahim were his favourite Hindi poets; he could repeat the whole of Hanuman Chalisa by heart. The widowed mother was a religious person and she would never take anything without a bath and puja. Jagjivan acquired the habit from her. His mother loved Jagjivan and lived long enough to see him achieve some great successes.

His elder brother Shri Sant Lal was 23 years senior to him and was just like father to him Jagjivan would never disobey Sant Lal. The brother too treated his younger brother like a son-he had no son of his own; he had a daughter. She died soon after her marriage.

From the earliest days Jagjivan had a distinct sense of self respect. Some persons told him that he would be given concessions in school fees if he pleaded that he was an untouchable-he rejected the idea. He was sure that if he worked hard he could secure distinction in his exams which would bring him the necessary concession and scholarship. By getting the second position in class exams he automatically got freeship amd scholarship.

One incident that happened in his school days deserves mention. There were two waterpots in the school for the boys-one pot was for the Hindus and the other for Muslims. Normally a peon supplied water to the boys but when he was absent, Jagjivan took water from the pot for Hindu.A boy noticed it and reported to the Headmaster observing that Jagjivan was an untouchables. Jagjivan did not like this arrangement but he did not get into an argument about it. He waited till he conveniently could and broke the third pot. It was replaced by another but that too was broken by Jagjivan on the sly. The H.M. Understood the significance of the two broken pots; he cancelled the order for the third pot.

On prize distribution day sweets were usually distributed to all the boys. Bansidar Prasad, one of the teachers, asked Jagjivan to take charge of the distribution of sweets. Jagjivan tried to point out that he being 'untouchable' the boys might not accept the sweets; but to his surprise, every boy in school accepted the sweets from his hands.

Jagjivan, even an a school boy, was fond of meditation and joined every meditation and religious instruction class available to him. He became a friend of a noted wrestler of those parts, one Nitali Bhagat and that also made him popular among the boys in school.

Jagjivan was sought out whenever there was a bhajan party either at school or in his village. At his village he had observed the evil effects of drinking and exhorted his fellows not to drink. Thus even before he thought of political reforms as most necessary. But soon the struggle for freedom was also to claim his attention.

Sant Lal was working as a compounder in the Medical College Hospital, Calcutta. Jagjivan accompanied his brother's wife from the village to Calcutta during summer vacaion in 1923. He saw an electric tram for the first time in Calcutta; but he went from the station to the hospital in a baggi. In addition to the trams, buses were also plying in the streets. He saw the museum, the zoo, the Victoria Memorial, Eden Gardens etc, along with a friend who took him round, In a couple of days he moved on his own and saw Shibpur, Kumar Hatti, lcchapur and other places; the mill areas especially attracted him. He would stand before a millgate lost in thought; he watched the people coming in and going out.

Soon his vacation and his visit to Calcutta were over and he went back to Chandwa, carrying Rs. 500 which his brother had given him. He was seen of at the Railway station by many friends he had in calcutta.

His village was visited by a devastating flood in the Month of August. Many houses collapased including Jagjivan's. The news of the flood was published in the Calcutta news papers and Sant Lal wired to.Jagjivan for information. Jagjivan had to wade through knee-deep water to Arrah to send a wire to his brother. Sant Lal's wife had secretly kept some of her money in a safe hole in the wall. Sant Lal wrote a letter to. Jagjivan telling him about it. Jagjivan enquired of his mother who had known about the money and had saved it.

After the floods subsided, Jagjivan worked day and night to rebuild the house. He was only 15 years of age at that time and he shouldered the responsibility like a well-seasoned man. But soon his elder brother at Calcutta develpoed some eyetrouble and retired from service and came back to shoulder the responsibility of the family in the village.

The Bihari Student's Association was a militant organisation of students of Bihar. It was imbued with nationalist ideals. It's 18th session was held at Varanasi (Benares) in the Hindu University premises. Though only a high school students town in public elocution. He won priizes for his speech. This was Jagjivan's first participation in public affairs.

The students conference was also addressed by Pandit Madan Mohan Malaviya. Malaviya's very appearance was inspiring to young Jagjivan. He felt the inner purity of the leader and saw his outer purity. Malaviya spoke at the session saying that India was at the crossroads of history facing great problems on the solution of which depended her future. "Whether we are big men or small, we have to undertake the work of big men because only big people-big in vision, big in determination, big in action and big in sympathies-can face and solve heavy and big problems." Jagjivan thought that the words of Malaviya were sparkling as the water of Ganges; it seemed to have a cleansing effect and moved him greatly.

Many things had happened in India in the near past and Jagjivan was compelled by the inspiring words of Madan Mohan

Malaviya to study them and think over them. Among them was the abolition of the Khilafat. After the first world war, the British Government had dethroned the sultan of Turkey and done away with the Khilafat. Mohammed Ali, Shaukat Ali, Abdul Kalam Azad, M.A. Jinnah, Asaf Ali and other Muslim leaders were enraged by this action of the British. Mahatma Gandhi who had by now won his position as leader of the Indians gave his blessings to the Khilafat Movement. Khilafat and Congress became synonymous. Hindus as well as the Muslims courted arrest protest against the abolition of the Caliph (Khalifa) regarded as the religious head of the Muslims.

The first non-co-operation movement and the Khilafat movement were not only complementary to each other but were actually two faces of the same coin. Those taking part in either of the movement incurred the wrath of the Government.

Gandhi caps were intolerable and waters were beaten mercilessly One day when Jagjivan was passing through Babu Bazar street to his school, a class friend came and told him that men wearing Gandhi caps were being beaten up. But the young Jagjivan who was wearing a Gandhi up. But the young Jagjivan who was wearing a Gandhi cap was not afraid. He neither removed his cap nor changed his route. Nothing untoward however happened. There was a Khilafat Conference in the school premises and Jagjivan listened to every speech that was delivered there.

Lord Irwin had just become the Viceroy of India. Irwin was not farsighted enough to visualise that his Viceroyalty of India would be the era of a great change in Indian politics; he did not anticipate the dimension that the Indian fight for freedom was to assume. Even when things happened he did not see them in their proper perspective as definite goal.

The Congress was propagating Khadi, removal of untouchabilitry was a moot point; the chief grievance of the Muslims was that they did not have enough representation in the services. The Hindus were the target of this attack and some of the Hindu leaders adopted a fighting attitude towards the Muslims. gandhiji castigated this sort of attitude in Navjivan. In the beginning it did not have much effect. In December 1924, Mahatma Gandhi Launched on his twenty-one days fast at the residence of Mohammed Ali. The fast had the desired effect and Hindu-Muslim riots at various places came to an end.

In 1926 Jagjivan passed his High School examination. When Malviyaji came to address the people at Arrah the same year the Harijans decided to present him a welcome address. The onus of reading it and presenting it fell upon Jagjivan. He did it so well and in such a fine ringing voice that Malviyaji was extermely impresseed. This was Jagjivan's first contact with a national leader.

Enquiring about Jagjivan, Malviyaji invited him to join the I.Sc. in the Benares Hindu University. Jagjivan was very happy He had an alternate proposal from the American Christian offer for free education.

Jagjivan decided to go to Benares. But a Benares he learnt that the principal of the college was in Gujarat as the college was closed for the summer vacation. Jagjivan left a letter for the principal and returned to his village. A while later, the Principal wrote asking him to report at Benares. The resident of the village were happy that one of them was going to Benares for higher studies.

Higher Education

In July 1926 Jagjivan joined the university. He was a young man with a mind open to impressions as wax. While national leaders were talking of Independence quite a few of the fellow scholars at Benares who came from families loyal to the British made fun of them; talk of Independence struck them as a wild fantasy.

Jagjivan had many arguments with them; he exhorted them not to think of Independence as a fantasy that was impossible of achievement.

Jagjivan won a scholarship. The recipient of the scholarship was entitled to stay in the hostel. Another Harijan boy also was staying in the hostel. But Jagjivan wanted to bring his mother to Benares and he arranged for a separate residence. The principal even suggested that if he thought the hostel unsuitable he could stay with him in his house.

Jagjivan was conscious of the rate honour done to him but still persisted in his request that given permission and he fixed a house in a locality called the Lanka. But when his mother arrived she did not like the colony which was only thinly populated and asked her son to look for a new residence. In due course they shifted to Assighat area.

The owner of the new house was a Kori by caste and when his caste people came to know that he had rented his house to a Harijan they made trouble. The house owner refused to allow Jagjivan appealed to a priest of whom the Kori was a disciple. For a priest the guru of the Kori was a man of liberal views and he brought round the Kori saying that "they are good people and why should they be returned out ?"

The house owner was reluctant to make an enemy of his priest and Jagjivan was allowed to stay. In course of time the Kori caste householder came to know the sterling character of Jagjivan Ram and his caste prejudice gave way before peronality and they became good friends, Added to Jagjivan's character was the presence of his mother Basanti Devi. She soon had all boys of the locality on her side. She won the acclaim of even the elders by her religious attitude; many persons in the locality came in due course for her advice. When she decided to return to her village, many persons wept while parting.

Jagjivan had other troubles too because of his being an untouchable. Once a barber refused to dress his hair. The boy took this to heart. He had to do something and he organised the harijans in the locality. This was his first attempt towards organising Harijans.

In a matter of days all the back-ward classes were organised and at a mammoth public rally Jagjivan gave the call for the boycott of the barbers. In this effort he was helped by Dev Nandan Dixit who later turned a revolutionary. In a couple of days the barbers came to their senses and came to him on deputation and apologised for the misbehaviour of one of them.

There was no doubt; the teenaged Jagjivan had emerged as a youth leader. Destiny was pushing him on to leadership on a national platform. But there was nothing arrogant or brash about him; those who knew him at the period bear witness to the fact that he was one of the gentlest and kindest of human beings they had ever met. He was not prepossessing at first sight but anyone who came into contact with him acknowledged his nobility. He was quick of mind. He was not given to condemning others. If he hit, he hit only when he himself was injured. He was never one to nurse a personal injury. He was sympathetic and reacted quickly when he came to know of any wrong done to the poor or the under privileged.

Jagjivan was more hard-headed; he had no such illusions. He could foresee a hard struggle a head and he told his friends as much. Mahatma Gandhi's ideas and appeal reached the educated middle-class and some of the enlightened persons in the higher income groups also. But the landlord lobby in the countryside and the gentry in the cities were hardly with him. Students in various Universities were moved by the Mahatma's appeals the Benares Hindu University was one of the foremost in this respect. It produced many illustrious young men who contributed their own weight to the national cause.

And then there was this question of untouchability. What was this untouchability? In what lay it's justification if any ? cannot the old structure of the society be changed to suit agitating the mind of young Jagjivan Ram. He had begun exploring the Shastras even when he was an I.Sc. Student; with the help of translations and commentaries. He peeped into the spiritual treasures of the Vedas, the Upanishads, the Gita and other scriptures. He was already familiar with the Ramayana. He gained thus a through insight into the Indian tradition through personal study and meditation. He not only read the books but discussed about the things found in them with friends and elders. His outlook, aided by the inherited devotional practices, represented the accumulated wisdom of the ages.

In this period he read many translations of the Bengali classic, He liked Bankim Chandra, Sarat Chandra, Dwijendra Lal Roy and Rabindranath. He later learned Bengali and read some more of their books.

In this labits he was regular. He had his dipdaily in the Ganges amd did his Pranayama, the breathing exercise. He attended many of the religious and devotional discourses of which there were plenty in Benares. For a while he got interested in The Arya Samaj movement and the Theosophical Society. He listened whenever there was a lecture by Annie Besant, anywhere in the city. But he could not find full satisfaction in any these activities; he did not consider the Arya Samaj progressive enough and was of the opinion that it's tenets would not help him to reform Indian society. But he conceded that it's activities had brought about a healthy change in society though it did not go all the way. He was equally unsatisfied with Theosophy; he thought was dry logic all the way.

He passed his I.Sc examination in 1928 and went to Calcutta for further studies and joined the Vidyasagar College. In calcutta he came into contact with various men, some of them from the backward classes. He helped in setting up various Ravidas Sabhas. His initial success was encouraging.

In Calcutta he began to wear Khadi; but he was not a regular user of Khadi till 1932. While in Calcutta he took to the charkha but because of his various other activities both as a student and as a leader he could not spin much. But in five or six months he had enough yarn to make a 4 1/2 yard dhoti. He found time for spinning, for meeting various types of leaders. And for political and social activities, for organising Ravidas Sabhas and reading literature. He organised a conference in Wellington park which made him a known man in nationalistic circles. The conference was a great success, nearly 10,000 persons attending it.

Some senior members of the Dalit Sudhar Sabha, which was started by the Congress attended the Wellington park conference. They began to make an interest in him. Among them were J.M. Sen Gupta, Subhas Chandra Bose, B.C. Roy and P.C.Ghosh; they took notice of him and encouraged him in his activities.

He discovered that Subhas Chandra Bose was pro-labour and pro-Harijan. Bose it was who convinced him that the depressed classes could be in the vanguard of a political and economic revolution in the country. Bose went out of his way to encourage him in all his activities and he promised him all help if he should at any time need it. Jagjivan enquipped himself for his task by reading all the political books he could lay his hands on.

Higher Education

In July 1926 Jagjivan joined the university. He was a young man with a mind open to impressions as wax. While national leaders were talking of Independence quite a few of the fellow scholars at Benares who came from families loyal to the British made fun of them; talk of Independence struck them as a wild fantasy. Jagjivan had many arguments with them; he exhorted them not to think of Independence as a fantasy that was impossible of achievement.

Jagjivan won a scholarship. The recipient of the scholarship was entitled to stay in the hostel. Another Harijan boy also was staying in the hostel. But Jagjivan wanted to bring his mother to Benares and he arranged for a separate residence.

The principal even suggested that if he thought the hostel unsuitable he could stay with him in his house. Jagjivan was conscious of the rate honour done to him but still persisted in his request that given permission and he fixed a house in a locality called the Lanka. But when his mother arrived she did not like the colony which was only thinly populated and asked her son to look for a new residence. In due course they shifted to Assighat area.

The owner of the new house was a Kori by caste and when his caste people came to know that he had rented his house to a Harijan they made trouble. The house owner refused to allow Jagjivan appealed to a priest of whom the Kori was a disciple. For a priest the guru of the Kori was a man of liberal views and he brought round the Kori saying that "they are good people and why should they be returned out ?" The house owner was reluctant to make an enemy of his priest and Jagjivan was allowed to stay. In course of time the Kori caste householder came to know the sterling character of Jagjivan Ram and his caste prejudice gave way before peronality and they became good friends, Added to Jagjivan's character was the presence of his mother Basanti Devi. She soon had all boys of the locality on her side. She won the acclaim of even the elders by her religious attitude; many persons in the locality came in due course for her advice. When she decided to return to her village, many persons wept while parting.

Jagjivan had other troubles too because of his being an untouchable. Once a barber refused to dress his hair. The boy took this to heart. He had to do something and he organised the harijans in the locality. This was his first attempt towards organising Harijans. In a matter of days all the back-ward classes were organised and at a mammoth public rally Jagjivan gave the call for the boycott of the barbers. In this effort he was helped by Dev Nandan Dixit who later turned a revolutionary. In a couple of days the barbers came to their senses and came to him on deputation and apologised for the misbehaviour of one of them.

There was no doubt; the teenaged Jagjivan had emerged as a youth leader. Destiny was pushing him on to leadership on a national platform. But there was nothing arrogant or brash about him; those who knew him at the period bear witness to the fact that he was one of the gentlest and kindest of human beings they had ever met. He was not prepossessing at first sight but anyone who came into contact with him acknowledged his nobility. He was quick of mind. He was not given to condemning others. If he hit, he hit only when he himself was injured. He was never one to nurse a personal injury. He was sympathetic and reacted quickly when he came to know of any wrong done to the poor or the under privileged.

Jagjivan was more hard-headed; he had no such illusions. He could foresee a hard struggle a head and he told his friends as much. Mahatma Gandhi's ideas and appeal reached the educated middle-class and some of the enlightened persons in the higher income groups also.

But the landlord lobby in the countryside and the gentry in the cities were hardly with him. Students in various Universities were moved by the Mahatma's appeals the Benares Hindu University was one of the foremost in this respect. It produced many illustrious young men who contributed their own weight to the national cause.

And then there was this question of untouchability. What was this untouchability? In what lay it's justification if any ? cannot the old structure of the society be changed to suit agitating the mind of young Jagjivan Ram. He had begun exploring the Shastras even when he was an I.Sc. Student; with the help of translations and commentaries. He peeped into the spiritual treasures of the Vedas, the Upanishads, the Gita and other scriptures. He was already familiar with the Ramayana. He gained thus a through insight into the Indian tradition through personal study and meditation. He not only read the books but discussed about the things found in them with friends and elders. His outlook, aided by the inherited devotional practices, represented the accumulated wisdom of the ages.

In this period he read many translations of the Bengali classic, He liked Bankim Chandra, Sarat Chandra, Dwijendra Lal Roy and Rabindranath. He later learned Bengali and read some more of their books.

In this labits he was regular. He had his dipdaily in the Ganges amd did his Pranayama, the breathing exercise. He attended many of the religious and devotional discourses of which there were plenty in Benares. For a while he got interested in

The Arya Samaj movement and the Theosophical Society. He listened whenever there was a lecture by Annie Besant, anywhere in the city. But he could not find full satisfaction in any these activities; he did not consider the Arya Samaj progressive enough and was of the opinion that it's tenets would not help him to reform Indian society. But he conceded that it's activities had brought about a healthy change in society though it did not go all the way. He was equally unsatisfied with Theosophy; he thought was dry logic all the way.

He passed his I.Sc examination in 1928 and went to Calcutta for further studies and joined the Vidyasagar College. In calcutta he came into contact with various men, some of them from the backward classes. He helped in setting up various Ravidas Sabhas. His initial success was encouraging.

In Calcutta he began to wear Khadi; but he was not a regular user of Khadi till 1932. While in Calcutta he took to the charkha but because of his various other activities both as a student and as a leader he could not spin much. But in five or six months he had enough yarn to make a 4 1/2 yard dhoti. He found time for spinning, for meeting various types of leaders. And for political and social activities, for organising Ravidas Sabhas and reading literature. He organised a conference in Wellington park which made him a known man in nationalistic circles. The conference was a great success, nearly 10,000 persons attending it.

Some senior members of the Dalit Sudhar Sabha, which was started by the Congress attended the Wellington park conference. They began to make an interest in him. Among them were J.M. Sen Gupta, Subhas Chandra Bose, B.C. Roy and P.C.Ghosh; they took notice of him and encouraged him in his activities.

He discovered that Subhas Chandra Bose was pro-labour and pro-Harijan. Bose it was who convinced him that the depressed classes could be in the vanguard of a political and economic revolution in the country. Bose went out of his way to encourage him in all his activities and he promised him all help if he should at any time need it. Jagjivan enquipped himself for his task by reading all the political books he could lay his hands on.

Jagjivan With Gandhiji

It was at the Calcutta Congress in December 1928 that Jagjivan saw Mahatma Gandhi for the first time. But he saw him then only from a great distance; there was no possibility of a talk.

Gandhi laid stress on spinning and he was listened to by a great number of persons all over the country. Hs sphere of influence was widening and growing fast. Even Jawaharlal Nehru who had western outlook on most of the things listened to gandhi with respect and took to spinning and Khadi which he called "the livery for freedom".

Mahatma gandhi's ears were turned to the beating of the hearts of the countrymen. His appeals always struck a note of harmony in the ears and hearts of common men. His greatest concern he said at Calcutta was the hardness of the hearts of the gateway of our salvation". The inspiring example of the Mahatma made young Jagjivan vow to devote himself to the masses.

At the same time as the Congress was being held there was an all party conference at Calcutta Jinnah attended it and spoke demanding one-third of the seats for the Muslims in the Central Legislature, reservations for the muslims in the Punjab and Bengal and the vesting of residuary powers in the Provinces in a Federal Constitution and the unconditional separation of Sind. This attitude of Jinnah was also later emphasised at a meeting in early 1929, presided over by the Agakhan. At this meeting were made demands of a more inflexible nature which opened the path for the later parition of India.

The young Jagjivan wrote a letter to Mahatma Gandhi urging him to see the Viceroy at an early date. It was decided that Mahatma Gandhi was to meet the Viceroy on 23rd December 1929 on his way to the Congress Session, Irwin returned that day from Hyderabad to take up his residence in the newly built Viceroy's house. But as his train neared Delhi at about 8 A.M. In a dense fog, there was the sudden explossion of a bomb in the middle of the train when it was passing at forty miles an hour a curved high embankment. The revolutionaries had laid a fuse from Purana Qila three hundred yards away to the curved railway track and had intended to touch the bomb off after the pilot engine had passed and just before the engine drawing the Viceroy's train reached the spot. Owing to the fog, the attempt was slightly mistimed and the Viceroy's carriage had passed the danger spot. The bomb blew a hole four feet wide on the track If the bomb had exploded thirty seconds before, the Viceregal carriage would have overtuned and rolled down the embankment.

Seventeen years before to the day a bomb was thrown into the midst of Lord Hardinge's procession in the heart of Delhi. Rash Behari Bose who threw that bomb had been working as a clerk in the Forest Research Institute, Dehra Dun. During his student days in Chandernagore near Calcutta he had come in contact with Swami Virlamba who inspired him to organise terriost actrivities in Bengal. Harding narrowly escaped the bomb when Rash Behari Bose threw the bomb; only an A.D.C. was killed and some others were injured. Rash behari Bose escaped from Delhi. That bomb was thrown from the residence of the grandfather of the present author. A teacher by vocation my grandfather was arrested for having known Rash behari Bose and jailed for a considerable period of time. Along with grandfather worked as a teacher in the same school the wellcaptured and hanged. Delhi had long remained a centre for terrorist activities.

Jagjivan on the way to attended the lahore Congress was anticipating that something important was about to happen in Delhi. But he had no prior knowledge of the Purana Qila incident.

The Viceroy newly installed in the Viceregal lodge met Mahatma Gandhi, Motilal Nehru, Vithalbhi Patel, Tej Bahadur Sapru and M.A.Jinnah. The Mahatma Gandhi told the Viceroy that Indian's future constitution should have been framed by the elected representatives of India and not by the British Parliment. Indians were capable of solving their own problems, Including the problems of defence. He further said that unless Dominion status was considered the immediate result of the Round Table Conference he for one was in no mind to participate in it. The Viceroy rejoined that there seemed no common ground of agrement betwee them.

"I propose to take an early opportunity" Lord Irwin wrote to his father, "of making it pain that if and when the extremists try any policy of what they call Civil Disobedeince, we shall lose no time in jumping on their heads. "It was evident that a conflict was developing and was inevitable. N.C. Kelkar and Sarojini Naidu advised the Mahatma to stay his hand. But many young workers all over the country were anxious for action and approached the Mahatma to tell him to begin early; they were only a waiting his green signal, Jagjivan kept on organising the people in his immediate circle anticipation the call to action.

The Congress met at Labore, Jawaharlal Nehru presiding. At midnight of December 31, 1929 the hour which marked the coming of the new year. The Indian National Congress unfurled the flag of Indian Independence on the banks of the Ravi. The Congress called upon all it's members in the central and the provincial legislatures to resign their sean and authorised the A.I.C.C to launch the Civil Disobedience Movement. Though he was not a delegate, Jagjivan was invited to attend the A.I.C.C Session.

Mahatma Gandhi suggested that a resolution condemning the attack on Irwin's life be passes at the Congress It was passed by a narrow margin of 38 votes, 1832 delegates voting. It seemed to prove that nearly half the Congressmen present did not condemn tthe revolutionary activity, the attempt by terrorists to kill Englishmen in India. Many of the Congressmen assembled knew some of the leaders of the revolutionary movement and were their friends and aided them secretly. Chandrashekar Azad of U.P. was a friend of many of the Congressmen. Jagjivan had met some of the terrorists at Calcutta and had helped them when he could, collecting funds for them and sending them to secret hideouts with friends when they had to lie low. Azad had often sought out Jagjivan in Calcutta and spent quite a lot of time with him.

On 12th March, 1930 at 6-30 in the morning mahatma Gandhi left his Ashram and began his 240 miles march to Dandi. Eighty satyagrahis followed him, old persons and teenagers, Herijans and mill workers, scholars and editors. The mahatma carrying his long bemboo sick led at so brisk a pace that even the young men found if difficult to keep up. The dust on the path was strewn with yellow leves.

Jagjivan's Meetings

Jagjivan organised many meetings in Bihar at which he spoke that the separate electorate idea was generally harmful to the Harijans. Ambedkar then demanded reservations for the Harijans. Mahatma did not agree immediately as he had consulted the other leaders about it. He was however willing to keep an open mind on it.

When Mahatma gandhi returned to India after the R.T.C. In 1932 the political situation had changed for the worse. The British officials and a few others did begun to dub the Indian National Congress as a Hindu Organisation. The Muslims, by and large, were found gullible. Riots broke out in many places and innocent persons suffered.

M.C. Rajah, the first Harijan to become member of the Central Assembly, supported Gandhi's stand, though he himself was not a member of the congress. The participants in the R.T.C. at Landon had not reached any conclusion regarding communal representation The Prime Minister of England Ramsay Macdonald announced his award on August 15, 1932. Special constituencies were carved out for the depressed classes and they could execise the votes in reserved as well as in general constituencies. There were numerous reserved constituencies in the then Madras presidency.

On August 18, Gandhi who was in jail wrote to Ramsay Macdonald saying that if the separate electorate provided in the Communal Award was not withdrawn forthwith he would begin a fast unto death. The British did not concede Gandhiji's point and he commenced his fast on September 20. Rajendra Prasad asked the Hindu community to throw open all temples, drinking water wells and schools to Harijans.

Malviyaji convened a meeting of the leaders on the eve of the fast. Sapru appealed to the British to relese mahatma Gandhi unconditionally. Rajendra Prasad, Tej Bahadur Sapru, M.R.Jayakar, C.B.Mehta, C.Rajagopalachari and B.R.Amb edkar conferred in Calcutta. Some of them had been shuttling between Bombay and Yarawada Jail. Mahatma Gandhi now made in clear that he was not against reservation of seats for Harijans but was only against separate electorate as it was detrimental to the cause of solidarity of the Indian people.

On September 24 a pact was signed between the leaders. The pact was a sort of Magna carta for Harijans. reservation of seats legislatures. Substantial portions of the expenditure on education would be utilised for the education of Harijan students. The pact was signed at Poona. The terms were conveyed to the British Prime Minister who announced his acceptance of these terms on September 26. The scotching of the dangerous separate electorate for Harijans was the greatest service that had been done of preserve the integration of Hindu society.

Many persons in the country did not understand the full significance of Mahatma Gandhi's fast. Ambedkar was surprised at the fact that Mahatma gandhi had not accepted the idea of reservation had written a letter setting out his case to the Mahatma before the Poona pact was signed and asking for the Mahatma's opinion Through Gandhi's secretary He got a reply which satisfied him in all it'essentials and he took the trouble of informing all his immediate friends that all was well.

The fast of Gandhi stirred the conscience of the Nation. A large number of high caste Hindus and others formed an organisation on 30th September for prompting the welfare of Harijans. In November this organisation was named the Harijan Sewak Sangh. Mahatma Gandhi changed the name of his weekly from Navjivan to Harijan. As a part of all the activity Dr. Subbarayan brought a bill in the legislature of Madras which was passed in 1932; but the Viceroy did not give his assent to this bill and thus it could not become an Act. Later N.G.Ranga brought a bill in the Central Assembly for Harijan uplift; but it was sturdily opposed by the nominated members.

Jagjivan attended the Anti-untouchability Conference in Patna. Dr. Rajendra Prasad was the chief speaker. Jagjivan also spoke and spoke impressively. Rajen Babu was notably impressed by the young man and when Jagjivan had returned to Arrah he wrote him asking him to come and meet him at Patna. Jagjivan immediately went back to Patna and met Rajen Babu. Rajen Babu invited Jagjivan Ram to spend some time in Organisational work in Patna also. rajen babu evidently wrote to Mahatma Gandhi who in reply called Jagjivan an "Anmol Ratna", priceless jewel.

Lord Willing now took over from Irwin as the new Viceroy and he initiated a campaign of ruthless repression.

In the meanwhile Jagjivan had occasion to meet the Mahatma once again. On his return from the R.T.C. Mahatma Gandhi was given a rousing public reception in Bombay. Jagjivan was invited to this reception and utilised the occasion for paying his respect to the Mahatma. Gandhi advised him giving him some guidelines regarding organisational work.

The events of 1931, 1932 left Jagjivan Ram more convinced than ever that the Mahatma was the leader whom he should followed and who was doing his utmost for the Harijan cause. He came into contact with other leaders also who thought similarly. He was getting closer to Rajen Babu also The protest meeting at Patna over the arrest of Rajen Babu was a mammoth affair and was organised ably.

Earlier here had been a big conference at Chapra in Saran District of North Bihar. Jagjivan had been the life and soul of the conference. Amrit Lal Thakkar, secretary of the Harijan Sewak Sangh wanted Jagjivan to devote himself entirely to Harijan uplift work and the affairs of the Sangh He tried to wean Jagjivan away from the political movement But for Jagjivan Ram both activities were only two sides of one movement.

A word about Dr. Ambedkar and what Jagjivan Ram thought of him at this time may be out of place here. Dr. Ambedkar was no doubt a learned person but his attitude towards the freedom struggle was not healthy. He had leadership thrust on him by the British authorities as a foil to healthy trends of a nationalistic kind that were shaping up in India. This was nothing new; the British for their own purpose had made a leader of T.M Nair in 1919; Overnight this person of whom no one had heard before assumed a representative status.

Once Mahatma Gandhi in a piece of his writings referred to the Harijans saying that they were like cows, Jagjivan wrote a letter to Gandhi claiming that the word and the comparison were unfair. The Mahatma wrote to him explaining the comparison and saying that the comparison was only in one aspect and that he had the greatest respect and regard and affection for Cows and Harijans.

Jagjivan understood that the Mahatma never saw the problem of the Harijans in isolation. It was a problem in the larger contect of the country's Freedom. Until India was free nothing much could be done for the Harijans.

Jagjivan took over a the secretary of the Bihar branch of the Harijan Sewak Sangh. This was the first ever public office he held. Needless to stay he discharged his duties to the satisfaction of every one concerned. He was out of college but he was not yet thirty. He was already recognised as a leader at the Provincial level; this was high achievement indeed.

Emergence As a Leader

It was the beginning of 1934 and Jawaharlal Nehru had announced his plans for celebrating Independence Day on January 26 and had taken his wife Kamala to Calcutta for a medical check up. It happened that Jagjivan Ram was also in Calcutta leaving Dr. Rajendra Prasad in the Patna Hospital.

There was a tremendous earthquake in Bihar with devastating results. Tremors were accompanied by noises as if a hundred engines were moving together. The damage was heavy in North bihar, particularly in Monghyr. Part of the civil secretariat of Patna had collapsed. Whole towns were ruined and hundreds of villages were destroyed. The area of devastation was over thirty thousand square miles with a population of about fifteen millions. The casualties were estimated at over thirty thousand dead. Nearly half a million homes were damaged or destroyed beyond salvaging.

Jagjivan rushed back to Patna and had preliminary discuassions with Rajen Babu about relief work. Nehru too visited the affected areas and made his suggestions before he returned to Allahabad on February 11. The day after he arrived back in his home town a police-van called at his house and he was arrested and within a few hours was taken to his old prison at Dehra Dun. His old cell was occupied and he was put in a new cell. A little earlier than his arrest Nehru had written a letter to Jagjivan offering to come Patna to take part personally in relief work. That was not to happen.

Rajen Babu and Jagjivan Ram attended to the relief work in Bihar ministering to those affected by the earthquake. They arranged for funds as well as blankets and sent them to various places in Tirhut Division. A few persons were sent out to various other places to find out and report on the extent of damage done. As the means of communication were competely cut, Jagjivan Ram and his fellow relief workers travelled long distances in country boats. As Rajen Babu was recovering from an illness and consequently physically weak the bulk of the heavy work fell on the shoulders of Jagjivan and he rose to the occassion magnificantly Later when Mathura Prasad and Satya Narayan Sinha were released from Hazaribagh jail they also joined in the relief work and took over some of the burden which Jagjivan was shouldering. A public meeting was earlier called in Patna and the announcement of a central relief committee was made. The members of the committee were named by Rajan babu taking Jagjivan Ram into his confidence.

Branches of the relief committee were set up in all the districts and the work was coordinated by Jagjivan.The committee began receiving contributions in the shape of money, rice, utensils, clothes, blankets and medicines from all parts of the country. They were stored in Patna and distributed to various centres according to their requirements Sardar patel was in jail and could not come to Patna; but Mahatma Gandhi and Jamnalal Bajaj visited the earthquake-affected areas and gave various valuable suggestions about organising relief on efficient grounds. Jagjivan was benefited by their guidelines.

Jagjivan Ram suggested to Mahtma Gandhi that some person expert in accounts should be sent to Patna for maintaining the accounts of the central relief committee property. Accordingly Mahatma Gandhi sent J.C.Kumarappa to take charge of accounts. There were over two thousand relief workers spread over twelve districts. Jayaprakash narayan was incharge of the central office. After his release from jail Anugrah Narayan Sinha took charge of the office. To keep donors, sympathisers and workers informed of developments, the central committee for relief began publishing a bulletin; Jagjivan Ram was incharge of the printing and distribution of this bulletin.

In many places drinking water was becoming scarce. Roads and bridges were damaged beyond repair. The work of reconstruction was arduous and long drawn out. But slowly relief was becoming equal to the needs of the devastated area. Bullock carts, cycles and a few motor trucks were secured and put into service; the roads were repaired; the bridges restored whenever possible or diversions provided. Jagjivan Ram was in the midst of all this work literally wiping off the tears of weeping humanity.

He helped build thousands of houses that had been destroyed or damaged considerably. New wells were dug; tanks had to be built and water stored in them either when rains came or through canals. Many water sources had mysteriously disappeared, thanks to the earthquake, Fields that had been productive were now covered with sand; the sand had to be removed and the lands reclaimed.

In North Bihar, sugarcane is grown plentifully and there are a number of sugar mills. The earthquake had spoiled the Machinery in the milk. The sugarcane crop worth millions of rupees was still standing beyond its season. Jagjivan supplied the villagers with a great number of indigenous crushers so that the sugarcane crop might not go compeletely waste. Every reconstruction work was undertaken with the co-operation of the willing villagers.

The beds of the rivers of Bihar, the Ganga, the Sarju, the Gandak and others were lifted by sand deposits. Soon after the rains started the rivers would soon overflow causing floods, Bhartua on the way to Sitamarhi from Muzaffarpur was once a fertile area; it had become waterlogged and was unfit for cultivation; the river Bhagmati had changed its course and the draining water from the lowlying areas could not be drawn into it. The stagnant water damaged thousands of trees in the area. When Gandhi arrived and toured in the area accompanied by Rajan Babu and Jagjivan people met him with tears in their eyes. Two English women had also accompanied Gandhi on this trip-miss Muriel Lester who had been hostess to Gandhi in London and Miss Agatha Harrisson, a public worker and sympathiser. The ladies have written about their experiences of this tour. C.F.Andrews toured in the area and wrote a book about it for circulation in England and U.S.A Dr. Cersole was in; doing manual labour.

It was a period when some groups were emerging even within the Indian National Congress, based on minor ideological defferences, A number of members inclined towards the left, decided, while in jail, to form a socialist party. It was founded in 1934 while Jawaharlal Nehru himself was in jail. Nehru's writings and speeches had obviously influenced the socialist minded young men. Acharya Narendra Deva and Jayaprakash Narayan were two of the prime movers of the Socialist Party. The Congress Socialist party was formed to give an alternate leadership to the country and to give Congress policies a more revolutionary bias. The attraction of its programme for socialism was deep and in the Congress Session of 1934 the C.S.P. Controlled nearly a third of the delegates.

Nehru was released but arrested again on the eleventh day of his freedom. While his wife Kamala was ill he was confined in Naini Jail. Soon afterwards Kamala Nehru was removed to a sanatoriumn the hills at Bhowali. Nehru was allowed to see her before she left Allahabad and found her bright and cheerful. He himself was transferred to Almora Jail which was a few miles distant from the hill sanatorium. Once in three weeks, Nehru was allowed to visit his wife.

Some of the Congress cause and capitalists who were sympathetic to the Congress cause and occasionally helped with money were alarmed at the emergence of the Congress Socialist party Apprehending a lack of funds for running the Congress establishment. The Indian National Congress came out with an attack on socialism and went on record as being of the opinion that "confiscation and class war are contrary to the Congress creed of nonviolence", Though Jagjivan was not a member of the Congress Socialist party he made a bold and antagonistic reference to this resolution in one of his speeches in Bihar. He said that ultimately the Congress should look to the masses for funds and not to the richer classes.

In the following month the Congress triumphed in the

elections by winning 44 seats in the Central Lagislative Assembly. A large number of members were to be nominated by the Viceroy. The contests in some constituencies had been particularly keen. Satyamurti defeated the well-known Justice party leader A. Ramaswamy Mudaliar. Venkatachalam Chetty defeated R.K. Shanmugam Chetty, a favourite of Lord Willington. In Bihar, Ramakrishna Dalmia tried to dictate that the candidature of Anugrah Narayan Sinha be withdrawn; but Congress had decided to set up candidates in every constituency. Dalmia flouted Congress discipline. He spent a large sum of money and was ignominiously trounced. Jagjivan had spent a lot of time in the constituency working for the Congress Candidate against Ramakrishna Dalmia.

The A.I.C.C. Met in the Shrimati Radhika Sinha Hall at Patna in May 1934. The official resolution recommended the suspension of the Satyagraha and were not for taking part in the elections. The newly formed Congress Socialist Party was one of the main opponents of the Congress participating in the Elections. Acharya Narendra Deva. made a brilliant attack on the official resolution. It was decided to have a special session of the Congress in October in Bombay many satyagrahis still were in jail. Sardar Patel was released in time for the session; Nehru was released much later. In October, Rajendra Prassad accompanied by Jagjivan Ram proceeded to Bombay for the special session of the Congress. A procession was arranged at Bombay to give a recepion was arranged at Bombay to give a reception to the leaders. Rajen Babu, Sarojini Naidu and K.F.Nariman sat in the first carriage. Jagjivan Ram was in the carriage that followed. The procession was two miles long. The city of Bombay was tastefully decorated and presented a festive appearance. Different markers of the city put up deorations made of defferent commodities; in the cotton market put up an arch of fruits. Bright flowers were strewn on all the leaders. The session was attended by a record number of persons. The chief streets of the speeches was on constructive work Khadi prohibition and removal of untouchability.

In August 1933 Jagjivan Ram's first wife passed away after a brief illness. In June 1935 he married Indrani Devi, daughter of Dr. Birbal, a well-known social worker of Kanpur. She is a well-educated lady and has been always of great support to Jagjivan.

In 1934 the all India Ravidas Sammelan was to meet in Calcutta. Jagjivan interested himself in the organisation of the meet and helped to make it a success. It was at this conference that Jagjivan met for the first time social workers like Dharam Prakash, Ram Prasad Jaiswal and others. Jagjivan suggested that all Harijan leaders of whatever shade of opinion should meet on one platform. An appeal for this organisation was drafted and sent to various persons at various places and the foundation laid for the Depressed Classes League. The Depressed Classes unity conference took place in Kanpur in May 1935. Ambedkar and M.C.Rajah did not attend it. The conference was presided over by Rasiklal Biswas; Jagjivan and P.N.Rajbhoj were the secretaries.

After his second marriage Jagjivan plunged into the work of the Depressed Classes League. By the end of 1935 he had organised the Bihar branch and was elected his president. Ambedkar and M.C.Rajah were known to be loyal to the British. Thakkar Bapa did not associate himself actively with the freedom movement though he was not a loyalist. Many in the league wanted Jagjivan Ram to Keep away from active political work; as a result of differences, before long, Jagjivan Ram resigned from the league.

Unfortunately after the Poona pact relations between caste Hindus and Harijans deteriorated instead of improving. In October 1935 there was a conference of Harijans at Bombay. Ambedkar urged that it was better for Harijans to give up the Hindu religion. There was some correspondence between Mahatma Gandhi and Ambedkar on this point; but Ambedkar was not to be easily satisfied. Maulana Mohammed Irfan met Ambedkar and argued that the Harijans should become Muslims, saying it was only under the banner of Islam that Harijans would get equal treatement. Some members of the Islamic council of bombay also met Ambedkar hoping to convert him to Islam.

Some Harijans met at Nasik and burned copies of Manusmriti, By now it was clear that only a small section of the Mahars in which community Ambedkar himself was born, was sympathetic to his opinion. M.C.Rajah came out with a statement opposing Ambedkar and saying that the Doctor's stand would be destructive of Harijan interests. Rasik Lal Biswas, Jagjivan Ram, R.Srinivasam, Solanki, Kajrolkar and Jaiswal declared themeselves opposed to Ambedkar. The depressed classes league met under the presidentship of M.N.Mondal and took serious and adverse note of Dr. Ambedkar's call to the Harijans to leave the Hindu fold. But underterred by all this opposing clamour, Dr. Ambedkar announced in December 1935 that he had decided that he and his followers would not remain any longer in the Hindu fold.

Jagjivan's Talent

In the first week of February, 1938, Jagjivan addressed two big rallies in Patna in which he told the people that soon they were going to ask for the release of those in jail still. He declared that if they failed in this attempt to release the political prisoners they would not hesitate to resign from office. He was instrumental in bringing pressure on S.K. Sinha to take up the matter with the Governor. Shortly after wards most of the political Prisoners in Bihar were set free. There was some difficulty about the release of some 20 prisoners who were serving terms for various convictions. Jagjivan worked for their release also.

February 1933 proved an eventful month. The Congress held its 51st plenary session at Haripura, in Gujarat, under the presidentship of Subhas Chandra Bose. Subhas Base observed on February 19 that "there is no possibility in my opinion of the Congress altering its attitude towards the Federal scheme at any time". The main resolution at the Congress read as follows: "The Congress is not opposed to the idea of Federation as much but should consist of free units enjoying, no more or less, the same measure of freedom. The Federation as it is now contemplated will instead of building up Indian unity, encourage separatist tendencies and involve the states in internal and external conflicts".

In 1937 Jinnah took a sharp communal turn. He accused the Congress of having "a most brutal oppressive and inimical attitude towards the All India Muslim League", The Muslim League wanted that in some particular provinces, like U.P. The Muslim Leaguers should be made Cabinet Ministers. They had secured on a few seats in U.P.Assembly and the claim was not based on any strength of achievement. Jinnah began to speak as if he were the lone leader of the Muslims all over the country. Congress Muslims and other independent Muslim leaders raised their voices against Jinnah's claims. The U.P.Cabinet had one Muslim in it-Rafi Ahmed Kidwai, but he was persona non grata with Jinnah. Jinnah played on the susceptibilities of the Muslims and raised the slogan: "Islam in danger." Speaking at the annual Session of the Muslim League in Patna Jinnah observed that "Muslims would adopt all possible means sanctioned in their religion in order to defend their rights and interests and would not hesitate to make any sacrifice to achieve that end".

Jinnah's speech was direct incitement of his followers to take the law into their own hands. Jinnah of course would not allow the Muslim League to take any action against the British.

His call for action was understood by his followers as a call to riots.

A few days after Jinnah's speech at patna Jagjivan had occasion to address half a dozen meetings in various towns. In Bhagalpur he declared; "Mr.Jinnah should Know that more Bihari Muslims have voted for the Congress than for the Muslim League. In towns and villages the Muslim brothers in Bihar have lived side by side with the Hindus. They have lived pacefully for the last so many generation. Jinnah's utterance at Patna not only amounts of a disservice to the country but would ultimately spell ruin the poor people living in the country side. Never has any Muslim been prevented from saying his nammaz and Jinnah's bogey of 'Islam in danger' is in fact the real threat to the poor Muslims in carrying on their normal work in paceful manner. We in Bihar will fight the evil tendencies through all peaceful means.

Jagjivan Ram's popularity rose to new heights in 1938. In public esteem he stood next only to Rajendra Prasad. The year saw the birth of his only son. Despite heavy work at office he found time to tour remote villages and rub shoulders with the people of the countryside. He met them individually and also in manageable groups, listened to their problems and worries and carried their grievances to their Departments concerned for quick action.

Jagjivan Ram had been elected a delegate to the Haripura Congress and he was also elected a member of the All India Congress Committee. He spoke on almost all the resolutions that came up in the Congress. The president Subhas Chandra Bose already knew him and he was further impressed favourably by Jagjivan's performance.

The Congress leaders decided that they would work for an awakening among the people in the princely states. The time was ripe for a political movement in the states. The All India states' people's conference met at Ludhiana on February 16, 1939. The conference passed a resolution appreciating the political awakening in the various states all over India". Nehru was president of this conference.

In Rajkot people demanded responsible government. The Thakor Saheb refused to accept their demand and there was a hartal followed by prolonged Satyagraha. Mahatma Gandhi went to Rajkot on February 27. When the Thakor refused to accept Gandhi's suggestions the Mahatma started an indefinite fast on march 3. Jagjivan went to Rajkot and stayed with the Mahatma for a week. A commission had been appointed and it had already named three persons who whould administer the state Affairs from day to day. The Thakor refused to honour his commitement and Gandhi had to intervene again. The Vceroy, Lord Linlithgow, referred the matter to the Chief Justice, Sir Maurice Hwyer. The Mahatma ended his fast on the 7th of March. Jagjivan Ram was with him that week.

The next plenary session of the Congress was held in Tripuri, near Jabalpur. It opened on March 12, 1939. There was a resolution on the peoples movement in the princely states. It said: "The great awakening that is taking place amongst the people pf the states many lead to the relaxation or complete removl of the restraint which the Congress has imposed on itself, thus resulting in the increasing identity of the Congress with the states' people. The Congress desires to reiterate that its objective, complete Independence, is for the whole of India including the states, which are an integral part of India.

Among the persons who spoke on this resolution were Hira Lal Shastri, Jai Narayan Vyas and Jagjivan Ram. Hiralal Shastri was an educationist who founded the Vanastthali Vidya Peeth, a few miles from Jaipur. The Vanasthali Vidyapeeth was an unique institution for girls. Jai Narayan Vyas hailed from

Jodhpur and had personal Knowledge of suffering under princely administrations.

Jagjivan's Speeches and Tours

Jagjivan Ram toured various parts of Bihar and addressed big rallies whenever he went. He asked the people to prepare for another struggle as the call might come at any time. He told the people that it was not possible for Congressmen to remain in office anymore. On his return to Patna he tendered his resignation along with others.

The A.I.C.C. debated the war situation and decided that no assistance of any sort could be rendered to the British regime. Some persons advocated that Britan ought to be supported in the War crisis. M.N.Roy was one of them. He had also delivered some speeches favouring the War effort Disciplinary proceedings were launched against him and he was expelled from the Congress. Some of his flowers received their position and stayed back in the Congress.

The Congress met at Ramgarh in second half of March, 1940. Abdul Kalam Azad presided. It endorsed the resolution passed by the Working Committee at Patna. The resplution said:"....The Congress cannot in any directly or indirectly be party to the war". It also said in clear terms that nothing short of compelete Independence was acceptable. Speaking on the resolution Jagjivan Ram said that "....No Permanent solution is Possible except through a Constituent Assembly (elected on the basis of adult franchise), Where the rights of all recognised minorities will be fully protected by an agreement as far as possible between the elected representatives of the various majority and minority groups, IOR by arbitration if agreement is not reached on any point....."

The nation was getting restless. The Mahatma's hand was on the pulse of the nation as usual. Sme action was called for. Vinoba Bhave began the Individual Satyagraha by delivering an anti-war speech near Wardha. Vinoba Bhave said that he had three reason for speaking against the war efforts (1) The British Government's rejection of the Congress demand for National Government; (2) The Viceroy's denial of freedom of speech against was efforts; and (3) The British government's refusal to admit that India was declared a belligerant country without the consent of Indian people. He was arrested and Sentenced to three months imprisonment. On October 31, Nehru was arrested and was sentenced to four years imprisonment on various counts.

Only the selected few were allowed to offer individual satyagraha. Jagjivan Ram was one of the persons selected. He delivered an anti-war speech and was arrested in December, 1940. He was kept in Arrah jail for a week and in the end of December he was shifted to Hazaribagh, the biggest jail for political prisoners in Bihar. People at Arrah had come to know that he was being shifted and thousands of them gathered at the railway station. The prisoners had to change trains at Patna and then at Gaya. The reputation for the honesty of these arrested men was such that at Patna when they wanted to go out for meals the policemen allowed them to go out unaccompanied. They had not an iota of doubt that they would return themselves. Some people saw them at a restaurant near the Patna railway station and the news spread like wild fire. The platform at the Patna station was thronged by the people. Many people squatted on the tails and didn't allow the train to move. People brought hundreds of packets of his favourite brand. Before getting in the train he distributed among children the entire quantity of eatables and gave away all the cigarette packets to the railway coolies. At Hazaribagh he had the company of Jayaprakash Narayan, S.K.Sinha, A.N.Sinha, S.N.Sinha, K.B.Sahay and B.N.Jha. Most of these leaders were given 'A' class, which merely meant that there was only to be one prisoner in a cell 14 feet long and a 9 feet wide. There used to be about 30 to 35 prisoners in a ward. The prisoners were allowed to keep money for cigarettes and supplementary food from outside. They were shut inside their cells at six in the evening and the locks were opened at about six in the morning. Jagjivan Ram remained in Hazaribagh Jail for about a year This Jail term did not have any adverse effect on his health. He spent his time studying and also in discussions with the other political prisoners. He spent some time in prayers too.

In 1941, his son, Suresh, got ill and emaciated Mrs. Jagjivan Ram came to her father's residence along with her two-year old child. Suresh's health gave anxious moments to his mother and father, a prisoner in Hazaribagh central Jail.

At Kanpur the child improved. When Jagjivan Ram was released on 10 September, 1941 the first problem before his was the treatment of his son. By mid-November Suresh was healthy again.

Mahatma Gandhi was at Wardha. Jagjivan Ram received a message from Gandhi asking him to visit Wardha. He first went to Benares to see Pandit Malaviya who was ailling. After spending a couple of days at Benares he reached Wardha.

The Mahatma kept Jagjivan Ram with him for about two weeks. He daily accompanied the Mahatma in his morning walks. The Mahatma walked briskly and during the walk he discussed many things with Jagjivan Ram.

On January 3, 1941 the Congress president. Maulana Azad, was arrested. Another important event of that month was that Subhas Bose disappeared from his Calcutta residence. Many people in the country have made varying conjectures regarding the reasons of Subhas Bose departure. Subhas Bose himself gave the reasons in a broadcast from Berlin. "We in India had always regretted that during the last war (World war I), the then leaders had not utilised the War situation to our advantage. It was, therefore, necessary for me to leave India this time in order to establish a direct personal contact with the enemies of British Imperialism and thereby link up India's fight for freedom with the struggle of the tripartite powers against out own enemy 'Britain'. Though the Indian people must rely primarily on themselves for achieving their liberty, anything that weakness Britain can automatically help them and it would be indeed foolish of them not to take the fullest advantage of such assistance which fate and history has provided for them". In another broadcast from Berlin on March 1, 1943 he said "Friends, when I took the unusual step of defying the British Government and departed from India my principal objectives were two-fold. Firstly, to find our myself the truth as to what is happening in the world and secondly, to see if India has any allies in her fight for freedom". The German propaganda machinery was put at the disposal of Subhas Bose.

The Viceroy, Lord Linlithgow, was meeting all sorts of leaders in 1941. He met Sikander Hayat Khan, Fazal Haq, Tej Bahadur Sapru and many others in order to see whether there existed any common ground between Britain and some non-Congress leaders in India. Linlithgow had succeeded to some extent in winning over the sympathies of some non-Congress leaders, but later on Churchill's comments on the Atlantic charter completely stunned all public men in India. Churchill clearly said that the provisions of the charter applied to the countries which had fallen victims of the Hitler's aggression and did not apply to India and other colonies of Britain.

This, in fact, removed the earth from under the feet of such Non-Congress people who were finding excuses to co-operate with the British War efforts. The Viceroy expanded his Executive council by including a few more Indians, but they did not represent even their own families, not to talk of the people of the India. Subhas Bose was completely night when he broadcast from Berlin saying that "India has no enemies outside her own frontiers." In another broadcast, he explained how British Rule was established in India. He said: "The foundation of British Rule in India was laid by Robert Clive whom history has convincingly proved a forger. The British Empire in India was built on treachery and fraud and not as a result of military prowess. During the long struggle for power in India, there is no cruely and there is no attrocity that the British have not committed in that country. Why does not know that in our revolution of 1857, innocent men were bound hand and foot and shot dead cannon fire."

Some persons had suggested that the Governments of the Allied powers and of the British Dominions should guarantee to India that Britain's promises would be redeemed when he war was over. Commenting on it from Azad Hind Radio, Germany, Subhas Bose said; "what value is there in such guarantees when we have no power to enforce their fulfilment". Have we forgotten that the American president's enjoy, Ronald Donaven, travelled all over the Balkans with letters from the president in his pockets urging the Balkan countries to declatre was on the Axis powers? And have we forgotten that all these countries that were provoked and instigated into joining the War were ultimately left to their fate by the all-promising president when the Axis forces overpowered them ? On such matters even if some people are still blind, the vast majority of our countrymen realise that the statements in United States of American are playing a role of father to the insane and they regard themselves as the heirs of the British Empire that has gone into compusory liquidation. It is comical to see men who have been and still are the slaves of Britain branding themselves as saviours of the British Empite.

But no power on earth can save that Empite which is now going the way of all other empires of the past".

Commenting on some people in India who and started talking in support of war efforts, Subhas Bose said. "They do not talk frankly of co-operating with Britain, but camouflage their real motives by asking Indian people to co-operate with China or Russia or American". He further said; "I may tell these propagandists, both British and Indian, that when I was president of the Indian National Congress I was responsible for giving effect to the Congress resolution to send a goodwill mission to China. Those were the days when marshal Chiang-kai-shek was fighting for his nation's principles and that is why he could win the sympathies of Indians in an werwhelming degree. But the Marshal who came to India the other day to ask the Indian people to fight or England was now a different man, the puppet of Anglo-American powers and the japan which the Marshal is now fighting is all along a different Japan, Japan that is willing to annihilate Anglo-American imperialism in the East, a Japan with whom Marshal Chiang-Kai shek can come to an honourable understanding today if he can emancipate himself from the grip of his Anglo-American masters."

Jagjivan and Congress

A couple of days before Jagjivan Ram's arrival in Patna, the British troops had fired upon a procession in Patna. Many people had been killed and several injured on that day. Curfew was clamped on the town. Rajen Babu, S.K.Sinha, A.N.Sinha and other leaders were already under arrest. Jagat Narain Lal had gone towards the rural areas. The responsibility of conducting the movement in Bihar now developed on Jagjivan Ram as he was the only leader who could not be traced by the authorities for a few days. British And American troops were being brought to Patna. In a couple of days the city was surrounded by the white troops. Some Congressmen in Patna wanted to disrupt the water supply in the city but Jagjivan Ram asked them not to do so. Instead, he advised and guided them to disrupt all telecommunications.

The Kadamkuan post office near Jagjivan Ram's residence was set on fire by the students. Another active worker in the cause of freedom, Annada Prasad chaudhary, was in Patna those days. He and Jagjivan Ram had frequent and long consultations with each other. Chakradhar Sharan, who later on became private secretary to the president of India, Dr. Rajendra Prasad, was also with Jagjivan Ram in some of his meetings with Annada Chaudhary.

Jagjivan Ram one day met Ram Dayalu Singh. The latter asked Jagjivan Ram to obtain a curfew pass in some different name. But he told Tam Dayalu Singh that he would move out without a pass if and when necessary. Ram Dayalu Singh also advised him not to wear Khadi for some time, but the letter did not think it proper to give up Khadi even temporarily. Ram Dayalu Singh was ill and was staying at the residence of Sir Ganesh Dutt. Jagjivan Ram moved to another part of dynamite sticks to blow off a bridge at Patna over which military trains used to carry arms, ammunitions and other supplies to the Eastern Front. The dynamite sticks were kept in some bushes not far from the inhabited area of the town. The British authorities got a clue that Jagjivan Ram was in Patna. His presence in Patna was now noticed. In the aftermoon of August 20, 1942, Khan Bahadur Umar, the additional District Magistrate of Patna, and the Senior Superintendent of Police came with two truck-loads of policemen.

The A.D.M. told Jagjivan Ram that he could have some time to prepare himself. Jagjivan Ram went to another room and handed over cash and some documents to Jamil mazhari, a trusted

Congressman, who disappeared through another gate and avoided arrest. Jagjivan Ram then came and informed A.D.M. that he was ready to accompany them. He was first to the Bankipur Jail near Patna. After a couple of days Devsharan Singh was also brought to the Bankipur Jail. He informed the leaders that the public was being terribly harassed. The resistance was growing stronger day by day. Jagjivan Ram passed world out side and informed some friends regarding the hidden bombs and dynamic sticks

One evening Subhas was to speak from Berlin. I turned the radio set and was thrilled on listening the voice of Subhas Bose coming over the electromagnetic waves from Berlin. When we caught Berlin he was saying : "Speaking to you over the Azad Hind Radio". I was advised to keep the volume of the receiver low as listening to broadcasts from Axis countries was banned. With thrill we listened. Many of the things he spoke were highly appreciated by all the listeners. In his speech on August 31, 1942 he said "It is also possible for us to obtain from abroad any help that we may need for our emancipation. Therefore, in the fight against all the modern forms of terror and brutality, if you feel overwhelmed at any time and if you desire your friends abroad to give you the hand of assistance, you have only to say so. But these friends who are anxious to see India free will not offer their help to you so say so, But these friends who are anxious to see India free will not offer their help to you so long you do not need it, and for our national honour and self-respect we should not ask for any assistance so long we could do without it... please do not be carried away by ideological considerations; do not brother about the do not be carried away by ideological considerations; do not bother about the internal politics of other countries which is no concern of ours. Believe me when I say that the enemies of the British Imperialism are our friends and allies it is in their interest to see the British Empire broken up and that India is once again free.....Gone are the days when kings and statesmen had to wend their way through London in order to have their problems solved. Gone are the days when the American president had to go to Europe to meet the British Prime Minister has now to run to new York and Washington and the Americans in Britain are declared to be outside the jurisdiction of British laws.... The most interesting phase of the metamorphosis that has taken over the British Empire is the fact that the high priest of Imperialism, the arch-enemy of Indian nationalism, the sworn opponent of all forms of socialism, the British Prime Minister, Winston Churchill, had to swallow his former imperialist pride and present himself at the gates of Kremlim in Moscow.... The British Empire will soon collapse and break up as a result of shattering defeat in all the theatres of war. And when the final dismemberment of the Empire takes place, power will automatically come into the hands of the Indian people."

In that very broadcast from Berlin Subhas Bose gave out to the Indian people a programme of action, which was a follows.

a. Boycott of British goods, including burning of British stalls and Government stores.

b. Total boycott of all Britishers in India and of Pro-British Indians.

c. Holding of public meetings and demonstrations.

d. Publishing of secret bulletins and setting up a secret Radio station.

e. Marching to the houses of British Government officials and demanding their departure from India.

f. Organising Processions for entering and occupying Govt. offices, security places and law courts etc., with a view to hampering administration.

g. Arranging to punish police officers and prison officials.

h. Erecting barricades in the streets where attack from the police and the military may come.

i. Setting fire to Government offices and factories which are working foor war purposes.

j. Interuping postal and Telegraph Communication, as frequently as possible and in different places.

k. Interrupting railway, bus and tram services, whenever there is a possibility of hampering the transport of soldiers and war materials.

l. Destroying police stations, railway stations and jails at islated places.

The clarion all of liberty had reached the ears and hearts of Indian soldiers at home and abroad. The fire was spreading from one place to another. A large number of Indian soldiers voluntarily deserted to join the Axis forces in Egypt. It really seemed that break up of British Empire was imminent.

The up surge was really very strong in Balia where the British administration completely broke down. There was some upheaval in Maharashtra where Patwardhan was the source of inspiration to the underground workers. In the month of August itself more than one lakh people had been arrested, thousands killed and tens of thousands injured. At some places the people were silenced temporarily but the movement went on unabated. Railway stations, post-offices, telegraph and telephone lines were the main targets, In some places a few teenagers were also arrested. This present author was one of them.

The movement was having its reverberations outside India as well. Naturally it gladdened the patriots in India that whatever happened here was given wide publicity by the news agencies of the Axis countries.

On August 31, 1942, Subhas said : "As a matter of fact every bit of news regarding India's National Struggle, very incident in Indian towns and villages, every case of shooting whether in Wardha, in Bikrampur or in Lucknow, is immediately flashed all over the world, is broadcast over the radio and published in the press in all of these countries that are either hostile to the Allied Powers or are neutral... The more we suffer and the more we sacrifice in the pursuit of our national freedom, the more will India's prestige to go up in the eyes of the world".

The War Situation In Europe

The War situation in Europe had already taken a new turn with Hitler and Stalin falling apart. There was now enough collaboration between Britain and U.S.S.R. and some people in India had termed the struggle in Europe as a "People's War. Though Swami Sahajanand had many friends among the communists, he did not agree with them in their analysis of the world situation. As Sahajanand had a considerable following among the Kisans of eastern U.P.and Bihar, Subhas Bose had to take note of his possible role. Speaking from Berlin on March 1st, 1943, he said, "Friends, I know that my friends like Swami Sahajanand may hesitate to believe in the sincerity of the Tripartite powers. But I would like to remind them that these powers have in their own interest resolved to fight British Imperialism to a finish and they will undoubtedly do so. And the destruction of British power will inevitably help India in throwing off the British yoke.... In this fateful hour in India's history, it would be a grievous mistake to be carried away by ideological considerations.

This internal politics of Germany or Italy or Japan do not

concerm us. They are the concern of the people of those countries. But even a child should understand that whatever the internal politics of the tripartite powers may be, their aim in international sphere is the destruction of the British Empire which is India's one and only enemy. Do we not see with our own eyes, how, regardless of ideological considerations, the British Empire is now cooperating with Soviet Russia ? .... The internal policy of India is and should be the concern of the Indian people themeselves, while the external policy should be one of collaboration with the enemies of Britain...... our salvation will not be long in coming and India will win for freedom and I repeat once again that when the hour strikes, I shall be at your side ready to participate in the final struggle. The power that could not prevent my getting out of Indiia will not be able to prevent my getting in. Meanwhile, friends, please send a word of cheer to our comarrades in prison, let them patiently bide their time for when they learn of fighting, they will be first to hail it. And we shall then bring them the arms and equipment which will enable them to be soldiers of India's last war of Independence".

Sporadic incidents were taking place in various regions throughout. the country. Railway communication was disrupted on and off between Delhi and Calcutta between Poona and Bangalore. Post offices and Railway stations were damaged at thousands of place. More than a lakh of persons had already been put under arrest. Many of them were receiving cruel treatment at the hands of jail authorities.

It may now seem surprising no many but it is a hard fact that the Viceroy Linlithgow took the momentous decision of suppressing the 1942 movement not himself alone but in full session of his Executive Council in which J.P. Srivastava, Mohammed Osman, Feroz Khan Noon, Sultan Ahmed and some other Indian members were present.

Speaking in the Central Assembly Sultan Ahmed, Law Member, said on September 18, 1942.

"Could any Government agree to negotiate with a party who came with certain demands in its right hand and a pistol in its left. It is too late in the day now for anyone to make the impossible arttempt to absolve thew Congress friom the fullest responsibility for all that has happened iin the country .... "In the Council of State at New Delhi, Mohammed Osman, was Transport member, observed; "The Congress alone is responsside for the present situation and for the destruction of life .... The Congress has done the greatest disservice to the country at a time when Japan is at the very doors of India. The action taken by the Government is, Therefore, throughly justified...." In the council of states I.N. Aspru and H.N. Kunzru diod not accept the view that Congress was resposible for the distrubances. They forcefully said that the Government of India was also fully responsible for the situation that did had arisen.

Mahatma Gandhi had delivered a soul-stirring speech on the night of 8 August, 1942. Speaking at the historic A.I.C.C. Session at the Gowalia Tank, Bombay, the Mahatma said. "Every man is free to go to the fullest length under the 'Ahimsa'. Satyagrahis should go out to die and not to live. It is only when individuals go out to seek and face death that the nation will revive. 'Karenge Ya Marenge', we shall do or die."

Feroz Khan Noon, a number of the viceroy's Executive council suggested that if India was divided into five dominions the constitutional deadlock would no longer exist. Here was a man who desired that India be broken up in five parts! The Muslim League working committee met in Bombay from August 15 to 20 at M.A. Jinnah's residence. It called upon the Muslim to abstain from any participation in the movement initiated by the Congress and to continue to purse their normal peaceful life.

How unjustified the stand was could be seen from a counter statement from Syed M. Hussain, secretary of the Muslim League party in the council of state. In a statement he said".....Decision reached by the working committee of the All India Muslim League has failed to give any lead to the Muslims at a juncture when it was urgently needed.

The Working President of the Hindu Mahasabha Dr. S.P.Mukherjee, in his press statement of September 4, declared. "..... India cannot be governed today by a mere policy of repression, the initiative for ending the present deadlock should come from the Briish Government".

The Movement had gone underground and a good number of persons evaded arrest successfully. They staked their lives to carry on the movement. Many of them died in encounters with the police. The soul of the nation was not fully stirred. The student community was by and large electrified.

Though many of them were not in a position to do much, still hundreds of students went underground and effectivelly carried on the Freedom Strugglé. Some girl students carried the messages from one place to another. At times these girls travelled long distances even through regions where there was no proper transport.

A very significant event occurred in Hazaribagh Jail a day before Diwali, the festival of light, in 1943. Jayaprakash Narayan, the Socialist Leader, who was about 40 years of age at that time, jumped the wall of Hazaribagh jail and escapes.

Jaya Prakash's escape was noticed only next afternoon when some visitor had come to see him.When he could not be traced any where there followed the alarm bell, better known as the 'pugli ghanti ? when this 'pugli ghanti' rang, all the persons were supposed to go to their cells. If they remained outside it was at their own risk. By the time his escape was noticed he had travelled a long distance from Hazaribagh. A good number of policemen in Bihar were not actually interested in arresting him.

A large number of policemen had been brought from other provinces. For many weeks Jayaprakash remained outside Bihar. During that period the underground movement took a fresh turn and postal and rail communications were again severely affected at hundreds of places in India. The British Government in India staked all its resources to track down Jayaprakash Narayan. He personified the idomitable spirit of the youth of India.

After this escape the prisoners in Hazaribagh Jail were in fact tortured very much, day and night. This caused a severe station on the health of many of the inmates. Jagjivan Ram fell ill and could not even sit up for many days. When his condition grew worse the Government decided to release him.

The Epilogue

Jagjivan Ram was scheduled to leave for Moscow on July 7, 1973. Among those who came to see him that day was Aruna Asaf Ali, the brave Freedom fighter.

In U.S.S.R. Jagjivan Ram met A. Kosygin. From Moscow he went to London where he met various leaders. On July 20, a Western new agency flashed from London a news about his visit abroad. It said;

"The Defence Minister, Mr. Jagjivan Ram, expressed fears that the huge quantities of American and British arms going to Iran ultimately may be used against India. British Government leaders, Mr. Jagjivan Ram said, have sought to allay these fears.

Mr. Jagjivan Ram has been in Moscow recently for talks with Soviet Government High-upsamid reports that India is seeking new armaments to counter-balance a big arms build-up in Iran. He told a group of news men that he asked the U.K.Foreign secretary, Sir Alec Douglas Home, to provide a list of arms that Britain could sell to India Mr. Jagjivan Ram made these points:-

1. President Zulfikar Ali Bhutto has acknowledged that Pakistan is receiving military hardware from Iran.

2. Shah Mohd. Reza Pahlevi has warned that Iran would come to the aid of Pakistan if Pakistan is attacked by India. Therefore, we have every reason to believe that the armament being supplied to Iran had every possibility of being used against India". The minister added; "We are apprehensive".

Mr. Jagjivan Ram said that "India made the United states aware of the fear when the American some months ago resumed arms sales to Pakistan. But India consideredity would be fuile to raise the issue of U.S. arnmms spplies to Iran, believing Washington would pay little heed". He said that "he pewrsonally had raised the matter with Sir Alec anmd the British Defence Secretary."

Jagjivan Ram returned to India in July itself. He was given a rousing welcome on his arrival at palam. On 26th of November, 1973, Leonid Breznev arrived in New Delhi. From Palam to Connaught Circus it was a sea of human heads. people were genuinely happy to see this friend of India. In recent years U.S.S.R. has stood by India as no other country has done. In the security council debates on Kashmir U.S.S.R. has always supported India. The economic co-operation between the two countries is also increasing. They have never failed us in times of need. Jagjivan Ram has contributed a good deal to this friendship.

It would be interesting for the readers to know the views of a couple of very eminent persons. Late P.K. Atre, a literary giant,: "Jagjivan Ram is irradiated with an intrinsic magnetism which captivates all gentlemen who confront him. His words as straight and meaningful, never meandering in an exercise of futility."

The Chief Minister of a big state said interalia. "Jagjivan Ram is a great man not only because his sympathies are big but also because he is a master in the technique of handling men, officials and nonofficials. He believes rightly that in times of stress, political and economic, anything is better than remaining at the same spot. He is pragmatic.

Among very large segments of Indian population he was quickened the imagination and noble vision of a new, splendid and healthy social order. He believes that minima in the standards of living of the vulnerable sections ought to be established and constantly protected. His sheer presence anywhere generates finer feelings.

During the first minute of Conversation he wipes out the atmosphere of selfishness, rigidity and dullness that hangs upon some high quarters in New Delhi. His tone is never threatening to many countryman.

He is warmhearted and quite lively. Unlike a couple of other senior ministers he knows how to extend his exuberance to other people. he is not parochial, never. At an A.I.C.C. Meeting sometimes back a member from Delhi termed another senior minister a political acrobat. Not even a political adversary ever hurled such a charge at Jagjivan Ram.

His initial sufferings and travel had created an important trait in his character which eventually got ingrained in his personality : an understanding of humilitation in life. He tries to be a benefactor to the people, never a bully. He wants to humanize the economic and political life of the country so as to make it more tender, more hospitable to the suffering community of have nots. A human factor invariably guides his thinking.

In his earlier days he struggled almost as an unknown youth for the resurrection of a big Section of Indian people to which the greatest injustice in history had been done; and all this happened in our country where every guilty conscience now unloads its spleen on the ideals of democracy.

6

Dr. A.P. J. Abdul Kalam

Birth

A nineteenth century house on Mosque street in Rameshwaram, Chennai state, saw the birth of a child on 15th of October, 1931 to Jainulabdeen Marakayar and his wife Ashiamma.

They named the child, one of their many children, Avul Pakir Jainulabdeen Abdul Kalam. The parents were tall and handsome but the child grew up to be average in height and looks.

His father had no formal education but had knowledge, wisdom and common sense more than what a formal education would have given him. Mother Ashiamma came from an illustrious family, with the title of Bahadur given by the British.

While father was deeply religious and secular, doing Namaz five times a day and participating in the activities of the Rameshwaram temple, mother was too good and kind-hearted a woman feedling quite a number of hungry souls every day.

Not that they were rich enough to run a charitable institution, but whatever she fed her children, she made it her daily routine to feed the same food to many who would be in her house at the time of feeding. Kalam fondly remembers the affectionate hands serving him simple rice and sambar with a variety of pickles and chutnies on a banana leaf. Kalam would squat on the ground and relish the tasty lunches and dinners-not a rich man's food at all, not even nourishing by medical standards. Kalam has given great credit to his mother for her culinary expertise in cooking many varieties of sambar, pickles and chutnies.

His father would start the day after Namaz in the early mornings and take the young Kalam to an old Mosque on their street. Though not able to understand what the Arabic prayers meant, he had full faith that whatever he prayed for reached Allah, the almighty. He also used to notice that people would be waiting for his father to come out of the Mosque with vessels. Containing water in which his father would dip his fingers. The people would take that water home and some of them would later inform that the sick were cured.

His father would ask them to thank Allah. This enriched Kalam's faith in God. The wise father told him that prayer enables the person to become a part of the cosmos irrespective of his personal religion and prepares him or her to face difficulties.

Kalam's doubt was why his father would go out of the way to help others instead of advising them in the same way.

Kalam's mother tongue is Tamil. His father would advise him in simple Tamil that people in distress would find solace and comfort in sharing their sorrow with others in whom they had belief. He was only a tool in the hands of Allah to help others. He would discuss spiritual matters with Pakshi Lakshmana Shastry, high Priest of Rameshwaram Temple. They were very close friends. Like wise their children, Kalam and Ramanadha Shasthry became not only close friends but classmates also.

Family Background

Apart from a small coconut grove, Jainulabdeen had to depend on ferrying. Pilgrims would go from Rameshwaram to Dhanushkodi, a nearby Island and return. A sailboat was a good idea and Jainulabdeen ventured into the ferrying business profitably. Income was good but luck was bad. Then Kalam was around six years old who had seen only the goodness of the sea.

One evening, the calm climate changed to a devastating cyclone with winds speeding over a hundred miles on hour. The Pamban Bridge itself coolapsed with a train-full of passengers. Coastal land at Dhanushkodi was grabbed and swall owed by the hungry sea. Jainulabdeen's boat was broken to pieces and found its grave in the sea. The adversity strengthened his faith in Allah to whom he prayed in silence. As it was, he was not a rich man but was able to make the two ends meet comfortably; no luxuries, but good food, clothing and shelter, tyes ; again, yes to elementary education to Kamal; but, no to his higher education.

Shemsuddin, Kalam's first cousin was the first to plant the seed of business sense in Kalam. Rameshwaram's literate population was a thousand strong. The sole distributor for news papers in Rameshwaram was Shamsuddin but, as they say, he was the whole and sole of the enterprise! It was a one man's show. By the age of eight, Kalam was able to understand one thing that when the second world war broke out, an unexpected demand for tamarind seeds rose and he had an opportunity to earn some money. He would collect the seeds from trees and other sources and sell them to a provision shop on the Mosque street.

His grand profit would be an anna (one sixteenth part of

a rupee in those days) per day ! But his first proud wages which Kalam has not forgotten came as a helper to Shamsuddin in catching the newspaper bundles thrown from a moving train ! The war had forced the railway authorities to cancel the stop at Rameshwaram. But the train was moving from Rameshwaram to Dhanushkodi and it was arranged to throw the newspaper budles on the Rameshwaram road from the moving train.

Shamsuddin appointed Kalam to do this important job of catching the budles of Dinamani ! Kalam recalls his great pride in handling has first wages as an eight year old boy.

The Education

Ahmed Jallaluddin, who perhaps sensed the bent of Kalam's mind encouraged him to develop the healthy hobby of learning instead of wasting time. He himself was the only one learned man who could read and write English in the entire island ! It was he would read or write English letters or applications for anybody who would come to him asking for it. It was he would educated young Kalam about the brave, new world beyond Rameshwaram and the great achievements and achievers in various fields.

Kalam was not a scorer of high marks but a studious boy who would want to know whatever was there worth knowing. If he could not real Dinamani, he would see the pictures on it. There was a revolutionary in Rameshwaram, Shree S.T.K. Manickam, who had a good library in his house.

Kalam would frequent his house for borrowing all sorts of books. The revolutionary would gladly tell him to widen his horizons. The School education at Rameshwaram came to a close and it was time to go to High School. Neither Kalam's brothers nor his near relations and neighbours had that much schooling as kalam had at that time. They had left school long back and engaged themselves in some sort of livelihood. But when Kalam expressed his inclination towards joining High School, Jainulabdeen, in his matured and wise way, told him that their parental love or their financial needs would never bind him.

A bird cannot be stopped from flying and reaching its goal. He convinced Ashiamma that children come through them and not from them and children have to grow into adults. He took Kalam and the other three sons to the Mosque and recited the prayers **Al Fathiha** from the holy Quran. He blessed Kalam saying that his soul dwelled in the house of tomorrow. It was again Ahmed Jallaluddin and Shamsuddin who gave company to Kalam while travelling to Ramanathapuram. They enrolled him in the Schwartz High School and also arranged for his boarding.

Kalam was accoustomed to the small town of Rameshwaram where every one knew every other one. He would become home-stick often but his father's great hopes in him that he would become collector would bring him to terms with his weakness. Added to that, Jallaluddin would always be there in such mental conditions to guide him. He would educate him about the powers of positive thinking. But again, Kalam was a fortunate boy for he got another great teacher in the High School Iyadurai Solomon, who later become Reverend Iyadurai Solomon. His affection for Kalam went beyond his status of good pupil. Kalam learnt the basic secrets of success from him which are mentioned here for your benefit: Desire, Belief and Expectation. Intense desire strengthened with belief in achieving it and faith would make you design your destiny. He elevated the self-esteem in his students. As a result, when Kalam finished High School, he had no second thought about higher education.

Kalam has mentioned that he did believe literally what the Reverend advised him. He had immense desire to soar and to fly like cranes and Seagulls. It resulted in his being the first child from Rameshwaram to fly later.

There was funny incident in High School which is worth mentioning. Kalam, while yet new in fourth form, wandered inadvertently, one day, into a wrong class room where Mathematics was being taught. The class teacher was Ramakrishna lyer, who believed in the old axiom 'spare the rod, spoil the child'.

He had no patience to hear 'excuse me' apologies.. With his cane and in front of the students, he punished the errant boy holding his neck. Perhaps, it induced Kalam to score full marks in Mathematics in the final examination ! That was the result of positive thinking taught by his brother-in-law Jallaluddin ! Perhaps, any other student would have cursed his teacher or brought his elders to scold the teacher.

The teacher was overwhelmed and again in front of all the students, he Praised Kalam that he would bring glory to his School and to his teachers. He however, did not forget to add that was the result of his caning ! Well, the boy did bring glory not only to Ramanathapuram Schwartz High School but to the entire nation !

The social concern of Kalam which was in the subconscious mind began to notice people around him at the age of eighteen. Whenever he returned to his home town, his elder brother would put him in charge of his provision shop and disappear with some excuse. And then, his younger brother would not leave him and would put him in his shop selling novelties to pilgrims.

Kalam noticed that in the provision shop, many poor people would buy beedies and cigarettes. In fact, they were the fastest moving goods ! Kalam could not understand how these poor people who earned just a little by a lot of hard labour could squander a considerable portion of that money on such injurious products. By 1950, the High School education ended and St. Joseph's College in Tiruchirapalli was calling him. Those were the days when higher education meant going to a College. There was neither expert advise or guidance not plenty of opportunities at his level. Like others, he also got admitted to the Intermediate course and then to the Bachelor of Science degree course.

Kalam got a room in the college hostel sharing with two other students, one an orthodox Iyengar and another a Syrian Christian. He has mentioned this aspect to educate the religious fundamentalists. They had a wonderful time all through the term and most interesting feature was that the Muslim Kalam was made secretary of the vegetarian mess ! ans their cooking was lavishly praised by reverend father Karathil ! Normally, Kalam prefers Vegetarian food.

Kalam was not a rank student bound to his curriculum. Apart from Science subjects, he used to study English literature and Philosophy. He could not help disagreeing with the argument that Science and Philosophy were different. Science ever since then, has been to him an enlightening path to spiritual awakening and self-realization. He reads books on Cosmology celestial bodies but would not interest himself in astrology, though he believed in the supernatural power of the almighty.

However, he could not proceed further in Physics. Lack of guidance made him to follow the line and join B.Sc. but his heart was in Engineering. Two years were spent after Intermediate to gain the Science degree with which he was not satisfied. He regretted he should have chosen the Engineering degree cours. He used his brain and decided to go for the D.M.I.T. in 1954. The Madras Institute of Technology is a prestigious institution in India and its post graduate Diploma is considered equivalent to an Engineering degree academically but carries more weight in employment circles.

Kalam managed to be on the list of selected candidates for admission to D.M.I.T. But he had one more problem the problem of finance. He could have got a job with his B.Sc. but Kalam was determined to become an Engineer. Jainulabdeen could not raise the required amount of thousand rupees which was a big amount. But his godfather Ahmed Jallaluddin came to his support. Kalam's sister Zohara whom Ahmed had married had shared the same faith in Kalam as her husband and raised the money mortgaging her jewels.

Kalam was overcome with emotions and took a vow that he would take the first opportunity to repay the loan. But he couldn't look for a part time job or business. All he, as a student, could do was to devote his entire time to his studies and earn a scholarship and with that amount, he did repay the loan and return the jewels.

Kalam's father could not think beyond the position of collector for his son; that was the height of his ambition and information. But Kalam wanted to soar and to fly like birds and that desire led him to choose aeronautical Engineering as his optional after the first year. His persistence gave him the key to the store house of his dreams. He put his first step forward. He was spurred to this choice by the two decommissioned aircrafts displayed for teaching purposes.

Kalam would spend as much time as he could before these aircrafts. His desire to fly the aircrafts was strenthening, though not his assertiveness due to his mind manners and introvert nature. Whenever he tried and failed in his effort to setup some sort of communication with others, he would remember his father; being learned is to know others but being wise is to know oneself; it is better to be learned and wise.

Kalam was always lucky in getting excellent and extraordinary teachers throughout his student days. That is the reason why he remembers all his teachers with great respect unlike many of us who certainly cannot boast of paying such high regards to our teachers, let alone, remembering their names after a short while. May be, the days have changed the old, sacred guru shishya relationship into the commercial and impersonal nature of the present system of education.

One of his teachers at MIT was Dr.Kurt Tank whom the HAL staff at Bangalore and other aeronautically minded people remember for the first jet fighter of India, HF-24 marut designed by him. He was a well-known figure in Bangalore. Kalam remembers an interesting point about Prof. Sponder, his techinical aero-dynamics teacher. As an Austrian, he had to spend some time in the concentration camps of Hitler. But unfortunately apart from Dr.Tank, his boss was also a German, a Prof. Walter Repenthin. His strong dislike for the Germans, however, never interfered in his teaching profession.

Kalam learnt another great basic secret of success which distinguished him in is his later life from this professor sponder.When Kalam went to him for advise in choosing his optional, the professor gave a small discourse which can be a turning point for the young Indians.

Why do you choose Aeronautical Engineering ? why not Electrical Engineering or Civil Engineering or Mechanical Engineering ? we may, perhaps, extend it present day young Indians; why do you choose Softweare Engineering ? Why not medicine or Electironics which were not subjects not long ago ? He said that the trouble with Indian aspirants was that they do not discriminate different disciplines and rationalize their choices.

They do not check their inclinations, natural enthusiasm and deep likings for a particular subject, instead, they go by the ambitions of their parents who are guided by the employment opportunities and income prospects.

{It is not irrelevant to state here that a few parents wish their children to apt for government jobs which, the parents are certain, would offer regular and additional irregular incomes, least work and easy and maneuverable responsibilities.} The students ignore the essential and decisive factor-whether their choice generates and fulfils their innermost aspirations, other landing a job that assures high income.

Kalam was fortunate to get a 'self-interview' through such a forthright professor before he choose his optional subject of Aeronautical Engineering. Prof. KAV Pandalai was a professor who taught, in addition to aerostructural design and analysis, to agree to disagree.

In later life, Kalam was respected for the 'Surgical Knife' with which the would review the aeronautical and rocket designes with surgical precision. This surgical knife, Kalam Picked up from Prof. Narasingha Rao, a mathematician who taught theoretical aerodynamics. His teaching was so forceful that Kalam preferred Mathematical Physics to other subjects.

The great teachers were noted for their intellectual approaches with clarity of thought and passion for perfection while they were on their jobs of imparting knowledge to their students. They created an excitement and attachment in their students for their subjects. Their methods were original and individualistic.

Kalam remembers one particular incident which, once for all, at his budding stage itself, rooted out holding others responsible for mistakes and imbibed in him the quality of taking the entire responsibility on himself like a leader in term work, Consequently, Kalam's greatness is recognized today in his leadership qualities. Five students including Kalam were assigned a project of designing a lowlevel attack aircraft. Kalam's part of the work was preparing and drawing the aerodynamic design. After a few days, Prof.Srinivasan, his design Teacher and Director, MIT, came to review Kalam's progress. He was totally dissatisfied with the state of affairs and looked at him He would't listen to any number of excuses genuine or otherwise.

Kalam was disheartened and requested for a month's time to complete the work. Prof. Srinivasan stared into his frightened eyes and said, "Look, young man, today is Friday afternoon. I give you three days time. If by Monday morning. I don't get the configuration drawing, your Scholarship will be stopped." It was a bomb that exploded. Prof. Srinivasan left the bewildered Kalam there and went away. It was scholarship money that was sustaining Kalam. It was not entirely his mistake that had caused the delay. But the situation was beyond his control. But it made him think positively as taught by his mentor Jallaluddin and made him take responsibilities in future. The enlightening encounter between the teacher and the pupil gave rise to a great leader of India.

That Friday afternoon, Kalam started the work and was nearing completion on Sunday morning ! He only knows how he was able to recompense his and his teamates' lapses and the sacrifices he had to make to achieve the progress. Prof. Srinivasan, in his tennis dress, was watching Kalam from a distance without his knowledge. He suddenly and impulsively came to Kalam, hugged him affectionately and patted him, "I never expected you to perform so well".

The lesson and the experience made deep impressions in Kalam's subconscious mind and kept him evercareful, everconscious and always ahead of his schedules and the team members and elevated him to the high post he occupiest-day.

Kalam is a proud Indian. He is justifiably proud because

he has proved what Indians could do in the most difficult circumstances. He showed this streak as a student also. The MIT Tamil Sangam (Literary Society) organized an essay competition for the students, Kalam's mother tongue is Tamil and he is proud of that also.

He choose the subject "Let us make our own Aircraft" and wrote the essay in Tamil and got the first prize from the editor Devan of Ananda Vikatan, a famous Tamil weekly of India ! The language he wrote it in is immaterial but the spirit of making India proud should be our motto also.

The DMIT course took Kalam to Hindustan Aircraft Limited, Bangalore for practical graduate apprenticeship where he acquired hands on experience in parts of aircrafts from the technicians. Kalam was convinced with the native Indian inteligence while learning from the technicians who, not with standing lack of academic education, were able to teach the graduate engineers. These keen and absorbing observations of our latent capabilities even at lower levels were forming the firm foundation for the astounding success of Kalam when the Developed Nations boycotted us.

Kalam's Fate

It was true for the man who had, all along his life, starting from the age when a child commences dreaming, dreamt of soaring and flying like a crane, like a seagull, but had rudely suffered the shock of his wings mercilessly cut off on the ground itself.

He felt that he could no more look at the skies. He felt he was at the end of the flight with nothing to look at back in satisfaction. His life had lost the purpose and goal for which his parents, his sister and brother-in-law had sacrificed their mites with great hopes and expectations in his ability and destiny.

The man Kalam narrated to Swami Shivananda how and why he was bitter with his luck. The proud aeronautical engineer had applied to Air Force selection Board for the post of a Commissioned officer and was called for an interview, he had faced an interview for the post of senior Scientific Assistant in DTD & P(Air), New Delhi,but he was concentrating on his ambition of becoming a Pilot. He had travelled two thousand kilometers to Dehradun from one end of our country to another end for the first time, observing during the long journey the Indian culture, varied in appearance but one and the same in the core, reminiscing the past history and dreaming about his future as a Pilot.

He was in for a shock ! He had no Air Force personality! Perhaps, the then Air Force authorities gave second preference to originality and innovative ability ; but the loss was to the Indian Air Force! The president would have come through the Air Force instead of through the DTDP ! Kalam stood ninth in the list but only eight candidates were selected !

Kalam stood still for some time unable to realize and accept what had happened to him. His dreams were shattered ! He literally dragged his listless body to the edge of a cliff in Dehradun. Looking at the lake far below the cliff from its edge, he brooded over the calamitous blow of the destiny for indefinite time. Slowly, recovering and refurbishing himself with the aid of positive thinking taught to him by Ahmed Jallaluddin and faith in Allah inculated by his father Jainulabdeen he started trecking.

He reached Rishikesh and bathed in the sacred Ganga. The purity and medicinal property of the Himalayan water cooled his mind. He had heard of Swami Sivananda and thought it might be a good idea to have his darshan. He wanted answers for the taunting doubts and uncertain fears.

Swami Sivananda was himself great man and a yogi who

had seen life in its myriad forms. The Muslim name made no difference to him but it was Kalam's personality that impressed him! For him, Kalam looked like a man in melancholy. The Swamiji transferred his confidence and happiness through his child-like smile to Kalam and explained the mystery of cosmic energy and the ageless promise.

"Accept your destiny and go ahead with your life;" he advised, "what you are destined to become is not revealed now but it is predetermined. Surrender yourself to the wish of god, rely upon the eternally unbroken promise of sunrise and of the spring".

Abdul Kalam was reassured. He had been lucky to get the right advices and guidance from the right people at the right times. Throwing off the mantle of despair which had covered his body and mind, he got ready to face the tomorrows whatever they would bring. Returning to Delhi, he went to DTDP to enquire about his interview. He was to given a letter appointing him as a senior Scientific Assistant in the Technical Centre (Civil Aviation) on a basic salary of Rs. 250/-per month. well, thought Kalam, my destiny is not to fly the aeroplanes but to make the aeroplanes airworthy! During the one year he spent in Delhi, Kalam carried out a design assignment on a supersonic target aircraft which earned a world of praise from Dr. Neelakantan Director. Then he was sent to Kanpur to gain experience in maintenance of aircraft at the Aircraft & Armament Testing unit. He was involved there in the tropical evoluation of Gnat MK I aircraft.

After returning to Delhi he was involved in several miscellaneous projects, which however, earned him the good will of his superiors. By 1961-62, Aeronautical Development Establishment was established in Bangalore, opposite the erstwhile Electronics Research and Development Establishment (ERDE) and on the other side of the road, Kalam was posted to ADE, Bangalore.

The long journey and the living styles of Rameshwaram, Kanpur and Bangalore were slowly churning the subconscious mind of Kalam. Indians were invaded by several foreigners from time to time, subjugated and forced to adapt to their cultures. As a result, Indians lost unique identity and began to imitate their umpteen masters. It may be chewing pan like wajid Ali Shah in Kanpur or walking dogs in Bangalore like the Brown Sahibs. We became Proud imitators of our masters.

Politics and Kalam

Abdul Kalam, senior Scientific Assistant, had been selected by Dr. Op Mediratta, Director, ADE, based on his past performance and experience, especially in his preliminary studies on ground-handling equipment to head a team of four members at his level.

The project was to design and develop a ground equipment machine on the lines of a hovercraft. A hovercraft is a vehicle that would not fly like an aeroplane or helicopter in the sky but would travel a little high on the ground or on water blasting downward a cushion of air under it. That way, it will be a very convenient utility vehicle. The team was given three years time and freedom to think and work! The pity was that no one of the team had ever built any machine, not to think of an aeroplane !

But that was exactly the opportunity Abdul Kalam had been waiting for-to show to the world what he could do ! But to discourage him and his team members, very many colleagues were readily available on hand. They had quite painstakingly coined some nicknames like 'eccentric inventors' and 'Navvies'. Their special target, of course, was the team leader.

But Abdul Kalam was not a hollow man. His confidence in himself and faith in Allah guided him in spite of paucity of literature on the subject. As he remembers, the challenge opened the windows of his mind. He took the inspiration from the makers of the Aeroplanes-the Wright Brothers themselves who were busy fixing bicycles for seven years before they succeeded in making an aeroplane. And now the times were not that bad as in those times.

The Wright Brothers were also being ridiculed by their fellow citizens until they shut their mouths with their grand success. Majority of the students with rural background and also those who study in vernacular media, seem to have some sort of complex that makes them shy a way from the English medium students. This aberration of slackened assertiveness continues until they realize that they are as good as or even better that others irrespective of the media of learning.

Abdul Kalam also had this hangover but soon cured himself with his successes. His native intelligence was enough to build Nandi, the native hovercraft step by step through trials, tribulations and errors. They got an extraordinary morale booster from none other that the Defence Minister, VK Krishna Menon himself.

After about a year, shree VK Krishna Menon visited ADE to know about the progress of the project. Abdul Kalam took the Defence Minister enthusiastically to the assembly shop, showed him the various sub-assemblies and explained how he was going to fit them all to make the final hovercraft.

Krishna Menon, known for his oratorical skills and cynical attitudes, extracted all the answers to clear his doubts. He was especially bent on making defence weapons within India. Sharing the enthusiasm of the 'Navvies' team, he certified to Dr. Mediratta, "GEM flight is impossible with the gadgets Kalam now possesses". In the near future, Krishna Menon visited ADE again, accompanied that time by a Group Captain Golay. The hovercraft was ready to drive and to fly.

Krishna Menon sat in the wonder vehicle disregarding thc officials' concern for his safety. The Group captain, who, later became Air Marshal, was Skeptical about Kalam, a mere civilian pilot, in the cockpit. He asked Kalam to come out so that he could take over the flying machine through gestures because he did not want the Defence Minister to know his fearful doubts about Kalam. Krishna Menon was a better observer and himself gestured to the Group Captain to shut up with his laugh.

After a successful demonstration, he was very happy and suggested a more powerful prime move and asked Kalam to be ready for his second flight with it. Dr, Mediratta was more that pleased, he was proud.

Reassured himself with the confidence and courage, he told, may be, retorted to, his colleagues, "Here is flying machine, not constructed by a bunch of cranks but by engineers of ability. Don't look at it is not made to look at, but to fly with. "As a by-product, his lack of assertiveness vanished !

The hovercraft was completed ahead of the schedule and was put in cold storage no sooner than it was completed after Krishna Menon resigned ! And along with it, went the hearts and souls of Abdul Kalam and of his team members, the Science and Engineering entrepreneurs. The hovercraft is imported to this day at the cost of out tax money but that is another matter that doesn't matter!

Kalam was disgusted and disillusioned. He had dreamt that for him too, as for a bird, sky was the limit ! Anyone with wings of imagination could do anything that he was capable of in his mother land India, that is Bharath ! Kalam went back to his childhood days for recoupment for he could not face the stark reality of some of our countrymen who would sacrifice their one eye if that could gouge out the two eyes of their neighbours.

He remembered Pakshi Lakshmana Shasthry who had advised to seek truth which sets the seeker free. He remembered Jesus who had said "Ask, and you shall receive".

The Destiny

Thirty one Years had passed after 1931 and Abdul Kalam was trying to forget the bitter truth.

Dr. Mediratta, another great Scientist and Engineer, had reckoned the merit of his assistant and one day, asked him about the condition of the hovercraft.

Kalam replied casually that it was in perfect condition. He was then told to arrange another demonstration for a visitor, No further details were given. Still, Kalam and his team felt happy and were ready with the machine the next day, A tall and handsome man with an attractive beard was welcomed by the Director and brought to the hovercraft.

He was quite inquisitive and finally requested Kalam for a ride. His request thrilled Kalam just as it thrilled the visitor while floating for about ten minutes above the very ground he was standing earlier. He enquired further about Kalam and introduced himself as Prof. MGK Menon, the renowned Director of T I F R, the Tata Institute of Fundamental Research! He thanked Kalam politely for the great ride and left.

A week had passed after returning the Indian-made hovercraft to its garage and the incident was forgotten. Unexpectedly then, Abdul Kalam received a call from INCOSPAR, the Indian committee for space reserch Mumbai. He was not aware much of the committee, though he had heard about it. WIth permission and good wishes of Dr. Op Mediratta,

Kalam came over to Mumbai to face an interview for the post of Rocket Engineer. The candidate who had tasted failure at the doors of Indian Air Force at Kanpur was nervous because he was not give sufficient time to prepare himself for the interview, nor had he anybody to take help from. But his faith in Allah was with him. He remembered what Shree Krishna had preached.

All beings are born to delusion overcome by the dualities which arise from wish and hate. But those men of virtuous deeds in whom sin has come to an end, freed from the delusion of dualities, worship me stead fast in their vows.

So, Kalam decided to remain unperturbed by the results of the interview; He was Pleasantly surprised to find Prof MGK Menon with two other dignitaries, Shree, Saraf, then the Deputy Secretary of the Atomic Energy Commission and the great Dr. Vikram Sarabhai, who became his mentor.

The atmosphere of the interview was personal, intimate and warm; Kalam forgot that he was being interviewed by great scientist who had by then carved their names in the history of Indian Science. No routine and textbook questions as in the case of thousands of interviews; only of the dreams of the candidate. He was treated in reference to a larger entity and a larger goal by the true scientists.

Hurtful Attentions

It was within a short time that Abdul Kalam fitted himself in the INCOSPAR like a fish in the water. The stifling, Congested and bureaucratic atmosphere of a government setup gave room to an independent, encouraging and throughly professional environment in the new scientific organization. Here designations did not justify one's existence. All that mattered was one's performance. And in this pursuit, the small town man Kalam excelled and escaped the hurtful and mischievous attentions of some of his excolleagues. Those were the pioneering days for Indian space research. The Indian committee was searching for a suitable place to locate their station to launch rockets. The place had to be near earth's magnetic equator. Dr. Chitnis of the Physical Research Laboratory, Ahmedabad, recommended Thumba near Thiruvananthapuram, Kerala.

Thumba is a small fishing village. A site measuring about 600 acres near the sea coast was finally chosen but it had a sensitive spot namely a church, st.Mry Magdalene Church under the jurisdiction of the Bishop of Trivendrum, Right Reverend Dr. Peter Bernard Pereira. The then collector of Trivendrum, Shree K Madhavan Nair handled the problem of evacuating the villagers very tactfully, Later, Dr. Vikram Sarabhai himself went to the house of the Bishop in Thiruvananthapuram and convinced him how the site was suitable for ionospheric research.

The next morning in Sunday congregation, his Excellency Bishop introduced Dr. Vikram is doing and what I am doing are the same-both Science and Spirituality seek the blessings of the almighty for human prosperity in mind and body. He then put the question to the congregation, "children, can we give them god's abode for a scientific mission ?" The response was a resonant "Amen !" The holy coincidence was that the prayer room became Kalam's first laboratory and Bishop's room, his first design and drawing officer ! The Equatorial Rocket Launching station started functioning vigorously at Thumba.

Abdul Kalam was immensely happy when he was selected to undergo training in sounding rocket launching rockets for about six months in America at their National Aeronautics & Space Administration (NASA) work centres. He wanted to convey the happy news personally to his parents and so took a few days leave. His father, Jainulabdeen took Kalam to the Mosque and arranged for special prayers. All his well wishers blessed him.

Kalam felt a current flowing from and back to Allah, first through his father and then from him through himself. When Ahmed Jalaluddin and Shamsuddin were at the Mumbai airport for send-off Ahmed, who was his childhood mentor and his teacher of positive thinking told him, "Azad, we have always loved you, and we believe in you. We shall always be proud of you". The true sentimental tears were quite visible in all the eyes. It is an irony of fate that while Abdul Kalam was learning at the various centres of NASA like langley Research Centre, Hampton, Goddard space Flight Centre, Greenbelt, and Wallops Flight facility, Wallops and making his impressions of the mental attitudes of the Americans towards life and their enormous success, the real fillip to his patriotic sense came from a painting!

The painting was displayed in the reception hall of the Wallops Flight facility. It was a good painting that would attract anybody. Abdul Kalam went near it and saw that it was a painting of a battle scene. A few rockets were flying in the background and a few were being launched. An appropriate painting for a rocket launching station, appreciated Kalam, But a keen observer that he was, he noticed that the rocket launchers looked like Indians in colour and war uniforms.

He moved closer to the painting and was simply astonished to learn that the soldiers throwing the rockets were Indeed Indians! It was the painting of a war between the British and the great Indian Tipu Sulthan of Mysore, nicknamed Tiger !

He left happier to learn that when Tippu Sulthan was killed in the war, the Briish were able to locate 700 rockets and 900 subsystems of rockets at Turukanahally ! Tipus every brigade had a company of Jourks or rocket men. The British, who had not much of knowledge of rockets and subassemblies to England

and subjected them to reserve Engineering to learn the Technology.

The pitiable fact in India, repetitive as in other fields, was, however, that Indian missile enterprise died with Tipu Sulthan ! The Rocket enterprise had to wait for more than a hundred and fifty years to raise its head again ! Very few Indians thought it fit to appreciate and continue the genius of Tipu Sulthan till we achieved our freedom ! But he was glorified as a hero of rocketry in England and America ! Whether any rocket has been named after the great hero is also not known, a few are destined to dust bins of history, regardless of their achievements. It is relatively worth mentioning what Abdul Kalam learnt from his mother. It is an ancedote from the Holy Book.

It was soon after God created the first man Adam. God was very much happy about his creation and asked all of his other creatures to prostrate themselves to Adam. Only lblis or Satan refused stating "You created me of fire and him of clay. Does not that make me nobler than Adam ?" Allah said, "Be gone from paradise.

This is no place for your contemptous pride. "Satan obeyed, but true to his nature, cursed Adam with similar fate, Not long after, Adam also disobeyed Allah and earned Allah's displeasure. He said, "Go hence and may your descendants live a life of doubt, pride and mistruct.

Interaction With Others

Kalam had to interact with scientists from different disciplines and from different countries like U.S.A., U.S.S.R., France, Germany and Japan. In this job he had the opportunity to know first hand how foreign scientists regard their work.

Kalam saw Prof. Oda, the X-ray payload scientist from

Japan, Shedding tears when his timers, which were used instead of the Indian electronic timer devices, at the professor's insistence failed to trigger in perfect time coordination the exploding of pyros and consequently the telemetry signal reported mission failure. Kalam was stunned.

Abdul Kalam wants the young Indians to remember and he proud of their forefathers. One of the jobs of Kalam at Terls, short for Thumba Equatorial Rocket Launching Station, was building jettisonable cones, a subsystem of rockets. He had to study the composite materials required to make the cones. We should be proud to know that the composite bows used by the Indians according to Archaeological excavations were made of wood, sinew and horn.

This was during the eleventh century, not less than five hundred years before medieval Europeans made such bows. Kalam and his team went further and created Rohini and Menaka rockets (not the Apsara dancers) and launched them without the necessity of the French Indra (rockets) !

Kalam gives full credit for all of their achievements to Dr. Sarabhai who had the knack of making things look quite possible of achievement by them even though it was not the fact, and then leading them gradually to success through his magical powers of persuasion. He would bring a visitor from the developed world, as if for technical collaboration, and would later put the challenge to his team to stretch their minds. A very enterprising and smart leader, indeed !

Kalam's understanding with Allah was that he would raise his ability by fifty percent and then put himself in his hands ! Kalam says that the partnership has been very fruitful ! But he remembers a quotation from George Bernard Shah, which he chanced reading in a business management book lying on a sofa in Hotel Ashok, New Delhi, when he was waiting at 1.00 a.m in the morning to meet Dr. Sarabhai ! All reasonable people adapt themselves to the prevailing ideas of the world.

It is the unreasonable people that force the world to adapt to their ideas. It is to them that the world owes its progress. Edison, Ford, Wright Brothers and so many like them experimented and succeeded in bringing the world round to their so called unreasonable ideas.

That was when Kalam was called from Mumbai to meet Dr, Sarabhai at New Delhi at 3.30 a.m in Hotel Ashok. That was the way Dr. Sarabhai used to work and expected his group to work. There was GP. Capt. V.S Narayanan from Air Headquarters also waiting to meet Dr. Sarabhai.

He called both of them to his room, orderd coffee and explained his plans to develop a Rocket Assisted Take -Off (RATO) system for military aircrafts to help them take off from short runways in the Himalayas.

After finishing coffee, he took them to Tilpat Range on the outskirts of Delhi where he showed a Russian RATO. After allowing them to study it for some time, he suddenly shot oa question at them, "If I get you the motors of this system from Russia, could you do it in eighteen months time?" Both Kalam and Narayanan shot back an answer at him in unison, "Yes, we can!"

Prof. Sarabhai went to have breakfast at the Prime Minister's house and in the evening, the news was out that India was going to take up manufacture of RATO for the Indian military aircraft under the leadership of APJA Kalam ! Dr. Sarabhai was a leader with a vision.

He was full of ideas and plans. He drew up a plan for ten years covering utilization of satellites for non-military purposes like television, education, weather forecasts, management of natural sources and so on. At the same time a missile panel was formed in Ministry of Defence with Kalam and Narayanan as members. Here again, we should know that these tactical and strategic missiles are. Though there used to be some difference between the two, now both are used to fly thousands of kilometers to strike the targets wherever they are situated.

The work on RATO was getting delayed for they had to depend on imports for every thing. And in India were we worship documentation as something bigger than the Almighty, importing was a colossal procedure which had and has to pass through an army of government servants.

Kalam and Narayanan wondered whether they have to continue to live with screw driver technology. One day Kalam happened to see a colleague Jaya Chandra Babu, a new entrant, going home after office hours. Kalam knew him as a man with positive attitude.

SLV-Part 1

Launching of our own satellite vehicle had been conceived but the stage of progress was at the ground itself. In 1968, the Indian Rocket Society was formed, transformation of INCOSPAR to an advisory body under Indian National Science Academy (INSA) was made and Indian Space Research Organization (ISRO) was created under the department of Atomic Energy (DAE). Prof. Sarabhai, the ever active man decided in 1969 that first a suitable ground had to be selected and took Personal initiative in the matter.

His intention was to take advantage of the earth's West to East rotation in helping the setellite's orbit. He, therefore, choose Shriharikota island, a hundred kilometers North of chennai along the coast line and set up the SHAR Rocket Launch Station.

Prof. Sarabhai, then choose his team exclusively for this purpose of making the Indian satellite. The team consisted of Abdul Kalam as the project leader. Dr. V.R Gowarikar, MR Kurup and AE Muthunayagam as members. Kalam had to design the fourth stage of the SLV also. Though Kalam was methodical in his work ensuring progress at every tiny step, he felt he was not able to give attention to certain crucial sectors.

At that time, Prof. Sarabhai brought Prof. Curien, president of space Organization, France to see our progress. Pro-curien was engaged similarly in developing their SLVs called Diamont aunch vehicles. After studying Kalam's methods of working he advised Prof. Sarabhai to take out routine jobs from the purview of Kalam, and let him concentrate in the main work.

However, the French scientist was so highly impressed with the progress here that after commending that what was achieved here in one year was more significant than what their counterparts in Europe had achieved in three years, he wanted to know whether the Indian scientists could take up the Diamont's fourth stage. The subtle smile on Prof. Sarabhai's face was a smile that could make every Indian happy. Though The airframes of Indian and French SLVs were incompatiable, Kalam accepted the work adding to his heavy work load.

Kalam, the keen observer, would watch carefully his colleagues and would catch whoever showed even a little promise in spite of his friends cautionary advice.

His management was to make leaders out of common people at every stage. This was not the traditional management and Kalam was put once in a very embarrassing position for his innovative spirit. It happened during one of the bimonthly progress review meetings chaired by Prof. Sarabhai. Presentations of the first three stages of the SLV were made as usual.

But for the fourth stage which was directly under the control of Kalam, he gave the opportunity of presenting the progress to the five staff members who had worked on the design. That was the way how Kalam used to encourage and bring out the potential of his junior colleagues to the noticeof his boss Prof. Sarabhai. But there was a senior Scientist with Prof. Sarabhai who thought otherwise which was tradition wise. He questioned Kalam. "what did you do ?" Exhibiting his gross ignorance of changing management techniques and team work. For the first time in his working under Prof. Sarabhai, Kalam saw him getting really annoyed.

The Professor was scathing in his reply to the senior scientist, "You ought to know what project management is all about. We just witnessed an excellent example. It was an outstanding demonstration of team work. I have always seen a project leader as an integrator of people and that is precisely what Kalam is." No wonder, Kalam regards Prof. Vikram Sarabhai as the mahatma Gandhi of Indian science-to transform ordinary people to leaders.

It was not that Kalam had some how impressed Prof. Sarabhai, as many of us are accustomed to degrade our brethren. His qualities as a leader, his orginality in approach to scientific goals, his business acumen, his concern for indigenization of mind and materials, all drew appreciation of not only Prof.

Sarabhai but his successors also. Prof. Sathish Dhawan, who succeeded Prof. Sarabhai after his untimely, mortal arrest of his overworked heart on 30th of December 1971, as head of ISRO, was equally appreciative of Kalam's work.

He himself was a great scientist and a multi-faceted personality. It is interesting to note that he had amassed unusual degrees like an M.A. in English literature and B.E. in Mechanical

Engineering along with several professional degrees from Indian and American Universities.

Prof. Dhawan consulted Dr. Brahm Prakash for choosing a person to handle the management structure of the mega project of SLV which included the coordination of a large number of work centres with their own ways of working and management. It was a big responsibility which required the observation of a scientist, capability of an engineer, efficiency of an administrator and above all an extraordinary communicator.

Both were unanimous in their choice of Abdul Kalam as the Project Manager. Dr. Brahm Prakash, who regarded Kalam as his son, cautioned, "you will require a tremendous amount of tolerance and patience. But the way progress was moving as government speed, made even the patient Kalam lose his patience with government procedures.

By then, ISRO had become a government body with the concomitant red tapism. In one of the review meetings chaired by Dr. Brahm Prakash himself, he squarely held the indifference and delay tactics of the controller of accounts and financial advisor responsible for procurement bottle-necks and insisted that the accounts staff have to change their methods of working in line with the goals of the national project and demanded transfer of their functions and powers to the project team. Every one was stunned at the outburst of Kalam. Dr. Prakash himself, without saying any thing, stubbed his cigarette and went out of the meeting.

Abdul Kalam spent a sleepless and disturbed night. But as efficiency respects efficiency, Dr. Prakash delegated the financial powers to the project team the next morning. One has to be as hard as a diamond and as soft as a flower depending on the circumstances. But there was a professional bitter shock and disappointment to Kalam as great as the ones he suffered at

Dehradun and Bangalore. The extra pains he had taken to complete the French Diamont satellite fourth stage using the spare time of his colleagues generated the shock treatment pains.

The French Government shelved their project and with it went all the efforts of Kalam and a few of his colleagues. But Kalam had the experience of absorbing such shocks and controlled his emotions in the success of RATO project.

As the SLV project Manager, Kalam took the executive responsibility of completing the project within the frame work of policy decisions, approved management plan and especially within the budget.

Dr. Brahm Prakash constituted four advisory committees to help Kalam in several specialized areas of rocket motors, electronics, materials, fabrication and soon with outstanding scientists like DS Rane, TS Prahlad, SC Gupta, AR Acharya, CL Amba Rao and many more.

The project activities were sorted into three groups: Programme Management Group, Integration and Right Testing Group and Subsystems Development Group with related functions under each group. Against the projected requirement of 275 engineers and scientists, Kalam got only fifty strength !

Kalam says his day would start with cleaning his table first, then proceed with work according to priorities. (But have we seen an Indian bureaucrat cleaning his table?). The ending of the day would not be in their hands. Sometimes, it would go round the clock. The working schedule itself would be drafted during the two kilometres stroll Kalam would 'indulge' in the early mornings. Prof. Dhawan, now head of ISRO, while discussing the Complex Programme for the next seven to eight years, stated that the SLV Programme would be assisted by all the manpower and funds of Vikram Sarabhai Space Centre and SHAR.

Kalam stressed the importance of design capability, goal setting and realization and the strength to withstand setbacks.

The mechanical structure of the SLV is its body, the control and guidance systems with their associated electronics is its brain and the musculature comes from its propellants.

The life part of the SLV is its complex electrical circuitry which sets the mechanical structure in motion. What is referred by "Avionics" in aerospace research is this vast spectrum of varied activities commenching from simple electrical power supplies to sophisticated instrumentation, guidance and control systems.

SLV-Part-II

Just when the activities were in an ascending tempo, India suffered the loss of its great scientist and visionary Dr. Vikram Sarabhai on December 30, 1971.

It was the loss of a leader who had influenced the path of the Indian Science. His real greatness lies in creation of many leaders who were able to take over the unfinished task from him. To Kalam, it was like a shocking loss. But the work moved as Lord Tennyson had said 'men many come and men may go, but I go on for ever.

By June 1974, the team was able to best successfully the three systems-heat shield if SLV, Rate Gyro Unit and the Vehicle Attitude Programmer using the Centaur sounding rocket launch and wide ranging expertise in composite materials, control engineering and software " The dynamic Prime Minister Smt. Indira Gandhi was very happy and on 24th of July, 1974 announced in the parliment, "The development and fabrication of relevant technologies, subsystems and hardware (to make India's First Satellite Launch Vehicle) are progressing satisfactory. A number of industries are engaged in the fabrication of components.

The first orbital flight by India is scheduled to take place in 1978. Just when Kalam was recovering from the death of his professional mentor, Dr. Sarabhai, he was subjected to a rather personal and more intimate loss in passing a way of Ahmed Jallaluddin.

He was many things to Kalam : his close friend, guide, teacher, cheerleader, helper in financial and other distresses and what not. The shattering news came to him when he was engrossed in the static test of the first stage motor.

His eyes blurred and he could not control himself and handing over the work to Dr. S. Srinivasan Dy. Pr. Director, he travelled overnight and reached Rameshwaram the next day. His father himself over a hundred years became pall-bearer for his son-in-law. Jalaluddin went a little too early. For many days, Kalal's inner self was agitating and his mind was going through the futility of every thing.

As if this was not sufficient, in 1976, Kalam's father passed away. He was 102 years old and had led quite an eventful life. He was just another Indian who passed away but to Kalam, he was the source of real affection and real wisdom and real faith in Allah. His father was like about Ben Adhem who loved and served his fellow men irrespective of who they were.

Religious tolerance came naturally and by birth itself to Kalam through his parents, brother-in-law, Kith and Kin and neighbours like Pakshi Lakshmans Shasthry and teachers like Sivasubramanya lyer.

Not before long, His mother also expired, unable to bear the agonies. Kalam was getting hit again and again disturbing him severely in his professional life. The Divine Messenger has said, "Your wealth and children are only a temptation whereas : Allah ! With him is and aternal award".

Kalam would remember how when the call for Namaz sounded his home would transform itself into a small Mosque with children and grand children following the parent. Kalam was Physically exhausted and emotionally shattered but 'The show had to go on' with such people forming the firm foundation. Dr. Brahm Prakash asked Kalam one day to receive at Madras and escort to Thumba, a VVIP of rocketry, German born Wernher Von Braun.

He is a legend, the creator of the lethal V-2 missiles, supersonic in speed, that enabled Hitler to shake London, However, with the end of the watr and defeat of Hitler, he was captured by the Allies. Genius respects ginius. American made him a top official of NASA. He developed for the US Army, Jupiter missile, the first IRBM to reach beyond 3000 kilometres. It was a great honour for Kalam to receive Braun.

The great rocket engineer listened like a student to Kalam when he was explaining about Indian recketry ! What a comparison to; us who exaggerate and assume superhuman stance presenting a mountain of a success out of a mole of achievement! It is very, very important and pertinent for our young Indians in whichever fileld they are, to keep in mind what the rocket legend told in reply to Kalam's questions :

"America is a country of great possibilities, but they look upon everything non-American with suspicion and contempt. They suffer from a deep-rooted NIH-Not Invented Here-complex and look down on alien technologies. If you want to do anything in rocketry, do it yourself.

SLV 3 is a genuine Indian design and you may be having your own troubles. But you should always remember that we don't just build on successes; we also build on failures.

"Hard work is not enough in rocketry. It is not a sport

where mere hard work can fetch you honours. Here, not only do you have to have a goal but you have to have strategies to achieve it as fast as possible. Total commitment is not just hard work, it is total involvement. Building a rock wall is back-breaking work. There are some people who build rock walls all their lives. And when they die, there are miles of walls, mute testimonials to how hard those people had worked.

But there are other men who while placing one rock on top of another have a vision in their minds, a goal. It may be a terrace with roses climbing over the rock walls and chairs set out for lazy summer day. Or the rock wall may enclose an apple orchard or mark a boundary. When they finish, they have more than a wall. It is the goal that makes the difference. Do not make rocketry your profession, your livelihood-make it your religion, your mission". Kalam felt as if he was listening to Dr. Sarabhai and Ahmed Jallaluddin.

Kalam sacrificed badminton in the evenings, weekends and holidays, family relations and friends to succeed in his mission. Kalam came across people of different categories of people during his career. Some would grumble working for 40 hours a week and some others would never know how many hours they had worked. Sivaramakrishna Nair was injured severely along with five others with acid burns when an oxidizer tank filled with red fuming nitric acid (RFNA) burst.

He regained conciousness the next morning and his first concern was about the loss of time caused by the accident. Success depends on such a team which would stand like a rock in success and failure. The first trial of SLV 3 was scheduled on 10th of August, 1979. Stage 1 was perfect but stage 2 went out of control and the flight was terminated after 31seconds.

The fourth stage along with the payload splashed into the

sea 560 kilometres off Shriharikota. The unbearable mix of anger and frustration stiffened Kalam's legs and he relived the agony of abandoning of Nandi, RATO (after successful trial) and abortion of Diamont fourth stage. Without caring to answer queries, the staggered to his room and slumped on his bed. It was when Dr. Brahm Prakash came for the third time that Kalam woke up.

Dr. Brahm Prakash had always treated Kalam as his son. He said "All your comrades are standing by you". He gave emotional support. encouragement and guidance to Kalam till he retired in November, 1979.

The postmortem diagnosed the reasons for the failure and Kalam was ready to resign accepting the overall responsibility in the meeting presideed over by Prof. Dhawan. The pin drop silence in the hall was broken by Prof. Dhawan himself when he got up and told, "I am going to put Kalam in the orbit !" The meeting ended. That was the tradition of the great Indian Scientists.

Sivakaminathan was entrusted with the work of bringing the C-Band transponder from Thiruvananthpuram to SHAR by air. The SLV 3 launch was depending on the integration of this equipment with the rocket.

On landing at the Madras airport. his aircraft skidded and overshot the runway. There was suddenly heavy smoke inside the aircraft. Every body started running out to save their lives. But the last passenger was Sivakaminathan who emerged hugging the transponder to his chest ! At another time, the rocket was saved from the gushing waters from the water ports kept for extinguishing fires minutes before they were rotated at the suggestion of Kalam to face the opposite directions.

Kalam's Talents

Kalam was lifted onto the shoulders of his jubilant colleagues and carried in a procession ! Parliament greated the achievement with the thumping of desks. In the culmination of national dream and the beginning of a bigger phase in the history of India, Prof. Sathish Dhawan, chairman, ISRO declared, "India is now ready to explore space !".

Prime Minister Smt. Indira Gandhi was a Proud Indian, Proud of herself and of India. She scheduled a meeting of the parliamentary panel on Science and Technology. About thirty members of parliament, Prof. MGKM Menon and Dr. Nag Chaudhuri were also present. Prof. Dhawan and Kalam, were the guests of honour invited by the Prime Minister to attend the meeting.

Kalam, as quipped by his boss Prof. Dhawan was beautifully dressed in his success. (Kalam's usual, regular and official dress were all the same : A bush shirt, a pant, and chappals. And his hair do is exotic) After the PM spoke and Prof. Dhawan thanked, Smt. Indira Gandhi asked Kalam, "Kalam, we would like to hear you speak. Hesitating, Kalam got up and responded, "I am indeed honoured to be in this great gathering of nationbuilders.

I only know how to build a rocket system in our country, which would inject a satellite, built in our country, by imparting to it a velocity of 25,000 km per hour."

There was thunderous applause. Happiness was visible on every body's face. India had admitted itself in to the small club of nations which their own satellite launch capability. But the glory of SLV-3 had not gone to every one who deserved it-but hardly any thing could have been done by Kalam about that. Some are destined to be the foundation unseen but only the learned know the whole tower and the crown stand as firm as the foundation.

Thomas Gray's elegy written in a country church yard praising the unknown geniuses is apporopriate for all people for all the times, especially for those who are destined to miss the public eye.

Kalam quotes the following poem in response to the overt and covert reactions of some of his colleagues and others. Kalam advises from the experience of his life, that there are forces in life working for you and against you. You must distinguish the beneficial forces from the malevolent ones and choose correctly between them. The big recognitions of meritorious work namely Padma Bhushan and Padma Vibhushan were given to Abdul Kalam and Prof, Satish Dhawan respectively on our Republic Day, 1981.

But more important, he was made the Director, DRDL, Hyderabad in February, 1982 after the usual government bickering. Though the main players were Dr. Raja Ramanna, Dr. Satish Dhawan, Dr. VS Arunachalam, the final and quick decision was taken by our then Defence Minister, R Venkataraman.

DRDL had its own history and sad story. GP Capt Narayanan, who had accompanied Kalam to see RATO systems at Delhi and had agreed they could build them in India, had been promoted as Air Commodore. He took over as Director, DRDL. But then, the new aircrafts did not need RATO and the project was shelved.

The Defence R&D Organization took up another project to develop Surface-to-Air Missiles. A code name of Devil was given with a funding of five crore rupees.

The project was handed over to Air Com. Narayanan. A man of tremendous energy and always in boost phase, he brought it up as his child. But for some or the other reasons, the Devil was buried after winding up.

The senior scientists were nursing their hurt sentiments, though they were engaged in some or the activities. Their feeling was that or the activities. Their feeling was that they had been cheated by the senior officials in the Ministry of Defence. That was the situation when SL Bansal, the then Director of DRDL, showed Kalam around the laboratory in Hyderabad in April, 1982. When Kalam was studying in St. Joseph's, he had learnt that an electron may appear as a particle or as a wave depending on how you look at it. Ronald fischer had mentioned "The sweetness we taste in a piece of sugar is neither a property of the sugar nor a property of ourselves.

"We are producing the experience of sweetness in the process of interacting with the sugar." But it was a fact that DRDL had not been lucky to have leaders like Prof. Sarabhai and Dhawan at the helm.

Kalam who always hated closed door meeting and always Zealously pursued openness in scientific matters took the first major decision of collective endeavour. A high level body was formed with the name Missile Technology Committee.

Middle-level scientists and engineers were involved. And after days of intellectual debates and thinking, a long term guided Missile Development Programme was drafted to know "Where you are going". The great thing in the world is not knowing so much where we stand, as in what direction we are moving towards."

The western countries may have the technological might to day but we know we have to attain that might and more. The representatives of the three Defence Services and Zp Marshall, NR Iyer, AK Kapoor and KS Venkataraman were consulted and a final proposal was prepared with an estimated budget of Rs. 390/- crores, spread over a period of twelve years.

The prsentation was made in the meeting presided over by the Defence Minister. All the three service chiefs, Defence Secretary, Cabinet Secretary and several other VIPs were present.

Dr. Arunachalam was there to support Kalam. Pros and cons were discussed and then R. Venkataraman asked Dr. Arunachalam and Kalam to meet him after three hours. The waiting was nerve-wracking. But they were totally surprised to hear from the Defence Minister his suggestion to launch an integrated guided missile development programme instead of developing rockets on piecemeal basis.

Dr. Arunachalam was flabbergasted and replied, "We beg for time to rethink and return, Sir !" However, the Defence Minister was not generous in giving them sufficient time. The next morning was fixed for the next presentation ! Both Dr. Arunachalam and Kalam spent the whole night in redrafting the entire workout involving countless variables and the necessity of delivering contemporary missiles with latest technology developed in India to the services.

The morning dawned and then at the breakfast table, suddenly, Kalam remembered that he had to attend his brother's daughter Zameela's wedding at Rameshwaram. She was like a daughter to him but as he always says 'nation is bigger than an individual.' Both finished their breakfast and hurried to the office of the Defence Minister. The Defence Minister, learning the far-reaching consequences, said, "Since I brought you here, I was expecting you to come up with something like this. I am happy to see your work.".

Kalam was turning towards the door, when Dr. Arunachalam, the scientific adviser, who had a command over the language and presence of mind, informed the Defence Minister about Zameela's wedding and the difficulty in reaching

Rameshwaram from Delhi that day itself. Shree R.Venkataraman lost no time in locating an Air Force helicopter which was doing sorties between Madras and Madurai and made quick arrangements to despatch Kalam to Ramesh waram via Madras.

Anukalpana

Kalam narrates several incidents where the ignited Indians proved he was correct in relying on their intellect.A wind tunnel was required in keeping the Agni under control which would re-enter the stmosphere at 12 times the speed of sound. American may or may not help, but even if they wanted to, India would be considered a competitor to their exclusive privilege.

Prof. SM Deshpande of the IISC found four young bright scientists working in the field of fluid dynamics to assist him and, it is no exaggeration to record, within six months, his team developed the software for computational Fluid Dynamics for Hypersonic Regimes. It is one of its kind in the world.

ANUKALPANA, a missile trajectory simulation softwere by IG Sharma of IISC was developed to evaluate multitarget acquisition capabilities of an Akash type weapon system. No country would have parted with it but it is our pride that we developed it.

His success in tapping local talent was so overwhelming that it brought along with the successes a fair share of disturbing pain to him in judging the persons, evaluating their performances and rewarding all of them. But the matrix system of organization adapted in 1983 was giving results.

The launch of Prithvi on 25th of February, 1988 gave rise to varied reactions among friendly and unfriendly countries. The Western Block could not digest their own shock and anger. The seven-nation group went so far as to clamp a technology embargo on the pariya (a member belonging to scheduled castes) India.

They could not tolerate India emerging as a Developed Nation in the field of guided missiles. They exercised their pressure through diplomatic channels to abort the trial of Agni and others. The Indian Government was not deceived in spite of some of our own 'Peace-loving patriots and special brand of Mahatma Gandhis.' The 1962 and 1965 experiences could not be ignored. After all, every Indian has to be protected !

It is always in our interest to know how the Developed Nations reacted to our achievements. The US Congressmen threatened to put a stop to aid. There was a Mr. Gary Milhollin, who calling himself a specialist in missiles, claimed in the wall street Journal that India made Agni with the help of West Germany and that German Aerospace Research Establishment had developed the Control Systems and it was tested in their wind tunnel.

American senator Mr. Jeff Bingaman claimed that Kalam picked up everything needed for Agni when he visited Wallop's island in 1962 ! (That reminds some of our Indians trying to prove that Shekespeare was an Indian, that Jesus christ came to India, that whatever is great in the world is form India!)

The Himalayan efforts that preceded 23rd May, 1989 when Agni was launched like a textbook trajectory were just superhuman and speak to the credit of the Indian Intellect. The physical and mental fatigue and the nervous anxiety tuned one 'High'of heavenly delight by a mere ten hours of Agni's celestial flight.

All the great leaders including the PM congratulated the team. President Venkataraman saw the fulfillment of his dreams. It was the fulfillment of the dream of many, many visionaries, perhaps starting from the pionner Tippu Sulthan himself !.

7

Chandra Shekhar Azad

The Childhood

Chandra Shekhar Azad was born amid acute poverty. His parents were so poor that sometimes they could hardly afford even two square meals in a day and a necessary clothes to drape their bodies.

In 1906 birth of a son to the couple brought happiness to their home.

Jagrani Devi, was so happy as if she had found a rate gem. Prior to the birth of her son, which was her fifth child, she had already suffered the loss of her three children. So, she began to look after her new born son with great care. Due to her acute poverty, she could not even celebrate the occasion.

The baby boy was of course, very handsome but somehow he had a very weak body. So his mother was always very much concerned about her baby's health. But she was so much short of money that it was not possible for her to feed her child upon other nutritious diets. Eventhen she continued to look at her son very carefully. The boy was the apple of her eyes.

Gradually the baby boy improved in his health. He began to walk on his knees. Then he was able to climb even a few stairs. As the days passed by the baby gained more health and soon he returned in to a handsome boy.

The women living in Jagrani's neighbourhood cautioned her to take care of the child lest someone should cast an evil eye upon him. And that was correct. The baby boy was so handsome and there was every possibility of someone casting an evil eye upon him. As a matter of fact the Villages were known centres of which-craft and black magic.

Jagrani became apprehensive she pondered over the matter and began to put a 'Tilak' on child's forehead, to save him from any evil according to the religious belief.

At the time of the naming ceremony of the child, it was the first occasion, when Punditji used his brains. The boy was christened as Chandra Shekhar in view of his handsome looks and other qualities. After sometime Chandra Shekhar had grown enough to take part in games and doing mischivious acts while playing in the company of other children

He was always very much afraid of his father's temper and tried to keep away from him where as his mother was always ready to fulfil his every wish. His father did not like too much dotage. He would rather chide his wife "You are allowing too much liberty to your son. Is not it bad enough to spoil him".

Hearing his father little Chandra Shekhar would take refuge in his mother's lap out of fright. His mother worked as a shield for him. How could his father know that a messiah of revolution had taken birth in his house.

Shekhar liked to show number of games to his friends.

Some games were dangerous. For example, pressing the trigger of a toy cannot, after loading it with a country made explosive. The cannon, when it went off made a loud noise. But the main hurdle for the boy was how to get money to purchase explosives.

Chandra Shekhar found a way to fulfiil his desire. He did not consider it a crime, to pluck a few fruits from the orchard, where his father was employed, and sell them in the market. So he plucked a few fruit from the orchard and sold them in the market. The money that he received. by selling the fruits were spent on purchasing the explosive for his toy cannon. When his father came to know about the incident, he hit the roof. It was just intolerable for him to think that where as he never allowed anyone to even enter the orchard without it's owner's permission, his own son not only entered it but also plucked fruit there and sold them in the market.

He did not show any mercy to his son and beat him black and blue. When the boy's mother tried to intervene, she was shoved aside. The boy was so much beaten by his father that the he was almost half dead.

That was the first spanking of the boy by his father ; the first and the last as well. The punishment given by his father served also as challenge to teenage Chandra Shekhar who was growing fast into a young man. It was a challenge in the sense that it was against his nature to get beaten by his own parents or by anybody else. He was unable to forget it.

Azad in School

Chandra Shekhar and his brother Sukhdev had attained the school going age. One of the bosom friends of Tiwariji, who was known as Pundit Manoharlal Trivedi, shouldered the responsibility of teaching both the boys.

Sukhdev and Chandra Shekhar both began to take lessons from him. Trivediji was in the habit of using cane, while teaching his students. One day, he pronounced a word wrongly and then asked the boys to correct it, while Sukhdev corrected it, Shekhar instead of answering his teacher's question picked up the cane and it his teacher twice. Tiwariji who was sitting nearby got up in great anger to beat Shekhar, but Manoharlal intervened.

"How dare you hit your teacher ?" Tiwariji asked Shekhar.

Shekhar replied fearlessly, "When we commit a mistake our teacher beats us. Now, when he has done the same thing he deserves the same punishment". Tiwariji stood shocked at his answer. The teaching classes were still in progress, but Shekhar was finding it hard to put his heart into his studies.

Tiwariji wanted his son to learn Sanskrit and bacome a Vedantacharya and a Scholar.

Shekhar used to go out wandering along with his friends on the pretext of attending the school. But instead of going to his school, he and his friends would go to the nearby jungles and enact a drama of police catching the dacoits. Shekhar was particularly very fond of practising archery, with the tribals living around.

Although Shekhar was by a caste Brahmin but all practical purposes he showed every sign of Kshatriya blood running in his veins. It was perhaps because of this that guns and bows arrows were his favourite items to play with. But he was equally aware that his father's hopes hinged upon him for a defferent matter. And this was the reason that Shekhar wanted to break all the domestic barriers and run away somewhere else to live on his own. It was only a matter of getting a suitable opportunity. By the time Shekhar reeached fourth standerd. The desire to run away from home got more and more stronger in him. Manoharlalji who was his family well wisher was aware of that.

Shekhar was not the least interested in his studies. He had an inkling for Shekhar and wanted to see him rise in his life.

Manoharlalji wanted to provide him with some job. He was of the opinion that, after coming into employment, Shekhar's movements will be restricted and also he will be able to provide some financial help to his family. Ultimately his own efforts and the popularity of Tiwariji as an honest man, brought results.

Shekhar got an ordinary job in Alipuraing Tehsil. Shekhar started to attend to his job in the Tehsil. But it was against his selfrespect, to honour someone as his boss and say, 'Yes' to him, despite the fact that, it was an essential requirment during the British administration of those days and was followed in letter and spirit.

Shekhar's friends would try to make him understand, "Shekhar it is not good on your part. This may cost you your job". Shekhar would just laugh over it and say, "I myself do not want such a job. Let it happen today only. After all I shall be a free man then. I am myself looking for such an opportunity".

And the fact was that Shekhar was never serious on his job. He would just wander towards the jungles move around and sitting near a pond. situated in the jungle, would day dream all alone for hours together. A strange thought was taking place in him, which consisted of the feelings of independence fearlessness, self respect, intolerance and excitement. The little spark of intolerance was soon to have turned into a raging inferno of revolt. A storm was building up in his heart.

Sitting at the edge of a pond Shekhar used to think to himself, "Is it a life that I live ? Strict control of father, hard discipline and slavery of others. His feelings of curiosity for other countries to visit them and roam there became more and more evident in him.

Shekhar's feelings turned defferently. There was a youngman who used to visit Alirajpur and sell artificial pearls. He was very social and knew the tricks of number of Trades. Shekhar became friendly with the youngman. Whenever they met together a lengthy conversation took place between them.

Shekhar decided finally to run away from his home. And one day, without informing anybody, Shekhar ran away from his home, along with that pearl selling salesman. Shekhar had an immense liking for Bombay. As soon as he got off on the railway platform, he was thrilled to find himself in a huge city.

Azad in Bombay

Shekhar had an immense liking for Bombay. It was his first chance to come to a metropolis. He came out of the station immersed in his own thoughts. Sky-scrapers all around, trams running on roads, motor cars....... huge crowds on the wide roads, noise, razzle-dazzle and a fast life of the people living there.

Shekhar looked at them all with immense curiousity. In the meanwhile his home, along with that pearl selling friend had already departed. Now Azad was all alone to trudge the roads. He began to think...... were will he go ? Where will he stay ?

Undaunted by all these problems he reached the sea beach. He liked the beach atmosphere. He was already tired. So he sat there and began to watch the ships sailing in the ocean. Finding a livelihood for himself was the biggest problem for Shekhar. It worried him a little. But somehow he was able to find a job, with a group of people, who painted the ships. He began to learn his job as an assistant painter. He was also provided with an accommodation by the painters.

The Painters used to run a mess for themselves. Once they invited Shekhar to have a meal with them. But being a conservative Brahmin, who believed in untouchability due to his family influences, how he could have wined and dined with his host in a mess ? He did not attend the party.

He began to live on grams etc. as his food till the time he was able to save some money for making arrangement to cook food by himself. But, not knowing how to cook food Shekhar had to drop this idea later. Then he began to eat in a hotel. The altogether new environment made him forget all those ideas regarding untouchability.

After Shekar's food related problem was solved he developed a new taste of watching movies in cinema halls. But Azad failed to find peace within himself in a city like Bombay.

Shekhar used to take his bath once in a week. There was little facility available for taking bath during the early morning hours. He was short of clothes also. So he bathed on Sundays only. Sunday being a holiday gave him enough time to sleep till late in the morning. After he woke up he will get ready to Visit the black market. There he used to purchase a nicker and a shirt. After having his meals in the hotel he will wander aimlessly on the roads, visit the zoological garden and when completely tired he will take rest under a tree in a park.

Shekhar never indulged in drugs or smoking, etc. His painter friends tried their best to make him an addict but he kept himself aloof from all these vices. After sometime Shekhar began to undergo a feeling of boredom. He was fed up with the life he was living in Bombay...... a mechanical type of living. A time came when he made up his mind to leave Bombay.

One day after taking his food in the hotel, he headed for the railway station. He boarded the train leaving for Benaras without ticket. Then, he got off at the Benaras railway station.

The Life in Benaras

At Benaras, Shekhar again began his studies. The problem related to his boarding and lodging was also solved. Those days rich philanthropists used to help poor Brahmin boys Shekhar too took shelter in one of them religious institutions. He began to study Sanskrit. He learnt 'Laghukaumudi' amd 'Amarkosh' by rote. However, along with his studies, a feeling for national freedom was also taking place in him. Shekhar by nature was religious and chivalrous. He often went to the banks of the Ganges river and swam in it for hours at a stetch.

Shekhar had a special liking for 'Ramayan', 'Bhagwat Gita', and 'Mahabharata'. He used to attend religious congregations. He listened to epic stories with great interest especially those which were related to bravery.

The day came when Shekhar began to visit library and read newspapers. He read about the freedom movement going on in the country. He kept himself informed through the newspapers. The call for non-cooperation movement had already reached benaras. First of all it started on a college campous by staging 'dharna'. Shekhar was also impressed by this indefinite sitting period.

His absence at home had left his mother ill and his father deeply shocked. After a few months when everything normalized, Shekhar informed his parents about his where abouts and asked them not to worry. His mother's worry was over to some extent. She often sent two or four rupees to Shekhar for his daily expenses. She believed that one day when her educated son will start earning money the financial position of her family will improve. Pt. Sitaram, Tiwari was himself busy making efforts to increase his earnings. And in 1921 Civil disobedience movement took place throughout the country. It was like a fire which engulfed the whole nation. It was a scene of disobedience all around.

The students community too did not lag behind. Instead of attending their classes they took out processions, indulged in agitations and slogan shouting. And it was Shekhar who led one of such agitations held by the teenagers. It was a red-letter day for them.

Shekhar joined India's freedom movement irrespective of the consequences that he would have to face.

Inquilab Zindabad (Long live the revolution)

Long live India-

Jai

Britishers ! Leave India

These were the slogans that rent the air in Benaras.

The procession was taken out by a dozen teenage boys on the roads of Benaras. Their faces exuded courage; confidence and firmness of ideas. Unmindful of the brutal punishment by British government, this procession was marching ahead.

The crowd standing on both the sides of the road was watching the procession with great admiration and astonishment. The people looked, surprised at the daring courage of the teenage agitators. The civil disobedience movement was gaining strength day by day.

The British government was keeping a hawkish watch over the people who were demanding freedom for the country but the freedom fighters were marching ahead with their aim of gaining India's freedom.

The teenagers procession was the burning symbol of the people's desire for independence.

"Speak loudly...." The fifteen-yearold boy leading the procession cried at a high pitch voice.

"Bharatmataki".... he gave a loud cry. "Jai" a collective reply rent the air.

The people in the crowd began to whisper to each other. A few coward people shut the doors of their houses. A few others hid themselves for the fear of the police. But those who loved freedom and were optimistic about it highly praised the enthusiasm of the boys. On the other hand, a few stooges of the British government expressed their view that the procession was stage-managed by some interested group. They were of the opinion that the boys were made the scape goats. They were too immature to fight a mighty foreign government. How would they be able to face the deadly guns of the British ?

But those processionists had no time to listen to all bogus talks. They were marching ahead on the road with just one aim in their mind-independence. They were not bothered that they would be arrested and punished. The processionists were still marching ahead with all the enthusiasm.

In the meanwhile the police arrived there. While a few boys moved out of the procession, their leader and a few more boys stayed back. They were surrounded by the police, handcuffed and ordered to march towards the court of law. But still there was no trace of fear on the faces of the arrested boys. They kept on shouting slogans in favour of the country and in the praise of Mahatma Gandhi.

"what's your name ?" The magistrate asked the boy who had led the procession.

"Azad", the boy replied in a fearless tone.

"What's your father'name ?" This time the magistrate

asked him in a harder tone while starting at him from head to toe.

'Swatantra', was the boys's reply in the same dauntless manner. Hearing the answers the magistrate became more and more angry. He knew that the boy was courageous, as well as a rouge and was committing contempt of court.

"Where's your home", the magistrate almost burst into anger. "The jail", the boy answered with the same fervour. The magistrate seathed with anger. If the boy would not have been a minor the magistrate would have definitely pronounced a harsh punishment for him, But in this case the magistrate was helpless. Any how, he have the boy a punishment of fifteen lashes.

Even that harsh judgment by the magistrate did not discourage Chandra Shekhar from shouting slogans for his country. He was brought to jail to undergo the punishment of fifteen lashes. Before whipping him the jail authorities began to tie the boy's hands and feet.

"Why do you tie me ?" The boy protested. "Lash me. I'll take it all without it".

The police personnel standing around were amazed to listen to him. A jail officer began to lash him. With the first strike of the whip the body shouted "Liong live India".

The official whipping continued and with every count of it the boy shouted slogans for India and for Mahatma Gandhi. Every lash on his body brought forth the words 'Vande Mataram' on his lips. instead of painful exclamations.

Those who were the witness to that were amazed at the bravery of that teenage boy. Many of them at the verge of fainting. The boy's body was badly bruised and blood was oozing out at many spots. But lashing never deterred the boy from shouting patriotic slogans. With the last count of the whip, the boy fainted for a moment. But even then he didn't give up, He recovered and started for his home without a trace of pain on his face and without a word of complaint on his lips. The boy's home was situated in Gyanwapi Mohalla of Benaras city.

When the residents of the city came to know of the daring act on the part of the boy, they became eager to have a look at this fearless and brave boy. The bloody incident earned the boy the name 'Azad'. Preparations were made to hold a public function in his honour. An article captioned 'Brave Boy' 'Azad' appeared in 'Maryada' Magazine, which was edited by Sampoornanand. The function was over crowded. The people were eager to have a look at 'Azad'. Amidst the shouting of slogans like, 'Hail Mahatma Gandhi, Long live India'. 'Azad'appeared on the stage.

Being a boy he was still small in stature which prevented the audience to have a good look at him. The crowd became restive. He had to be elevated by making him stand on a high table. Only then the calmness prevailed over the audience. They were mesmerised by the boy's natural charm and glamour. 'Azad' was presented with so many garlands that his face was literally covered by them. At that function 'Azad' delivered his most enthusiastic speech. The next day's newspaper carried his speech and details of his other courageous deeds along with his photograph.

'Azad' became popular in the whole Benara's city. He became apple of the eyes of the people. It was perhaps that occasion when 'Azad' had vowed to remain 'Azad' or 'free' for the whole of his life.

"It's highly improbable that I shall ever be arrested by the British government. Once they have done it. Now they can come over my dead body only".

God knows whether his father Pundit Sitaram Tiwari was happy with his son's vow or not, butt his mother Jagrani Devi was certainly glad to know that, she was proud of his brave son.

'Azad' raised slogans for his country and for Mahatma Gandhi at the Gyanwapi square of Benaras. He was lashed again by the police, but he didn't stop shouting slogans till the moment he remained conscious. The people were amazed at the courage and firmness of this boy. After the incident Azad got his admission in Kashi Vidyapeeth. After his admission in Kashi Vidyapeeth Azad became a centre of student's attraction and their admiration. The students looked at him with amazement. Azad was a kind of a peculiar genius for them.

Azad, no doubt, got his admission in the Vidyapeeth, but he was not interested in his studies. He was obsessed with only one idea, how to drive away the Britishers from the country and make it independent.

Azad was more interested in reading stories of revolution and war than his course books. He was also very much eager to join a revolutionary organization. As the time passed, he made friends with some of his classmates and persuaded them to work for country's freedom. It was the time when the enthusiasm for non-cooperation movement was dying down. After the 'Chauri-Chaura' incident Mahatma Gandhi had suspended the movement. Then youths were very disheartened over that decision.

But Azad did not leave courage. The youths in north India became active to establish their own organization. They were those youths who returned a dream to make India free.

Azad and Ramkrishna Khatri

A haggard looking and frail bodied sick person was lying on a cot in a dark room. Two youngmen entered the room. Once was Swami Upedranand Brahmanand and the other was a robust fellow. The patient got up and wished the visitor. But the youngman asked the patient to keep resting on the cot. He said, "You are suffering from high fever. Take rest from now on I will take care of you". Since that day, the young man started looking after the sickman. He used to attend on him daily for two three hours. The Sickman was Ramkrishna Khatri. He was famous for his radical ideas.

As the days passed he began to recover from his illness and soon he was able to discuss political issues with the young man attending on him. The youngman followed the Gandhi ideology, while Khatri was opposed to it. He was of the opinion that Gandhiji's decision to withdraw the movement of giving ultimatum to the British government was not appropriate". The young man would simply laugh over it.

Such type of political topics came up for discussion between them. There ideologies were quite different. But in any case he was influenced by the youngman. His ideas were gradually changing with time. After sometime Azad again met Khatri and gave him a book captioned 'Bandi Jeewan'. He said, "It is an interesting book".

Later, he gave Khatri the sedition committee report. Khatri was irritated to see the book "It will make an interesting reading to those only who love Britishers. Have you too changed sides in their favour?" Azad smiled and said 'better you read the book. May be it was criticised our country's youths. But, at least you will come to know how brave they were".

One day Azad suddenly met Khatriji. He had a bag on his shoulderes full of books and newspapers. When Khatriji after bolting the front door came near him, he took out an interesting article from his bag which Khatriji was looking for a long time. It was a mouser pistol. Khatriji snatched it from Azad and kissed it. Then he touched it with his forehead.

Azad said, "What are you doing I am just a middleman. When a friend gave me a book I showed it do you. Now he has given me a pistol. Have a look at it and return it to me so that I could give it back to my friend.".

"Don't try to make a fool of me. I was not wrong, you are really a jack of all trades".

There is no other alternative "Azad said." The secret institutions have to function in a secret manner. Now that yourself chosen to join us, you too would have to remain alert. After his talks with Azad, Ramkrishna Khatri formally joined the Azad's party.

Azad's only aim was to make the country independent through revolutionary means. He used to travel also from one place to another place for organizational work. It was his dynamic personality which impressed every one, who happened to meet him. He was by nature a very gentle, truthful and hard working person.

It was not a mean feat that a huge organization had come into existence, but a massive financial backing was also needed for it's smooth functioning. Nearly all the members of the organization had come after renouncing their families and resigning their jobs of work for the country's independence.

A Pamphlet on Revolution

A pamphlet on revolution was circulated in the country for the purpose of expansion of party and it's activities. The aims and objectives and the activities of the organization were highlighted through this pamphlet and an appeal was made to the young blood of the country to co-operate with the organization for it's success. The member of the organization were highly successful in the distribution of the pamphlets, and letting the people know about it's message. There was not a single youth-related educational institution which did not receive this pamphlet. A large number of supporters throughout the length and breath of the country drew initiative from the contents of the pamphlet.

Some revolutionaries like Bhagwati Charan, Bhagat Singh, Sukhdev and Yeshpal also came across this pamphlet. In Punjab 'Naujwan Bharat Sabha' was active with the country's Independence struggle with great enthusiasm. In Benaras Azad himself looked after the circulation of this pamphlet. Despite all precaution and vigil taken by the school and college authorities, those pamphlets were delected, hidden inside the pages of registers even. All the activities of the organization helped boost it's prestige and reputation in the eyes of the people.

Not much publicity could be achieved for this movement. But as a result, a new trend started among the people to go for political reading. In those days the concept of intellectual work was missing, so other methods were employed to impart political teachings.

Secret letter boxes were installed to drop letters secretly. A letter which was meant for a particular person bore the address of such a person who was considered to be out of the suspect lists of the police also it was difficult for a person to know the other person easily. No questions were asked without purpose.

The rules and regulations of this organization were specially very strict so much so that if any member ever played any fraud upon the organizational activities, he was removed from the organizations membership and shot. The membership and activities of Azad's party was expanding by leaps and bounds, but a major problem was that in the absence of the finance the party's activities were coming to a naught. Besides, the finance were also needed for the boarding and lodging of the members, publication of the material, and to purchase the arms and amunitions. Donations and contributions were not enough to run the organization.

Azad was highly worried over this issues. He was himself ever ready to forego his food and sleep for the sake of the organization, but that was not the solution.

Azad started his day by his physical exercises in the early morning. If he had any breakfast available after it, it was all right for him otherwise he would just forego it too. He was a care-free type of person. He did not care even for himself. His worries were only concerned with that of his organization. One of the causes of his worries was increasing day by day, and so was the expenditure, which was the main reason of his concern. He employed many tactics for fund raising, but nothing was successful. A meeting was called to discuss the financial state of affairs. The persons who participated in this meeting were, Pandit Rajender Lahiri, Roshan Singh, Ramkrishna Khatri.

Yogesh Babu was the chief participant in the meeting. The participants Suggested that political docoities should be committed to improve the financial condition of the organization.

Some parties functioning in the state of Bengal and in some other provinces were already doing it. They were Committing docoities. One or two participants opposed the suggestion. They said, "These activities will bring us in sharp focus of the government and it may prove disastrous for us." But then there was no other way except committing dacoities to raise the party funds. So Ultimately all agreed over the decision.

Dacoity for the Party Fund

Azad, Khatri, Roshan Singh and others discussed in a meeting about dacoities in order to collect party funds. It was decided to first start the work from the villages. The dacoities were to be committed in the houses of rich businessmen only.

There would be no killing and women folks,would not be harrassed or tortured. A detailed blue print was prepared under the guidance of Ram Prasad 'Bismil". At the time of dacoities special coded words were used for communication. A coded message like 'Gyan jo hai so Brinda' meant that the attempt had failed.

The person who took part in dacoity was called 'Gyan' and he who did not know how to commit dacoity was known as Bhagat. An expert in committing dacoities was reffered to as, 'Awadhoot'.

The whole terminology related to Dacoity was coined by Azad himself. This secret coded communication was limited to its personal use only, while one was busy with party's work. The party members started committing dacoities under the leadership of Ram Prasad Bismil. The first dacoity was committed in a village of district Fatehpur. But the attempt failed. But the revolutionaries looted, some of the other rich families at other places and came out successful.

This incident happened in a village near Pratagarh. There lived a wicked money lender in the village, the gang of revolutionaries entered the money lender's house. One of the gang members was firing in the air to frighten the villagers. The gang was led by Bismil. He was guarding the main entrance with a pistol in his hand.

The women folk in the family were quite courageous. They put up tough resistance. One of the woman grappled with one of the gang members. She was quite bulky and bold. She caught hold of Azad and began to shower blows on him. But Azad did not react. He simply Stood calm, and quiet tolerating her beating. In the meanwhile Bismil shouted "Let us go now".

Everybody had to retreat. The second dacoity was more paying and organized. This time Bismil wore a police superintendent's uniform. The other members too attired themselves in police dresses. The dacoity committed this time was highly successful. The villagers thought that, it was some sort of police search. Meanwhile the revolutionaries thoroughly ransacked the house and collected all the booty kept in the house. However these small engagements did not bring relief to the organization.

At this critical juncture Ramkrishna Khatri chalked out a new plan to raise money. He had been an important member of a sect of sadhus and also a favoured a disciple of a serving Mahant. He informed his other colleagues that a wealthy mahant was in search of a disciple as his successor. He was very wealthy and lying on his death bed. In case he died his disciple would take over and become a legal heir to his property.

The party decided to plant Azad as a disciple of that particular Mahant. First Azad was hesitant to do that. But later in view of party's command and the impending need for the finances for the party he agreed.

Katriji made all the arrangements. Azad was introduced to Mahant in a dramatic manner and he took over as Mahant's disclipe. The purpose for which Azad was making efforts was not less challenging. He had to learn Gurumukhi language. He had to devote himself to religious performances like pooja and aarti. For Azad it became diifficult to pull on it.

One day Azad slipped away from the math without informing any one hand came back to Benaras. The city had by then become a hot bed for revolutionary activities.

The Kakori Dacoity

It was the evening of 7th August 1925. Three youths came

to the station. They were looking very rich and talking to each other merrily.

"Three second class tickets to Lucknow" said one young man and handed over the money to the counter clerk.

The tickets were to be issued for 8 in train going to Lucknow from Shahjhahanpur. The ticket clerk was surprised. Second class tickets from Kakori station were hardly sold. He gave an intense look at the passenger.

Sachindranath Bakshi got the inkling as to what the clerk was thinking about. He returned his face with a hand kerchief. Then he returned to the platform. Rest of the party members were also ready according to the modus operanoi decided earlier. When the train arrived at the station all the three young men boarded the second class compartment.

One more member friend boarded a third class bogie. The train started and soon it gathered speed. There was one more passenger in the compartment. The darkness had fallen. There was light in the compartment. When the train reached near the signal. Sachindranath asked Ashfaq, "Where is our jewellery box ?" Ashfaq replied "Oh! that we have forgotten at Kakori station!"

Bakshi and Ashfaqulla got of the bogie and walked Ashfaqulla got of the bogie and walked onwards. The train guard was comming from the opposite direction. He asked. "who is pulled the chain ?" "We have lost our jewellery box at Kakori station we were going to fetch it" they answered. The cash box was lying in the guard's cabin. When the guard reached near them all the three youths pounced upon him.

One of them fired in the air and warned other train passengers. "don't get off from the bogie we are robbing the cash and we will shoot you." The passengers were frightened.

Not even one moved from his seat. The guard pleaded for mercy. "Please spare my life, Don't shoot me." Sachindranath said "Lay down on the grass quick."

The guard followed the instructions. The other two youths dashed in to the guard's cabin. They broke the light bulb of the cabin. It was darkness all around. A few more youths entered the guard's cabin and took heavy steel trunk out of the cabin and began to hammer it's lock. While Ashfaq was trying to break open the lid of the box, others stood guard. There were thirteen armed passengers in the train at the time of dacoity. One of them was a British major. But every one looked scared. Ram Prasad Bismil was supervising the dacoity. After sometime Ashfaq was able to break open the heavy steel trunk. It was opened and was of currency notes were taken out.

Meanwhile another train from the opposite direction was seen approaching. The revolutionaries got nervous. They all became apprehensive. But the other train passed at it's full steam on the the side track. They all felt relieved. The cash was tied in to a cloth bundle and all the revolutionaries got ready to leave.

The train was still standing there. In the meanwhile, Sachindranath asked his colleagues to move on, while he himself addressed the guard. "My dear guard Dead people don't talk. Should I now shoot you my dear ?"

The guard was almost frightened to death. He again pleaded for mercy. "I swear in the name of God. I will never dare to identify you. Bakshi pitied the guard and left him go. All the members of the party then left the place and disappeared in the jungles.

The Arrests in Connection With Kakori Dacoity Case

As a result of arrests made by the police in connection with dacoity case, a number of party members had parted away from each other. But their arrest did not disheartened Azad. He continued with his efforts on organizing his party.

Despite all the surveillance mounted by the police and the criminal investigation department all over the country, Azad kept travelling from one place to another in disguise. He was prepared to die every time. He used to recite the following poem of Bismil.

"Sarfroshi ki tamanna ab hamere dil mein hai.

Dekhna hai, Zor kitna bazue qatil mein hai."

Azad stayed at Kanpur for some days.

One day Vidyarthiji (He was a great supporter of revolutionaries). received a letter from Nagpur written by a youngman named Bhagat Singh. He had expressed his desire to work in Pratap publication.

Vidyarthiji ignore such an offer from a youngman. He immediately invited him to come and meet him at Kanpur. By that time the pamphlets published by Hindustani, Republican Association had already been distributed at Lahore.

The India's independence programme was almost ready. The new organization had come into existance. Jaichandji was it's founder. This organization's first task was to enrol as many members as possible. But even after all those activities Jaichandji was not satisfied.

Bhagat Singh visited Delhi and kanpur and some other provinces and tried to contact the revolutionaries there. But Bhagat's father Kishan Singhji was not too pleased with Bhagat Singh's devotion to political works. He wanted Bhagat Singh to pay attention to his domestic problems.

After reaching Delhi Sardar Bhagat Singh first started working in 'Arjun' daily. But it's publication was soon discontinued.

Vidyarthiji's invitation filled Bhagat Singh with a new hope and enthusiasm and he immediately left for Kanpur by the first available train. At Kanpur, when Bhagat Singh met Vidyarthiji he was embraced by the latter.

Bhagat Singh began to work in the editorial department, of Pratap under the pen name of 'Balwant' In one occasion Azad met Bhagat Singh. Both Azad and Bhagat Singh were happy to hear the remarks of Vidyarthiji. At Lucknow, court proceeding started on connection with Kakori dacoity case. Azad and Bhagat Singh went to Shahjaha npur in connection with giving a practical shape to the plan of escaping.

At Shahjahanpur, the revolutionaries gathered at the house of Ashfaqulla. It was noon time. Riyasatulla, the elder brother of Ashfaqulla was having his lunch when somebody knocked at the door. When he opened the door he found a youngman and some other people standing outside.

"Yes what can I do for you ?"

"Here is some money your younger brother has sent for you" said the youngman.

"How can you do it while you are still in jail ?" He had asked him with surprise.

"Leave it to me I can do it." His younger brother had said with all his seriousness.

Now Riyasatulla became sure that the money that the youngman had brought had really been sent by Ashfaqulla. But before he took it's possession, he wanted to know the identify of the youngman. In those days Azad used to help his revolutionary friends escape from the jail, besides giving them financial help. The trial for Kakori railway station dacoity case went on for about eighteen months. It is said that British government had to spend rupees ten lakhs on the trial of the case.

The Meeting of Revolutionaries

An Important meeting of senior revolutionaries of India was held on 8th December 1928, in the ruins of Ferozeshah fort, in Delhi. The main agenda was to coordinate the working of all the revolutionary groups functioning in different provinces. The revolutionaries who participated in this meeting were Sukhdev, Shiv Verma, Brahma Datta, Vijay Kumar, Kundan Lal, Surendra Nath Pandey, etc. A control committee was also formed through a proposal tabled in this meeting

There were seven members of the committee, viz, Sardar Bhagat Singh, Sukhdev, Chandra Shekhar Azad. Shiv Verma, Vijay Kumar, Phanishwar Nath Ghosh and Kundan Lal. The names of coordinators were also announced in the meeting. Phanishwar Nath Ghosh was appointed the coordinators of Bihar. Sukhdev and Bhagat Singh of Punjab and Shiv Verma and Vijay Kumar Singh of Uttar Pradesh.

Chandra Shekhar Azad was the chairperson of the party. But he was exclusively given the change of army wing of the party. The party's name was changed from 'Hindustan Republican Association' to 'Hindustan Socialist Republican Army' Factories were opened at many places to manufacture bombs. Bigger factories were established at places like Agra, Lahore, Saharanpur and Calcutta.

It was also decided at the meeting that issue of public only should be undertaken by the party for action. In line with the above discussion, first of all, Simon Commission was chosen for further action by the party.

Simon Commission had come to India in the beginning of 1928 in response to the demand for administrative reforms and to study the prevailing condition in India. The commission was headed by the renowned lawers of England, Sir John Simon. Congress and all other parties opposed the appointment of Simon Commission.

Slogans like-'Simon go back' rent the air in the entire country.

On 20th October, the commission arrived at Lahore. A big rally was organized there to oppose the working of the commission. The rally was led by Punjab Kesri, the aged Lala Lajpat Rai. All around there was huge crowd and black flags were fluttering. . On the orders of Lahore Police chief, a lathi charge was made on the demonstrators.

But even in the face of severe lathi charge by the police the demonstrators did not stop shouting slogans and marching forward. Their slogans shook the earth and the skies. Suddenly. Dy. S.P.Scott hit Lala Lajpat Rai with a lathi. Lalaji's umbrella was broken and he received injuries on his shoulders.

The demonstrators standing around Lalaji were adamant to march ahead, but Lalaji instructed them, "Post Pone this demonstration in protests against the police atrocities."

The demonstration came to an end. In the same evening, while addressing a large gathering near Mori Gate Lalaji said, "The government which makes brutal attacks on it's unarmed subjects cannot be called a Civilized government. Such governments do not govern for long. Today I predict that each and every lathi-blow in my chest shall prove no less than a nail in the coffin of the British Empire".

The above address which was delivered in Hindi was translated by Lalaji himself in English, so that the British officers who were present in that public gathering could comprehend his message.

On December 17th 1928, Lalaji Passed away. The entire nation was overtaken by grief. But the lathi below which was inflicted on Lalaji definitely proved fatal for the British in the long run. A lot of confusion prevailed after the death of Lalaji. At the time of his death. The members of the revolutionary committee were present at Lahore.

A meeting was immediately called and it was decided to avenge Lalaji's death. Pt.Jawaharlal Nehru had described this incident like this "Lalaji died as a result of police lathi blow inflicted on him. But his injury was shared by each and every countryman and it soon turned into a revolt against the Briish Empire."

Before evening the death of Lalaji, Azad had chalked out a plan to rob the National Bank. But the plan somehow failed. Then the revolutionary committee decided to kill the police officer who had hit Lalaji during the public demonstratiion.

The committee then formed an action group and assigned the task of keeping a watch on Asst. Superintendent of Police. J.P.Saunders, to Jaigopal. He was in fact mistaken for Scott, who had hit Lalaji with a lathi. Jaigopal began to keep an eye on Saunder. There were four members in the killing squad, viz, Bhagat Singh, Chandra Shekhar Azad, Rajguru and Jaigiopal.

Then on 17th December. 1928 A.S.P. Saunders was killed by these four revolutionaries. Lalaji's death was avenged in a 'bullet-for bullet' manner. This was a successful operation.

The Punjab police force went mad over this incident. The criminal investigation department launched a statewide hunt for the killers. All those people who were suspected to have taken part in the crime were taken into custody. House-to-house searches were made and more arrests followed. The Police left no stone unturned to capture the revolutionaries.

All the members of the party secretly gathered at the 'Majang' house. Before the meeting could be started the patrticipants had to be served food. But unfortunately, there was no money with the party to even buy food for the participants.

In order to solve this difficulty, Azad somehow borrowed rupees ten from someone and offered food to the party members. It was decided at the meeting that all the members should leave Lahore and go somewhere else.

But this proposal was hard to be implemented because of want of money A huge amount was needed to be given to the members. A few members were sent to such places where was hope of getting monetary assistance. While Yeshpal contacted Dr.Gopi Chand, Sukhdev met Bhagwati Charan. The future plan of Bhagat Singh was to go out of Lahore with Durga Bhabi after giving a slip to the police.

Durga, wife of Bhagwati Charan, disguised herself as a European lady, whereas Bhagat Singh got his hair and beard shaved offs. He donned overcoat, trousers and a hat like a British gentleman in order to confuse the police. Rajguru acted as their servant.

At the railway station the boarded the Calcutta bound mail to go to Calcutta. Nobody at the railway station. Even the police dared question them because they looked sophisticated and displayed Western manners. Other members of the party had already left Lahore to reach some other destinations.

In the Calcutta bound mail train, a mahatmaji clad in a saffron dress was also travelling. When he walked past that compartment in which Bhagat Singh was also travelling, he uttered in a loud voice 'Alakh Niranjan'. When he repeatedly uttered these words, Bhagat SIngh smiled and then disclosed the indentify of sadhu to Durga Bhabi, "He's Punditji"- Durga Bhabi smiled.

The bomb manufacturing factories at Agra were working well. They were located in two different mohallas.

Sukhdev and Kundanlal were expert bomb makers. The outer cover of the bombs were being manufactured in a different unit altogether. These two factories were not only the hiding places for the revolutionaries, but also a centre for discussion and future planning.

Azad's Dynamic Personality

Everyone was highly impressed by Azad's dynamic personality. his sacrificial nature perseverance and strong character. He was in favour of observing strict discipline. It was so hard that his colleagues would sometimes find it quite difficult to withstand the rules and regulations.

Azad possessed a high character. He always respected women. He used to say for the country. The nation which was lost it's character has lost every thing'.

Vaishampayan writes, "Azad possessed an ideal character. This was the reason he was a successful leader. He was revolutionary madly trying to make the country independent. He was fully devoted to his duty and saw that the others carried their responsibilities with the same devotion. He used to say enthusiastically and fearlessly, "I shall fight till my last breath."

Azad had his own self respect. He never introduced his family. After many efforts Banasari Dass Chaturvedi gathered the information that Azad's mother was spending her days in acute poverty.

Azad had devoted himself to the country's cause. For him India was his family; Bharat Mata was like his mother. He tried to overcome all his difficulties through perseverance and in a peaceful manner. He had a strong body. He was never afraid or nervous of any situation in his life. He was self-restrained in all the circumstances.

After sometime the British government launched a new terror tactic. It tried to introduce the public safety bill and trade disputes bill. If these two bills would have come into force that would have meant the curtailment of people's freedom. The central committee of the revolutionary force decided that, the day, this bill takes the shape of an act by an order promulgated by the viceroy, the assembly should be bombed in protest. For the successful operation of this plan a new branch of revolutionary council was opened in Delhi.

Bhagat Singh and Batukeshwar Datta were given the responsibility to carry out this task. First of all Azad surveyed the gallery of the Central Assembly. He came to the conclusion that will not be very difficult for the revolutionary mambers to run away from the assembly hall. The only facility required was a motor car, Which would serve as an escape vehicle.

However Bhagat Singh did not favour the idea of Azad that the members should run away from the Central Assembly after lobbing bombs in the assembly hall. He was of the view that, it was not sfficient to bomb the Assembly and distribute pamphlets to make the public aware of their views.

"We should instead get ourselves arrested and later explain our point of view in the trail court. This would enable the people understand out views and efforts for gaining India's independence".

The Public Safety Bill

On 8th April 1929. The public safety Bill was tabled in the assembly. A debate was going on from both the sides. Two youths in the meanwhile, entered the main entrance and walking past the gallery reached the upper floor. There they took their seats at such a spots from where the government members were in their full view.

As soon as Sir Shuster got up to announce the promulgation of the bill, Bhagat Singh threw a bomb on the floor of the Central Hall. The other bomb was thrown by Batukeshwar Dutta. Next Bhagat Singh fired at Sir Shuster from his revolver but shuster saved himself by hiding beneath a table.

There was perfect opportunity for both the youngmen to run away from the Assembly after throwing the bomb. But they did not move an inch from their seats. They shouted the slogans like, "Inquilab Zindabad".

"Down with colonialism."

They also threw red colour pamphlets on the floor of the house. These pamphlets contained the aim and objectives of the revolutionary party. The police arrived there and arrested them. They were put in the Delhi prison under heavy security.

Azad was highly upset over their arrests. With the arrest of Bhagat Singh one of his confident had gone. After the Lahore conspiracy and the subsequent arrests in this regard the revolutionary party began to face organizational crisis. However

Azad was determined to carry forward the party's cause. The party started functioning again. There were also a few women. members in it. Mrs. Sushila and Mrs. Durga were some of the senior women members. In another incident a bomb exploded under the Viceroy's car. The Congress condemned the attack and wished Viceroy a healthy life.

Azad was again highly upset over this gesture, of the Congress party. He began to make efforts for the release of

Bhagat Singh and Dutta from the jail. At Saharanpur bomb making factory Shiv Verma was leading a torturous life. Azad was at that time putting up at Jhansi. He was very anxious about the well being of his party members.

Sukhdev and Kishanlal and a few others had already arrested at Lahore. Azad was sure that after Bhagat Singh and Dattas are convincted in the Delhi assembly case, they too will be taken to Lahore jail. Azad was looking for this opportunity. He planned to attack the police party and set the prisoners free. But the reports that he received later were not very encouraging. At Lahore a house to house search was going on and party members were being arrested one after another.

The organization was at the verge of collapse. The police had become highly active. The government seemed to have bent upon finishing the party altogether. Azad had been quite successful during all these days to keep himself away from the watchful eyes of the police.

Bhagwati Charan's Death

Azad, Yashpal, Bhagwati Charan, Dhanwantri, Vaishampayan had gathered in a bunglow at Bahawalpur road. The plan was to throw a bomb at the police party which was scheduled to pass through that police escorting Bhagat Singh and Datta and Set free the prisoners.

It was decided to test the quality of the bombs before they were thrown at the police party. Sukhdev Bhagwati Charan and Vaishampayan went to the banks of Ravi river for random testing.

As soon as Bhagwati Charan lifted his right hand to throw the bomb it exploded in his hand. Bhagwati Charan screamed in pain and fell down on the ground wounded. Vaishampayan an Sukhdev rushed to his help. Both hands of Bhagwati Charan had blown off, A fountain of blood was gushing out. Blood-soaked torn pieces of flesh were dangling from his both hands. Bhagwati Charan was feeling thirsty. He asked for water. But in absence of any utensil water had to be dropped into his mounth by squeezing a wet cloth.

As the minutes ticked by the condition of Bhagwati began to deteriorate. The place where they had come to test the bomb was quite fra from the city limits. Vaishampayan asked Sukhdev to rush back and inform Azad about the incident. Sukhdev somehow managed to reach Azad. When Azad reached there, Bhagwati had already breathed his last. Bhagwati's death gave Azad a servere blow. He had lost one of his most hard working and enthusiastic friends.

Before dying Bhagwati had said to Vaishampayan, "If this accident would have taken place two days after, we could have at least been able to set free Bhagat Singh and Datta." The police raids and searches were countinuing. Their campaign against the revolutionaries was much more harder at Delhi and Kanpur.

Azad decided to open a new centre at Bombay, under the supervision of Prithvi Singh. He was an old comrade in the revolt cadre and was a hard working man. This new arrangement brought some relief to Azad. He again devoted himself to re-organising the already battered party.

Azad and Nehru

A meeting was arranged between Jawaharlal Nehru and Azad by some people. In the beginning, Azad was not ready for it, but later he gave his consent. A time was fixed for their meeting.

Jawaharlal Nehru was a true follower of Gandhiji. But Azad never favoured Gandhiji's ideology of peace and nonviolence. He favoured a direct method of struggle for the country's independence. Keeping his own ideology of armed struggle in view there was little hope of his talks with Jawaharlal bearing any fruit. But on the insistence of his collegues he agreed to attend the meeting.

Azad secretly reached Anand Bhavan to meet Pundit Jawaharlal Nehru. Earlier he already had a meeting with Pundit Motilal Nehru. The main objective of the meeting was to discuss the pros and cons of Round Table Conference. Also, the future of the revolutionary party had to be decided.

Later Pt. Nehru while writing his autobiography had described his meeting with Azad. Yeshpal had also written about the Nehru-Azad meeting. He says that one cannot understand how Nehruji came to the conclusion that Azad was a fascist. Fascism is based on the rule of suppression and atrocities. Azad never thought of administering the country through his party. He infact was opposing British fascism, and the government's brutalities inflicted on the Indian people.

In the third week of February, Yeshpal himself went to see Nehruji at Anand Bhavan. "He made it very clear that, by saying," we are not terrorists. We want to simply launch a widespread armed revolution. Ours is also a part of India's freedom struggle.

We will fight the government's repressive methods and tell them that we are not afraid of it's armed power. Out views are socialistic. We do not believe in terroristic idealogy".

Nehruji replied. "whatever it is I cannot help you in your terrorist like activities. Where as your desire to visit Russia is concerned. I will think over it."

Everyone was astonished to see Azad's dynamism and talent developing day by day. Who soever had come across his mental abilities a month before would find it hard to believe the altogether changed Azad in one month, more matured with a widened mental horizon. with more newer responsibilities coming on his shoulder. Azad would develop new capacities in him.

Those days eveyone was praying for Azad's long and healthy life. He was considered to be the only leader who knew what the revolution was and how could that he adopted to become a way of life for a common Indian. So whenever there was an opportunity Azad's friends would insist upon, his going to Russia.

Nehruji gave a financial help of Rs. fifteen hundred for the purpose. In the night of 26th February. Yeshpal met Azad. He wanted to hand over his the money given by Nehruji, But Azad showed his unwillingness to take the money.

Search for Azad

The British government had left no stone unturned to arrest Azad. The police was looking for him all over the country. Special efforts were made at Benaras, Jhansi, Kanpur and Delhi to apprehend Azad. Those informers, who were able to recognize Azad, took their positions in these cities. But Azad skillfully gave a slip to them all everytime he had to go out of city, or move arround in the city itself, or mover around in the city itself. Whenever the police came to know that Azad would be leaving the station, that day all the trains passing through Kanpur, Delhi and Tundla were throughly searched at the station by them.

One day, Azad accompained by one of his friends, reached Kanpur by train. At the station he was surrounded by the police. The police had also engaged two persons who claimed to know Azad minutely by face. At the main station exit A.S.Shambhu Nath and Tikaram were standing with pistols in their hands.

That day Azad was attired in coat and trousers and was wearing a hat also. He looked like a police inspector. A coolie was carrying his luggage.

Azad walked ahead of the coolie and reached the main exit along with his friend. Both handed over their journey tickets to the ticket checker standing there and came out of the railway station.

One day, Azad some of his other party members were taking a stroll on the Mall Road in Kanpur. All of a sudden, a person dressed in a long coat and trousers came near Azad; stared at him and then walked away. Kashiram then remarked, “It looked like he was Visheshwar Singh. He had probably recognized us”.

Visheshwar Singh was a police inspector. Azad said, “All right, let’s be ready. Let him come here again. Then we’ill see to it”. As expected. Visheshwar Singh came back for the second time and began to stare at Azad. Azad put his hand inside his pocket. An expression of brutality came over his face. Sensing danger to his life Visheshwar Singh fled the spot in utter panic and never returned. Kashiram asked Azad, “If we’d to run away after shooting Visheshwar, how could have we done that ?

Azad smiled and said, “You seem to have gone mad. Don’t you see those two bicycles pedalled by two British over there. We could have snatched those for our purpose. The presence of mind is what is required in such situations.”

There is one more similar incident, which took place at Kanpur. It was the winter members used to put on shawls. These shawls were manufactured at Ludhiana. The shawls, no doubt were very comfortable to wear but proved very inconvinient at the time of handling a pistol or revolver. In order to solve their problem, Azad had ordered for stitching of a few coats.

While proceeding towards railway station Azad, all of a sudden, remembered the coats. He said to his friends accompanying him, “why not we visit the tailor on our way to station ? It is quite likely the coats are ready to wear. There is still time to catch the train. Besides, there is no use reaching the station so early".

They visited the tailor's shop. The coats were ready by then. They took off their shawls and put on the coats. The shawls were folded and kept in the steel trunk which they were carrying with them. There were also some bottles of carbolic acid kept in the trunks. Azad and his party friends boarded the train.

As soon as the train started to move an armed constabulary entered the compartment and took its seat. The train entered the Kanpur railway station at a very slow speed. There were a number of armed policemen standing in a row on the platform.

Azad said. "They must be waiting to welcome the arrival of some high ranking official." However, after looking around carefully he said to his friends, "Keep yourself ready with your revolvers, in case we've to shoot."

Then he looked at the luggage and said irritably, "This luggage is a nonsense. Hand over these to a coolie and follow immediately behind me. If there is a shootout, start firing with your back against mine". When the train came to a halt. Azad was first to get off. The luggage was handed first to get off. The luggage was handed over to a coolie; his token number was noted down and Azad and his party members came out of the station safety. The coolie emerged out of the station a little late. Azad was annoyed. He asked the coolie "Why did you come out late"?

"The ticket collector wanted to know who was the owner of this luggage," the coolie said. So, this was yet another example of Azad's cleverness.

Once Azad had gone to Kanpur in connection with an important work. The party was short of finances. It was proposed that the office car of the party could be sold out to solve the financial crisis of the party to some extent.

Azad's mother was spending her days in acute poverty. It was a matter of great concern for the party. However, Azad was least worried over the matter. He was more occupied with the conditions prevailing in the country. When Ganesh Shankar Vidyarthi came to know about the condition of Azad's mother, he gave rupees two hundred to Azad. But Azad, instead of remitting the money to his mother, spent it for party's cause.

When Vidyarthiji asked Azad about the money, Azad said with all his seriousness, "Why worry for my mother. Only two shots are enough for that poor old women. Vidyarthiji, there are millions of families living in this slave country, who go hungry everyday. My mother, at least, manages to have her meals. every alternate day. Even if otherwise, I shall never let our party people go hungry for her sake.

It is my first duty to look after the interest of my party members. Even if my parents sacrifice their lives on the altar of the country, it would not make any difference what so ever. To speak the plan truth there are millions in our country who either die or take birth daily." Azad went away leaving Vidyarthiji surprised. Later Navinji remitted money to Azad's mother.

27th February 1931

The day was Friday 27th February 1931. It was morning time Azad entered Alerd Park along with Sukhdev Raj to discuss some important matters. They sat under the shade of a tree and began to talk. All of a sudden he looked on the road running along the park out side and said with a start, "Look, perhaps it is Virbhadra Tiwari coming ! I hope he did not notice us sitting here."

But it did not further arouse his suspicion. De reverted to the ongoing topic of discussion. But by then the police had already laid seize to the park then all of a sudden a bullet came whizzing around and found its mark into the thigh of Azad. Azad fired back. The bullet tone of the police vechile's tyre to pieces.

By that time the police fired another round and a bullet pierced Azad's lungs. The warm blood ozzed out of Azad's lungs and flowed down on his body. Then the Superitendent of Police ran helter in great panic and pain. He was badly hurt. He rushed towards his car. Azad fired again from his revolver. The bullet damaged the engin. Nott Babber jumped out from his car seat. He was afraid that another fire from Azad might take his brains out of his head.

Azad pulled the trigger, and the next mement one of the police inspector's Jaw was blown off he dropped dead on the ground. Azad checked his gun. There was one last bullet remaining in it. Azad's thigh bone was fractured. Another bullet had pierced his right arm and had entered his lungs. Blood ozing out all over his body, he fought tooth and nail and put up a brave defence for nearly half an hour forcing the police force to take up a defensive position and lick dust.

'Azad' shall never remain 'Azad', he murmured in his last moment of eternal journey. He put the nozzle of the revolver on his temple and pulled the trigger. The last bullet shattered his brains making an end to all his revolutionary activities of which each and every attempt was direted towards the sole aim of achieving country's freedom.

Azad's motionless body was resting solemnly in the park. The body which was full of vigour and vitality a moment before was now lying in a state of tranquility Even after his death on his bloodsmeared face. He looked all the same scene determined and courageous. The crowd swelled further. Thousands of mourners entered the park to pay their last homage to the great revolutionary.

8

Subhas Chandra Bose

Childhood and Education

Janaki Nath Bose was a noted lawyer. In 1885, he had migrated to Cuttack; he was working as a public procecutor as well as social worker. Janaki Nath's wife Prabhabati was from the well known Dutt family Hatkhola. To this religious couple Subhas was born, on January 13rd 1897. Janaki Nath, like most parents of that period believed that the future of his child by in English education.

Prabhabati inspired the love of motherland in the heart of young Subhas, by making him aware of the great traditions of India. The childhood of Subhas was an amalgamation of an English education. Subhas was an extraodinarily briliant student. His childhood was greatly influenced by his mother, as well as by his teacher, Mr. Beni Mahav Das. Subhas's early schooling took place in an Anglo-Indian school at Cuttack. So he was not able to learn his mother tongue Bengali, in his childhood.

He worked very hard to learn Bengali. Subhas felt very humiliated, when his teacher read out his poor Bengali composition, in the class room. At home he worked very hard to learn Bengali. In the matriculation exam Subhas stood second in the whole university. In B.A. examination he got first class honours in philosophy and was placed in the second in the order of merit, in the Calcutta University.

In the year 1919 at the insistance of his father he sailed for England to try his luck in the ICS. He joined the Cambridge University. He had to study English History, European History, Economics, Geography, Political Science, English Law, Philosophy, Sanskrit and English composition. However Cambridge had an everlasting effect on the personality of Subhas.

Cambridge in those days was a place where students of many parts of British empire gathered, and had later greatly affected the history of their respective countries. There existed an atmosphere of, free discussions and evaluation of problems faced by different countries.

Infact Cambridge shaped Subhas into a complete man known to every one as the great leader he was, he had been still a boy when he left India. But his experiences, and interactions with people from different walks of life, at Cambridge brushed of all the uncertainities. leaving behind a polished human; being sure of himself and certain of his goals and ambitions in life.

Subhas was able to see how people lived in free countries. He compared them to the people of India, who lived under the British rule, in a sense of fear and in security. He realised that India had remained several centuries behind other countries in the march of progress. He realised that, if India was to be equal with other nations, it has to be a free country.

Without knowingly Subhas considered himself an enemy of Britain in many aspects. His stay at Cambridge had given him an insight not only into the nature of the British people, but also the imperialistic system of rule which worked effictively without destroying the virtues of the population; who were not aware of what is being done in their name.

When he sat for ICS examination Subhas was not sure of his success. Having studied European history from the original sources he came to acquire a new perspective of international politics, some thing which was not possible in India, where only the English history was taught. However when the ICS results were declared he was quite surprised to find his name fourth on the list of merit. But he later resigned from the ICS.

Subhas had an outlook similar to British and the sense of discipline and honour almost English-like. This was evident from the sense of discipline and honour which he inculcated while managing the Indian National Army later in his career.

The Long Wanderings

Subhas came fourth in the Civil Services Examination; but he had decided by that time that he would not serve in the Indian civil service under the British Government. He had made up his mind to devote his life to the service of the country. Subhas was greatly influenced by Swami Vivekananda since the young age of 15. He studied many books on religion and Yoga. He loved to spend most of his time, in the company of holy men, as he was impressed with their way of life.

One day during the summer, while studying in college in Calcutta, he along with his friend left for a long pilgrimage without informing their family members. For months they kept wandering all over the North. They visited many places of religious and historical interest. Often they stayed in the ashrams.

At haridwar they had a bitter experience. The priests would not allow them to eat in the common dining room, sincce they were nonvegetarians. However, Subhas and his friend attended many religious discourses and mixed with all sorts of Sadhus. At Benaras, they also happened to meet Swami Brahmananda of Ramkrishna Mission, who knew Subhas's family.

During the long wanderings Subhas had a very mixed experience. He was very disillusioned about many religious customs and practices. One fine morning Subhas walked in to his house to the great relief of all his members. And within a few days, he was down with typhoid fever. However Subhas's search for a 'Guru' was ended.

Incidents In The Presidency College

In the year 1916 two incidents occurred in the Presidency College where Subhas was studying which changed the very course of his life. In those days there were two types of teachers in the colleges. The English lecturers and Indian lecturers.

The English lecturers were paid more than he Indian lecturers. Many English teachers were behaved in a very haughty manner. One of them E.O.Oaten was known for his rude behaviour towards the students. One day Mr. Oaten entered the verandah, infront of his class room and pushed some students who were walking there. The students felt very offended, and went on strike. This incident caused, silent anger amongest the students.

Professor Oaten continued his rude behaviour. Another day he slapped a first year student. Within a short while all the students gathered around him. They knew well that, if they complained to the college authorities, no action would be taken. So the students surrounded the professor. Students were aware that, the professor was very rude. They decided to each a lesson to him. The professor was beaten up by them in the college corridor. This incident caused a great stir in Calcutta.

The Government closed down the college and ordered an enquiry. Subhas was very critical of the new Indian society existing at that time, which was a mixture of Indian and Western culture. When asked about the incidence, Subhas told the enquiry commissioner, that were was a grave provocation for it. Since he was a well known leader of the student union. Later Subhas was expelled from the Presidency College. This particular event highlights the fact that Subhas was very critical of the new Indian society, existing at that time, which was a mixture of Indian and Western culture.

Subhas was frustarted mainly because, this new society was more intiative rather than imaginative. At an early age Subhas was convinced that Indian society could never be real unless the Indians are masters in their own country, and unless the western influence ceased to be something imposed on Indians by their alien rulers. When Subhas was expelled from the college, he had not even a trace of regret in his mind. He was indeed glad that he had stood for the national honour at the cost of some personal sacrifice. Sometimes, small things in life lead to greater events in future !

Subhas and C.R.Das.

The success at the civil service examination brought him face to face with the greatest crisis of his life. He was in a dilemma. For a long time Subhas corresponded with his father Janaki Nath Bose, about this issue. The later advised him that, soon India would get home rule, and then the service conditions for men like him.

Subhas wrote to Deshbandhu C.R.Das. a great patriot expressing his desire to work under his guidance. Later Subhas went straight to C.R.Das, and helped him in all his works. Very soon Subhas became the right hand man of C.R.Das and an important Congress leader.

For Subhas, it was the service to the Motherland which counted most and he was prepared to pay any police to uphold his ideals. On meeting Mr.C.R.Das the great Bengali leader, and having exhaustive and lengthy discussions with him, Subhas realised the situation. Once he was convinced of the Congress ideology, he decided to join the Congress.

After joining the Indian National Congress, the first activity undertaken by Subhas was organising the boycott of the visit of the Prince of Wales to India. Subhas was arrested for his offence, along with C.R.Das and hundreds of their supporters. This was the first instance that Subhas went to jail.

In the meanwhile Lord Reading the then viceroy of India, felt the volatile political environment and offered a negotiated settlement to the Congress. For this Congress leaders agreed. However Lord Reading changed his mind at last movement. In 1922, the non-co-operation movement was abruptly stopped by M.K.Gandhi after the Chaura-Chauri incident.

Gandhiji was arrested and sentenced to two years imprisonment Subhas was a mere spectator and watched all this from prison feeling utterly helpless.

Subhas As a C.E.O.

When Deshbandhu C.R.Das was elected as the mayor of the Calcutta Muncipal corporation, he in turn appointed Subhas as the Chief Executive Officer (CEO). In those days Calcutta Muncipal Corporaion was one of the most powerful team for civic administration, and social reforms.

The first thing Subhas did also was to bring the education department under the corporation,so that redical educational reforms could be introduced. Free Primary Schools were opened by taking the help of social workers, Subhas formed, Health

Associations in very ward of the Corporation. This way greater health consciousness was promoted amongst the general public. He also opened free dispensaries, in every district to provide medical aid and medicines to the poor. He started free clinics and milk distribution centres. All in all it was a service oriented Muncipal Corporation that took care of the poor people.

Subhas would personally look into the problems of welfare of the masses. As a C.E.O.Subhas showed remarkable, organis ational abilities. He was a stricker for discipline and punctuality. He worked round the clock to supervise the muncipal affairs, be it water supply, sanitation, health services, lighting, road repairs or anything that affected the well being of the people. Subhas proved his mentle as an able administrator. After some days he started a weekly journal, Calcutta Muncipal Gazette. He also setup a commercial museum to promote domestic goods. Subhas introduced new norms in the administration. He made the rule to hold special receptions to honour the visiting nationalist leaders.

The Great Ideals and Principles of Subhas

After his release from the prison Subhas was engaged himself in relief work, as Bengal was affected by severe floods during those days. In the meanwhile Subhas became the Editor of the Bengal Daily, the "Banglar Katha".

For any other young man passing the ICS exam would have been a matter of great achievement. But for Subhas it was the greatest crisis in his life. He knew that being in the civil services would mean leading a life of luxury something that he had always wanted. But on the other hand the fierce nationalist in him could never agree to work for the British. For Subhas working for British amounted to slavery. It was not an easy decision to make, since his parents had pinned all their hopes on his joining the ICS. But his ideals led him another way. For a long time he had been in touch with his elder brother, Sarat Bose, who he loved and trusted deeply.

Subhas poured his heart out in these letters and asked for his advice. He then wrote to Deshbandhu C.R.Das offering his services to work under him for the nation. Once Subhas made his final decision. He wrote the letter of resignation to the secretary of the state for India, on April 22, 1921. His decision caused great stir in India. The patriot Subhas would only agree to serve his Motherland. On his return to Calcutta he joined the National College, run by C.R.Das as the principal. Subhas also contributed articles to the Congress party's news paper 'Swaraj'. In the mean while Pandit Nehru and C.R.Das had formed Swarajya Party. The main aim of the party was to avoid any chance of the freedom movement loosing it's movementum.

The Swarajya Party had been formed o contest the elections to the legislative councils and offer resistance to the British Government from within. Subhas joined the Swarajya Party and was made the secretary. In 1925 Subhas experienced a shock due to the death of C.R.Das. This was unexpected turn of events for Subhas. He had become so much used to the presence of C.R.Das, that whenever he encountered any hurdle in his triad for the freedom movement. Subhas who could have been an ICS officer, gave up money and confort to be able to live up to his ideals and principles in life.

The Helping Nature

Subhas was widely known for his compassionate nature. Through out his life he never missed an opportunity to help people. During his study at presidency College one such incident happened. Subhas's college was over four kilometres from his house and his parents would give him the tram fare for going to the college.

Once while travelling he caught sight of an old poor woman begging near his house. Seeing her in such a helpless state, young Subhas gave her his tram money. He then decided to walk back home that evening, This routine continued for a long time. By sacrificing his own comfort Subhas helped a poor needy woman.

As a student Subhas was actively involved in Community service. In those days cholera and famine occurred frequently. He would often organise student groups and work in areas affected by the cholera epidemic. Once a poor student who was lying sick in the hostel but nobody attended to him, because he belonged to a lower caste. When Subhas heard of this he went over and started nursing him regularly.

Later on when his mother came to know of it, she was over joyed at her son's spirit. Service to his people and his country was the guiding principle of Subhas's life. He always lived for others. He lived according to Swami Vivekananda's ideals of serving God through serving the poor and the needy. Subhas's faith in his fellowmen and his sense of service inspired more and more fellowmen to come forward and help him. As the chief Executive officer of Calcutta Corporation Subhas would accept only half of his monthly salary. He used his money to help poor and the needy students.

Subhas started a 'Detenus Fund' for the welfare of the families of the under trials kept in jail for long periods. Most of them were poor and illiterate and their families would almost be starving. Looking after and attending to the sick and suffering soon became a way of life for subhas, even when he was very involved in politics.

In 1922 heavy monsoons led to flooding of many rivers in North Bengal. Thus Subhas organised Volunteers in the Congress party and then set out to help the flood victims. Subhas was also busy with the relief work that he did not even join in Durgapuja celebrations. His devotion to social work in the face of many difficulties won him all round praise. The success of this work to help the victims of the flood earned the Congress Party great credit. Even the then governer of Bengal praised Subhas for his selfless service. Service to his people and his country was the guiding principle of Subhas's life. He always lived for others. He lived according to Swami Vivekananda's ideals serving God through serving the poor and the needy.

The I.N.A.

From the beginning discipline was very much a part of Subhas's character. When he was a young student he happened to meet a ex-officer of the Bengal Ambulance corps. Subhas was reviewed by the heroic exploits and the adventure of this officer who had earlier been captured and taken prisoner in Turkey.

This was actually what inspired Subhas to join the army. Mean while, the government of India decided to start a University corps of Territorial Army. For this the selection tests were not so difficult, as in the case of army selection, and Subhas had no problems getting accepted into the unit. This military training proved very useful to Netaji in his later life in the Indian National Army. (I.N.A.) In the beginning the British officers incharge of the unit had a poor opinion about the Bengali boys.

The British feared that, Bengal; boys would be failures as soldiers. But during the course of their training period, these boys performed wonderfully. Some of them even beat their Briish instructors in shooting. When their unit marched into Fort William, they marched with an increased sense of confidence. At that movement Subhas felt as if he was marching into, take charge of something which belonged to them.

The early military training and sense of strong discipline became a positive factor when Subhas started heading the Congress Seva Dal. Subhas not only raised the volunteer force but also systematically organised their training in military discipline. These volunteers were expected to dress and behave like soldiers.

When Netaji Subhas Chandra Bose as the general officer in command inspected the parade it was a wonderful sight that inspired confidence and strength. The volunteer corps had three sub units-a motor cycle uni, a cavalry unit and a women corps. This way Netaji progressively introduced character and disclipline in the volunteers.

All the experiences from his college days contributed immensely to the organisation an early success of the I.N.A. which fought many heroic battles against the British army. Throughout his life Nataji showed a lot of concern for all those around him. He would always think of the welfare of his people even at the cost of his own needs and comforts.

This sense of concern was displayed even during the worst days of the Indian National Army's struggle fpr freedom. At the end of April 1945 early and heavy monsoons caused a severe set back to the INA. It was decided that troops should with draw from Rangoon and move to Bangkok.

The Japanese suggested that, Subhas should leave the front at once for his personal safety. But he insisted that he would not move until all the troops especially the girls of Rani of Jhansi Regiment were taken care of. The Japanese then offered fifteen lorries and six cars for the withdrawl of his troops. Due to heavy air attacks, the troops used to travel only at night about 2 am on April 26th they reached a small place Waw, where they had to cross the river by ferry. The Japanese General suggested that Netaji should cross over first and then the other troops would follow. But Subhas disagreed, saying that, unless all the girls of the Rani of Jhansi Regiment crossed over, he would not move.

Subhas supervised the ferrying of the girls through the night till day break. By them the enemy planes were expected any time, yet Subhas choose to cross the river only after the others.

The Rani of Jhansi Regiment was once resting in a village by the riverside. At 3 pm. Six British fighter planes arrived and started hovering over the area. Many of the troops ran and hid themselves behind the trees. General Chatterjee tried to push Netaji into a small pit, but he once again refused, insisting that he would not take shelter, since the girls had no place to hide themselves. Netaji stood calm in spite of the enemy planes attacking with heavy machine guns, for half an hour. It was one of the worst enemy attacks. Five lorries were destroyed and bullets went flying everywhere. It was almost a miracle that Netaji remained unhurt. But to Netaji, the safety of his staff was more important than his own life.

During the retreat Netaji did not travel in his car. Since most of the troops were moving on foot. One day while they were resting, one of the girls asked Netaji to take off his boots and socks so that she could wash them. When he took of his boots and socks the girl was shocked to see that, his feet were full of blisters. As usual Netaji never spoke of his own pain and discomfort to any one.

Once Netaji was taking a salute in a ceremonial march past at Rangoon. About 3,000 troops were taking part in that parade, After he had delivered his speech, the march fast started. As the Rani of Jhansi Regiment started marching, the British fighter plans were seen approaching Rangoon. Sensing danger most of the visitors including the Japanese Generals ran for cover. But Netaji did not move. And the girls too kept on marching as if nothing had happened.

Bombs were falling in all directions, but still Netaji stood there till all the troops had moved and taken shelter. It so happened that the planes were flying very low with in a hundred yards of Netaji and could have easily shot him and girls. But the brave soldiers and their supreme commander did not move from their ground in the face of all the danger.

The Sense of Humour In Subhas.

On his return from England Subhas went to the great leader C.R.Das, and offered his services to him. Subhas was proud, to have found a dedicated leader as his master. Likewise C.R.Das was equally proud of his brilliant young lieutenant. Subhas began teaching in the National College.

There he was involved in the running of the English and Bengali journals of the party. For Subhas the nationalist service to his leader was the foremost duty. He was first imprisoned in December 1921. It was the time when thye Prince of Wales was visiting India. For having organised the boycott Subhas was arrested and produced before the magistrate in court. The latter handed down a prison term of six months. In all he was jailed eleven times and the worst term was in the Mandlay Jail in Rangoon. These long jail terms ruined his health. The sense of humour in Subhas was uncountable. It helped him cope with the stressful life that he had chosen.

Subhas got a golden opportunity of staying very close to his leader, in the Alipore Central Jail for eight months. During this time he tried to study his master's character, and habits and learn from his experiences. Subhas found C.R.Das to be an excellent organiser and extremely devoted to his comrades. During the eight months spent in jail, Subhas served his master with great devotion. He would take care of all his needs. He could even cook for his leader.

The Lofty Character of Netaji

The lofty character of Netaji was evident when he was a student in England. When he resigned from the ICS he wrote to the British Government that he would refund all the stipends that he had received from them. He borrowed 100 pounds from his classmate Dilip Kumar Roy and paid it back to the British government. Netaji was equally generous to other associations. He made large donations to the Thailand government for their help and other facilities offered to the I.N.A. Many great are not known for being careful in handling large sums of money or in returning the money borrowed. Netaji was not like other great men ! when it came to money he never once cheated anybody. When Subhas mobilised the Indians in East Asia he appealed to them for funds. A large amount of cash and gold jewellery was donated by the Indians, living in South East Asia.

The donations were kept in the newly formed Azad Hind Bank. Netaji kept his promise. He paid back millions of Yen to the Japanese Government. Similarly all the money borrowed was returned to the Germans. Yet another sign of the greatness of the man was his sincerity and honesty in all matters, whether they he ralated to his beliefs his patriotism or money.

In 1943, when he came to Singapore to set up the provisional government of Azad Hind, he had to borrow a lot of money from the Japanese, for which an Indian-Japanese Loan Agreement had been singed. Earlier in 1943, when he had set up the Indian Independence League in Berlin, he had to borrow money from the German Government with the assurance, it would be duly paid back.

The Boycott of The Simon Commission

The boycott of the Simon Commission was followed by

popular discontent among the Indians against the British Rule. According to Subhas in one of his address he said that the boycott would result ultimately into a series of events leading to the freedom of India.

The boycott of the Simon Commission by the Congress was also joined by the dissident Muslim League, and leaders of both the communities joined hands in a united move against the British. After the publication of the Simon Commission's Report, the Congress appointed a committee, which was headed by Motilal Nehru. This committee was entrusted with the task of framing, the future constitution of India.

This was to be submitted to the British Government as the minimum political demand of the Indian people. In the fiftieth session of the all India Congress held in December 1928, This report was submitted by Motilal Nehru. It was at this session that Subhas once again began to express his strategies more clearly. He organised a group of youth as volunteer corps trained on military lines whose duty was to maintain order at the location where the Congress Session was held. The corps had been dressed in military like uniforms and they had handled the situation in a military manner. Subhas was severaly criticised by the British press for his actions, but in contrast he was highly praised by the Congress President, Motilal Nehru. Soon after the session of 1928 several youth organisations had been formed all over India. All the youth organisation were constantly supported by Subhas; who had realised the immense potential of the youth force in liberation of India.

The A.I.T.U.C.

Soon after the Congress session of 1928, several youth organisations had been formed all over India, the most prominent being the all India Youth Congress presided over by Yusuf Mehrali, the All Bengal Students Association and the Bengal Presidency students Association. All these youth organisations were constantly supported by Subhas, who had realised, the immense potential of the youth force, in the liberation of India.

Subhas was also in contact with Several revolutionary organisations, such as Hindustan Republican Armed Group led by Bhagat Singh the Anusilan Samiti, the Jagantar Group and many others. These revolutionary groups had realised that, Subhas was their supporter and held him in high regard.

A few months after the Calcutta Congress, Subhas was elected as the president of all India Trade Union Congress. This was a turning point in the life of Subhas. Working with C.R.Das, Subhas had become used to work as a second man to some one whom he respected. C.R.Das's death had left a void with in him which he had taken a very long to fill. Unused to act on his own, he was not very sure of himself in the beginning and searched his way up.

However with his election as the president of all India Trade Union Congress he became conscious of his own leadership, abilities and was convinced of acting on his own without depending on others. He became, the uncontested, leader of the youth and the leftist elements in the country. He had learnt as the President of the Trade Union Congress that he could utilise the so-far untapped strength of the working classes, in India for the freedom movement. As a result by 1930, Subhas became the third most important political leader in the Congress.

The Strong Principles of Netaji

Netaji was a man of strong principles and character. The honour of his community and country was something be valued immensely. When Subhas was the mayor of Calcutta the government had imposed a ban on all political meetings. But Subhas wanted to organise a Congress meet in a befitting manner. So, he led a big procession of Congress volunteers up to the Ochterlony Monument, where the meting was to be held.

On the way, Netaji, along with other local Congress volunteers were assaulted by the police. Many people sustained injuries and some started bleeding profusely. But they kept on advancing and shouting slogans.

The Police tried to snatch the Congress flag which Netaji was holding. But the would not give in easily. Many policemen charged towards him with lathis. He was beaten very badly; still he clung to the flag, till he was completly exhausted and his right hand fingers were fractured very severely. By this incident one can understand that, Netaji was always prepared to defend the honour of his party and his country at any cost.

Subhas's Travel to Vienna

In 1932, Subhas went to Vienna for receiving medical treatment for suspected Tuberculosis. In Vienna he met the famous Vithalbhai Patel, who had also come to Vienna and was staying there. Both of them used to have lengthy discussions and as a result they came to a conclusion that India would not be free till they have support from foreign countries, especially thiose cpuntries who are opposed to the British.

Together they issued manifesto, which was a result of their constructive thinking, convinced unless, India develops international contacts, Indian national movement would not be featuring on the international scene. It was also stated that to hasten the attainment of freedom by India, the freedom struggle should be reffered to as an issue between nations. So impressed was Vithalbhai Patel, who was suffering from serious ailments, that he left all the money he possessed through a will to Subhas so that, he can carry on anti-British campaign, in other countries. This manifesto released by Subhas and Vithalbhai Patel forms a landmark in the history of India's freedom struggle.

Until then, except Nehru's participation at the Congress of league against imperialism at Brussels, no other important leader involved in the freedom struggle in India; had taken an initiative to develop international contacts in general international sympathy and awareness to the sufferings of Indians.

After Mahatma Gandhiji's decision to adopt non-voilent non-co-operation. even the small Congress office located in London had also been closed. This office had earlier been established to create an awareness among the English peoople, about the miserable living conditions of the Indians under the British Raj.

Apart from the above this office also was striving to establish contacts with liberal English politicians. But with the closing down of this office, there was no official organisation outside India, to bring the Indian problem to the notice of other countries.

Patekl and Subhas in their Manifesto, totally disagreed with the view of Gandhiji. No one knew outside India how the British treated the people of this Country. Ten years of better struggle from 1920-1930 by the Indians against the British rule, in the non-violent, non-co-operation manner, had yielded very meagre benefits.

The Sense of Diplomacy

The manners and sense of diplomacy exuded by Subhas was evident his stay in Europe. Very few Indians before him and the opportunity of conducting discussions with foreign leaders.

But when the necessity came Subhas handled the situation in an admirable fashion and came out with flying colours. Subhas was elected as president of the Indian National Congress, in January 1938, when he was still aboard.

Subhas returned to India in February 1938, and presided over the 51th National Congress Session. He formed a national planning committee and he made Pandit Jawaharlal Nehru, it's first chairman and he himself was the convener of this committee. As his term of office began to come to an end, Subhas expressed his desire to try for re-election an the president of the Congress.

Mahatma Gandhi however did not approve of his intentions. He instead chose Dr.Pattabhi Sitaramayya as the next presidential candidate. This resulted in sharp differences between Bose and Gandhiji. Most of the prominent leaders in Congress resigned because of this rift. However Subhas contested the presidential elections, against the wishes of Gandhiji, and was elected as the president of the Indian National Congress for a second time. All the members of the Congress working committee resigned in protest.

At the 52nd session of the Congress held at Tripuri in Madhya Pradesh in 1939, Subhas was elected as president. At the Tripuri session Subhas indicated to adopt a proposal to be sent to the British government demanding independence with-in 8 months. This proposal was opposed by Mahatma Gandhiji and his supporters and ultimately, the proposal was dropped by the Congress. It was the conviction, Subhas felt that, world war would break out anytime that made him frame the proposal and demand to send it over to the British.

The Sense of Service of the I.N.A.

A remarkable sense of service prevailed among the soldiers of the I.N.A.One day in october 1944, Netaji was visiting the base hospital at Myanmar. There were about two thousand sick and wounded soldiers in the hospital at that time. Most of them were in a very bad shape either suffering from septic gunshot wounds or dysentery or malaria. A unit of the Rani of Jhansi Regiment was looking after them. One of the girls Bela Datt Barely 16 years old was nursing eighty-five cases of acute dysentery, she washed their soiled clothes, gave them medicines, a sponge bath and also helped them dress.

When Netaji went on a round and talked to the soldiers, they all spoke about the extraordinary service rendered by the nurses. They told Netaji, "Even our mothers and sisters could not have looked after us better". There were tears in Netaji's eyes and he gave a special pat to Bela Dutt for her devotion to duty.

Netaji's Hard Character

Men like Subhas are born revolutionaries. They are meant to be leaders. Such people are known to overcome hardships and emerge a winner. It is faith which ultimately helps them succeed in their mission. In the early 1930's when Subhas was serving a long prison sentence. his health deteriorated very badly.

The British would not agree to release him eventhough he needed treatment. They believed that once Subhas was released, he would be source of serious trouble for the government. He was however, permitted to travel to Europe for treatment at his own expense.

Once Subhas was there he acted as a one man mission, contacting all the important leaders in those countries. In his meeting with the Italian leader Mussolini, he was asked as to what path he would adopt-revolutionary or reformist. Very emphatically Mussolini replied, "Revolutionary" satisfied the Italian leader said that he had a chance.

In 1941, when all the other leaders were in jail waiting for things to happen, Subhas took the initiative, and planned for a very daring escape from Calcutta. Disguised as a beard Muslim Mohammed Ziauddin, he slipped out of his home and then reached Peshawar. Aided by his colleagues there, he disguised himself a deaf and dumb Pathan and crossed over ro Kabul in Afghanistan. It was very difficult task to hood wink, the British police and the C.I.D.

The most challenging task was Subhas's journey from Germany to South-East Asia in a submarine, which took over three months. Despite heavy patrolling of the sea by the British, he managed to give them a slip. Subhas's life history of a real hero, who would undergo any suffering and take any risk to accomplish his mission.

Formation of The Forward Bloc.

Subhas intended always to utilise the problems and difficulties faced by the British Government to the advantage of the freedom struggle of India. He was however strongly opposed by the Rightist group within the congress. With all the efforts to solve the dispute between Mahatma Gandhi and Subhas having failed, when the All India Congress Committee met in Calcutta in April 1939. Subhas resigned from the post of the president of All India Congress.

In one of his addresses after his resignation Subhas had clearly brought out that he had no desire to be a dummy president or to hang on to his post. After resigning from the post of the president. he formed the Forward Block within the Congress in May 1939.

Subhas's intention of forming the Forward Bloc was to offer stiff resistance to the non-violence, policy, propagated by the Congress. The peaceful stance taken by Congress was damping the violent mood of the people of India to fight for freedom struggle in the real fighting manner. The second World war broke out in September 1939. Subhas was waiting for the opportunity, with the help of the Forward Bloc, launched a very strong anti-British propaganda, throughout India. With the result the British arrested him and he was imprisoned in July 1940.

In November 1940 Subhas threatened the British Government that he should be released immediately, failing which he would go on an indefinite hunger strike. Realising the seriousness of the situation and the volatile climate existing in India, at that time the British released him but interned him at his house. But Subhas was not one to be continued for a long time. One fine day, to the astonishment of the British and Indians, he disappeared from his house.

Not a soul knew the where abouts of Subhas. The British were puzzled at his sudden disappearance, inspite of all the security measures they had taken. This very escape from the cluthes of British, by Subhas single handedly shows how smart and intelligent a person he was, His every move was organised and had a sense of discipline.

The two great leaders of Indian freedom struggle namely Subhas and Gandhi, shared the same aspiration to liberate India, but in their own ways. Subhas's young mind was buddling with ideas and plans. He had a long discussion with Bapu tried to answer all his queries.

Later Subhas admitted that he was disappointed in his first meeting with Gandhiji. Subhas became very active leader of the Congress Party and he had frequent meetings with Gandhiji. Subhas had very strong views and advocated total freedom or Swaraj as opposed to gandhiji's plan of Dominion status.

But Subhas had a great respect towards Bapu. In fact it was Netaji who first addressed Gandhiji as the "Father of the Nation". The great man, Subhas was never showed, the feeling of difference with Bapu, to the public.

The Spirit of Subhas.

Netaji's life is an extraordinary story of courage. His dare devil spirit could be seen in the times of danger. Only the 'Born Great' are capable of doing such heroic deeds. The second world war broke out at the end of 1939.

For a fire brand nationalist like Subhas Chandra Bose, the war offered the best opportunity to free India from the clutches of the British. He believed in the golden principle, that the enemy one's enemy is a friend. If only he could get out of India and join hands with the Germans, the Japanese or the Russians.

Towards the end of 1940, Netaji was serving his eleventh prison term. Like all other leaders, he too could have taken it easy and marked his time in the prision, but his spirit could not remain contented with the sort of a "vegetable existence".

On January 16, 1941 at midnight Netaji slipped to Kabul in the guise of a respected elder Muslim. After a long wait, under an Italian name Orland Mazotta he left for Moscow, from where he flew to Berlin. Let us see why Subhas choose Germany. During world war second, the German forces headed by the Dictator Hitler had created great in roads into France and had caused great damages to the Allied forces.

Not all the Germans approved the ideas of Hitler. But he was so powerful, that no other group in Germany could openly cristicise his Fascist policies. The Nazi force which followed Hitler were ruthless in their endeavours and achieved great victories before the Allied countries joined forces to humble them,

So, the question arises in one's mind that why Subhas selected Germany to put his ideas into action.

The Theroy of Subhas

The theory of Subhas was to try and make friends with countries, which were against the British. Sensing that even Soviet Union was an ally to the British, Subhas had decided to proceed to Germany. Eventhough he went to Germany Subhas never approved of the Fascist idealism of Hitler and his Nazi followers. He even was a part of German movement of resistance against Hitler. So under these circumstances, it is highly erratic to recognise Subhas with the racist fanatics of the Nazi group who blindly followed Hitler in his mindless violence. In that time many countries had made an Allied force to fight the very strong German military machine.

However Bose saw a chance in this great war that if utilised fully, India would attain freedom. Subhas's idea was to garner support from Germany, since they were anti British. It was in Germany during 1941 to 1943 did Subhas laid the foundation of the Indian National Army.

He negotiated with the German authorities and formed the free India centre in Berlin. It was Baron Von Trott Zn Solz who launched Subhas in Berline. If one goes about pondering about Subhas there is not a single piece of evidence which shows that, Subhas approved the Fascist ideas of the Nazis. Infact he was closely associated with against the Nazi movement.

During his stay in Germany, Subhas was associated with the foreign office and he had made it clear to them that India's co-operation with Germany was limited to Germany's war, with Britain and the Indians were not involved in Germany's quarrels with other countries or it's internal quarrels.

Subhas used to give very effictive and moral rising speeches on the Azad Hind Radio to keep the Indian people on their toes in their demand for total independence.

The Habit of A Strict Disciplinarium

Long before Subhas formed the I.N.A.and became it's supreme commander in 1943; he had acquired the habit of a strict disciplinarian. In 1928, the Congress party was holding it's annual session at Calcutta and Pandit Motilal Nehru was to preside over it.

For his session, Netaji had organised a special volunteer corps and was operating as it's commanding officer. It was the first time in the history of the Indian Congress that a large national volunteer corps was formed by any leader.

The men were dressed in military unioform and were given proper military training. The volunteer force had it's cavalry, infantry and medical units. Subhas became the idol of his men. He was very much liked by others for his sense of duty and courage in the of all odds.

Netaji was very attached to his men and always thought of their welfare. Promoting a sense of oneness and brotherhood was the most important task for Netaji. He was the first national leader to introduce the concept of Bharatiya or 'Indianness'.

The Travel to Singapore.

Subhas Chandra Bose arrived in Singapore on July 2, 1943. To his delight he found that, the Indians over there, were an enthusiastic lot who were eager to fight for India. The people of Indian origin in South-East Asia belonging to the business class, workers, clerks, lawyers, poor or rich welcomed Netaji with open arms. Before his arrival in South-East Asia, Ras Behari Baus a well known revolutionary who had fled from India having thrown a bomb at the British viceroy, Lord Hardinge, was trying to head and organise the Indians in South-East Asia.

When Subhas arrived in South-EastAsia, things changed for the better as both the groups had (in S-E-Asia) equal respect and regard for the great leader Subhas.

Subhas met, General Tojo the Prime Minister of Japan and received firm assurance from the japanese that he would be supported by them. They also promised to deliver arms and equipment to the Indian National Army.

After this, Subhas toured extensively to, Malaya, Thailand Burma, and appealed to the Indians living in these countries to come forward for financial aid. Even today Subhas will be remembered as a man of action, who believed in the freedom cause and went to any extent to achieve it.

In our country, Netaji has created a sense of oneness, witthout any distinction of caste and creed.

Biography of the Great Indians

Biography of the Great Indians

Part- II

Parameshwar Hegde

Neha Publishers & Distributors
Delhi- 110002

Neha Publishers & Distributors

4832/24, Prahlad Lane, S- 207

Ansari Road, Daryaganj, New Delhi - 110002

Tel. : 011- 43570976, 23278261

Email- nehapubdistributors@gmail.com

First Edition, **2013**

ISBN: 978-93-80318-25-7 (Set)

978-93-80318-26-4 (Vol 1)

978-93-80318-27-1 (Vol 2)

Price: ₹ 1695/-

Laser Typesetting by: Tamalika Computers, Delhi

Printed at: Nagri Printers, Delhi

PRINTED IN INDIA

Published by Neha Publishers & Distributors, Delhi- 110002

Contents

9

Swami Vivekananda

Swami Vivekananda's Birth And Childhood

Babu Vishwanath Dutt was a Barrister of Calcutta. His wife Bhuvaneshwari Devi was a gentle and religious lady. For years the couple remained childless. When the Barrister was busy in his work, his wife who was religious in nature. filled her time in going temples and religious singing sessions.

Bhuvaneshwari Devi's firm faith in God proved very helpful, to get happiness in her life. One day she realised that she was in the family way. Babu Vishwanath Dutt heaved a, sighn of relief. He prayed to God that it should be a male child.

On 12th January 1862 the baby arrived. Bhuvaneshwari Devi's happiness knew no bounds. To Babu vishwanatha's delight it was a male child. Bhuvaneshwari Devi Started fondly calling her child "Billay". Later the child was formally christened, 'Narendranath'.

Bhuvaneshwari Devi continued her religious work. The day was rocked to the runes of religious Songs and Bhajans, and breathed in a spiritual atmosphere. In afternoons women would gather in large number, of Dutt mansion to sing hymns or to hear 'Katha'. The child Narendra had a very sensitive mind. He had millions of Questions to ask from everyone regarding things and situations around him.

Babu Vishwanath had his own horse buggy and driver. Whenever Narendra rode the buggy with his parents he would pester the driver with questions all the way.

Often the driver was asked to take Narendra for a ride; then he had to brace himself for a barrage of questions. The illeterate driver would answer the questions according to his own level of knowledge. When Narendra was a four years old, Mr.Pathan Khan had came to their home.

Narendra asked him 'what are there' in his bags ? Mr.Khan answered that,

"A lot of sweets" Narendra said,

"I like sweets."

But Khan knew well that Narendra's mother was religious and orthodox.

Mr. Khan was in confusion. He Knew better about the religious nature of Bhuvaneswari Devi. But the kid's face flushed with sweet expectations and his pleading eyes swept away all the hesitations and other considerations.

Mr.Khan gave varieties of sweets to Narendra. Then Narendra ran away to his mother, to show the gift given by his Pathan uncle.

Bhuvaneshwari Devi was too shocked to react instantly. The sweet given by a muslim was a poison for their religion, so she understood. As the stood thinking about how she could take away the sweet from her child in diplomatic way;

Narendra walked up and put a piece of the sweet in her mouth. Bhuvaneshwari Devi was horrified as if someone had put filth in her mouth. It all happened so suddenly. Her orthodox mind recoiled. She spat out the sweet in disgust and ran to the water pitcher to wash her mouths.

She returned to find her son eating the remaining piece blissfully. It enraged her. The imphal defiled her piety. She flew at him and spanked his hand to brush of the remaining particles of the sweet. She slapped on the cheek of her kid, and screamed "You have desecrated my religion'.

Nerendra was stunned. He could not understand, what wrong he had done. There was no one to console him or to answer his questions. He sat on a chair and tried to think what could be wrong with him.

Once before his mother had thrashed him when he had touched the women who used to sweep and map their house.

Narendra-The Cute Child

The Barrister, Mr. Vishwanath was surprised that his son's inquisitive mind was being troubled by many questions. The Barrister had little time to spare to hear the long story of his son and to provide answers to his questions. So he decided to pass on the problem to his buggy driver. The buggy driver was fearing to the long drive, because of barrage of questions. The sight of the kid frightened him. He could see that the kid had become a pressure looker of questions. He used to gritted his teeth and used to say, "come Billay Master ! Let us go for a ride."

Narendra always like to lisson about stories. He liked Hanuman Katha. When the kid's primary education began at home, Mr. Vishwanath Dutt decided that his kid henceforth be called by his christened name, Narendra Nath, or Narendra only. A tutor was engaged to teach Narendra letters as was the custom in upper class families.

The teacher was a well educated elderly person who was held in high esteem by the Dutt family. He wanted Narendra to concentrate on his primer book. But Narendra's mind wandered over other subjects, he wanted to know about and his curiosity demanded answers of.

The teacher would not entertain extracurricular queries. It resulted in Narendra playing pranks and naughty games with the teacher to let his steam of which kept building up in his mind. The teacher would often find his things like cane shoes or his bag missing. Then the missing articles would appear at strange places miraculously.

One day teacher's can was found missing. The teacher appeared very vexed. The sisters revealed that it was the doing of Narendra, when they found their mother worried. Narendra's sensitiveness was perhaps the manifestation of his deep spiritualism born within. He on his own used to sit in meditation. His meditation was no act. Other children were merely trying to copy him.

One day the other kids saw that a cobra snake stood with his hood up behind Narendra. He was lost in his meditation unaware of the fact. On being informed, Bhuvaneshwari Devi ran to the spot and found the snake departing the spot, to her great relief.

What irked young Narendra was that the adults were not straight forward who avoided the telling truth. Their thoughts intentions, speech and the acts were not in harmony. It greatly disturbed his mind. Once it happened like this. There was a tree in a ground near the colony where the Dutt house was situated.

The children used to play monkey games of climbing and swinging by its branches. Somehow an elderly person did not like it. To scare away the children he warned , "kids stay away from this tree. It is a hunted tree. A horrible demon resides on it." He devours or puts a curse on anyone who disturbs this tree. So for your own good stay away from it.

Narendra was among the kids who used to play on that tree. He did not believe in demons or ghosts. So one day when the elderly person was around, Narendra got up on the tree inspite of the protests of his mates, who believed in the ghosts.

Narendra announced, "See friends there is no demon on this tree, or it would have devoured me." The elderly person departed being outwitted.

When Bhuvaneshwari Devi learnt about it, she was enraged. Being an orthodox woman having a penchat for blind faiths she eared for her son. For her, demons ghosts, evil spirits, and witches were real threats to mortals.

Upon Narendra's arrival she flew in a rage. In sheer anger she slapped her son. It greatly hurt Narendra. He knew that even his mother was not being true to him. She was infact afraid of ghosts, demons and evil spirits.

Narendra felt a great revulsion against the falsehood of the adults. In its hear he spoke some very bad words to his mother which shocked the entire family. At that time the Barrister Mr. Vishwanath was also at home. He too heard at those of fending words. He did not react violently to the misbehaviour of his son. He desided to make his son realise his folly in a different way through a subtle psycholigical rebuke.

He wrote down all the bad words used by Narendra against his mother on a wall in bold letters under the caption Narendra uses following words for his mother. When Narendra saw it he was very ashamed of himself and duty aplogized to his mother and the other family members. He never again used any foul words against his mother.

The reason of his anger, the falsehood and hypocrisy of the adults was never understood. No one tried to fathom the depth of his hurt feelings.

Narendra's Education

Narendra completed his primary education at home. He was enrolled in Calcutta Metropolitan Institute for normal education and higher studies. The School and the company of other students greatly agreed with Narendra. He made a lot of friends who used to go to his house.

Narendra became a very active youngman. He studied, played, learnt music, rode horses and took great in physical exercises. Very soon he had a muscular body which surged with energy.

Narendra was a conscientious boy. His physical power found release in wrestling, friendly fights jasting and pushing around. In the mean while his mind also kept pace with physical growth.

Being a student Narendra always maintained the moral character. Once by looking his morality, the teacher was moved and praised Narendra's moral character.

At the age of 14 Narendra suffered a health set back a stomach ailment. No medication worked. It worried Bhuvaneshwari Devi. At that time Vishwanath Dutt was living at a far off place Raipur situated in the central, India. On a professional demand, he could not able to comeback.

Mr.Vishwanath was very worried at hearing the news of his son's illness. He called his wife and the son to leave Calcutta to live with him at Raipur. There was no School at Raipur. Bhuvaneshwari Devi was worried about her son's education, But her husband reasoned.

"Dear, our son's health should get priority over his edcation. The education can wait. First we must have him in health again."

Narendra was very happy in Raipur. Because Raipur was situated in central India set in scenic beauty with salubrious climate. All around were lush green forests, velvety pastures, enchanting hills, and rivers, cascading water falls, bird calls and animal calls. The new scene brought dramatic change in the health of Narendra of the better.

Narendra felt his soul at peace in the company of the nature. He would go in the forests for long walks, and sit at home. Scenic point to gaze at the beauty of the wild.

Fluttering leaves and branches of the trees, swaying bushes sweet calls of birds, rippling waters flushing streams whispering winds, sweet smell of the soil passed on spiritual lessons to the heart of Narendra. He would sit under trees for hours under the spell of the nature, imbibing its spiritual message.

For the teenager Narendra walking through the winding hill paths that tunnelled in to the thick forests felt like pilgrimages. Then Narendra started going akara, the traditional wrestler's gym. The push ups and other exercises resulted in growth of his body in wide chest, broad shoulders and muscular arms and legs. He looked like a wrestler for more mature than his years .

Narendra spent two years in the company of his father. During this period the father and son came closer. Mr. Vishwanath was a good look. He could prepare several delicacies and enjoyed being on kitchen. He taught Narendra cooking. Narendra did not feel shy of asking uncomfortable questions to his father.

Narendra's Higher Education

Narendra joined Calcutta Presidency College for further education at the age of 18. The College was based on western styles, education system and the medium was of course English. There was nothing Indian about except dark complexioned pupil.

The main aim of the education was to produce people servile to the British who would make the desks and the posts of the British Raj. The scenario pained and hurt young Narendra. He was no more adolescent but was away from the adulthood. Agewise he was in no-man's zone. But he was a thinking youngman. His mind automatically analysed the social and cultural goings on around him.

Narendra never worried about himself. He was worried for his mother and the sisters, who were solely dependent on the Barrister's income.

Narendra new in his heart that becoming a family man and carrying on the burden of the family traditions was not his aim of his life. He had become a very conteplative young man. That was the time when the western influence was increasing in India. Social evils and castism had ruined the native society, and religion.

Reformist movements were petering out after eighty years of struggle. After joining the College he fell ill again it was as if. Whenever his mind felt sick it passed or suckness to his body.

So Narendra again had to disrupt his education to regain his health. He stopped going to the College. Then he joined general assembly College. Here he developed serious interest in music, cricket and wrestling.

The subject he took to heart was philosophy, because it was the most likely platform, where the answers to all the questions that had troubled his mind since his early childhood could appear. It was not only the principal but other teachers too who admired Narendra's quest of inner knowledge.

His classmates and other students too who came in contact with him got immensely impressed by his knowledge led others on the road to the learning.

Narendra's venture to seek the ultimate knowledge was not only confined to the College only. he used to go to every congregation or to meet sages, holymen, gurus, scholars or philosophers. He would listen to their sermons or speeches. He used to ask question "Sir have you really seen God, or felt his presence or sensed his existence ?" The answers he got were not clear cut.

Mostly they were long winding explanations, without focussing on the specific issue which revealed their own confusions and lack of clear vision. It disapointed Narendra.

Narendra used to sing a special song, that was infact the prayer of his heart. The Song was to the following effects.

"Where's the sun that will drive away the gloom of my heart. Where is the holy light to brighten up my mind dull and innert. It is somewhere at the feet of an exalted spiritual guru.

To whom I should surrender and forget myself and confussions too. O Saint Exulted ! Come to show me the way.

Lead me to God, whose power holds everything in sway.

The Universe, times, dimensions, speeds and all forces "Speeds and all forces at play."

Narendra had sung the song with such emotions, and so

melodiously that the entire gathering was spell-bound. The words had come straight from his heart.

Once Narendra went to meet Saint Ramkrishnadev. Narendra touched the feet of the Saint. Who put his hand on Narendra's head to bless him. A current of ecstasy ran through the body of Narendra. At the very movement Narendra decided that Ramkrishnadev, would be the one and the most very hearted guru for him.

Narendra's Meeting With Ramkrishnadev

Once Narendra was singing a hymn, with all his heart. Saint Ramkrishnadev asked Narendra by hand signal to approach him.

Narendra respectfully touched the feet of the Saint who put his hand on Narendra's head Narendra felt a new experience.

Ramkrishnadev said, "Youngman ! why don't you say something ? I want to hear you speak."

Narendra heard him speechlessly. Narendra again touched the feet of the saint and departed. He had gone through a strange experience. It was like a spiritual Union between two persons. No one else could realise the importance and depth of the feelings of the two for each other created by this meeting.

Strange telepathic sympathy vibes experienced by Narendra on his first meeting with Ramkrishnadev made him wonder if he was the person for whom he had always been praying for to guide him ?

After attending M.A.exams, Narendra decided to go to Dakshineshwara to meet the Saint who had stirred him emotionally on his very first encounter.

Narendra With Ramkrishnadev

Narendra decided to go to Dakshineshwara to meet Saint Ramkrishnadev. Same time his family members declared that he was old enough to get married. Narendra refused. He was marooned in the sea of spiritual and emotional confussions.

According to him, the society was largely plagued by the social evils, blind faiths and illeracycum-poverty. A foreign culture, education, religion and political rule was rushing the country. Therefore Narendra decided to meet Ramkrishnadev to seek guidance.

Narendra set out for Dakshineshwar along with many of his friends. When Narendra reached the abode of Ramkrishnadev, he was over joyed to see the young man. He had not forgotton Narendra.

Ramkrishnadev got up and held Narendra's hand. He said,

"Now I will find my peace as you are finally here."

Ramkrishnadev had started crying like a child which shocked and baffled Narendra.

Ramkrishnadev said, "you are no ordinay soul, Narendra. I realised it the first day. I set my eyes on you. I know that you extra-ordinary destined to be a great."

Narendra had heard that Ramkrishnadev, was a devotee of Kaali and showed blind faith in the Goddess.

The Saint was often dancing before the idol of the Goddess Kaali entranced. In those days all the reformists were dead set against the practice of idol worship.

Ramkrishnadev a man with child like simplicity could not be play acting or defrauding He deserved a closer look.

Narendra met many holy men and scholars. He used to ask the question:

"Sir, have you seen God ?" But No one had the answers to his simple questions.

All the books of philosophy and the religion he had read had failed to clear his confusions.

One day early in the morning Narendra set out for Dakshineshwara to see the Saint, Ramkrishnadev.

Narendra went straight to him and stood before him as a life size question mark.

Ramkrishnadev looked at him curiously and asked.

"Narendra Do you want to ask any question ?"

Narendra said,

"Yes, I want to ask you a question."

"Then ask."

Narendra folded his hands and spoke "holy sir, tell me frankly have you seen God?"

Ramkrishnadev, smiled and said, "youngman, Yes, I have seen God as I see you clearly standing before me now."

That was the first time when someone had replied to his question straight forward. The Saint was making a confidence claim. There was some murmur among the people present. Some looked at the Saint somewhat in surprise.

Ramkrishnadev further added, "Son, I can even introduced to him. You will see for yourself, "But there is a condition. You must come to me after serving your relationship with home, family, society and worldly trappings. It requires full and total commitment.

Narendra was overjoyed to hear it. He felt that at last, he had found the spiritual guru, he was looking for to lead him. But the condition put by the Saint was not easy to meet. But his mind was made up that, Ramkrishnadev was the man he would seek guidance from as soon as he was free of all the wordly obligations.

Deep Devotion of Narendra, Towards Ramkrishnadev

Narendra started going to Ramkrishnadev more often that not. He was becoming deeply devoted to the Saint. But, he was to blind follower. He openly criticized the Saint for, many of his childish acts, and wailing like a woman, when emotionally moved.

Many of the disciples of the Saint disapproved of the outspoken behaviour of Narendra. Narendra ignored their frowns. He stood by his outspoken righteousness and held his belief in selfrespect, hard meditation and penance.

One day Saints eyes were boring into the eyes of Narendra who was feeling like being hypnotised. As the sun went down the Saint got up suddenly and put his right foot on the youngman's shoulders. It sent Narendra through an astonishing experience. He felt his surroundings, things connected to him, and all relationships melting away leaving him alone in a vaccum.

Narendra's frightened mind echoed that,

"What are you doing to me a Saint ? What ! I had my family and parents.......sisters.........what is happening to me ?"

Then, the Saint Ramkrishnadev removed his foot off his shoulder and placed his right hand on the young man's chest. Narendra found himself returning from the strange vaccum to the normal state of mind and the surroundings.

Narendra realised that, Ramkrishnadev was no ordinary being. The Saint was indeed a psychic or a miracle man, May be some kind of a divine person of spiritual world. Narendra's mindset also changed with that experience. He was no more egoistic or selfconscious about his possessions and the attributes. The broom of humility had swept his mind clean. Narendra felt at complete peace in the company of Saint Ramkrishnadev.

Narendra's Philoshical Thoughts

On the education front Narendra had studied all the works of the leading Philosophers of India and the foreign lands. To him no philosophy looked complete in itself. Every philosophy had gaps and weak points. A meaningful and purposeful thought could emerge only after together the good points of each thought or religion.

Dutt house most of the time hummed with distracting activities. There always were friends and clients of his father around who were in the habits of talking loudly and debating in legal jargon.

For his own benefit Narendra created a hybrid philosophy by borrowing the process of reasoning from the west, the idea of common God from the samaj, wisdom from Buddha, mercy and nonviolence from Mahavira, and simple emotionalism from his guru Ramkrishnadev.

Narendra hired a room in another street (just far from his home.) and furnished it with bare necessities.

Vishwanath Dutt wanted his son to become a famous attorney of Calcutta. The parents were just waiting for the nod of their sun to set them off an a bride, hunting drive.

Vishwanath Dutt had put his son, to work as the assistant with famous attorney, Mr. Nimaich and Babu to learn the primary lessons of the 'legal' world.

Narendra lived in his hired room like an ascetic. He did a lot of philosophical thinking and Meditation. No indulgence in any luxuries or Mery making for him.

Going to meet Ramkrishnadev at Dakshineshwara was his daily ritual. The company of the Saint was very spiritually inspiring experience for Narendra Ramkrishnadev himself had become very fond of him.

One night Narendra was playing his music at one of his friend's house, when the sad news arrived that his father, Mr.Vishwanath Dutt, had passed away suddenly due to heart failure.

Narendra ran home. The whole family was in a shock. His mother and sisters were beyond any consolation. He himself was dazed.

Narendra's grief was loaded by the fast that he was the provider of the family, Narendra had always dreaded this situation. His father had never saved money for the future. With him died the very source of the income of the family. In no time the family fell on bad days.

Narendra knew not what to do. he became a picture of misery. He went out looking for some work. His friends and well wishers deserted him. The relatives would turn their faces to the other side whenever they sighted him. No one came to help Narendra. He was desperate.

Narendra began speaking out of his mind. He aired his doubts about God being fair. The people heard his new thoughts in shock. Many believed that Narendra had turned an athiest and passed on barbed remarks.

As we know, in our society the people push further down a person who is down already. The people started ridiculing him and making fun of him. It angered Narendra and multiplied his misery. These were his most frustarting days of life. He was getting nowhere but down.

Narendra's Grief

In difficult situations maximum number of people choose the easy way to blame God.

Narendra could not understand why God was punishing him? He had done no wrong. In fact, from his very childhood, he had been singing his praises and dancing for God.

Narendra reviewed the entire situation. At last he realised that blaming God won't solve his problems. It was clear that he was missing some point or viewing the problem from a wrong angle in the negative frame of mind. Narendra decided to seek the help of Ramkrishnadev to see the situation in a correct perspective.

Narendra went to Dakshineshwara to see the Saint. RamkrishnaDev, noticed the entry of Narendra.

The Saint was shocked. Because Narendra looked like a scarecrow, lean and gloomy figure. In an instant reactions Narendra's eyes worked up tears and he started sobbing uncrollably.

Ramkrishnadev rose up and patted Narendra on the head comforting him.

He said, "son, I feel the grief you are suffering. You were not born to go through such a pain and misery of life.

In the material world humans create sufferings for themselve, by their own narrow minds and shallow thinking.

Only spiritual thought of India can redeem the mankind

from the misery. Our message must go to the world before it's too late. I know that you have the capacity of see the world through my eyes.

The mission is waiting for to be taken up by you. It is time you left the family to god's care and accept the responsibility you are born to bear."

Narendra was only overwhelmed. His life was regaining its meaning in the Saints words. But he was very confused. Ramkrishnadev embraced him. Narendra felt at ease. He spent the night there, to clear his mind in the benevolent presence of the Saint.

Meanwhile another problem was waiting for him. Some greedy relatives had filed a case in the court of law disputing the claim of Dutt's over their house.

Narendra lied down in bed paralysed by the new developments. His mind was benumbed and the heart is silently cried. Narendra's mother was screaming deliriously. She was tearing her hair. Narendra was shocked. His mother's outburst and grief pierced his heart.

Narendra went again to see Ramkrishnadev. The Saint heard the tale of his woes. The Saint was a great believer in the power and the divinity of Goddess Kaali. So much faith had he in her, that he thought she could solve any problem of a devotee if prayed in earnest.

The Saint advised Narendra "Go and ask for anything you wish from Kaali Ma. She will solve your problem.

Narendra stared at Ramkrishnadev. He knew that the Saint had blind faith in Kaali Ma. He himself had no such faith. For once he thought that he would become a laughing stock if he had that. But he decided to do it just for honouring the advice of the

Saint. He went into the Kaali temple and stood before the idol of Kaali. He did not ask for any wish. He felt it very embarrassing to do it. If Kaali was really a devine Goddess she should read his mind and know his wish he reasoned. After spending some time before Kalli idol mutely he returned to the Saint and told him what had taken place.

Ramkrishnadev said, "I can see that you are not born to beg for worldly spoils. These petty things are not in your nature. Narendra realise yourself. My son awaken your at man and redeem the world."

Narendra fell at the feet of Ramkrishnadev who for his disciples was, '**Ramakrishna Paramahansa**.' Narendra returned home having made up his mind to solve his domestic problems at his own level in practical way. The very next day a lawyer gave him a job of translation work in his office.

Narendra decided to fight the legal battle regarding his property himself without hiring any lawyer. Narendra became very busy youngman doing translation work looking after the family as the man of the house and pursuing his property case in the court of law. After doing all the work he would go to his guru.

Meanwhile Ramakrishna Paramhansa was suffering from throat cancer. His body had been slowly dying. After meeting Narendra he had become a content man. In Narendra Paramhansa had found his worthy heir. He was quite sure that Narendra, would carry the torch of his thoughts further and would keep its a light for posterity.

The Last Days of Ramakrishna Paramhansa

In Calcutta a garden house was hired when the Saint was put up and meditation was given. It was an ideal place for recuperation. Good location and treatment appeared to work. Ramkrishna Paramhansa's condition stabilized. He was kept in Calcutta, a garden house, for several months.

Legions of his disciples looked after him taking turns. Many of his followers, were men with families and jobs to attend to. They managed to steal as much time as they could to serve their spiritual guru and to be near him.

Narendra was devoting all his spare time to the service of his guru, Ramakrishna Paramhansa. The Saint guru was bravely going through his pain making least possible, bother for others. He did not like being a problem and avoided seeking help.

One day the Saint was in a good mood and full controll of himself. He called all his disciples to him. It was apparent that the Saint wanted to make some important announcement.

Ramakrishna Paramhansa said, "Sons ! In this auspicious hour, I wish to pass on to you the holy mission of the spiritual liberation and uplifrment of the people. I firmly believed that our philosophy is the sole hope for mankind which deserves to be made a mission. I want to initiate you through proper custom into the mission."

The Saint further said, "I admit that all of you are very good humans. who live to the high moral values. Let me tell you that you are the sweet rewards of my spiritual penance of the entire life.

All of you are very capable and very deserving Yet I have chosen Narendra to lead our spiritual mission, because has a little extra thinking mind and exceptional leadership qualities. The initation rite will make you the ordained missionaries of our spiritual philosophy bound to live by its rules and regulation. I will ask Narendra to come forward to me.

Narendra came forward, and he was asked to take an oath. Others followed him to go through the same ritual. Each one of them was given a saffron rob and the mendicant's alms bag. All the disciples stood in line headed by Narendra.

Ramakrishna Parmahansa surveyed the field with satisfaction and proclaimed, "You are my spiritual force. Narendra is your leader, your commander."

I wish the commander to lead the spiritual force in to the battle to defeat the armies of evil and the forces of darkness namely narrow mindedness bigotry, blind faiths, Material craving and all kind of exploitation. Your valiant commander hence forth shall be called **"Swami Vivekananda."** All the disciples bowed to Ramakrishna Paramhansa including Narendra.

Swami Vivekananda had put on his saffron rob and turban. His face glowed in the Saintly attire. Now all the disciples of Ramakrishna were brothers of the mission. They greeted their leader Swami Vivekananda, who humbli accepted the salutations of his brothers.

For Ramakrishna Paramhansa Vivekananda was the essence of his lifeful of penance and spiritual quest. Ramakrishna Paramhansa's condition, suddenly aggravated on the night of 15th August, 1886 and he breathed his last on the same night, liberating his soul, A great spiritual guru had departed. His disciples were grief stricken and looked spiritual orphans.

Vivekananda was beyond consolation. He wept like a child. The beacon of his life had gone out. He again found himself floundering in darkness of pain and despair. Mournful silence prevailed even after the funeral rites of Ramakrishna paramhansa. All of his disciples continue to be shell shocked. For days Swami Vivekananda did not utter a word. His mind stayed benumbed and blanked out. It look a long time for everyone to regain the normal state of mind and communicate with one another.

All the disciples, decided to construct a monastery, in the memory of Ramakrishna paramhansa, which could serve as their headquarter to plan the spreading of the spiritual message of the Saint.

The monastery came up at Varah Nagar. The ashes of Ramakrishna Paramhansa was put in a bronze Urn and ceremoniously taken in to the monastery and installed as the holy relic of the Saint. Vivekananda led this ritual and the monastery was declared open.

Narendra As Swami Vivekananda

When Ramakrishna paramhansa passed away, Swami Vivekananda took charge as the head monk. Regulated life doing penance, recitals of religious scriptures and devotional singing-cum dancing were activities the inmates kept themselves occupied with. No missionary tasks were taken up or planned.

Mean while Vivekananda won his court case. For him it was the great moral victory and solution to all his wordly problems. Vivekananda placed all the property papers and the verdict copy at the feet of his mother, and prayed with folded hands.

"Ma I have completed my duty. I owed to you and the family. This large mansion can earn enough money to take care of all your needs and that of the sisters.

The society and the country is calling me for a bigger mission. Release me from the family bondage and allow me to take leave you."

The mother stared at her son. He was no more a kid who used to pester with silly questions. A stranger stood robed Swami whose face glowed with some inner aura and magnetic eyes bore through her to gaze at a mystic point younder. There was no trace of her Billay. !!

She had lost her Billay in the mystic saffron robes. Tears rolled down her cheeks as Swami beat down to touch her feet. She put her hand on the hand of Swami in the gesture of blessing. Her lips mumbled, some unintelligible words.

Swami Vivekananda rose up bowed his head again and turned his back to her. The departing figure did not look back. When Swami Vivekananda arrived in the monastery the brothers were lost in singing and dancing oblivious of the happenings around.

Vivekananda's arrival went unnoticed. The music drew him into its quick-sand magic and he too began swaying entranced. He was dancing for joy being liberated from the wordly bondages. The dancing went-on all through the night.

In the morning Swami Vivekananda revealed that he was free of all the wordldly trappings. The brothers were overjoyed. Vivekananda was heartily congratulate by them.

Then onwards Vivekananda kept all his time to the monastery and pay attention to its working. Swami Vivekananda wanted to set up a definite mission. It required to be strictly regimented to in fuse the spirit of purpose and duty.

He decided to lead by example. He got up before dawn and woke up others saying, "wake up O sons of light, the sun invokes you."

Swami Vivekananda had developed certain habits in which other disciples had to follow him. In the evenings he used to go for a stroll among the trees. One evening he was taking a stroll at sunset time. The merrily twittering birds were flying homewards for a restful night in their nests. They appeared happy like bundless of contentedness so free of cares and worries and so liberated. He sadly wondered, 'why the people of our country are so different from the other creatures of the land ? Why are they doing slavery of others ?

Why a spiritual culture of India was being trampled upon by a cheap materialistic western culture ? Why is God allowing this Does he want it to be so ?'

Swami Vivekananda's Thoughts

According to Swami Vivekananda, 'No God, support injustice and naked exploitation. The countrymen themselves are responsible for their own plight. God can't help the people who are hell bent on destroying themselves by prepetuating illeteracy, poverty social evils, castism, slave mentality and defeatist mindset,' The people are resigned to their fate to be the fodder of the cannons of vested interests.

People cling to their blind faiths to justify their misery. The need of the hour is to awaken the people to their own spiritual power and legacy.

'The bones of the society, the casteism, untouchability, illiteracy blind faiths and the strange hold of the orthodoxy must be dealt with. It will lead to a society really great free of hunger & poverty.

'Then and only then the masses will resume their spiritual tradition and repel the forces of materialism.'

Swami Vivekananda came to the conclusion that he must inspire and work for the spiritual awakening of the people to liberate them from the miseries they were suffering.

Then Swami Vivekananda returned to the monastery for good out of disillusionment with the life there which had become a routine with no aim, sooner or later others too were bound to get fed up with rituals serving little purpose.

Ramakrishna paramhansa wanted to make free the people of narrow thinking, backwardness evils poverty, and diseases through spiritual upliftment.' Swami Vivekananda said to other brothers,

"Brothers you may remember that, our guru Ramakrishna paramhansa had entrusted a special mission to us and to me in particular to lead spiritual renaissance.

Building up this monastery was not our sole aim. It was merely stepping stone. For the time being my usefulness here is over. Don't shed tears or grieve for me.

I wish you to stay here and carry on the traditions of our late guru. We all have separate roles to fulfil to realise the dream of guru. Now my role is to go out and find the meaning of what he had said to me."

Swami Vivekananda departed from the monastery as his brothers bid him tearful farewell.

Swami Vivekananda's Expedition

Swami Vivekananda decided to visit prominent pilgrim centres to meet the religious heads, priests, the pilgrims and the people to gauze the depth of the religion at work, at that grassroot level. Swami Vivekananda had a muscular body. And his face glowed. His eyes had hypnotic charm.

Swami Vivekananda visited pilgrim centres of Bihar and U.P.Where he met religious scholars priests, theologists, holymen and devotees. He talked to them about primary concerns of common people, poverty, hunger and their exploitation by vested interests.

He pleaded for the liberation of the masses from their suffering. To his shock, Swami Vivekananda found that the religion people were not all bothered by the problems of the masses. For most of them it was not their business to worry their heads off for the wretched people.

In Kashi Swami Vivekananda stayed at the ashram of guru Dwarkadas. There he met brother Akhadanandaji who was a loved disciples of Ramakrishna paramhansa, who had made Kashi his home.

Swami Vivekananda found Guru Dwarakadas' own views very educative and enlightening. In Kashi the religion was at its ugliest. The poor masses were being treated as fodder of the cannons of the upper class vested interests with the people of religion, acting as their hatchet men. Then Swami Vivekananda went to Ayodhya.

In Ayodhya Swami Vivekananda interacted with the people of religion. Some were mildly agreeable to Vivekananda. Some of them were orthodox but not as bigotic as the priests of Kashi and were not hyper reactive. Later Vivekananda visited all the places connected with events of Lord Krishna's life. The journey tired him. He stood at Hathras. He had not arranged any place to stay or meet anyone in that town. He was in a fix. The railway station master invited the monk to be his guest.

Swami Vivekananda's assionate appeal for spiritual revival of Indian society. so deeply in fluenced Sharachandra, that he resigned from his past and became the disciple of Vivekananda for life. In the real sense he was the first person to join his spiritual revival crusade.

Sharachandra was duly renamed, Brother Sadananda. Vivekananda took him to Varah monastery and introduced him into monkshood through proper rites.

Sadananda served the Ramakrishna Paramhansa mission till his last breath, and remained a trusted disciple of Vivekananda.

Vivekananda stayed in the monastery for a year. During this period he revised all the scriptures and other books available in the monastery. He analysed his experiences of the various pilgrim centres and did into spection.

Swami Vivekananda wanted to meet Sharda Mata, the wife of late Ramakrishna Paramhansa, who was still alive and lived in a village situated on the bank of Bhagirathi river. He wished to seek her blessings in his spiritual endeavour.

The very sight of her evoked a great feelings of reverence in Vivekananda. She was a Saintly figure, the feminine dimension of Paramhansa. Vivekananda introduced himself and revealed his mission of spreading the spiritual message of Paramhansa, Sharda Ma was very happy, at meeting her husband's disciple. She offered her good wishes and blessed Vivekananda.

Swami Vivekananda decided to go to hills where there were some piligrim centres, besides the inspiring, mountains, forests snow and natural beauty. Since ancient times hills and forests have nursed Hindu thoughts and philosophy and seasoned them.

Countless theologists, writers, saints, sages and thinkers took shelter in the hill forests to clear their minds, polish and cut their thoughts, and ideas into precious gems of wisdom.

Swami Vivekananda too wanted the hills to provide spiritual guidance to enable him to chartout his path. He visited the snow-storm washed piligrim sports of Kedarnath and Badrinath. Then he descended on a small and quiet hill town of Almora. With the forests arround and the views of snow caped peaks were soothing to the eye and peace giving to the mind. A religious merchant named Badrisahai hosted his stay.

Talking walks on the serpentine hill paths walled up greenery and snow peaks peeping younder enchanted him. The salubrious climate as a dessert in the nature's menu. Swami Vivekananda felt perfectly contented in that lovely back drop.

The Seminars On Spiritualism

According to Swami Vivekananda, Escaping from the dreadful realities in the safety of the peace of the remote hills was a sin for a spiritual crusader.

Swami Vivekananda walked down through the hills. Then he met a famous disciple of Ramakrishna Paramhansa, named Swami Turananda. Many other followers were also there.

Over the years of Paramhansa had created number of followers, who were living at various places.

Vivekananda held discussion with them on the subject of spiritualism, religions, their guru's legacy and their duties. Vivekananda was still in a confused state. The discussions were proving helpful. Gradually a line of action was emerging in the mind of Swami Vivekananda. He decided to meet all the people of power, Kings, Rajas, Nawabs and Landlords to discuss with them the condition of the society, and the country.

During 1981, in certain circles, Swami was becoming a familiar name. His boldly fresh interpretations of the scriptures and wise thoughts made a great impact.

Swamiji's outlook was pleasantly secular. Hindus and Muslims flocked to his discourses alike, In his view all the humans were brothers and children of the same God. Swamiji oposed dividing humans in sections based on caste, creede or religion. The natural calamities, poverty and hunger, made no distinction between Hindus and Muslims.

Swami Vivekananda advised the people not to play in the hands of religious bigots. His brave new thoughts became the talk of the town.

The King of Alwar talked to him for sometime to get the feel of the Swamiji's thoughts and beliefs. Then Raja remarked "Swamiji you are very learned and a man of wisdom."

Swami Vivekananda went on to Jaipur and Ajmeer. The secretary of the Raja of Khetri one day paid a visit. He was narrow minded communal person. He brashly poked a question "Swami, you are a Hindu Monk, why are you staying at Muslim's?"

Vivekananda said, "Because I believe in God, and his omnipresence. A monk is trained to see him in all human beings. I am staying with my brother who is another child of God. We are human beings first, and other things after that."

The Secretary was shup up. He invited Vivekananda to Raja's palace. The Raja wanted to see Swamiji as he had heard a lot about him. Raja personally came tosee Swamiji. He asked point blank, "Swamiji can you tell me what is life "?

Swamiji Replied, "Life is a inner power of a person that is relentlessly trying to manifest itself. Quter forces keep it pressing inwards to keep it trapped. This on going struggle is the life." The Raja had no admit that there was something very different and original about Swami Vivekananda.

Swamiji moved on after visiting several places, in Rajasthan and Gujrath, he reached Porabandar where he stayed with Pandit Panduranga. Swamiji's fame had preceded him. Swami Vivekananda delivered a brilliant speech, which was heard in great owe. His understanding of Hindu philosophy was astonishing.

In Baroda he stayed with Diwan Mani Bhai for about 20 days, during which he gave discourses and met several Rajas, Princes of Gujarat, Kathiawar and Bombay areas. Swamiji met Bal Gangadhar Tilak while going to Poona from Bombay by train. Their Conversation brought them closer as their aim was one.

Tilak was doing same thing on political level while Swamiji was working on spiritual level. Swamiji stayed at Tilak Bhavan in Poona for several days and their confabulations continued. Upon resuming his journey Swamiji reached Belguam. Then Swamiji went to Mysore, thinking and wandering about it.

The King of Mysore gave enthusiastic welcome to Swamiji. His fame as new exponent of Hindu philosophy and scriptures had spread around. Every one wanted to hear Swamiji. The meeting was attended by Pundits. scholars and theologists. His talk on Vedanta was deeply appreciated by all. After the speech even his detractors and critics became his admirers.

The King asked Swamiji about, the exact plan he had in Mind. But Swamiji did not eleborate. He said, "the idea is still at embryonic stage. I will let you knew when it takes shape." The King assured Swamiji that he would finance his compain and meet all his expenses of any endeavour he would take up. Swamiji thanked the King for his Generosity.

Swamiji's Expedition To South India.

Armed with an introduction letter from the King of Mysore Swamiji reached Cochin and stayed at Trichur as the state guest. From there he reached Madurai. At Madurai he came in contact with Raja Bhaskar Setupati of Ramanad.

Swami Vivekananda was fast growing in stature as the

beacon of spiritual wisdom and leaving everlasting impression on the people he came in contact with.

He went to other places and won more admirers and made legions of followers. At the sunset of 1892 Swami Vivekananda walked on foot from Rameshwaram to Kanyakumari, the southern tip of India.

Swamiji felt lifted at the sight of the sea. The setting sun rays were painting the rippling waves in golden and number red colour, presenting a fascinating picture.

Swami Vivekananda climbed an a huge rock that extended into the sea and sat down to meditate. His eyes were closed but his inner vision had awaken that saw his country. In his dream he found that his country became free as a bird flying high singing merrily returning to its spiritual nest.

Swamiji returned to Ramnad and departed for Pondicherry a french colony in India. He contacted youth and gave them its message. Swamiji confided his admirers his wish to go Chicago to attend the World Religions Conference. The idea was greatly liked by all because Vivekananda could show the world sublime face of Indian philosophy. Swamiji's followers at once got busy to make arrangements for his travel.

The Chicago Religious Conference

The Chicago Conference began on 11th September 1893.

An American, lady Mrs Hail took Swamiji inside the conference Campus and arranged for his food and stay. The Conference began on 11th September 1893.

At zero hour Swamiji's name was announced. He gracefully got on the stage and faced the mike. His impressive figure and glowing face made possitive impression on the audience.

Swamiji began his speech.

"My brothers and sisters of America........."

A thunderous flow of words came from his heart as he resumed speaking.

"The religions do not teach hatred. Not do they divide people. A religion brings hearts closer."

Religion is another name of love, compassion, sympathy, mercy, brotherhood and mutual respect. The man is born to create with love. One should not make religions an excuse for destruction or expansion by force. A religion must teach to live and let live. If religions are used for confrontation, the human race will go astray......"

When Swami Vivekananda finished his short adress the people stood up to give him a standing ovation.

His address was so appreciated that the organisers were forced to include him in the list of main speakers. When Swamiji left the stage, the newsmen from U.S.A and Europe Mobbed him. The next day, the news papers printed his speech prominently.

The World Religious Conference became a seminar on Vivekanandas thoughts. This made him a much sought after figure respected and loved.

The Sabior Ashram And Swamiji's last Breathe

Swamiji met Mrs Savior. They met like mother and son and comforted and consoled each other. Swamiji's stay at the ashram became a news. The people started going to the ashram to meet him.

Swamiji started the publication of Prabhudh Bharat, a periodical from the ashram. Due to work overload, his health deteriorated alamingly as the cold winter set in. He was at once shifted to Belur monastery. There his condition stabilized.

Swamiji was always worried about the progress of the mission which was falling short of his expectations and goals. When Swamiji's health worsened his favourited German disciple, Nivedita hovered around him. She used to calm him down when he got agitated at the inaction and the apathy of his countrymen.

One day Swamiji sat down in lotus position, to meditate. Swami Vivekananda's lips quivered, with a child like whimper his rolled to one side. Swami Vivekananda had passed away, on the night of 4th July 1902. The great flame of spirit was put off !

10

Dr. Bhimrao Ambedkar

The Untouchables In India

In our country once upon a time the 'untouchables' were forced to live in the outskirts of village in dirty and un hygienic surroundings. These people were also called by different names like Atiudras, Avarnas, Namashudras etc. These people were denied the use of public wells. They were not allowed to send their children to the schools where children belonging to higher castes studied.

Untouchables were not allowed to enter Hindu temples. The higher caste people treated the untouchables worse than beasts. Those people were very poor. The men wore only a cloth at their waist a blanker or, their shoulder and walked with a staff in their hand. The women wore saris above their knees.

The men worked on low jobs like picking the garbage, drawing water from the village tanks for the farmlands. The other names of these people were like sweepers, water boys, scavengers etc. The other Hindus did not touch these people.

The conditions were so worse that, the barbers never cut their hairs and the washermen could not wash their clothes. People believed that they would become unclean if the shadow of these people fell on them.

The higher caste people made them to wear a particular type of dress, eat particular type of food, and wear particular type of sandals. Maximum number of these people had chosen their occupation as the cobblers. And some others came-basket weavers, and some of them were farm labours. The society called them as "untouchables".

Dr. B.R.Ambedkar's Birth and Childhood

Bhimrao, the son of Ramji Sakpal a serviceman of the Indore army, born on 14th April 1891. He was the fourteenth child Bhimbai (his mother) and Ramji Sakpal. Bhimbai was a beautiful lady. She had a happy married life and had fourteen children. The fourteenth child was named as Bhim who really left his mark in the Indian history. When Bhim was only two years old his father retired from military service, and came down to Dapoli in Konkan from central India. A calamity hit the family when they came to Dapoli, When Bhim Rao was 6 years old his mother was passed away.

After Mother's death, he and his two brothers, Balaram and Anand Rao, and two sisters Manjula and Tulsi, besides his father remained in the family. All his other brothers and sisters had already passed away. Bhimrao was brought up in the care of his aunt, Latoo Meerabai. Bhim's father Ramji Sakpal was a gentle and good fellow. He led a religious life. He was a devotee. He prayed to God both morning and evening. Their house was an ideal home. Devotional hymns and spiritual lyrics were heard in house every morning and evening.

Ramji used explain stories from the epics Ramayana and Mahabharata to his children very interestingly. He used to sang hymns of Maratha, saint-poets like Moropant, Mukteshwar and Tukaram. In childhood only Bhim developed a command over the Marathi language. Ramji never touched liquor or meat. In 1892 the Government stopped the in take of lower castes to the Indian army.

The Mahar people protested strongly against this orders. Ramji took the leadership of this protestaion. Mahar people submitted their petition to the government with the help of justice Ranade. Bhim completed his primary educaion at Satara and began to study in high school.

Once Bhim was drinking water at a public water course. Some high caste Hindus saw him there. They dragged him away from the water course, and beat him mercilessly. The crowd warned him not to repeat the performance. That was not the end of the story for the boy. Society had yet to teach, some more lessons.

One day Bhim went to barber shop for haircut. The barber was suspicious of the boys caste. He suddenly put down the scissors and the comb, and asked Bhim to go out of the shop as he would not cut his hair. He told Bhim that even the buffalo shaving was a much more holier affair than tonsuring the human being.

Bhim was quite shocked over this incident. He returned his home, where his sister cut his hair. These incidences made an indelible impression upon Bhim's young mind that was so strong and full of intelligence. Under the pressure of such maltreatments, Bhim was cultivating a spirit of patience.

Different Incidences In Bhim's Childhood

Bhim was fearless and resourceful boy. One day he went to school in soaking rain. His dress was dripping. His class teacher was a kind hearted man. he was moved at the sight. He asked his son to take Bhim to his home and give him a hot bath. Then Bhim was brought back to school and made to sit in the classroom half naked.

There was another teacher in the school. His surname was Ambedkar. He loved Bhim very much. Bhim drew his surname Ambedkar from his native village Ambawade. The teacher liked Bhim so much that he changed his name from Ambawadekar to Ambedkar. Bhim and his elder brother had to carry gunny bag with them on which they squatted in the classroom and that too in the corner.

Most of the teachers would not touch their note book for of being polluted. Bhim's father moved his children to Bombay. His daughters were already married and lived in Bombay.

Bhim and his brother got admission in the Maratha High School. Bhim made a notable progress in his studies. He was well grounded in translation exercises by his father. This method increased his vocabulary of the English language. In the school Bhimrao proved to be a bright student. Bhim's father managed son's education even though he had a limited income.

Bhim was sent to Enphinston high school which was one of the leading high schools in Bombay. Bhim studied hard.

One day teacher called Bhim to solve an Arithmetic problem. Bhim was happy. Because he knew how to solve the problem. The teacher called Bhim to the black board. As soon as Bhim came to the black board. there was an uproar in the class room. In fact the caste Hindu children used to keep their tiffin-boxes behind the black board. They feared that Bhim's presence near the black board will pollurte their food. So they rushed to the black board and lifted their tiffin-boxes before Bhim could reach the Black board. This incident hurt Bhim. The school life of Bhim was full of hardships. In the school Bhim and his elder brother were not allowed to take up the Sanskrit language, as the second language.

Untouchables were not allowed to read Vedas, and other holy scriptures. Some students even had to take Persian against there will, Bhimrao studied himself partly with the help of some pandits after few years, he developed a command over the language.

Bhimrao's Marriage

When Bhimrao had passed his matriculation, his father began to look for a suitable girl for his son. Finally Bhim's father selected a girl who was barely ten-year-old. The marriage was consumed in a strange surrounding which was in reality a market place. At night, after the shops were closed the marriage parties of bridegroom and the bride occupied two separate places in the open shed of the market. A big stone slab and a few little strone platforms served as benches. The marriage was celebrated with due ceremony and ritual. The whole market place which served as an open marriage pandal was cleared by the marriage parties before the break of dawn.

Bhim's wife's name was Rambai. She had belonged to a respectable family. She was the daughter of Bhiku Walangkar who was a potter at Dapoli.

Bhim's College life

Bhimrao Ambedkar joined Elphinston college in Bombay. Where he passed his Inter Arts Examination. Maintaining college fees was not an easy thing for Bhim. The help soon came from, the rule of Baroda. Sayjirao Gaekwad who had earlier announced that he would support any worthy untouchable by financing his higher studies.

Bhimrao got another help from prof Muller of Elphinston College, in the shape of Books and clothes. Bhimrao had to face certain problem regarding castism. The hotel keeper (in college) who was a Brahmin many times refused to serve tea and snacks to Bhimrao. He would not even give a glass of water to Bhim for the fear of desecration of his religion. For Bhimrao education was worship. Studying was the greatest joy of his life.

Bhimrao wanted to develop a master over books and various subjects. He aimed at preparing himself for a new role in his life. Bhimrao was looking upon the possiblities of a great career. He passed his B.A.examination in the year 1912.

After his graduation Bhimrao Ambedkar landed a job in Baroda. He was appointed on the post of a lieuteant in the Baroda state Forces. He had hardly served on the post for about fiifteen days that he received a telegram informing him about the illness of his father. He left Baroda immediately to look after his ailing father. All hopes of his father's recovery from illness had died down.

The sinking eyes of dying man moved on to his son for the last time, he moved his land over the back of his son and his hands become motionless.

Bhim's father had left his heavelnly abode. February 2, 1913 was the saddest day in Bhim's life. The grief of Bhimrao was limitless. The words of consolation failed to sooth his heart.

Bhimrao had no alternative but to support himself by his own initiatives and efforts. He decided not to return to his old job.

In the meanwhile, Maharaja of baroda had announced sending some Indian students to the U.S.A. for higher studies, at Columbia University. Bhimrao was also selcted by the Maharaja along with a few other student for higher education.

Bhim's Arrival In New York

Ambedkar arrived in New York in the third week of July 1913. The life in New York was free for Ambedkar. To Ambedkar the life at Columbia University was a revolution. It gave him many experiences of life and broadened his mental horizon.

Ambedkar's was one of the finest examples of self-help, self-respect and a revolt against the philosophy of helplessness, which makes the ignorant people resign themselves to their fate and accept their position at will of God.

Ambedkar was all alone in the great city of New York. He had no acquaintances except for a few Indian students. He realized it very well that, he well have to create a niche for himself if he had to survive in this world of cruelty and prejudice. He could have attain it by developing his native worth and for that he would have to work hard to achieve his goal. Bhimrao directed all his attention to his studies. Really speaking Ambedkar left all his idleness. There was no time for it. Even the through of going to theatre did not come to his mind. He tried to every hour for his studies.

The subjects of his study had included Political science, Anthropology, Sociology and Economics. At last after two long years of hard work Ambedkar passed his M.A. Examination. In 1915 Ambedkar was awarded the degree for his thesis "Ancient Indian Commerce." He also submitted another thesis to the Columbia University.

The title of the thesis was "National Divident of India-A History and Analytical study." The thesis was accepted by the Columbia University. He was awarded the degree of Doctor of Philosophy by the University. Later an extension of the thesis was published by a reputed publisher of London. In this thesis

Ambedkar had traced the growth of the financial arrangements from the act of 1833, under the Imperial system.

The students and professors gave a special dinner in his honour. After successful completion of his studies at Columbia University Bhimrao turned his attention to the Universities of London. He reached London in the middle of June 1916. He took his admission in the Grays In for studying Law. For the study of Economics he chose London school of economics and political science. When the time was over (scholarship) Ambedkar was called back to India.

The Difficulties Faced By Ambedkar

After the arrival of Ambedkar in Bombay a meeting was called to felicitate on his great academic achievements. Ambedkar did not attend the meeting.

According to an earlier agreement with the state of Baroda, Ambedkar had to serve the Maharaja for ten years. Ambedkar was first appointed as the military secretary to Maharaja. But there also his status as untouchable became a headache for him. He was treated by his staff and peons in a most disgraceful manner. The peons did not like to hand over his files and other papers to him. Not even a glass of water was offered to him.

The peak of the humiliation came to him when he was asked by the parse community leader to vacate the city hostel where he was staying and go somewhere else. The reason, he was an untouchable and his stay in the hostel would defile the whole building. He brought this matter to the notice of the Maharaja of Baroda. But there was no use ! Ambedkar was now all alone without any help from anybody. He returned to Bombay and sought help from his long time well wisher Kaluskar into the matter.

Kaluskar made some staying arrangements for Ambedkar with a professor at Baroda who being of progressive ideas agreed to keep Ambedkar as his paying guest. But as soon as Ambedkar reached Baroda station at the instance of Kaluskar, he received a note from professor requesting Ambedkar not to come to his house as he said, his wife had strongly opposed the proposal. With no other alternative left to him. Ambedkar again returned to Bombay bidding farewell to the state of Baroda.

The I.N.C. And Untouchables

During 1917 and 1918, a new consciousness was gradually taking place in the Indian National Congress, regarding the existence of depressed classes as the party wanted to take the support of the untouchables for the Congress-league scheme.

In consideration of the Congress-League demands, the two conferences which were held adopted two different resolutions, the one appealing the government to protect the interest of the untouchables, by granting them the right to elect their own representative to legislatures and the other impressing upon the caste Hindus to remove all disabilities imposed upon the untouchables.

Later on March 23rd 1918 the Depressed classes Mission Society of India held its first conference on all-India level inviting among others, His highness the Maharaja Sayajirao Gaekwad of Baroda who presided over the conference. Ambedkar did not associate himself with the conference. He was sceptical about the movement going on for the uplift of untouchables.

Ambedkar appealed for the post of professorship on Sydenhem College of Commerce and economics and also hot appointed on it to teach political economy. He accepted the post in the year 1918 in tthe month of November. with in few months

Ambedkar became popular among the students of economics. But even the holy atmosphere of learning in the college could not mitigate the evil of untouchability. Some of his colleagues objected to his drinking water from the pot reserved for them.

In the meanwhile Maharaja of Kolhapur who took great interest in the removal of untouchability. Later Ambedkar came in close contact with him. He started fornightly paper 'Mook Nayak', with the financial help given by the Maharaja.

Ambedkar wrote forcefully articles in the paper denouncing the Hindu Society for it's illness. Ambedkar wrote that Herculean effort was needed to save the depressed classes, from slavery and poverty.

In March 1920 Ambedkar presided over a conference convened by the untouchables at Mangaon in the Kolhapur state.

Ambedkar drew a handsome salary as a professor, but still he lived a frugal life. He lived in the same old two room apartment in the chawl. His wife Ramabai as usual ran the daily chorus of the house. She was always dutiful and self respecting woman.

Ambedkar's London Tour

Ambedkar's immense thrust for knowledge was unsaturated. So he left for England again after arranging finances for his travel and other expenses for his studies in London with the help of Maharaja of Kolhapur.

In London Ambedkar began his studies at the London school of economics and political science. He lived at a semi-boarding house conducted by a lady. She was harsh and terrible. Here again Ambedkar spent most of his time in reading books.

In London Museum he used to spend long hours in reading books. He would be the last man in the museum to be driven out by the watchman after the museum was closed in the evening. His research work was not only confined to the museum. He regularly visited India office library in the university of London and other city libraries noted for books on economics.

Ambedkar was living with minimum of expenses on himself. He did not spend on restaurants or theatres. His expenses on dresses and fares were rate. He trudged in the great metropolis from one place to another.

After submitting his thesis to London University, he went to study at Bonn University. But he was called back to London by his professor Edwin Connon who asked him to revise his thesis as portions of the thesis, had given offence to the imperialist examiners. As Ambedkar had no money to extend his stay in London, he returned to Bombay and submitted his revised thesis, after a few days from Bombay. The thesis was accepted and he was awarded the degree of Doctor of science.

Ambedkar had dedicated his work to the memory of his parents for their great sacrifice for the sake of his education.

The Upliftment Of The Untouchables

Ambedkar always used to think about the upliftment of the untouchables. Ambedkar borrowed money from one of his friends and obtained his Sanad, to start practising as a barrister in 1923.

The stigma of untouchability haunted him even in the unhelpful surroundings in the high court. But he was not disappointed. He worked hard to get name and fame. The fast changing world brought about a visible change in the mental and moral outlook of the depressed classes.

The prejudiced ideas of untouchability began to change giving place to progressive-ideas. The rise of the textile industry improved the economic conditions of the labour classes. It helped the depressed classes as well. An important resolution was moved by S.K.Bole, which was adopted by the Bombay Legislative council in the month of August 1923. The resolution aimed at promoting the interest of untouchables.

Bole warned that if the government did not take effective steps to improve the social conditions of the depressed classes, they might take recourse to satyagraha. The resolution recommended that the untouchable classes be allowed to use public water places, wells, schools, offices etc.... The Bombay government directed the authorities concerned to take effictive steps in this regard.

The Bombay muncipal commissioner was also requested to take similar steps for giving effect to its resolution with regard to the places under his control.

Ambedkar convened a meeting on March 9, 1924 in Bombay to consider the establishment of an institution to promote the interests of the untouchables and placing their grievances before the government. Accordingly An Institution known as "Bahishkrit Hitakarini Sabha" was established with the aim of protecting the rights of depressed classes, and promoting the education among the untouchables.

Ambedkar's Aim

Ambedkar's aim was to establish a powerful state on the foundation of oneness and unity of the Hindus. His initiatives powerful as he himself had emerged from amongst the untouchables. He was well aware of their social barriers. For over a decade he had experienced and studies their appalling poverty. As Ambedkar arised as a leader for untouchables, they got phenomenal energy.

Ambedkar did not approve of the organizations and institutions which were established in the name of depressed classes. These institutions and organizations functioned to suit their own purpose. Ambedkar did not join the national independence movement.

This was because he had no faith on certain national leaders. These leaders were doing lip service to the nation by crying for democracy and independence, while their real goal remained to grab power after the exist of the British from India. Ambedkar aimed at the progress of the untouchables for getting then civic religious and political rights. Ambedkar had the noble aim to rejuvenate the gasping Hindusim and to restore it's honour. He gave a clarion call to the untouchables to unite and demand their rights.

Ambedkar's, "Bahishkrit Hitkarini Sabha" came the ray of hope for the untouchables. In the begining it was meant for, high school students of untouchables. The sabha bore a major part of expenses which were incurred by the students. Under the supervision of sabha the students also conducted a monthly magazine named, 'Saraswati Vilas'.

In the begining Ambedkar had to move almost all alone, unsupported by their the press or by any other institution through the hamlets village and towns. Bhimrao Ambedkar presided over the first conference of untouchables at Malwa in Ratnagiri district in April 1925.

Hindus V/S Untouchables

The Untouchables got a boost in their struggle for social equality when Ramaswami Naiker a Non-Brahmin leader sponsored satyagraha or passive resistance at Travancore state.

Ramaswami Naiker, with other followers entered a Hindu temple Ambedkar himself was shocked over the incidence. Being a lawyer Ambedkar had started gaining popularity. He was engaged in a very important law suit. It was a suit against three non-Brahmins. They were charged with libelling the Brahmin community by publishing a pamphlet in which they had declared them, as the destroyers of India.

Ambedkar argued the case and won it. This was the resounding victory for Ambedkar. The efforts for rejuvenation of the society were at time nullified by the reactionary forces. Ambedkar had an uphill task of fighting such forces.

Ambedkar was leading a simple life. He was putting up in the same one-room improvement Trust Chawl. People of Authority and eminence came to see him, Ambedkar used to say that, he had decided to devote his life to the service of the untouchables. However he took a part time job as a lecturer in the Balliber's Accountancy Training Institute to teach Mecantile law. He served this institute for almost three years. When Ambedkar lost his dearest son Rajaratna, he fell in deep sorrow.

He wrote one of his fast friends, "......we have in all buried five precious children, three sons and a daughter.....all handsome children. My last boy was a wonderful boy.....with his passing away life to me is a garden full of weeds." During his hard days a sense of helplessness creeped into his mind. Herrassed men of depressed classes came to him for legal advices. He heard them with great patience and gave them legal advice free.

In the 1927 Ambedkar was nominated to the Bombay legislative council by the governor of Bombay. Two months later Ambedkar was felicitated by the Bombay depressed class teachers and a purse was also donated to the "Bahishkrit Hitkarini Sabha".

The Mahad Muncipality Committee had thrown open the Chawdar Tank to the untouchables. But the untouchables could not use the tank property because of the hostile attitude of the caste Hindus. A big conference was held in Mahad to protest against the attitude of the caste Hindus. Every care was taken to make the conference a success. People from backward and downtrodden classes came from far and near to attend the conference.

According to an estimate ten thousand delegates participated in it. As there was no provision for drinking water at the conference site, the organizers made it available to the delegates by purchasing it from caste Hindus.

Ambedkar delivered a message to his people saying that no lasting progress could be achieved, unless the untouchables put themselve through a three fold process of purification. Ambedkar further urged his people to agitate against the government for barring the entry for untouchables into army, navy and police.

Important resolutions were passed by the conference. Most of these resolutions were addressed to the caste Hindus asking them to help to improve the social status of the untouchables.

The Rights Of Untouchables

The Mahad Muncipality had thrown open its tank to the untouchables way back in 1924. But the same was not utilized by the untouchables for fear of incurring wrath of caste Hindus who were hostile to this move of the muncipality.

All the untouchables decided to visit the tank and assert their rights. They took along with them leaders of the upper classes when they marched towards the Chowdar Tank.

As the events turned Ambedkar marched to the tank with an army of men and women to assert The civic rights of millions of untouchables throughout the country. This March led by Ambedkar was more significant and risky because this was launch of a ruthless attack to liberate society from its ills, and evil customs.

Bhimrao Ambedkar took water from the tank and drank it. The mammoth procession followed suit and the processionists returned peacefully to the pandal. A few hourse after this event some rowdy elements among the caste Hindus spread communal rumours in the town of Mahad against untouchables. The anti-social elements spread the news that, their religion was in danger and the untouchables were planning in enter the Veereshwar temple. The atmosphere was spoiled by anti-social elements.

Ambedkar rushed to the spot with a few of his friends, and pacified the caste Hindus. He told them that they had no intention of entering the Veereshwar temple. But by then a large number of untouchables had been injured. A doctor was sent for. He came and jeered at the wounded people, and dressed their wounds.

When Ambedkar returned home after pacifying the caste Hindus, he found a hundreds of Maharmen, waiting for him. Their eyes were blazing with anger, and they were ready to take revenge for the attacks made on them. All of them simply wanted their leaders nod in the matter. But the struggle of untouchables was constitutional and non-violent. However Ambedkar averted a serious riot.

After everything returned to normalcy in the city, the police appeared on the scene and arrested few rowdies. Some of them were sentenced by the magistrate to four months emprisonment. The untouchable's first public attempt in the state of Maharashtra was ended. This changed the personal life of Ambedkar to a great extent.

The Orthodox Hindus

After what happened at Chowdar Tank, the orthodox Hindus purified the tank water, which was supposed to have been pulluted by the untouchables by dipping into the tank a spacific number of earthen pots, full of cowdung, curd and milk amidst the chanting of Mantras.

The Orthdox Hindus were not satisfied with what they had done, to untouchables in Mahad. They felt offended and adopted evil methods to harass the untouchables still more. They dislodged them from their lands and refused to sell their corns and even prosecuted and jailed a number of untouchables under false charges. A few caste Hindu leaders supported untouchables civic rights. However the fact remained that not many of them could gather courage to speak openly in favour of the untouchables for the fear of incurring the wrath of orthodox reactionaries. Ambedkar had to face a flood of criticism. He felt a strong need to air his views now. For this nothing was more suitable than publication of a news paper.

Ambedkar started replying to the critics of his movement through the columns of his journal. Sometimes there were fiery exchange of views through the columns of the journal. There were some Hindus who failed to do justice to the untouchables by staying that the society was not prepared for such drastic changes in the matter pertaining to the untouchables.

Ambedkar asked such people why they were fighting for the independence of the country while people as a whole were not prepared for it. He said that hardly one in a hundred, understood the significance of national independence. Ambedkar exposing the selfish views of some people, said that they were the same people, who raised violent protests against the insulting treatment meted out to the Indians in South-Africa. But at the same time denied human rights to their own countrymen.

Ambedkar appealed to the leaders and public at large to transform their sympathies with the untouchables into practically in the day-to-day life of the untouchables. Ambedkar said that the solution of the problem of untouchability depend not in the spread of education but on the removal of selfishness and peculiar fame of mind of the high caste Orthodox Hindus. Ambedkar asked the untouchables to unite their forces for the achievement of their own social and political rights.

Ambedkar's Idea About Equality

Presiding over a meeting at Badlapur in Kolaba district in 1927 in connection with the centenary birthday celebration of Shivaji the Great, Ambedkar dwelt upon the great warrior's different facts of life and told the audiences, that the main reason for the downfall of the great empire was invidious in equality in the social field.

In the same year Ambedkar was nominated no the Bombay Legislative Council. The newly-formed legislative council commenced its working in February 1927. Ambedkar who was the nominated member representing, untouchables delivered his maiden speech in the Bombay council on budget on February 24, 1927.

Ambedkar had a very broad idea about education and equality. Ambedkar said that "If all these communities are to be brought to the level of equality, the only remedy is to adopt the principle of inequality, and to give favoured treatment to those who are below par level.

According to Ambedkar, no real progress could be achieved in the field of education, if this work was given to the teachers, belonging to the Brahmin Community.......

Once Ambedkar fixed up an appointment with the head of the newly built, Thakurswar temple in Bombay and went to see him there. The mob gathered the temple and asked the Ambedkar to get out of the temple. Ambedkar told them that he had come to the temple with the permission of the head and cancelled the interview with Ambedkar. He even purified the temple amidst the chantıng of mantras after Ambedkar had left the premises.

Ambedkar warned the depressed classes that education alone would not solve their problems; they would have to adopt an aggressive attitude. He concluded that, the untouchables must assert themselves by taking water at public water courses and forcing their entry into temples.

Ambedkar always used to ask the question to the government that, why there was no strong government provision for appointing deserving members of the depressed classes to the higher posts in the government.

The untouchables received a blow, when the Muncipality of Mahad revoked its earlier resolution of 1924. Which had declared Chowder Tank open to untouchables. Ambedkar formed a committee with the ultimate aim of reestablishing the lost rights of the untouchables to the Mahad Tank.

According to Ambedkar, it was not possible to always stick to the golden principle of 'Non-violence' Concluding his remarks Ambedkar said, "Truly speaking the law should be non-violence wherever possible, violence wherever necessary."

In the Chowder Tank issue Ambedkar called upon the people to join the Satyagraha in Large numbers and make it a success. The proposed Satyagraha evoked a gale of bitter criticism from Hindu institutions.

Ambedkar replied that since the untouchables wanted to remain in the Hindu fold, they were strungling for their civic rights, and demanding an equal treatment. Ambedkar defined religion as something which showed prosperity or elevation in this world and then salvation.

Ambedkar's Ideology

Ambedkar presided over a conference of the backward and depressed class students in Poona. This was the first effort to bring all the intellectual forces from the backward and depressed classes into closer identify with Ambedkar's ideology and his aims.

Ambedkar exhorted the untouchable women also to contribute to the progress of the community if at all they found some spare time after doing their household work. Ambedkar's firm resolve and his movement began te attract lot of attention of people from all walks of life.

People began to flock to Ambedkar as disciples or as sympathisers. Most of his revolutionary activities were carried out through the social Equality society which was composed of members from all communities. Every member of this society was bound to invite at least once the co-member to dinner. So the class distinction attached to the caste may be totally removed.

In Mahad, the management of Ambadevi temple had expressed it's helplessness in allowing the untouchables to enter temple and play their in view of the traditional customs. A meeting was held. Ambedkar presided over the meeting. Ambedkar in his address said that image of God in the temple was the property of all and should be accessible to all those who wanted to worship it without any consideration of caste or creed. He said that a temple is not defiled by the presence of an untouchables in it.

Ambedkar opposed the idea of a separate temple for the untouchables. He said Hindutva belongs as much to the untouchables as to the touchable Hindus. To the growth and glory of this Hindutva contribution has been made by untouchables like Valmiki. While the conference was going on Ambedkar received a telegram informing the passing away of his brother Balasaheb in 14th November.

Ambedkar was grieved at his brother's death. The conference proceedings were stopped for a day as a mark of respect to the memory of Balasaheb. The news that untouchables under the leadership of Ambedkar would again march to the Chowdar trank, to take water from it, stirred Mahad town again.

The opponents of the struggle held a meeting on November 27, 1927 o chalk out a plan to thwart the attempt of Ambedkar and his followers to take water from the tank. Some Hindus tried to persuade the caste Hindus not oppose the struggle but met with no success. The District Magistrate of Mahad refused to take any against the untouchables.

December 25, 1927

December 25, 1927 was a red letter day in the history of India as it was the day when Ambedkar consumed the old Smiriti to fire and asked for a new one, so as to reshape the Hindutva that will treat all the untouchables as touchable Hindus. The third resolution passed by the conference called for reducing the Hindu society into one class only. The same conference adopted the fourth resolution saying that the preiestly profession should be opened to all those who wanted to be priests and must not be restricted to a selected class of society.

Ambedkar supported the Satyagraha, and he impressed upon the delegates to observe rigid discipline in their action. He asked the Satyagrahies to be ready to court arrest if the circumstances so demanded and once they do so, they must not tender apology or appeal for their release.

Ambedkar said to his people, "My heart leaps with joy to see that you are prepared for launching Satyagraha." The majority of the delegates who had attended the conference agreed to the launching of Satyagraha. Thousands of delegates registered their names for the struggle with in a span of few hours. The delegates had vowed to either capture the water tank, or court imprisonment in the attempt.

The collector was informed about the decision taken at the conference. Ambedkar asked the conference to postpone the struggle. Ambedkar said, "........postponment of the struggle will not mean that we have given up the struggle; the fight will go on........"

A wave of disappointment swept over the conference. But even then there was implicit obdience to their leader's call. The Mahad struggle ended for the time being. But this struggle opened a new era in the country.

Ambedkar's Leadership

Ambedkar's leadership over the depressed classes was more or less established fairmly. He had emerged as an unquestionable leader of the untouchable masses. He had turned in to a savant.

Once again the bonfire of Manusmriti came up for controversy. Ambedkar said that the burning. Of Manusmriti took place only to draw the attention of Hindus, toward the plight of untouchable classes. Ambedkar was always against the views of the caste Hindus, that untouchables had no right to use their temples.

Ambedkar asked them the reason for this discrimination. This was then that the untouchables wanted to construct their own temple at Trimbak near Nasik. Ambedkar said that poets of Maharashtra did never preach directly against the cast system, social inequality and social injustice. Ambedkar wanted that a Brahmin a devotee of God should meet another devotee of God, a Shudra, as gladly as he would have met his own brother. Ambedkar's careless efforts for appointments of talented persons, from amongst the untouchables class to the covered government posts bore fruit when an untouchables was appointed to the post of deputy collector.

The Governor had expressed his displeasure, over, Ambedkar's critizing the government policy in the capacity of a nominated member. Ambedkar had replied that he had said only what was right in his opinion. He had said to the governor that due to the governments' faulty policy even qualified men from the untouchable class were not selected for higher post.

Ambedkar never lost an opportunity to put his views boldly even in the legislative council for the acceleration of the untouchables. He always showed intensity of feelings for the poor and downtrodden. Ambedkar showed his great interest in the introduction of an important bill by tabling it himself. It's sole aim was too amend the Bombay Hereditary officers act 1874.

Ambedkar And Textile Workers

The important activity that Ambedkar engaged himself with was textile workers strike in Bombay, which brought the textile industry's working at a grinding halt for over six months. The workers had struck work to protest against the retrenchment of workers which came into the effect due to the adoption of a new system in the working of mills by managements.

During the strike the untouchables proved to be the worst suffers as they were the poorest of the poor. Ambedkar did not favour strikes because it had given a hard blow to the economic condition of the untouchables. Ambedkar saw the workers strike as a means of achieving some kind of political ends. The only happy recourse that Ambedkar found for his striking people was that they returned to their work. In those time Bole was one of the pioneer leaders in the labour movement of Bombay.

Ambedkar succeed to a great extent in bringing a large number of workers from his community that is untouchables back to their work in the mills.

Ambedkar's act must have caused a great resntment in the labour related political circles because from the day onwards his men began to guard their leader, whenever he moved out of his house. With regard to the Muslim demand for separate electorate Ambedkar said there were other countries in the world where the Muslims were in minority, but they had managed without the benefit of separate electorate and also without any definite ratio of representation allotted to them.

"Then why do they ask for it in India ?........ Therefore these cases fail to carry conviction".

Ambedkar argued that separate electorate is highly objectionable. The joint electrorate with reserved seats is the most appropriate system.

Ambedkar's Popularity In The Nation

Ambedkar's popularity was increasing day by day on the other side, labour conflict was going on. Ambedkar was invited to address a big conference at Chitegaon. Ambedkar's advice given to the untouchables was not taken seriously by the caste Hindus of Jalgaon. They thought it was yet another rhetoric by the leader of the untouchables.

The untouchables held more conferences. They became more hard in their attitudes towards the caste Hindus. They took drastic steps to further strengthen their position in society. They refused to carry away the dead animals.

For this they were harassed by the caste Hindus. Ambedkar asked the caste Hindus to desist from harassing the untouchables.

Arriving in Bombay the first task that Ambedkar took was to open negotiations with the caste Hindu leaders, who had closed all the doors to the untouchables to keep them away from worshiping the image of Ganapati at a public place.

After a lot of persuasion by Ambedkar the caste Hindus allowed the untouchables to worship the image of Ganapati side by side with other Hindus. This was the great victory for the untouchables. Number of times Ambedkar himself experienced the insulting treatment at a school he was inspecting, when he was not allowed by the headmaster of the school to enter the classroom.

The untouchable community taking inspiration from its leader Ambedkar, was not sitting idle. Several of its leaders launched satyagraha to establish the untouchables rights of worshipping the diety in the temple of Parvati in Poona.

Ambedkar, the leader of the untouchables had spent every moment of his life in the service of his people, securing them their civil and constitutional rights wherever the right opportunity came across.

The First Session Of The Depressed Classes Congress

The first session of the Depressed classes congress was held in Nagpur on August 8, 1930, under the presidentship of Ambedkar. Ambedkar in his address to the congress said that if countries like, Hungary, Latvia and Russia, with all their difference in race, language and culture could function as a united community and government and progress, why India could not ?

Ambedkar added, as the fundamental principle of a democratic country involved recognition of the value of it's citizens must be given an equal opportunity to attain his maximum development.

Ambedkar blamed the Indian aristocracy for being responsible for the continuance of the course of untouchability, under which about six crore people were denied elementary human rights. Ambedkar demanded a fair treatment for the untouchable class of India their adequate safeguard in the constitution to their strength. He also denounced the Simon Commission's recomendation that authorized the governor to certify the fitness of a candidate representing the untouchables. He said that it meant that, it was pure and simple nomination.

Ambedkar, referring to the issue of civil disobedience movement and Dandi March expressed his opinion that it was all extremely ill timed. Ambedkar said that a revolution is always for a change but there was every possibility of disaster in the process.

Referring to the independence of India. Ambedkar said that the ideal of the dominion status seemed to be superior. Ambedkar, on his part was never bitter. He based his judgement on realities. He described the British government as the costliest government in the world !

Ambedkar As The Y.S.S. Viceroy Of India

The whole country was in turmoil at the time when Ambedkar left the country for London on board Y.S.S. Viceroy of India. Everybody was not happy, when Ambedkar departing to London to take, part in the conference. While Ambedkar's supporters and the untouchables expressed their gratitude to him for his selfless services to their cause. There were many other especially the congress men who were abusing and cursing those leaders who wanted to cooperate with the British in solving the Indian crisis.

Ambedkar found the political atmosphere in London more conductive to the cause of untouchables. Ambedkar in his forceful speech said that he was representing one fifth population of the British India, the population which had been reduced to the position of a slave. He said that the existing government needed to be replaced with a more responsible and popular government.

He asked, "Has the British Government secured us the right to the well ?".........can we enter the temple now." What the British government has done in this regard ?

He said, "of what good is such an irresponsible government to anybody ?" Ambedkar added, the government did not know about the sad plight of the untouchables.

Ambedkar upheld the demand for the dominion status. He said that to accord social prestige to the untouchables should be the first priority of the government. This can be achieved more easily by the untouchables, provided they are given political power in their own land.

Concluding his speech, Ambedkar emphasized on the need of drafting such a constitution for India which was acceptable by the Majority of the Indian people.

"Let the consent of the people........be the touch of the new constitution." Ambedkar said.

Ambedkar's bold remarks had a remarkable effect on the conference. The delegates were impressed much by his brilliant speech. The newspapers of London described it as one of the finest bits of oratory. His highness the Maharaja of baroda was extremely happy with what Ambedkar had said.

Maharaja invited Ambedkar to a special dinner which he had thrown to his choice friends in London. Ambedkar's popularity had reached a new high Newspapers and even prominent people of London were convinced that Ambedkar was not doubt a great revolutionary and true nationalist.

Ambedkar had become a subject of discussion among the statesmen. Ambedkar employed every source and availed of every opportunity to propagate problems and views of untouchables, to the world and in particular to the British. The end result of this propaganda was, that the world came to know for the first time that, the condition of untouchables in India was worse than the Negroes in America.

Mahatma Gandhi wanted to see Ambedkar and hold discussion with him regard to latter's demands to be made at the round table conference.

Ambedkar went to see Gandhiji. During the discussion Ambedkar told that, all the claim made by Gandhiji and the Congress party, the untouchables were treated worse than cats and dogs. They could not draw water from wells for drinking. They have no home of their own.

Their civil rights were badly curtailed Ambedkar asked what use it was for the party to invest lakhs of rupees on the upliftment of the untouchables when their economic and social conditions still remained poor. Ambedkar told Gandhiji very boldly that Congress was not the least sincere about its professions.

Gandhiji praised Ambedkar for his great patriot feelings. Ambedkar like Vir Savarkar declared absolute political independence of India as his goal.

Ambedkar The Architect Of The Constitution

Ambedkar began to draft the constitution. He was working on it heart and soul. T.T. Krishnamachari in his speech, which he made in the constituent Assembly on November 5, 1948 said, "Ultimately that the burden of drafting the constitution fell on Dr.Ambedkar.... we are greatful to him for having achieved this task in a manner which is undoubtedly commendable."

The draft constitution prepared by Ambedkar contained 315 articles and 8 schedules. The whole constituent Assembly listened to him while he read out of the constitution's salient features.

Ambedkar explaining the form of Government proposed in the draft constitution said that under the draft constitution the president of India occupied the same position as the king under the English Constitution. He presented the nation but did not rule the nation, with regard to the executive, Ambedkar explained that a parliamentary form of government was recommended for the country in the draft constitution as was the British parlimentary executive.

Ambedkar further explained that there was a provision of single citizenship for the whole of India with a single integrated judiciary whereas under the constitution of the U.S.A., there was a citizenship of the U.S.A. and a citizenship of states. Ambedkar said that the conazstitutiion was workable. It was fiexible and strong enough to hold the country united, Ambedkar was paid glowing tributes for his lucid speech and brilliant analysis of the constitution as the chairman of the drafting committee.

Describing article 32 of the fraft constitution Ambedkar said that the powers of supreme court and the parliament in respect to the Fundamental rights of the citizens were the very soul of the constitution.

The Chief Architect of the Constitution Dr. Bhimrao Ambedkar rose to reply to the debate on the third reading of the constitution. He asked the Assembly to accept the constitution as drafted. Speaking about the future of the country Dr.Ambedkar observed that India lost her freedom by the infidelity and infighting of our own people. He cited examples from the history to prove this point.

He said, "It was Jaichand who invited Mohammad Ghori to invade India..... when Shivaji was fightiing for the liberation of the Hindus the other Mahatma noblemen and the Rajput Kings were fighting battles on the side of the Mughal experors.

Ambedkar appealed to the people India to discard castes which brought about separation in social life and gave birth to hatred between castes. The house listened to his speech spell-bound.

On November 26, 1949 the constitution with its 395 articles and 8 schedules was adopted by the constitution Assembly. The Assembly worked further for nearly three years on the draft constitution. There were over 7,500 amendments of the draft constitution. The constitution bestows sovereignty upon the people of India and parliament as representatives of the people carry that sovereignty.

Ambedkar's Last Days

On Dec. 14, 1956 Ambedkar had to go to Bombay to carry out programme of conversion of his followers there. He had also finished the writing of his book captioned. In the evening a deputation of Jain leaders came to meet Ambedkar. They casually enquired after his health and prsented him with a copy of a book, which described Jainism and Buddhism.

Ambedkar was feeling very ill. In the morning of December 6, 1956 Mrs. Savita Ambedkar went to her husband's room to wake him up but it was too late. She found that her husband was no more a denizen of this world. Babasaheb had passed away.

The shocking news of Dr. Ambedkar's death spread like a wild fire throughout Delhi. Soon his followers and devotees in thousands collected infront of his residence at Alipore road, to have a last glimpse of a great man. The body was received at

Santa Cruz Airport in Bombay by thousands of mourners and was taken to Ambedkar's former residence. Lakhs of people had gathered there to have a last glimpse of a great leader.

Leaders of political parties and trade unions paid their homage to the departed soul. Factories, Schools, Cinemas and a number of other private and Government establishments remained closed on December 7. The two-mile-long funeral procession attended by lakhs of mourners started for the Dadar crematorium. For hours traffic came to a standstill. Huge crowed lined a route, people showered patals and garlands over the body which was kept in a truck bedecked with flowers and wreaths with incense burning on all the four corners and a small image of the Budha kept near the head of the body.

More than half a million people witnessed the last rites performed by Buddhist priests. The pyte was lit by Ambedkar's son Yashwantrao. Hundreds of thousands of people embraced Buddhism at the crematorium as a mark of respect to their departed leader.

Ambedkar's death was a great loss to our nation. All the political parties mourned his death. Newspapers described his as valiant and relentless Champion of depressed classes. Growing tributes were paid to him saying that he was an able, gifted and versatile man, who prominently played for over thirty years a vital and varied role in the affairs of the nation.

11

Raja Ram Mohan Roy

Ramakant, a gentleman was the Mukhtar of the queen of Vardaman. He was well versed in maintaining and managing the estates of the queen. Ramakant's wife Tarini Devi, gave birth to a child on 22nd May 1772. At that time Indian society was enveloped with the ill fated customs. There was a lack of education Indians were under the full control of East India Company.

No one dared to raise voice against the Britishers, and also about the ill customs in the society. If someone dared to raise his or her voice against the religion and the ill fated customs then he or she was tortured in one way ot the other.

Pandit Ramakant Roy lived with his family in a village Radha Nagar of Vardhaman district. In 1792 Ramakant Roy got a new house built in Langoor Para. He and his family started living there. Ramakant's son had grown up. He used call his as Rammohan. Jagamohan was Rammahoan's elder brother. Rammohan had only one sister.

Rammohan was a talented boy since childhood. He got well versed in Bengali and French languages at the tender age of nine only. Then he got the knowledge of the Hindi and Arabian languages. By gaining knowledge he was approaching towards adulthood. When he noticed the worsening situation of India and it's people he was very upset. He wanted o remove all the evils prevailing in the society from the grass root level. So decided to educate the society.

In those days due to illiteracy males were unaware of their strengths and females were bond to live inside the walls of their houses. They hid their faces in the veils. Females were not allowed to speak before the elders and older people. They were the slaves of their husbands. If their husbands died then they were also forced to get burned along with the dead bodies of their husbands. They would quietly suffer the tortures done on them by the society. Once there was a mishap in Rammohan's house. His elder brother had died. Everybody in the house was crying bitterly.

Rammohan was a samll child at that time. His father told, crying, "Son your elder brother is no more. He is dead. God has taken him away from us forever".

On hearing this Rammohan also started crying bitterly. That was the first time he had ever seen a dead body. The dead was to be carried to the cremation ground. Indside the house, his sister-in-law was being decorated as newly-wed. The society people were about to burn her along with the dead body of her husband. When Rammohan saw his sister-in-law, decorated as a newly wed women, he was very much surprised.

Various questions came across his mind. Everybody was in deep grief. The dead body of his elder brother was being carried to the cremation ground.

In this procession men and womens were there. Males were carrying the dead body where as females were taking the widow along with them, to burn her live along with her dead husband. The widow was retaliating forcibly to be burnt alive with her dead husband but in vain. She was, being forced by the women to be 'Sati'. She was crying bitterly. A funeral pyre was prepared. The dead body was laid on it. Then the widow was forcibly brought near the pyre.

Nobody was listening to her miserable condition. Rammohan who was in between the crowd was very upset. He went near his father and pleaded. "Father !, please be kind to my sister-in--law. You are the one who can save her."

Rammohan's father did not heed to his request at all. The dead body was burnt by fire. Rammohan's sister-in-law was also burning along withe the dead body. This incident left a very bad effect on Rammohan's heart. He was very much moved by the incident.

From that day itself he took on oath to eliminate the 'Sati' system prevailing an the society. With age this desire become more and more strong. Along wiith this he had an earnest desire to eliminate other evils of the society, also from the grass root level.

Rammohan wanted to transform the society completely which believed in sacrifice of manhood. Tortures done on the people in the name of rituals and customs were on their high and had strong hold over the society. Therefore, Rammohan had an earnest desire to finish their hold from the grass root level so that the society has a totally new face for itself. People would live pacefully and not be thirsty of each other's blood.

Education

Rammohan got his primary education at home. After that he was admitted to a village school. Later he wished to get higher education in Arabic and Persian languages, because these languages were mostly used in the royal court. In patna he seeked higher educatiobn for 2-3 years. After that he come back to his home. Rammohan was so highly impressed by the sufi religion that he started reading the compositions of the sufi poets. After a few days his parents sent him to Varanasi to learn sanskrit language. That time Varanasi was considered the primary cantre for learning sanskrit.

In theVedic books Rammohan felt the presence of Brahma and one god only. When he returned home from Varanasi he was totally transformed. He considered many things as humbugs He had doubts about the true religion. rituals and idol worship.

Hating Idol Worship

Rammohan started hating idol worship. Rammohan's father, was utterly surprised by his son's strange behaviour. He felt highly depressed upon his attitude.

In a few days there developed differences between father and son on the question of religion, ritual and customs. By criticising idol worship through his modern way of thinking, Rammohan created a sensation around. He became a disputed man in the eyes of people. When he severely criticised the 'Sati Pratha' and supported widnow remarriage, then many people turned against him.

Though Ramakant was criticising his son Rammohan, yet he could not stop himself from helping him out as his father. Despite being angry with his son he helped him financially. Rammohan was unmoved by his father's anger. He was firm against all the evils prevailing in the society. Inspite of severe criticisms from people all around, he continued his struggle against all the evils of the society.

Rammohan had a through study of religion, politics, science and economics. He studied each subject with very keen interest.

Besides studying he was continuing with his reforming activities for the upliftment of the society.

In 1800 with the establishment of Fort William College in Kalkata a new chapter began in his life. William Kary was appointed the principal of that college. That college was established to provide education in main languages, to the workers of the east India Company. But after a few days many India and European experts began gathering in the college. People were fortunate enough to know about two different cultures. Rammohan showed his decency by visiting that college. Professors of the college were surprised by his intelligence.

In 1803 Rammohan started working as an officer in East India Company. He got this job because of Thamas Woodford. Woodford was a high ranked officer in East India Company. In their very first meeting Rammohan got the chance of working with him. Not many days had passed when Rammohan's father died. He was highly shocked by this episode.

After a year Woodford was transferred as a Registrar to Murshidbad. Rammohan also went with him, After coming here a change occurred in his way of thinking. Here he started writing about one God only.

Gift For One God

Rammohan wrote his first book in Arabic and Persian languages. 'Tuhfatul Mujahideen'. In Hindi it means-'Gift for one God'. This book criticised firmly those people who believed in non fundamental principles of religion.

Those people feared their recognition. That is why they criticised Rammohan's book. Rammohan was unmoved by their criticism, because he was by then used to such kind of attitude of people. Such kind of criticism gave him inspiration and strength to do revolutionary activities. All the words of Rammohan's book were proving disastrous for the stanuch believers of religion. These people were feeling hurt by this. Being moving in the darkness and illeteracy. they considered Rammohan as their biggest enemy. The reason of this was that Rammohan had proved their centuries long belief in God wrong.

The way he was criticising the idol worship it was not acceptable to any religious person. He suggested people not to worship idols. He believed that even without idol worship one could make god happy with his simplicity and high thoughts.

Rammohan severely criticised 'Sati Pratha' and said,-"After husband's death burning his wife with his dead body is equal to murder. This is no less than a brutal sin. I desire all women to get equal rights as man because she is the one who gives birth to a man. We should honour all women." People were continuing with their criticism against hiim. They never realised that there was how much truth in his reasoning. The way a mirror displays a clear picture of a person, there seemed to be undefeatable truth in his views in the same way.

Once Rammohan was sitting with his friend Kashi Ram, a person came to him with a conch in his hand. He said to Rammohan, "I am selling this conch. It costs merely five hundred rupees. The one who wants can buy it. The buyer will be fortunate enough in his life."

Kashi Ram said to Rammohan, "Friend ! I want to buy this conch. What is your suggestion ?"

Rammohan said smiling. "Kashi Ram see this man. He himself is not a big man. if this conach has not fetched him happiness and satisfaction in life. then how can it provide the same to others. This man is only showing his speaking skills to sell his conch. You can buy this conch, I do not disagree, but friend! This conch will not get you rid of poverty. On hearing this the conch seller went away from there. They both bursted into laughter. Rammohan always wanted the people to be freed from the clutches of those betraying people. He decided to make the people. aware and transform their inside feelings about the cheaters.

The Transformation Of The Society

Transforming the structure of the society was not an easy task for Rammohan. He was very much keen to accomplish his abjective. Some days later he come to know that the Britishers were not interested in transforming the Indian Society.

So he alone decided to eliminate the evils prevalling in the Indian society. He started his campaign against the social evils like, child marriage. Costeism, 'Sati System, torture on women etc. He also decided to fight those widows who had no relatives of their own. He considered illteracy to be the root cause of the evils prevailing in the society. Rammohan firmly believed that illiteracy and ignorance were responsible for the evils in the society which should be removed only by making the society literate.

Britishers did not do anything regarding literacy. The kind of education provided in the schools was not enough to improve the future of the Indians. So Rammohan decided to establish his own school for importing education. Rammohan considered all religions equally important so he had throughly researched all the shastras of all religions.

Various Gods, Goddesses and Ill Fated Customs

In Hindu Society people used to worship various gods and goddesses. Some worshipped Shankar others Hanuman.Some worshipped Durga others Kali. Even today the same situations prevailing in the Hindu society. Hindus don't believe in one God, only that is why there are as many gods and goddesses, worshipped as there are various sections in Hindu society. Rammohan wanted to tell, the Hindu society that, God is only one. Then why worship various gods and goddesses?

Rammohan considered this as superstition. He wanted to get rid of this superstition from the grass root level. So he decided to lit the flame of knowledge inside the people so that they could see the truth hidden in that flame. English was considered as modern language, those days. So Rammohan studied the English language. He regularly studied the English newspaper. This way he got well versed in English language. He could speak English very well as a Britishers.

Even Britishers were astonished by his fluency in speaking English. By reading the newspaper he would know very well that, what was happening, in the outside world. He felt the Indians were not progressing as the Britishers. Rammohan had a keen desire to inscribe new and developed thoughts inside the people's minds. He had accepted this fact that, the people of India were approaching towards the ditch of superstition. because of the lack of rationality.

People of our society think that our sins will get washed away by bathing in the holy rivers or worshipping the peepal tree or by giving alms to the saints. Those who think like this are committing a grave mistake. They can't attain salvation by bathing in the holy rivers. They are wandering in the darkness of suspentition. They have forgotten about likes and dislikes, because of superstition.

God considers everyone equal because he is unique, where as a person is filled with the discriminations be it racial or of untouchability. Every individual has the ability of thinking and taking various decisions, then why do they accept any fact foolishly. If they desire they may accept the truths prevailing in the religious customs. If a human being does not go by the ways of others and followed his own path of truth and wisdom, then no one in the world has the courage to stop him in the path of his upliftment.

A person can progress only by eliminating all the discriminations. There are many rituals and customs prevailing in the society today. Those who believe in those rituals and customs only give way to ill fated customs. They do not gain anything by this. They why do accepted these types of customs ? The reason behind this is that they are forced to accept those customs and they follow those blindly.

Today the most foolish ill fated custom prevailing in the society is that, when a person is not able to perform or do something better then he considers it as God's grace, and tries to hide his weaknesses. This is very disgusting that a person does not fight for his problems. By watching others he goes on entering into the ditch of superstition. If thinks rationally, then he can transform the structure of the society completely.

Rammohan considered the transferring of those rituals and customs to the forth coming generation as wrong which had no scientific base at all. There were some such rituals and customs which contributed only to misleading people instead of giving them proper guidance.

Rammohan firmly opposed these types of customs and rituals and also engaged other people fight against them. People used to talk about religion but their views had no firm base at all. The views people presented were always opposed by others. They themselves did not believe in their views too, as they would bring changes in their views every now and then.

Followers of single religion were always engaged pulling each others legs. If a person joined their religion, then he had to go according to their rituals, and customs.

Rammohan was very much against this. Those who kept themselves away from hypocrisis only could understand the modern views of Rammohan. Today's modern India is standing firmly because of modern views. (of Rammohan).

Rammohan's Fluent English

Rammohan had an earnest desire to learn English. He wanted the dream of modern India to come true. To provide his motherland a higher status around the world Rammohan wanted to acquire various kinds of viewpoints. That is why he chose the English culture, because it was considered more developed than the Indian culture.

In August 1805 woodford resigned from his post. Rammohan also handed over his resignation to the government. Both now decided to leave Murshidabad. At that movement Rammohan got the new of his being appointed as the clerk in the revenue department by the government. A few days later he was sent to Ramgarh. Here he worked under the supervision of John Dighy. Now he had good chance to learn English because all the people in his office were very well versed in speaking English.

In 1809 Mr. Dighy was transferred to Rangpur. Rammohan also got ready to go with him. When Dighy heard, Rammohan speaking fluent English, he started respecting him more than before. All the public coming to Dighy went through the hands of Rammohan. In debates also he used to speak in English. He had a keen interest in the politics of foreign countries, So he read the English newspapers very carefully. Unless he read the newspaper he did not engage himself in other activities. Through news papers he acquired the details of the political and economical scenario of European countries. When Rammohan spoke English people used to gather in large members to listen to him. Eminent English officers used to praise him for his outstanding quality of speaking fluent English.

Jeremi Benthem and James Silf Bakingham were among the admirers of Rammohan. Benthem was considered famous among the British philosophers, where as Bakingham was the editor of Calcutta Journal. To build modern India Rammohan had acquired the knowledge of English language. He wrote many books in English language. Those who read his books appreciated his writing skills. After reading his books Benthem wrote.

"If your book would not have a Hindu name of the author would certainly have thought of it being written by a prominent English writer because your writing skills are highly impressive."

Rammohan had acquired much knowledge. He was considering those points, by which he could transform India into a more self dependent and a strong nation. This was his maiden effective step which could make India modern. He had developed magnanimity for politics. He had become a rational person towards religion. He had a deep knowledge of, Hindu, Persian and Vedanta cultures. He also acquired the knowledge of the Upanishads and the Arabian cultures. The knowledge of those culture had no boundaries.

Rammohan had the solution for every problem, be it economic, political or social. He was now capable of transforming the economic instability of India. Whatever mission he planned, he accomplished it. He brought forward all social evils in the eyes of the people. He was firm in his objective. Rammohan fought in his own way to bring the problems to an end, and thus helped in the progress of the society.

Acts Before and After Independence

The rules and regulations and acts by the Indian government before and after independence to get rid of social evils are as follows.

* Sati Prohibition Act 1829.
* Child Marriage Prohibition Act 1929.
* Hindu women Property Rights Act 1937.
* Rights of women regarding separation and Livelihood Act 1946.
* Special Marriage Act 1954.
* Untouchability crime Act 1955.
* Hindu widow Remarriage Act 1956.
* Hindu inheritance Act 1956.
* Hindu minority and creation Act 1956.
* Hindu Adoption and Livelihood Act 1976.
* Dowry Prohibition Act 1961.
* Citizen Rights safety Act 1976.
* Child Marriage Prohibition Act (rivised) 1978.
* Muslim Women Act 1986.
* Sati prohibition Act 1987.

Hindrance In Women's Education

For a long time women had no rights of attaining education. Education was considered as a means of profession or service, but women were having no rights of doing service.

That was why they were not provided education. Pardah system and child marriage were proving to be a hindrance in their education. Women were not allowed to move out of their houses because people considered, this against their honour and respect. Before independence girls were not found doing service. People dreampt of making groups of girls, but it was not possible due to pardah system and lack of education. Before 1937 women had no rights relating to property.

The condition of woman was not proper in the family life. They were the slaves of their husbands. Their husbands used to beat them. Their parents used to consider them as burdens. So they were married in very young age. They did not feel the necessity of knowing about their likes and dislikes for marriage.

The condition of widows was much miserable, be it mother sister daughter or daughter-in-law. If at the time of travelling any widow came in some one's way it was considered as a bad women. Nobody like to see a widow's face. She was forced to live the life of a slave. Till 1919 no woman was having the right to vote. After that British parliament left the decision of giving the voting rights to women in the hands of the provincial council.

According to the legislation Act, 1935, women were given voting rights according to their education, condition of their husband and properly. During British rule Rammohan initiated steps to educate women. This strengthened the social upliftment. Aftre the Bhakti movement the Christian Missionaries also showed interest in educating women.

In 1824 the first ever school for girls was opened in Mumbai. In the leadership of Rammohan Lord Dalhousie announced that no other changes would develop people's lives except providing education to children. Universities. They were allowed to have higher education in 1887. From that day girls are touching higher skies every now and then. Rammohan had never forgotten his mission. He remembered how his sister-in-law was burnt along with the dead body of his brother. His eyes got wet when he remembered this episode.

Rammohan's Aim

In 1815 Rammohan established the Spiritual Sabha. This was established in Calcutta. Debates on 'Sati Pratha' took place often in this Sabha. The most daring aspect of 'Sati Pratha' was that the widows who did not want to get burnt along with the dead bodies of their husbands were forced to do so. They were tied with the dead bodies. When they shouted loudly, their shouts were suppressed by the loud beats of the drums.

Some widows beaten very harshly when they raised their voice. They were made unconscious by giving some intoxicating drink and then burnt with the dead bodies of their husbands. This was done so that those windows would not claim their part in their husband's property. The organisations working for women's development were as follows.

* Indian Women's Organisation. (1904)
* Indian Women's Board. (1910)
* Indian Women's League. (1917)
* Indian Women's National Council. (1925)

All these organisations made great efforts to educate women. They decided to eliminate the social evils liks the pardah system and child marriage. They raised voices for the moral and material development of women. Apart from this all the organisations get their questions of giving equal rights to women as men, before the government. All of Rammohan's friends were social reformers like him. They joined hands together in support of widow marriage. All the organisations engaged in social reform activities gave the right of widow marriage the primary position.

Rammohan opened up his struggle against evil customs. He wanted widows to get their rights by eliminating the 'Sati Pratha'. In the spiritual sabha Rammohan prepared such a platform upon which everybody raised their voices against the social evils. The debates going on there proved to be disastrous for the supersitions people, who were facing difficulty in saving their existence in the society. Progressive people gave their full support to Rammohan. Firstly very few people were in supporting India modern, but slowly their number began to increase. Many people began to support Rammohan. Among those who supported him were the religious politicians who were somewhat in support of Rammohan's thoughts.

Rammohan made his best efforts to raise their suppressing voices. Some people who opposed Rammohan's condemning their religion, also understood that he was not against their religion but against the superstitions prevailing in their religion.

The Main Aim of The Sabha

The main aim of the Sabha was to give good speeches to the people. Rammohan did not go hand-in-hand with one particular community. Rammohan adopted all the good thing of all the religions. That was why people from various religions became the members of this sabha. When there commenced any kind of debate then many people from various communities took part in the those debates.

Some people hesitated in participating in that sabha, due to social constraints. They had keen desire to take part but had to step backward. Seeing this Rammohan started a method through which any person would ask his question in writing relating to social and religious topics. Rammohan himself answered their queries. In this way Rammohan had to face the debates in public, but he continued to express his modern views in public.

Firstly Utsavananda and Vidhya Vaagish sent their questions in writing to Rammohan in which they had put up some serious questions. Rammohan answered their queries in a straightforward style After this letter writing got a kick start. This went on for many days. Rammohan's answers were sharp and pinpointed. Later Utsavananda's questions and Rammohan's answers were complied in the form of four books.

The author who first wrote his biography made it clear that Utsavanand was highly impressed by the straight forward answers of Rammohan. Those who heard Rammohan's speeches praised him a lot. Utsavananda also praised him. Many representatives of Hindu religion highly praised the talent of Rammohan. People used to get inspired by Rammohan.

The Brahmo Samaj

The Brahmo Samaj was started in 1818 by Rammohan. Brahmo Samaj had a firm belief in the vedas and the Upanishads. The disciples of this samaj spread the knowledge of the Vedas and the Upanishads in the Indian Society. Many social reform movements were taking place to eliminate all the superstitions, prevailing in the Indian Society.

Brahmo Samaj criticised the social evils of, child marriage and "Sati Pratha". To eliminate the religious discrimination and supersition, devotional song troupes were established. They would go around the society and sing devotional songs. They also spread the inspirational thoughts of the Brahmo Samaj. They also did a commendable job may making people aware through media like magazines and books.

One day Rammohan was returning home with his friends from the prayer meeting. On the way he met his friends Chandra Shekhar Dev and Tarachand Chakravarty. Both of them, suggested him not to go to the British prayer hall. We should have our own people hall.

Rammohan liked this idea very much. This was the point for the formation of Brahmo Samaj. Rammohan had discussion about this with his friends. It was decided that, prayer meetings should be organised in a rented house. For 13 years continuously prayer meetings were held in that house continuously. In 1818 Brahmo Samaj was given it's name in that house. A book titled 'Brahmopasana was published for the members of Samaj'.

The credit of all these words goes primarily to Rammohan, and then the other members too. Those days, Adam Saheb was running the unitarian otrganisation. Both Indians and Britishers were involved in it. Adam Saheb was considered as the companion of Rammohan. Due to the establishment of Brahmo Samaj, Rammohan is considered the founder of modern India.

The Aims of Brahmo Samaj

Brahmo Samaj had ignited a struggle against various superstitions spread in India. Because of this struggle a law was passed against "Sati Pratha" in 1829.

Brahmo Samaj tried hard to get the feelings of untouchability from the hearts of the Hindu Society. At that time lakhs of people were stopped from accepting the Christian religion. Inter-caste marriages were extended full support ignoring all the barriers of castism. Many leaders of Brahmo Samaj like Rammohan ignited new hope in the society They pushed forward the nation towards the path of development. One of the social reformist leaders Rajnarayan Bose established 'National Spiritual

Development Society'. The aim of this society was to strengthen the young blood through exercises. So that the youngster one filled with new strength. Vedas and Upanishads were considered as the base of the Hindu religion. Vedas are the primary sacred books of Indians as well as the people around the globe.

Veda constructed with the help of 'Vide' metal is called 'Gyan.' Legends have it that the hermit heard the voice of the vedas from mouths of the Gods. After one thousand years Vedas were complied in the form of a book. Vedas are known by some people as 'Samhita' Vedas are of four types-Rigveda, Samveda, Yajurveda and Atharvaveda. Rigveda is the oldest of the all. It contains 10,000 Shlokas which are known as 'Sukta'. It's each sukta is associated with the name of either a saint or a god. The second base of Hindu Dharma are the Upanishads-Upanishad means- attaining knowledge by sitting near the guru for the attainment of Brahma Vidya'.

Upanishads conatain the knowledge of the Vedas the Upanishads for which the Shankaracharyas had written the Teekas are as follows Ish, Kenkath, Prashna, Manduk, Taitirya, Atreya, Madukya, Brahadaranykya, Swetaswara and Chandogya. Including these the total of Upanishads, has been estimated two hundred. Many books on Vedas written by Rammohan had been published. Through these books Rammohan had strongly condemned the superstitions, prevailing in the Society. Those who had felt their existence in the Society in the name of religion, now were fearing their existence. They called Rammohan as an atheist and condemned him.. But Rammohan was unmoved. He continued suggesting people of worshipping unique God.

The Public and Vedas

Rammohan translated the Vedas and Upanishads in very easy language. The Veda knowledge known to a very few brahmins was now in the hands of general, public through the medium of books. The general public were lightening the flame of Vedic knowledge in their hearts by reading these books. Rammohan's efforts were a severe blow to the people engaged in superstitious activities.

When he translate the Vedas into Bengali language, then the monopoly of the scholars came to an end. This proved to be correct according to Rammohan's Views. The Brahmin society considered him as a religious culprit as he was campaining about the Vedas among all the sections of the society.

In 1816 Vedanta was translated in a summarised way in the Hindi and Bengali languages, which was published in the name of 'Vedantasaar'. As soon as it was published many scholars and Brahmins criticised Rammohan to a very large extent. 'Vedantasaar' was so easy to understand that even the gereral reader was able to acquire it's knowledge by reading it. This way Rammohan gained recognition amongst the general public. People had lot of respect for him. The European missionaries had no full knowledge of vedas. So they began to criticise Rammohan. He could not bear the fact that some body criticise him on the issue of truth.

After hearing their criticism he translated the Vedanta into English language, and got it published in other countries. He got huge success in this. The reality of Vedanta left the criticisers spell bound. After some time, the European missonaries also started thinking in his favour. The Society was progressing towards enlightment. The hypocrites were unable to stop the society, from progressing.

The number of criticisers of Rammohan was much more. They blamed him as an atheist. In this issue, Rammohan had only one answer. "I have criticised superstition and religion blindless not the Hindu religion. Those who are blaming me of criticising the Hindu religion are first suggested to prove me wrong."

Rammohan kept himself busy with the social reformist movement. He did a commendable job by making the people around the globe aware. After reading the Vedantasaar people's feeling began to change. After the publication of Vedantasaar, European missionaries began to believe in Rammohan.

Rammohan had impressed the Europeans as well as the Americans The intellectual had various discussions on Vedantasara. They concluded that there is clear cut uniqueness involved in Brahmanism.

Rammohan's Views About Common People

Sati pratha had spread to a very large extent. It had caught hold of the society. In this situation Rammohan raised to the reformation and development of the society. All the Hindu sections of the society opposed the social reform movements of Rammohan. At this time nobody supported him. He was left all alone. Very few true friends of his and members of the Sabha were in his support. For the people who left him Rammohan said.

"I am very much sad over the reaction of my beloveds leaving me all alone only because of the criticism of very few people. Today, the number of people who want to hide the truths of life is much more. Only few people today have the courage to enlighten the truths of life. I cannot understand why the people of society want to live in darker side of life ? don't have any answer to this.

There are also those who want to enlighten themselves as well as others with the light of knowledge but they are unable to do so, due to criticism of others. The ones who want to rule freely can't do so because of the criticism of the people. They are superstitious people. They want to spread darkness all around the society because they want to benefit for themselves in the Name of religion.

"If some body wants to change himself then the superstitious people feel jealous against him. They only think that he is going to do something wrong. If someone tries conceal his weaknesses they name it as cannected to religion. But if that person desires he may bring the truth before the world. For this he must have keen desire and inner strength."

Rammohan believed that the one who has an earnest desire to work for the welfare of the people, nobody can stop him from doing so. He was unmoved by any kind of criticisms. What he decided was decided finally. Nobody could change his decision. His every effort was for the welfare of the people. He worked for social welfare by considering the development of the country. He said, "Good crops are needed for happy living. For good crops, good area is required. Good irrigation facilities are required.

Every citizen of the society should leave the feelings of superstition. We have lost much time by living the darker side of life. Today everyone wants to fulfil his desires. For this he needs to be literate first. Without education he would not be able to distinguish between good and bad. If some one works with the knowledge of good and bad then he would be certainly successful in his mission. Something done in the name of customs and rituals is always harmful. I want those people to beware who blindly follow the old customs and rituals even today. They should leave this way otherwise this would make life dark. They should identify themselves, their likes and dislikes.

The social customs which Rammohan criticised were proving beneficial in one way or the other to the staunch believers of religion. The developed western countries accepted Rammohan's views very easily, but the Indian Hindu society was not ready to accept his views at any cost.

Rammohan's Dreams

Rammohan wanted India to lead towards the path of development. For this It was necessary to gather supporters. By this he wanted to make people aware of his views. Rammohan wanted to transform the society through edcation. Those days, there were Sanskrit School for the education of the Hindus. There educaion was imported by keeping in view the ancient principles. This education was limited to Sanskrit language only. The development of the nation was not possible in this way. In those school no subject was taught other than Sanskrit.

Rammohan decided to get the society aware of the subject which would be for the benefit of the society. Seeing the criticism, Rammohan tried to get the support of some English and Hindu scholars. Through their support he made an organisation in Calcutta. This organisation established a University there. In this University education was imparted in subjects like Science Mathematics and politics.

Rammohan wanted social welfare at any cost. To achieve his aim he established an English College by spending money from his personal assets. During this period his criticisers or rivals made several attempts on his life. But Rammohan was firm in his mission. He was aware of the present situation of the country. He wanted to enlighten the hearts of youngsters about education. Rammohan did each work considering the respect of his motherland. He wanted to push India towards modernisation. In his college, studentrs were taught Science, English, Sanskrit and bengali, languages. When anybody debated with him over education he would say, "In Europe people give equal importance to Greek and Latin language as they give, to Mathematics and

Science. If he education of Science and Mathematics can be important for them, then why not for us ?" Nobody had any answer to Rammohan's questions. His vast knowledge would impress the scholars a lot.

Rammohan had his hold on both the Hindu religion and as well as the Muslim and the Christian religions. He was well versed in various languages. Many missionaries were happy with his interest in Christian religion.

Rammohan was very much sure that he would succeed in modernising India. This success was only a dream for him for now. To make this dream come true he strongly accepted the criticisms. History has it that all the social reformists had to face the criticisms, of their opponents. Then also they did not lose hope. They moved to their way of success without any difficulty. Rammohan was trying to awake the people but they were happy by scalping only. They did not want to get their sleep disturbed. They were not aware of the fact that they had darkness all around. They considered them as their enemies who tried to awake them.

Such was the viewpoint of Mahavira also. His criticisers killed him by throwing stones at him. His crime was that he was enlightening the society with truth. Selfish people wanted to put off this lifght of truth. Rammohan was never moved by the criticism. Even after the lot of criticism be did not separate himself from his mission.

Relation With Christians

Rammohan had a thorough knowledge of the Bible. He wanted to know whether Christians followed that which was written in the Bible. Thinking this he established contacts with them. Rammohan talked to the missionaries of Rampur. There established cordial relations between them, which proved beneficial for both. Rammohan used to attend the prayer meetings held by the Christians. He used to get impressed by the teachings of Jesus Christ delivered in those meetings. He wrote a book these teachings titles the Precepts of Jesus. At that time Christianity was more simple than the Hindu religion, but it had the same evils as in the Hindu and Muslim religions.

When Rammohan saw the behaviour of the Christians, he expressed his views about them as follows, "Torturing the people of Hindu religions and to press them to change their religion is not good. The steps taken by the Christians to make the Hindus adopt their religion are unlawful, so they should avoid this."

Hindus and Christians both got angry with him when he said this. Now Hindus were much more against him. His criticisers look him as an atheist and corrupt.. Upon this he commented. "I would not be an atheist or a corrupt by the words of criticisers". When Rammohan's book 'Precepts of Jesus' got published he had to face severe criticism. To pacify his criticisers Rammohan expressed his views as follows. "God is the one who has sent us on this earth, who has given us the strength to fight".

God is one. He has made all the human beings part of happiness, sadness, hope, disappointment and death too. God considers everybody equal be it a king or a begger. He is kind to every one. He has established each and every system of nature in a very systematic way. Nature returns to a person in the way he deserves. Those who are sinners get back worse in return.

The Unitarian Press

Rammohan wanted to establish his own press. In 1823 he established a new press named. In 1823 he established a new press named, 'Unitarian press'. In the initial period he published his own book. Now he was self dependent for publishing of books.

When the missionaries came to know that he had opened up his own press, they become furious. They were already angry with his articles against them. This had added further to their anger. Nobody could lie his revolutionary truths as explained in his articles. The Christian Missionaries wanted join Rammohan in large numbers. Knowing this the other missionaries outsted those Christians from their missions.

Rammohan had a deeper knowledge of Bible. This was the reason that Missionaries were jealous with him but they were afraid of debating with him. To hide their fear they blamed Rammohan of being against God. The missionaries by repeatedly criticising Rammohan, turned insane, and considered the Hindu religion as untrue. Rammohan was against the Hindu superstitions, but he supported the teachings of the Vedas.

Rammohan severely criticised the baseless rituals and customs which were superstitous. He was such a courageous social reformist, who was not afraid of raising his voice against the social evils. Rammohan was against all those organisations which were giving rise to many social evils. He wanted enlighten the people. The way he criticised idol worship in the Hindu religion he also criticised the bigoted Muslims.

The People of the Missionary used to bride, the people of other religions and considered their religion as of law standards. By doing so they wanted to involve them in their own religion. These kind of problems aggravated day by day. But Rammohan was standing firmly against all such adds. The cause of such problems was religion. It was the base of all such evils spread in the society. Those days the condition of Hindu religion was much more worse as compared to the Christian and Muslim. On seeing the Hindus it would be made out that each and every person worships different gods and goddesses. Hindus considered the strengths and power of each God as different from each others.

In 1825 Rammohan established the Vedanta College. Through this college he wanted to spread the principle of uniqueness. Rammohan worked very hard for his organisation. Due to his efforts his organisation reached greater heights.

Rammohan had invented many big fundamental principles. Through these principles he wanted to convince, the people that God is one. He said, "Don't put yourself in a state of confusion by involving yourself in different kinds of worships."

Efforts to Enlighten The Indian Society

Brahmo Samaj Played a very important role in transforming the Indian society. There was no caste discrimination in Brahmo Samaj. In this everyone was considered as the child of one God. There children of Muslims as well as Christians gathered for prayers. Indians as well Britishers gahtered in the prayer meeting. All had the feeling of considering God as one. Here people of every caste and background met cordially with each other. Rammohan was very good at heart. He was kind to everybody. He had no malice against anybody.

Everybody considered his prayer hall as no less than a temple. It was like the depth of sea in which people would dive in the worship of God. There was a feeling of love and brotherhood. His prayer hall was the place worship for people of every caste and religion.

Once an atheist conference was held in Calcutta. Sir Venkatratnam Charied the conference. He said, "Brahmo Samaj has published it's memorandum. It contains the details about the objectives of Brahmo Samaj."

"According to it in Brahmo Samaj only one God is worshipped. Here people worship without any kind of discrimination." Brahmo Samaj acted as a strong link between persons. It taught mannerism and simpicity to people. It helped a lot in developing a personal traits. Rammohan played a remarkable role in bringing together people of different religions together people of different religions and sects.

Brahmo Samaj was inherited with the feeling of universal brotherhood. He believed that if man wakes up then the world would also rise. To accomplish this aim, he wanted the society to get rid of superstition and illiteracy. He wanted to enlighten the spirit of people so as to make his life brighter and happy. To achieve this aim he worked through his life to bring the people together. Rammohan believed that freedom is everybody's basic right. The person would only be satisfied who is free. If some one tries to snatch away someones's freedom then he commits a severe crime.

The Last Journey

During 1833, Rammohan was suffering from financial crisis as well as weak health. His health was deteriorating. Financial Crisis made him very weak. Nobody would dare to raise voice against casteism as Rammohan did. He worked freely for his mission. He worked for the human society inspite of severe protests.

Rammohan spent all his wealth for the welfare of the human soiety. When foreigners faced trouble they would come to him for financial help. Rammohan always stood there for help. Time was ticking usual. Black clouds covered the sky. Destiny was doing it's job on 27th September 1833 Rammohan Roy left for the heavnly abode. He died leaving some of his incomplete desires. He was sad that, India was not still completely self dependent.

Rammohan Roy had destroyed the superstitions from India in his life. He eliminated the social evils from the grassroot level. He stood firmly against all social evils. He had showed a new light to the people of the modern society today.

12

Mother Teresa

The Angel of Poor

Mother Teresa who was an angel of poor (and also rich) people, observed the basic Nature of reality as comprised of multi dimensional continuums of energy which are preceived from a multiplicity of perspectives.

Unbroken continuums extend throughout the fabric of reality, such as the nature, human spirit continuum, the physical emotional mental-spiritual continuum, the unconscious conscious-supra-conscious continuum the individual-group-society nation-world continuum, and the continuum of human values.

The very name 'Mother Teresa' itself indicates, how great the lady was ! she was a beam of rays for the millions of the poor, all over the world, She sacrificed herself for the poorest of the poor.

God never lies in stones and statues-but in humanity. She made it true. Her heart was full of mercinees love, affection. Not only in India but all over the world people recognized her as their ultimate mother.

Birth And Childhood

Mother Teresa was born on 26th August 1910 in a remote place Skopje in Yugoslavia people were astonished by looking the cute female baby. Her eyes were shining.

People did knew, the same eyes in future may give sight for millions of people. Her father Nicholas Bojaxhiu was a grocer. He was building contractor. Some authors argue that, he was running a small provision stores. Her mother was Dranafile Berani She was a devoted woman. The people of Skopje were middle class, and use to speak many languages, such as Albanian, Serbo-croatian and Turkish.

In her childhood Mother Teresa was like a flower bud. In contarast she was called by a nick name 'Gonxha' which means flower bud'. In her childhood mother was neat in her dress and also in her behaviour. [The childhood name of Mother Teresa was Agnes Gonxha Bojaxhiu. So next paragraph onwards let us call Mother Teresa by the name Agnes]

Some characteristic features of Agnes in her day-today life was as follows.

* Agnes always like to chatter with her friends.
* She used to play number of games.
* She loved animals and birds.
* Bird watching was her favourate hobby.
* She use to read number of stories.
* She never liked her friends to over ride her.
* She was fond of sweets.

Agnes was living with her family in a big house with a garden. Many times Agnes use to quarrel with her brother.

Because her brother was also fond of sweets. (His name was Lazar. Agnes also had a sister, Age.)

Lazar had a habit to eat sweet, meats, frequently, Agnes disliked his habit. All the family members of Agnes were closely united Agnes loved her mother very much.

Difficulties In Childhood

Agnes's father was passed away when she was 7 years old. So all the difficulties were should infront of her family. Being a religious lady her mother took on the role of bread winner of the family. When Agnes was four years old first world war broke out. Calamity not only struck her family but all the world. In that small age only Agnes was influenced by the distressed people, poor and the people in difficulties. In that early age she decided to help the needy. When Agnes father, was passed away, both daughter and mother were in deep sorrow.

In the meanwhile her father's business partner deceived her family. Her mother who mader mind had faced all the difficulties and problems. The most important, incident was held once in the childhood of mother Teresa. It was like this. Once Agnes brought a basketful apple. She kept it aside in her home.

Her mother kept a spoiled apple in the basket. WIth in few days all the apples were spoiled. This incident influenced. Agnes very much. She learnt a lot by this incident. She learnt a lesson that, one worst can spoil the whole society. After this episode Agnes never washed her time, in speaking, without any work.

Agnes's mother thought many things to her daughter. Helping nature was carried Agnes from her very early age gave importance for reality. Mother Teresa knew well that, reality is both one and many non-dual and dual, absolute and relative infinite and finite spirit and matter.

Education

Agnes got her early education at the sacred heart church school. Agnes went to non-catholic school. Agnes was a noble student. She was always busy in reading or writing work. The main thing what we have to notice here is that Agnes had born in Roman catholic family. But in strange circumstance she got a time to go to non catholic school. But she was mentally strong.

She was taught in the Serbo, Cration language. In the school only her spiritual ideas were moulded up to certain extent. The first world war made a great influence on her attitude. By observing human sufferings her mind was very much influenced.

The first world warcontinued up to 1919 (5 years) caused lot of loses and sufferings all over the world. As a student a Agnes had developed certain special qualities.

* She was always clean and neat.
* She never talked hard words to any-body.
* She never refused help to any one who depended on her.
* Agnes was interested in parish activities. (After her school hours).
* She was a model student.

Arival of Agnes to India

In her early age Agnes wanted to serve the people. When she expressed her feelings, she had to face opposition from her mother. She convinced her mother and succeeded to join Lore to abbey. (In Ireland). Agnes learnt English first time in Ireland. From Ireland Agnes travelled to India. In 1929 Agnes came to India. She liked to stay at calcutta.

Later Agnes decided to stay at Calcutta, and desired to serve the poor and distressed. With the following motto she began her work in India.

* God loves cheerful giver.
* The fruit of love is service.
* Death is nothing but a continuation of life.

The Bigining of Service

From 1929 onwards calcutta became Agnes's real home. She liked the city very much. She look training from the members of the Loreto order.

Agnes made to sink herself in the service of poor. She joined St. Marry's School in Entally, Calcutta. Agnes began her service without any hesitation. The surroundings of the school campus was cool and beautiful. It was covered by green plants. Irrespective of cast and religions number of girl-students were studying in the school.

All the students in the school. (Hindus, muslims and Christians) liked and respected Agnes. This was because Agnes never turned back white helping others. This was the main cause to earn love and respect from all.

To spend perfect life Agnes fiollowed certain things.

* She (and also other nuns) wore long dresses with black white shawls.
* She liked to eat simple food.
* She liked to spend more times for reading good books.
* She loved poor people and also the distreessed.

* She kept her face always smiling.
* She never worried about her own needs.

Agnes Became Sister Teresa

Agnes was very much influenced by the lifestyle of Theresa Martin, who had worked for the uplift and success of the missionaries. Theresa Martin had died of tuberculosis at on early age of 24. The mode her life and selfless service influenced Agnes verymuch. In the St.Marry's school all the nuns used to talk about Theresa martin. Agnes was also very much influenced.

Later Agnes desired to take the name of this French nun. Theresa Martin. Agnes had faced number of problems in taking Martin's name. There was another nun who had just changed her name as Marie Theresa. This was the little confusion in which Agnes faced.

Later Agnes Changed her name as 'Teresa'. In the meanwhile Agnes learnt Bengali language fluently. So she was called 'Bengali Teresa'. Whereas other nuns called Agnes as sister Teresa. Sister Teresa always remembered the sacrifice of French nun. Theresa Martin sister Teresa never refused help or assistance to any one who depended on her.

The Service For the Poor

Near St.Mary's School where sister Teresa was working. there was a slum; it was called "Motijhil" people bellow the poverty lived in that area.

The dirty water which was flowing in the particular area was causing several diseases for the people who lived there. The people who were living in Motijhil. were almost Uneducated, and unemployed. Men and women of the area, were working hard to meet their needs. The worst sight in the area was bare bodied children who were always used to play in the filthy water.

Number of children were suffering from diseases like fever. smallfox etc. By observing all these sister Teresa decided to dedicate her life to fight hunger, poverty and for the welfare of the destitutes.

Sister Teresa always kept the followning things in her mind.

* Selfless Service.
* Help for destitutes.
* Helping poor.
* Smiling service.

Sister Teresa always believed that God is in selfless service. She was always fond of helping poors. Her motto was smiling service. She practiced it from her young age. While serving poor and destitutes sister Teresa used to think about God.

In 1936 sister Teresa became the principal of the St.Mary's School. India was ruled by the British. Mean while Indians were fighting for the country's freedom. At that time Mahatma Gandhiji had started his Harijan movement. Gandhiji had started untouchables movement.

Sister Teresa was influenced by Gandhiji she learnt number ideas by observing Gandhiji. Sister Teresa loved to work for poors and destitutes.

Amidst the Poor

On September 10, 1946 sister Teresa had a very strange and good experience. She was travelling by a train Darjeeling. During her travel she was watching beautiful mountains, valleys, springs. Suddenly sister Teresa felt that God was advising her entrusted a mission to her.

Sister Teresa thought that Lord christ had ordered her to serve the destitutes, and the poor in need. From number of years, in her mind some doubts were prestering. By this strange experience she felt that, she got the answer for her inner doubts. At the same moment she decided to dedicate her entire life to fight poverty, ignorance, hunger, and disease, particularly for the welfare of the destitutes,

She thought herself that, she had a lot of work to do to relieve human suffering.. She also felt that it was not enough if she just became a nun. At last sister Teresa's goal and the aim of life was cleared. Sister Teresa remembered two points is her mind. They were as follows. God had entrusted a mission to her. God had ordered her "to abandon easy life and serve the destitutes and the poor".

After having the strange experience sister Teresa reached Calcutta. She explained all that she felt during her journey,' to superior of the convert. Sister Teresa told to the superior that, She would go to the people in difficulty and help them.

The superior of the convent agreed for the request of sister Teresa, Church Authorities gave permission to sister Teresa to leave convent and to help the poor. Sister Teresa kept certain strongest motto in her mind.

* Helping poor.
* Struggle against poverty.
* Selfless service.
* Neglect of self-comfort.
* Prime Importance to hard work.

* Service to the poor is service to God.

With these motto sister Teresa began her work. She joined the Medical Missionary Training centre at Patna in Bihar and got training as a nurse there. Sister Teresa's main aim was to fight against diseases. There was a organization in Calcutta by by named 'Little sister of the poor".

Sister Teresa worked in that institution for some time. The activities of this organization were limited. Their services were not extended to the disease-stricken and the dying people. So sister Teresa was thinking to start her own organization/school in which she can help to the poor. She had a strong will to open her school which may help dying people. (with poverty, and diseases).

Motijhil School

In achieving illumination or spiritual understanding one must go beyond the realm of verbalized expression-the realm of concepts, notions cetegories and images-and enter into the trascendental realm of silence which is ultimate truth.

Sister Teresa found the truth of life through service to the poor. She began her life's mission with the Bible in her hand, a cross on her shoulders and with very less money. The Important thing one would observe in Sister Teresa ws her non-breakable confidence. Sister Teresa's mind was always enchanting about her goal. Sister Teresa started a school in Motijhil. It was on December 21, 1948. Sister Teresa had no money to run the school. At the same time she had to face many oppositions and obstacles. People living around the area. never had confidence on her work. They underestimated her work. Sister Teresa never botherd about these things.

She used to wear simple white saree with a blue border. She got ready to serve the poor in the slums of Calcutta. Sister

Teresa believed that "Service to poor is service to God", She also had a idea that, it was essential to live like commoner, to serve the common man ! So, sister Teresa, spoke local language, weared simple dresses. In 1948 Sister Teresa got Indian citizenship. Sister Teresa's school had no roof, furniture, books ! and even she had no money. But plunged into hard work in order to serve poor people.

In the school slum children sat on the ground and learnt alphabets. The bare bodied children loved sister Teresa like anything. They shared their feelings. With their loving Mother. The classes commenced with prayer and ended with prayer. The people around the motijhil area watched all these developments, with their wondering eyes.

Many poor parents wondered, about that, how the lonely lady is taching and running the school. Some people around the Motijhil area came forward to help Mother Teresa. When they came to know, Mother is teaching without benches, they donated benches some people gave money also. Thus Mother Teresa's real war against poverty and diseases had begun. Since the school was smaller, many people never noticed the great work of Mother. But later many donars came forward to help Mother. Mother never refused the goodhearted donations.

A Band of Helpers to Mother Teresa

Those who have had personal spiritual realization testify that when the heart centre opens, anybody can feel the true spiritual flame of divine love. Same thing happened in the case of Mother Teresa. She understood her inner motto and goal of life. She never took her step back while helping the needy.

Many people were watching mother's hard work without seeking anybody's help. Michael Gomes a good hearted man, was also one among those people. He entered the missionary life of Mother Teresa. He had heard more about Mother. So had lot of respect towards her.

Michael Gomes was ready to give his home's upper floor to Mother to stay. Mother Teresa stood in his house, from 1949 to 1953. Gomes was not ready to take any kind of rent from Mother. Michael Gomes was a simple and good hearted man, He was the man who understood the goal of Mother Teresa. He felt that his house would be sanctified if a person like Mother Teresa was allowed to live there.

Mother along with other sister's lived there about 4 years Gomes and his wife helped her and also respected her a lot. The sisters of Mother's mission were very much qurious to solve the problems of the poor. They used to wander in the city searching for the people who are dying with poverty and desease.

Mother Teresa's mission was hard working, and it was working to remove the poverty of the people. In 1950 the goals, aim and also the constitution of the mission was written. The chief aim of the mission was marked as follows. Wholehearted and free service to the poorest of the poor. Service to the poor is service to the God. In october 1950 the congregation of the missionaries of charity was erected. Subhasini Das one of the student of Mother, joined her mission.

In 1953 Mothera Charity was shifted to Lower circular road. (today it is known as a Jagdish Chandra Bose Road). The building where the Mother's charity was resided later came to be known as 'Mother House'.

Missionaries of charity

A person experiences the genuine love of God, purged of all selfish motivations and egotistical desires. This was true in the case of Mother Teresa. The service organization of Mother gained more and more strength. Subhasini took more care about mother. Following subhasini many other sisters came to Mother Teresa. Infront of Mother all the sisters took oath that their life is for the service to the poor/God.

One of the followers of Mother Mr.Michael Gomes extended his help to, missionaries of charity. By begining her work mother declared that, she would be dying doing God's work. (Means Service to the poor) A Muslim who was the student of St.Xavier school came to help Mother Teresa. He became ready to sell his house for a low price. Mother adapted number of ways in servicing poor. Her policies attracted, many great personalities in the world.

* Service to poor is the service to God.
* Poverty is not a curse.
* Dying for the poor is the duty of one's life.
* One can find God in the service of poor.

With these ideas Mother Teresa advanced her duty. When Mother Teresa was willing to purchase the house for the charity many helping hands extended to her and money flowed like anything.

Mother purchased the house from the Muslim and continued the service of the poor. All the sisters were working restlessly. The service organization of Mother Teresa gained in strength day by day.

Service to the Poor

Mother Teresa believed strongly that service to poor is service to God. She never worried for the amenities. People recognised the goodness and kind heart of Mother Teresa.

Mother's hard work gained the attention of the surrounding people. Many helping hands extended towards Mother Teresa. People admired her work. Mother always dressed in a simple manner. She wore a simple Khadi saree.

Subhasini Das was helping Mother in her service. Subhasini took oath and got the name sister Agnes. Number of incidents indicate that how kind Mother, was !

Once Mother Teresa was returned to home. She was drenched with rain water. And also she was too tired. At that time two guests who were hungry came to her home. It was late in the night.

Mother was not worried she sent a slip of paper to her patron. (Gomes) Micheal sent some eatables. This type many incidents happened, in mothers life. But she never lost will power and confidence. The service organization of Mother Teresa gained in strength day by day. The number of sisters also increased.

Mother Teresa worked very hard along with other sisters. All the time she thought God Christ was inspiring them in their work. All the sisters who were working with Mother thought that upplifting the down-trodden, is their duty.

Sister's duty consisted number of type sevices.

* Both to the poor and dirty-looking patients.
* Cleaning the wounds of the helpless patients and applying medicines.
* Serving poor and bare-bodied children.
* Restless Services to the people who are in the urgent need.
* Showing affection to the old people who were suffering from diseases.

Mother Teresa was telling to people that all of them are children of lord, and also she added, one must have his love and affection for each other. Mother had her own motto to serve the poor people. Money never posed any type of problem for Mother Teresa. The sisters who were working with Mother, were given only two saries to wear. They were getting up early in the morning before sunrise.

Mother herself was the great model for others inorder to spend the good kind of life. Mother Teresa was telling sisters to be kind always. Sisters had to go to slums daily to serve the destitutes, and the dying people. Sisters saw dignity in their labour of love. All the sisters were thinking that, God was inspiring them in their work. The sisters under the guidance of Mother Teresa worked continuously for the welfare of the poor.

The Rules of Charity

The sisters who belonged to missionaries had to follow certain rules. (Even today it is like that only) They had to wake up at 4.30 a.m. Their first two hours. were devoted to meditation prayer and Yoga. They used to do prayer second time which was called community prayer. They used to take simple breakfast.

They were in two or three batches, used to start their duties without any lazyness. When the city was active (in the morning sisters were on their duty. They were found in lanes, slums or main roads. They were devoted in their duties As we know calcutta is the mega city. Here every day hundreds will die and thousands born.

The sisters have taken up some responsibilities of picking up some new born babies, found in dust bins. This was not an easy work to feed them and educate them. But Mother maintained all these hard works with the help of other sisters. Kindless was the guiding principle for the sisters to follow. Mother Teresa always use to give advice.

"I do not like you to do miracles if you are not kind, I can forgive you for your mistakes only if you show kindness".

As we have noticed eariler Mother used to wear only Khadi saries, So sisters were also following this hobby of mother. Sister never received anything from the friends and relatives, who come to meet them. They washed their clothes themselves. All the sisters had statue of crucified Jesus christ and they had only two saries to wear. The food-stufs that came as a charity were shared by all. In Mother's house.

* There were no fans.
* No washing machines.
* No mixer or Grinder.

This clearity shows the kindness and good heart of Mother Teresa. Once it happened like this. A donor offered a washing machine to Mother Teresa. But Mother declined this offer. Mother, would accept only buckets, soap and water facility for washing the clothes. Except in the visitors room there were no electric fans in The Mother's home.

Mother declined the washing machine and said to the donor that, She and her co-sisters had enough air, provided by the lord. All the sisters were bound to strear byict rules and regulations of the missionary charity.

Orphanage For the Destitutes

Mother Teresa was always worrying about destitutes and poors. One day it was raining,.mother saw a woman dying on a road side. Mother, without any late lifted her up and took her to a house near by. But unfortunately the poor woman breathed her last in the arms of Mother. When the poor woman died on the road side, Mother was moved. At the same moment she decided to start an orphanage, for the destitutes.

Mother thought that the destitutes must be in peace at least at their end time. They were not animals who die on the road side ! A doctor realised the feeling of Mother. The doctor gave the hall of his hospital to mother, for the care of destitutes. Even though the hall was small it was the begining of a great work. When the doctor provided the hall, some others came up to provide table & chairs. The hall was small and the equipments in which the mother had was very less. Surprisingly Mother got the solution for the problem. There was a small house, just beside the famous Kali Temple. This house was occupied by some anti-social elements. (Gundas and drunkards etc).

Mother requested to the related authorities of corporation to hand over this small house to her for running the home for the destitutes. Then corporation cleared the house from the hold of the anti social elements and handed over it to Mother Teresa. Mother was happy, when she got a home for the protection of the destitutes. Mother called this small house 'Nirmal Hriday". By seeing Mother's popularity the local priest began to protest against her telling people that she was has come there to convert all poor people into christianity.

Mother denied this meaningless statement and she said that, she is converting a bad Hiindu into a good Hindu. and a bad Muslim into a good Muslim, but never make Christian out of the Hindus or the Muslims. The local priest kept quiet. The protest was ended. Nirmal Hriday became the orphanage, where the doors were always opened for the poors. The holiness and open hearted service of the mother attracted people to help. Mother Teresa developed her own motto;

* Rendering service to the poor and destitutes.
* The reward of doing noble work lies in doing the work itself.

Mother's unaffected will power made her greatest personality in the whole world. She said "I only pray the Almighty to give me sufficient strength to continue this service, in the years to come".

In, "Nirmal Hriday" the sisters were engaged themselves in treating the dying patients, the homeless persons gor Nirmal Hriday as their happy home.

Mother Teresa's ambition to open an orphange was fulfilled. Mother had very strange experiences in the orphanage.

The last wishes of people before dying. (in Nirmal Hriday) were as follows.

* Smoking cigarettes.
* Drinking holy water (Ganga...........if Hindu)
* Hearing holy scriptures like Bible or Quoran.

Some people were asking some food. The nuns were happily meet their last wish.

Some patients while breathing their Last, were happy and satisfied. Some incurable patients would die with a smile on their faces.

The selfless service of Nirmal Hriday become popular not only in Calcutta but also all over the world.

The Activities of Mother Teresa

Nirmal Hriday had the place for the destitutes and patients for ever. Nuns were carrying dying destitutes to the Ashwaradham.

Service-minded people came from foreign countries to participate in the mission of Mother Teresa. They did knew About Bengali or Hindi. They minded only service.

The activities of Mother Teresa attracted the people from all over the world. Many youths male and female came to Calcutta during holidays and visited Mother. They thought their life is sanctified by looking Mother Teresa. Society has the dual nature like good and bad. Some people who did not knew, about Mother's work gave complaint to the police.

Police Commissioner reached 'Nirmal Hriday' His eyes became wet. He saw a nun serving a destitute with affection. Commissioner told to the complainant, I can get this place vacated by these sister of mercy, but on one condition that your mothers and sisters take up the mission of these nuns. The complainants realised their mistakes.

Nirmal Hriday had all the facilities like toilets, bath food, love and care, for the destitutes. Time turned, the priests of Kali temple appriciated the service rendered by Mother Teresa, and respected her. Mean while a strange incident happened.

One of the priests of Kali temple was attacked by cholera. As the disease was commenicable, he had to go out of the temple. No hospital would admit him. He was left in the lurch....! then sisters of Nirmal hriday brought him and treated him with love and care. He got cured.

The Mentality of priests turned. They left their hatredness and jelous nature. They came to knew that Mother is doing Godly service. All the priests of Kali Temple appreciated Mother Teresa's services. Nirmal Hridya consisted of two large halls. Nuns were always careful about the cleanlyness of Nirmal Hriday. The rooms were kept very clean. The destitutes who got entry in Nirmal Hriday, were living with peace at their end time. Some patients get cured, and were back at their work. Mother Teresa guided her assistants to go round Calcutta and bring the orphans and abandoned children.

Service to the Orphan Children

Mother Teresa loved children very much. She was always telling people to provided all affection and love to children. She gave instructions to her assistants to bring orphans and abandoned children. Mother regarded children as the existence nearest to God. She used to give food and Medicine, and heartful affection.

In 1956 Mother Teresa established Normal shishu Bhavan, close to Mother house. She decided to serve orphan children.

Her policy was as follows.

"The poor expected love in addition to service".

Mother always use to say "It is not sufficient if only is given; you have to give then your love and affection too".

The newly-born orphan babies, were being handed over to sister of the Bhawan, by the ayas of the hospital. once in a winter mother had no enough beds and bed sheets, for some children. Unexpectedly a stranger came in and told her that, he had decided to donate his few belongings like, bed, cot etc. Mother accepted and enabled children.

Many times, Mother observed newly born babies thrown into the dustbins and gutters in the city. The sister were being asked bring such babies without delay.

Once a boy was handed over to Mother. The boy was doing pick pocketing. Mother gave him proper treatment with affection and love. Later he became a good man, he left all his old habits. Some children who had gone astray were also admitted to

Shishubhavan. Mother was always produced more than 10,000 good citizens during the recent years.

Mother was always careful about children, inorder to make them good citizens. Money started coming from almost all corners of the world. Mother always believed that God would provide money, when she was in difficulties. A large shed near bSealdah railway station was handed over to her. She made it an orphanage.

Later she started a small cottage industry. She made children to work independently. Children became experts in crafts. The sisters of Mother house protected the children till they grew up and got jobs. Girls they grew up in the Shishubhavan were being married of to a good family. Larges sums of money was needed for running the Shishu bhavan. But Mother was believed God with good faith.

Mother Teresa was awarded with award magsaysay. The award was consisting Rs. 50,000/-and certificate of honour. Mother always used to say that God always likes to save and help the people who actually help the poors. By 1963 Mother Teresa had moved out to Delhi, Mumbai, Jhansi, Ranchi, for setting up homes for destitutes.

Mother Teresa faced number problems and difficulties in maintaining Shishubhavan, and the orphan house. But Miracles always used to happen. Donors used to come themselves and they were always providing the money or whatever the things needed to Ashram.

Dr.B.C.Roy was on eminent physician of interational fame. He was calling Mother Teresa as a divine healer. Dr.Roy showed interest in the work of the Mother. He sent memo to all the concerned departments of the state of Bengal to help her to maximum extent. Mother Teresa was always an optimist. She firmly believed that anything could be achieved if one had faith in the Almighty. She had strong faith that Lord was always on the side of the suffering people and would never leave them in the lurch.

The Temples For the Destitutes

The organisations like Shishubhavan, Nirmal Hriday, Mother house, were like temples for the poors and destitutes.

In 1957 Mother Teresa started an Ashram for lepers in Gobra. She began to treat patients her self, she would personally, clean the patients wash their wounds thoroughly In those days (Today also) people were very much afraid of leprosy and those afflicted by it. Such patients were even being thrown out of the villages. There was a social boycott of leprosy patients. Mother made strong desire to serve leprosy patients.

However, the leprosy home is transfered from Calcutta to another place, Which was later known as Shantinagar. The patients liked this place. It was a beautiful place. (120 km away from Calcutta). The people from all over the world used to come to this place to observe motto of the Mother. A clinic was also established near Asansol. Number of liprosy patients got cured there. (Today more than 100 leprosy centres run by Mother Teresa's missionaries; where nearly one and half lakhs patients are being given treatment). Mother Teresa held many seminars, training courses to educate people about the disease. Mother always used to tell that the disease is curable. She tired maximum to remove the misconceptions about the disease. She used to tell that, "Touch the lepers woth your Kindness".

In those days people in India believed that leprosy is the most dreadful disease. Many felt that it was curse on account of the divine wrath. Nobody wanted to go nearby the leprosy patients. About leprosy people had many types of misconceptions.

Even though modern world hyad found a medicinal cure for leprosy people use to fear the disease and those afflicted with it. Mother never hesitated to serve the patients. She was a lady of great humanity. Very soon Mother Teresa became a revered figure all over the world. All her centres begun to function smoothly.

Mother Teresa's Hospitals

The sisters of Mother Teresa's hospitals have been will trained in the cure and treatment of deseases. Mother was opened number of treatment centres, with the help of donations. Today more than 120 leprosy centres are being run by Mother Terasa's missionaries.

On the Outskirts of Calcutta at Titanagar Mother has established "Prem nivas" the treatment centre for the leprocy patients. This place has become the shelter for those who are totally cured by leprosy they are working for their independent life. In this place, ropes, mats, bags are prepared out of jute, and waste coconut husk. Once mother was treating a leprosy patient in slum area. One of the patients raised his finger, which was rotting with puss. Mother thought to cut that finger so that the affliction may not spread to other fingers.

Mother took a scissor and cut off the rotten finger and treated the patient. This was the way, Mother Teresa used to take desires regarding the way of treatment. Observing Mother Teresa's achievements Pandit Jawaharlal Nehru said that "What is being done by Mother Teresa is unachevable by all the prime Ministers, President and Kings of the world". What a statement! It was true. But Mother Teresa said that what she is doing is just a drop in the ocean.

In 1965 Mother set up her first overseas centre in Venezuela. She got an award in the year 1970 namely Pope John

XXlll peace prize. The prize amount was 21,500 dollars. Mother Teresa used all the money for the treatment of leprosy patients. of west Bengal.

Once Pope paul VI came to India. He presented his ford car to Mother. But Mother did not used the car for her own happiness. Mother kept the car for an auction. By the auction she got nearly four times the value of that car. She used all the Money for Leprosy centre.

Today Mother's missionaries are running everywhere. Newyork Moscow, Madrid, Athens, Germany Belgium........etc.

Mother's Hard Work

The famous Bengali writer Sudev Ray Choudhary observed mother's hard work and exclaimed like this; "She is not a humanbeing. She is above all. She is a bundle of energy".

Once it happened like this, Near Kalighat temple a beggar-imposter pretended to be a leprosy patient clad in rags and with artificial wounds on his legs. This pretension did not last long. To his luck he really become a leprosy patient. This man was brought to 'Preemadaan'. When he was cured of his affection after some days he had mentally and physically changed. He become a active man Mother Teresa has been spent all the moneys she got through national and international awards for the cure and rehabilitation of the stricken people of India.

Mother Teresa extended her service to public. She established "Nirmala kennedy home" on the Jssore road. In the year 1971 Bangladesh was fighting for freedom. Later it was separated from Pakistan. Thousands of people fled East pakistan and came to west Bengal. The Kennedy Home was being used for the sake of these refugees. Mother realised the difficulties of refugees. She extended the hand of help, to them. When the violence against refugees stopped in Bangladesh all the refugees were returned to their country.

Mother Teresa was founded "Brother of Charity" The main aim of this organization was to help the misguided and poor youth, and bringing them to right path. Andrew was the first servant or superior general among the Brothers. Mother wanted that these brothers had to have a separate religious dress. But Andrew did not thought about separate dresses.

Mother had got permission to start Brother's wing. It was started in 1963. Iyan Travers Bull of Australlia took over the leadership of the wing. Mother Teresa was the guiding force for him. Mother Teresa and her missionaries were dared to enter riot and even war zones, whenever found necessary.

6th December 1992 the babri Masjid was distructed. In that occasion Mother Teresa was on the streets; personally she was conducting her mission of peace by taking people from place to place. Though the area of operation of Mother started in Calcutta. Later it extended to the entire world.

Mother Teresa's Work Field

Mother Teresa belonged to poor and also to middle class people. She was the embodiement of the ultimate human quality. Mother's work field was India. Millions of poors and destitutes, loved her. On the otherhand no one in the entire world has shown so much compassion and piety of destitutes and poors. She was an optimist she did not like publicity. She never wrote any book or article to praise herself or her organization. Mother Teresa never advertised herself.

Many daily papers, and magazines, periodicals admired Mother and her service to the mankind till she breathed her last and even afterwords. Mother Teresa was the great believer of the almighty In every one,she saw the God. She was spending all donations given to her for the welfare of the destitutes.

About the prayer she had the great faith. She said, "The fruit of silence is prayer, the fruit of faith is Love, the fruit of love is service and the fruit of service is peace." What a statement......! she believed death as a continuation of life.

Mother used to say "Death is going home, yet people are afraid of what will come so, they do not want to die. If we do if there is no mystery we will not be afraid. The heart and soul live for ever. They do not die. Every religion had got enternity another life. This life is not the end. People who believe in it fear death. If it was property explained that death is nothing going home to God, then there would be no fear".

Awards and honour

No other person has won so many prestigious awards as Mother Teresa. She has utilized all the money for the establishment of Ashryadamas.

The Awards

* Magasasay, 1962.
* Padmashri Award, 1962.
* Award by Pope Paul, 1970.
* Joseph Kennedy Junior award, 1972.
* Nehru Award, 1972.
* Templeton Award, 1973.
* Nobel Prize, 1979.
* Bharata Ratna, 1980.
* Order of Merit, 1983.

* Presidential Medal of Freedom (U.S.A) 1985.
* Templeton Award, 1973.
* Pope John XX lll peace prize.
* Albert Schweitzer International Prize.
* Bharat Ki Suputri, 1992.
* Rajiv Gandhi Sadbhavana Award, 1993.
* Albania's Golden honour, 1994.
* Honarary Citizenship of America, 1996.
* Congressional Gold Medal, 1997.

Apart from the above awards Mother got number of other honours and awards. Mother Teresa received Leo Tolstoy international award.

Reality speaking Mother was not a human being, above all.....! Like an angel..........!

The area of operations of Mother Teresa, which was started in Calcutta extended to the entire world. Mother Teresa never aspired for publicity. She has never written any book or article, either about her or organization. Many Newspaper and periodicals praised Mother Teresa and her services to the society. The whole world knew that she was an extra-ordinary woman.

Mother Teresa had an unflinching belief in Almighty. In an interview Mother has said.

"People in the rich nations of the world are hankering for love and affection, that is why I have had to visit England, U.S.A, Australia and other nations. There is no scarcity of food there, but only scarcity of love. All the countries in the world agree that Mother Teresa was one of the most influential women. The former prime ministers, Indira Gandhi and Rajiv Gandhi,

Used to meet Mother Teresa quite often. Mother Teresa was loved and respected not only in India but in many other countries of the world. Every where she was known to help the poor and the downtrodden.

The Last Breathe of Mother

In 1991 Mother Teresa suffered from pnuemonia which led her to congestive heart failure. The age had withered her. In January 1992 Mother Teresa became seriously ill. She was being treated in a hospital at California. When Mother's health was falling down, millions of people all over the world prayed God for the recovery of her health. When the war broke out between Iraq and the US, Mother wrote o the presidents of both the countries.

She said, "This war might bring victory to either of you. But the lethal weapons used by both of you will bring death, destruction and misery which is not bearable by anyone. Mother had impressed upon the presidents of both the countries, the need to abandon the path of war and violence.

Mother did not had any formal education and did not go to universities for education. But many prestigious universities the world over have conferred honorary doctorate degrees upon her. K.R.Narayanan, the former president described Mother Teresa as an angel of mercy, who spread love and compassion throughout the world and brought succour and relief to the poorest of the poor.

In 1993 Mother visited Rome at her ripe age of 83. She fell and broke her ribs. Later she developed Malaria. Her case was global concern. The Missionaries of charity became worried. The members of missionaries of charity became worried, and thinking who is the successor. Later sister Nirmala was appointed as the order's new superior General. Sister Nirmala said "We are all Mother's children and will continue doing her work".

I.K.Gujral, the farmer prime minster of India said, "A beacon of light and poor had gone out of our lives. Mother demonstrated to us the beauty and power of the ulltimate and most difficult from of worship.

Mother Teresa was an apposite of love and peace in the real sense. On Friday 5th morning Sister Shanti one of the most senior nuns sensed that Mother was in great pain. Mother Teresa said "I cannot breathe, I cannot breathe". Alferd Woodward. Mother's long time physician knew well that, she was sinking. An hour and a half later at 9.30 p.m. Mother was passed away.

Mother's Message

* Service to the poor is the service to God.
* Poverty is not a curse.
* God helps them who help the poor.

The following one was Mother's prayer. "Lord make a channel of peace; that where there is hatred, I may bring Love; that where there is wrong I may bring The spirit of forgiveness; that where there is descord, I may Bring harmony; that where there is sadness I may bring joy!."

* Sacrifice does not cause often sadness, especially when one give upto God.
* God loves a cheerful giver.
* Faith is a gift of God and it becomes true, through the prayer.
* One should not have doubts, doubts disturb, Doubts take our freedom.
* Abortion is a murder in the womb. A child is gift of God."

Really speaking, Mother has give thousands of messages to us, it becomes our duty to understand and follow her message.

13

Sarojini Naidu

The Formative Years

Sarojini the eldest daughter of Agorenath Chattopadhyaya was born on February 13, 1879. Her father, Agorenath Chattopadhyaya was a scientist and a pioneer educationist. He had an extraordinary family life.

Describing her father to the English, Sarojini wrote, "My ancestors have been great dreamers, great scholars and great ascetics. My father is a dreamer himself, agreat man whose life has been a magnificient failure. I suppose in the whole of India there are few men whose learning is greater that his, and I don't think there are many men more beloved. He has a great white beard and the profile of Homer and a laugh that brings down the roof.

He has wasted all his money on two great objects to help others and on alchemy. But this alchemy was only the material counterpart of poets craving for beauty the eternal beauty. The makers of gold are the makers of verse, they are the twin creators that sway the world's secret desire for mystery; and what in my father is the genius of curiosity."

Nothing could have summed up Sarojini's drive in life more than these words to this man who trimmed and shaped her later poetic gift. But what is significant was her recognition as a young woman of twenty five, that her father's alchemy and her poetry sprung from the same roots.

In her father's laugh "that brings down the roof" one can see the profound influence upon this otherwise deeply serious child. In the court of her parent's home where thinkers, poets and revolutionarists, relatives, and friends, gathered in constant comings, and goings, and where her gentle mother presided over a tiny kitchen from which with limited resources, she produced prodigious meals for the endless hospitality of this home.

Rajagopalachari, Indias first Governor-General after Independence was to write about Sarojini; "Sarojini Devi was undoubtedly one of the few personalities in whom were combined a sense of humour along with perception of realities in the struggle for freedom". Robert Bernays called her the, "Court jester of the Mahatma's little court".

But in all the tales of her humour which seem to be more easily recalled than more momentous events by all her hosts of friends and in all the stories of her scant respect for the respect is the deep undercurrent of her wisdom and humanity, which provoked Arthur Symons to write; "I have never known any one to exist on such large draughts of intellectual diet as this child of seventeen, to whom one could tell all one's Personal troubles and agitations as to an old wise woman. In the East maturity comes early and this child had already lived through all a woman's life.

But there was something else, something hardly personal, something which belonged to a consciousness older than the

Christian which I realised, wondered at and admired, in her passionate tranquility of mind. Symons goes on to say that her desire always was to be a wild frecthing of thc air like the birds, "with a song in my heart."

Much has been written about the family of Agorenath Chattopdhyaya and his wife,Varada Sundari Devi for when men or a woman like Sarojini achieve national fame, there is a sudden desire to study the soil in which such genius has been nurtured.

If the father dominated the atmosphere of activity and creative thought in the house, it was the mother with her soft, Bengali ways who was its presiding deity. Her youngest son Harindranath considered by some critics a greater poet than his eldest sister, Sarojini.

Infact in all the descriptions of her one finds the 'ideal' Hindu woman whose life from waking to sleeping was a saga of devotion-whether in the culinary gifts she lavished upon her husband's court of friends and admirers, which gave Sarojini her robust love of good food, or in the simplicity and total "giving" of herself to her family of eight, vital children.,

Her simplicity profoundly affected Sarojini who developed a rate capacity to treat people as equals no matter what their walk of life. This simplicity gave her clear in sight and a freedom for cant. For there could have been no false pretensions in a woman of the calibre of Varadasundari Devi, nor did there seem to by any pull in her nature to life outside her home.

This to a child provide no greater security. If she had any inner drive unrelated to her family it probably came out in her poetry and the songs she sang.

As Harindranath remembers she would sit singing on the window still overlooking their gate, with tears brimming our of her eyes. Perhaps Sarojini's term for herself often said with half-laughing half serious voice, "I am just a poetess-singer". What reached the girl perhaps unconsciously was the woman's soul expressing itself in songs that made her weep.

But apart from the deep inner things this must have been a house of endless activity, a home in which the world moved through with its trials, and triumphs and in which challenges had to be met and the lamp of freedom always burned high. When Agorenath went abroad for studies his young wife as generally happened in those days was left behind. She lived in the Brahmo Samaj Ashram of Keshab Chandra Sen learning to become a good housewife.

Her husband, however having earned the scholarship sailed for England, and in 1877 took his Degree in Physics at Edinburgh, winning in the process the baxter prize and the Hope prize in Chemistry. It is said that he was the first Indian to win his Doctorate in Science. From England he went to Bonn in Gernany where he impressed Scientists with the breadth of his mind and accuracy and insight in research.

His career in pure Science was not fulfilled. In the case of both, father and daughter the needs of the country, were too vast and imperative for the luxury of Science or Poetry.

Both Agorenath an the devoted Varadasundari Devi had the cause of women's education a rather rare phenomenon in that period very much at heart. It is not surprising, therefore that in 1878 when he became a teacher in a Hyderabad School with English as the medium of the instruction, he should in time become Founder and principal of the Hyderabad College, the famous Nizam's College of later years, Subsequently, with his wife and some friends, he created the girl's college affiliated to Osmania University.

One of the reasons why Agorenath was a remarkable educationist was the fact that he could not resist teaching. His grand-daughter Padmaja said of him, "One of my earlist recollections was grandfather showing me the flowers in the garden and reeling off latin names he expected me to remember".

Agorenath's influence on his children was indeed profound. He would say, "If my children cannot live by their wits let them die". Once when Suhasini came home shouting that she had come first in her class he said bravely, "Is that so body ? What is the nature of the sun, do you know ?" she answered "No".

Then he said "Broaden your knowledge When know many things it is more important than being first." What different kind of youth we would have in India today if teachers were like Agorenath, and their homes an open house in which discussion and debate took knowledge and learning into the realm of the students everyday thinking. It was invitable that the new Hydrabad College rapidly became the Cultural Centre of Hyderabad, when classes were over, students would flock to Dr.Chattopadhya's home.

Infact the atmosphere of learning in this modern" setting where the emancipation of women especially their economic independence, distaste for child marriage among and encourag-ment of widow remarriage among other social reforms, were the constant topics of discussion, must have in essence, resembled the old Forest Universities of ancient India, where the relations between pupil and teacher were based upon many disciplines and constant contact with the teacher who was virtually a guru.

As time went on the stimulus of this gathering in the Chattopadhyaya home drew to it all the cultured active minds of Hydrabad and became known as the "Darbar of Dr.Agorenath". Invitably these informal gatherings began to crystallize into action groups based upon like-thinking. Soon the Anjuman-E-Akhwan-us safe was born whose organizer's main concern was how to tackle the social and political problems of the country.

At that time the British rule in India was probably at its apogee. The English by various means had established law and order, local administration revenue collection, communicaions through an extensive railway system and through English as the medium of instruction assured themselves of a well trained Indian cadre of humble and sub servient lower officials to carry out their rule.

Every British official lived in comfort with a large household staff, their wives ruled this little kingdoms and the exclusively English clubs and all megrated in summer to the joys of the hill stations in the Nilgiris and the Himalayas. If among the civilians and educators of those days before the turn of the Century were Englishmen of learning and humanism who contributted richly to the development of this country, the bulk were men and women of much calibre who enjoyed quite egotistically their status comfort and power.

When Salar jung the Diwan of Hyderabad died in 1883 the administration was entrusted to a council consisting of some prominent noblemen with a Nizam as President. Hydrabad was then part of Nritians treaty of Paramountcy with the old princely states where the ruler governed under the watchful eye if a British resident.

In the perpective of time, the "Chanda Railway Scheme" which led to the deportation of Dr. Agorenath Chattopadhyaya from Hydrabad revolutionary according to the acheme. The existing state Railway from Hyderabad to Wadi was to be taken by a British Company.

Few years later Dr.Agorenath was reinstated. His great friend and loyal supporter, Mulla Abdul Qayyum who had left for

Madras also returned to Hyderabad Sarojini wrote of him; "How happy I am to add a flower of affection to the memorial garland woven by many hands in honour of my father's beloved friend, Mulla Abdul Qayyum Sahin, whose picturesqe figure and fascinating personality are integral parts of my earlist recollections seldom have two persons divided by such diverget circumstances of birth, education, racial heritage and religious tradition achieved such perfect friendship as these two gifted and distinguished people.

"Both were men of vigorous intellect and versatile knowledge, nobility of character and righteousness of conduct. Both were kindled by the fire of deep moral indignation against every force of falsehood, injustice and tyranny. Both were sustained and inspired by radiant from the tragic evils of ignorance, poverty, exploitation and oppression."

The eight children of Agorenath Chattopadhyaya and Varada Sundari Devi wwere understandable unusual children and their collective vitality was of epic proportions. Gifted in different ways, each one of them was to make a distinictive contribution in the world.

Sarojini was the eldest and became the most famous. She was essentially a liberal and in a less revolutionary period, would probably have been a leader in literary salons in India and abroad.

Virendranath born in 1880 however would have been a revolutionary anywhere. He was exiled from India for his activities and during the Stalin era died of a heart attack on December 2, 1942. The news of his death in Europe however did not reach his family till much later. Bhupendranath the second brother was born in 1882. He became the Assistant Accountant General in Hyderabad.

Mrinalini was born in 1883. She became an an educationist and later as principal of the Girls College. She dedicated her life to teaching.

Sunalini Devi was born in 1890 and became an artist and dancer. Ranendranath was born in 1895, he died of cancer in 1959. The youngest brother and most flamboyant member of the family, Haridranath was born in 1898. Poet, artist, dramatist, Harindranath was the classic picture of the bohemian poet. His only son Rama was a consulting engineer. The youngest sister Subhasini was born in 1901, Subhasini was an ardent communist. By 1969, Harin and Subhasini were the only surviving members among Sarojini's brother's and sister.

Women's Education In India

In 1891 women's education in India was a far cry from what it is today, and a girl in school was something of a rarity. Agorenath Chattopadhyaya however was a man born before his time and it seemed perfectly normal to him that his twelve year old daughter should become a scientist or mathematician.

There had been governesses in the Chattopadhyaya household to teach the children in English and French as was customary in many homes in England and later Persian studies were added, but no High School existed in Hydrabad, where Sarojini could take her matriculation examination. 'She was consequently sent to Madras where her English teacher was to say later that she was so brilliant that she mastered there years' work in one year.

While it was a tremendous achievement for a girl to have passed her Matriculation with a First class at the age of tweleve her mental age must have been much greater than that of her contemporaries not only because of her natural intelligence, but because of an atmosphere of learning had been part of her babyhood and upbringing. By the age of fourteen she had read all the English poets; what is more there could have been no element of excluding children from adult life in their family. In fact children probably woe in and out of the discussions and disputations that were a normal feature of this household.

Philosophy, Science, Botany, Alchemy, Mathematics and Politics would have been such concrete elements of daily life that learning was alsomt by osmosis and a process infinitely more fascinating and stimulating than routine studies in School.

It was probably in the gatherings in her father's house that Sarojini met Dr.Govindarajalu Naidu. That she fell in love with this young man who had just returned from, Edinburgh after his medical studies, is brought out in her earlist poems, and the precocious love affair must have been of some concern, to her parents. It was not because he was a non-Brahmin, as some have said, but because she was very young and so sensitive that her health was health easily and constantly upset. This dogged her all her life leading to a complete break-down when she was in England in 1896.

It was the three years after her Matriculation in Madras that she claims were among her happiest years. During this period she was to write of herself. "I don't think I had any special hankering to write and dreamy nature. My training under my father's eye was of a sternly scientific character.

He was determined that I should be a great mathematician or a scientist. Padmaja says her mother spoke of herself at that age as, "having been a great prig." Quoting her girlhood statement uttered with a great solemnity. In families this would been a subject of mirth for Sarojini discovered with her usual precocity that the most serious things must be hidden and that they are most effectively hidden uder laughter.

A poetic rendering of the democracy she was a champion in later years. It must have been the effect of such episode that gave her the realisation that her words could move people whom she could command and lead. But in thos early years what seemed predominant was on odour of life which expressed itself most aptly in poetry.

She wrote the tender lyric love in November 1894.

"I love thee a love whose face
Is changeless as the stars of night.
My love is stronger far than death,
My love is pure as morning light.
I ask not if though lovest me,
It is enough to me thou art.
The noblest, dearest, best-to thee
I yield treasures of my heart."

Sarojini's Brilliance

Sarojini wrote a little Persian play called "Meher Muneer" which her father got printed in a local journal. A few copies of this play written in English were sent to friends. Among them was the nizam of Hyderabad, who was so charmed that he made a typically princely gesture.

Aware of Sarojini's brilliance and her love of poetry and perhaps to encourage a young genius, he said to her father that the young lady should tell him what she would like as a royal gift. History does not relate whether the choice was actually hers or not. Arthur Symons in fact states in his preface to her poems that she went to England against her will.

In her very young Sarojini sailed too England along with Annie Besant. For the moment, she was attending lectures at King's College. She studied for her "Little Go" at cambridge and was admitted two years later to Girton college. By that time she was a personality in her own right.

At Miss Manning's she had met leading literary figures, such as William Archer who did so much to popularise Ibsen in England. Those two years before she went to Girton were formative in the extreme. They also explain why she soon got tired of university life and what to her must have seemed a great deal of meaningless discipline both in the way of life and the form of study.

Her colleagues were very likely patronising too and Sarojini could have tolerated such attitudes with ill grace. They wrote of her, "You have a little Indian girl here who does nothing but write poetry."

Arthur Symons, in his intoduction to her first book of poems in 1904 stated, "To those who knew her in England, all the life of the tiny figure seemed to concentrate itself in the eyes; they turned towards the beauty as the sunflower turns towards the sun opening wider and wider until one saw nothing but the eyes. She was dressed always in clinging dresses of Eastern silk and she was so small and her long black hair hung straight down her back, you might have taken her for a child, She spoke little and in low voice like gentle music and she seemed, wherever she was to be alone.

The Early Poetry Work

In the early poetry work, Sarojini's intellectual power can be seen. The centre of her inner being can be understood. This was understandable living as she did in the heart of the finest Islamic culture; for Hydrabad had retained all the glamour and values of princely Persia and it's ruling prince was a poet of great distinction.

Here as in the past in Islamic societies, poets were the conscience and sensitive heart-strings of the people. They used technique of versifying to explore the depths of the soul and emotions all of which was closely akin to the Bhakti element of the Hindu search for higher consciosness.

Poetry to them was linked also with song and played a great role in community life as the Mushaira of today, continues to do in a rather limited way. Poets could do no wrong; their vision was acclaimed, their wisdom and insight became the catch words of the people. It is not surprising that all this should subconsciously affect her choice of poetry as the vehicle for her deep and passionate emotions, and under the influence of the English, language and the poets of the, another land, she began to write her colourful melodious verse.

Edmund Gosse put his finger exactly on the reason why her early work was stilted derivative and without life when he told her to write of what she knew. Her return from England to everything love, happiness, family homeland-was also a key that unlocked the door to her inner self; It was then that her rich treasure house of words for she revelled in the rechness of words for their own sake and their own music-led her to write some of the lovelist lyrics in the language at times she could be so carried away by words, however that meaning itself was lost such as in her celebrated poem on Indian dancers;

Eyes ravished with rapture celestially panting. What passionate bosoms aflaming with fire. Drink deep of the hush of the hyacinth heavens. That glimmer around them in fountains of light. O wild and entrancing the strain of keen music. That cleaveth the stars like a wail of desire. And beautiful dancers with houri-like faces bewitch the volumptuous watches of night.

This extra-ordinary dimension which she was able to give

words- leapt, in later years from poetry to such Oratory that audiences were caught swept away bewitched and so bemused that they often ended up without knowing what it was that she had actually said. But if the fountain of dazzling words continued to her last days her published writings were actually slender. 'The Golden Threshold' was published in 1905 and became a best-seller in England earning reviews of great acclaim from all the leading journals and literary crities in 1912 William Heineman published, "The Bird of time' and in 1917 "the Broken wing".

There had been of course, early writings when she was a girl, some of which were published in local papers. In the archives of national Library, Calcutta are some of her earlist poems dared october 3, 1896 and include, Traveller's Song written when she was thirteen, a verse on her own birthday when she was fourteen. These poems were written in Hydrabad and at the summer holiday resort of Shorapur near Hydrabad which reveal her budding love for her future husband.

In a prose poem "Nilambuja' she wove a fantasy of lush eloquent bejewelled prose which described her own dream world set in princely romance and splendour. But the dreamer is alone and apart. Here was the lyric child who saw the world with clarity and foretold in poetic language her own future.

"Yet must I go where the loud world beckons'

And the urgent drum beat of destiny calls.

For from your white domes luminous slumber

Far from the dream of your forest walls.

Into the strife of the throng and the tumult

The war of sweet love against folly and wrong.......

Nilambuja was indeed a vision of girlhood with all the awareness that delight, comfort and beauty were life. In the introduction of her collected poems published many years later under the title, “The sceptred Flute”.

Joseph Auslander wrote “for this lady who is conceded to be the greatsest living poet of India is in spite of the apparent contradiction a passionate philosopher. From first to last she is the lyric poet, the singer of songs. Like Keats she has suffered ill health almost all of her life. We detect this in a certain strange of feverishness of texture. Her poems Flush.

We touch heart... if she sings as the birds do, she sings out of a darker passion. Her song is not ephemeral. For that matter neither is the birds song. It is no more transitory than truth and her bird music was always true. She never writes for the mere sake of writing. There is no artifice in her poetry. She sings from the heart.”

The titles of her three volumes of verse were regarded by sir C.P.Ramswami lyer who had known her since her school days in Madras to be of significance.

According to him the first volume, “the Golden Treshold was linked to her happy domestic phase, the second Bird of time to her developing phase when the great noble ideals of humanity began to move her directly and she started work for the, emancipation of women. The last, “The broken wing’ was the saga of her emotions. Her poem in response to Gokhale’s question “why should a song bird like you have a broken wing ?” Significantly underlines the triumph of her spirit, for the poems that follow are with few exceptions songs of life, death and love.

Sarojini Naidu’s Great Poetry

Sarojini Naidu’s poems are not only great questions but also the answers for life problems. The following are the exception songs of life, death and love.

The great dawn breaks the mournful night is past,
From her deep age-long sleep she wakes at last !
Sweet and long-slumbering buds of gladness ope
Fresh lips to the returning winds of hope our
Eager hearts renew their radiant flight.
Towards the glory of renascent light.
Life and our land await their destined spring
Song-bird, why does thou beat a broken wing ?

The above poetry looks like questions, Sarojini naidu gives answer also. Shall spring that wakes mine ancient land again.

Call to my wild and suffering heart in vain ?
Or Fate's blind arrows still the pulsing note.
Of my far reaching frail, unconquered throat ?
Or a weak bleading pinion daunt or tire
My flight to the high realms of my desire ?
Behold I rise to meet the destined spring
And scale the stars upon my broken wing !

In some ways it is fortunate that her poetry was published before the birth of Modern Poetry with its harsh emphasis on truth without philosophy and meaning without lyricism.

Her era was that of the sonner with it's discipliness of form, the ode with it's call to higher thoughts and the small gem of verse with it's emphasis upon imagery and colour. It has been said she wrote at a time when English poetry had touched the rock bottom of sentimentality and technical poverty and it is certain that her gem like use of words would at a time like that have touched many chords, particularly in England, not only because they had in transic merit but because they came from a very young women from a very old country.

She was convinced and told the author so herself in 1946 that Modern Poetry had no future, and the trend would inevitably return to the disciples and beauty of the metrical form of lyrics. Such a statement did not imply that she had greater pre science about the futue of poetry than, others but that she sincerely believed modern permissiveness and lack of form to be a passing fad.

What is, more like many people of her generation who find modern art hideous simply because it is not visually beautiful, so too did she feel that modern poetry honestly lacked her concepts of beauty. If this were studied more deeply it is very likely that the real reason for her distate of modern forms was something much closer to her intrinsic nature.

In this type of poetry there is truth perhaps but no exaltation of spirit. What rings through many of her poems is this heroic transformation of the mere mortal, into a divinely possessed person translated into higher realms such as in her "Ode to India".

Rise Mother rise regenerate from the gloom

And like a bride high-mated from the spheres.

Beget new glories from thin ageless womb.

The future calls thee with a manifold sound.

To crescent honours splendours Victories vast;

Waken, o slumbering Mother and be crowned

Who once wert Empress of the sovereign past. It is certainly this aspect of her nature that took her into the service of her country, first through the redress of ancient wrongs which inevitably concentrated upon the lot of Indian women, and later to active political and revolutionary life.

It was only in the lyric period however, from the time of her marriage in 1898 till her emergence into full-fledged national life in 1915 that Sarojini Naidu was whole-heartedly wife, mother and poet.

The Life In High-Born Families

At the turn of the century life in High-born families in Hyderabad was placid and revolved around cultured exchanges between people in their own homes, with women leading a separate life. Weddings and other ceremonies might bring them together or the occasional tea party but care of home house hold children and the clan was their major preoccupation.

For festive days very elaborate saris and jewellery were mandatory and Sarojini adored beautiful jewels and clothes as much as any other woman

In fact permeates all she wrote but she was herself and equal devotee of colour, loving rich silks and the golden chains, shoulder brooch and bangles, so favoured in Bengal.

Later twin tiger claws mounted on a gold pendant and a gold pendant and chain were a permanent feature of her jewellery and in a photograph taken of her in her sick bed in 1918 she is decked with ear-rings necklase and bangles.

There is also a picture of her as a girl in a bustled dress with long frilly sleeves, her brothers in velvet suits and long white stockings and boots and her mother in a dainty sari with chinese embroidered border and ivory bangles, her father always wore the Hyderabad dress, and with his beard and Nizam turban the dastar-looked a perfect Muslim gentleman.

Others who have described the Chattopadhyaya household and later that of the Naidus, always talk of luxury and opulence enough a friend who new them very well, more perceptively stated that, they were "Simple generous and Cultured". If this had not been true it is doubtful whether Sarojini could have endured what proved to be decades of camp life, moving from place to place from hotels to huts and even to jails with equa ease bringing to each an aura of civilized, cultured sophistication.

But when she was in her own house or that of a friend whose home she considered her own no time was last for marvellous dishes to be created for a well laden table and all round her where the tasteful appointements, from flowers to carved blackwood furniture of a woman who loves a home filled with beautiful things.

Woman like there was a struggle too in her inner spirit between her attachment to these purely feminine aspects of life, the comfort security and fun, but the drive of energy within her never left her wholly at peace, while she revealed in meating people gossiping and telling stories in great detail about this person or that interlarding her tales with her boisterous chuckle and laugh. Another side of her was the reformer committed totally to work outside the home. And in the end this life claimed her.

To begin with the reformist aspect of her nature took the fom of involvement in the lot of women. With her gift for trenchant language, she once in an early speech called the joint family system "a domestic rat". But there is no record of all the speeches of Sarojini Naidu. even if there were her eldest daughter contends almost none would really reflect the actuality of her words. The combination of rich language fiery delivery, wit and pathos that as a born orator, she could weave into structured from filled with imagery was always more than a mere reporter or listener could absorb.

Yet in the few speeches that have been captured and imprisonment in print, the idealism and passion articulated in exquisite style pour out of her mouth as effortlessly and without notes as a waterfall on a high mountain. Of her contemporaries only Annie Besant had this same electrifying gift.

In a speech in Madras in 1903, she declaimed, "Having travelled having conceived, having hoped, having enlarged my love, having widened my sympathies having come into contact, with different races, different communities, different religions, different civilizations, friends my vision is clear.

I have no prejudice of race creed, casre or colour..... Until you students have acquired and mastered that spirit of brotherhood, do not believe it possible that you will ever cease to be sectarian.... If I may use such a word....... that you will ever be national......"

This early speech on unity was to be the grace not of her entire career. In another speech to the social conference in Madras where unity was again the main theme, She started that, she hoped than in ten years the resolutions they were passing on human brotherhood and integration in society would not be needed, and that the whole country would be one. With considerable insight she advised young people to travel to come into contact with men and minds rather than depend upon books and the written word.

She put her finger on the basic reason for disunity and discord, for in India tolerance may have been an accepted part of religious doctrine. But each community lived in isolation and the nation was mentally separated from other nations. Decades later this very isolationism of normal social life and attitudes was to be the root cause of separatism, civil strife and partition of the country.

She said, "I say it is not your pride that you are a Madrasi, it is not your pride that you are a Brahmin, it is not your pride that, you belong to South India, it is your pride that you are a Hindu, but that it is your pride that you are an Indian.

Sarojini Naidu's Meetings

During the year 1902 Sarojini travelled to calcutta for meetings, and in Bombay addressed large crowds and ladies meetings dwelt on social disabilities of women, child marriage and widnow remarriage polygamy and women's education.

She passionately exhorted women to come out of seclusion to work and to take up careers. With the trammels of tradition to bind them she took women to ask for ignoring the poverty and misery around them, the sick in hospitals, the neglect of children, the misery of orphans and the handicapped. For she saw with complete clarity than the very isolation of religious creeds which permitted the existence of other creeds did not foster any elementof ordinary human concern for the troubles and miseries of others. Herself "a Hindu very, much at home in her Muslim environment a Brahmin bound by ties of love and marriage to a Non-Brahmin bound by ties of love and marriage to a Non-Brahmin she was a citizen of the world who yoelded to none in her attatchment to the motherland."

The bulk of her audiences however were locked in their limited words and it was the dynamism of her personality, the shock of her words combined with a pervading love and humanity making these words heeded and acceptable, that in great measure contributed to her success as a pionner creating the moment for women's emancipation in India.

It is not as though she were the first, for there were other great women reformers like Pandita Ramabai, Dr. Mrs. Muttulakshmi Reddy, Rambai Ranade, but she had the rate gift of touching the heart of listeners in such measure that they gave themselves to her and were influenced, If one analysis the work she did in her life time, it is surprising to find that she did not perhaps have the organisational abilities of the women of the thirties and forties. But she had the unique gift to inspire others to action.

Her contribution was almost entirely based upon speeches and the vision of an exalted and truly universal mind. Her frank and lucid analysis of social ills especially in regard to women, generated a leadership with direction and purpose that was to start the emancipation of women centred as it was later in the organisation of the All India Women's Conference.

The most significant event of these early years was her meeting with Gopal krishna Gokhle. When he died in 1915 she wrote a touching tribute "Gokhale the Man" which was published in the Bombay chronicle in which she describes many significant episodes.

"One morning a little despondent and sick heart about national affairs in general Gokhale suddenly asked me what is your outlook for India ? 'One of hope' I replied what is your vision of the immediate future ?' Hindu-Muslim unity in less than five years' I told him with joyous conviction. 'Child' he said with note of yearing sadness in his voice, 'you are a poet but you hope too much. It will not come in your lifetime or in mine. But keep your faith and wish if you can. ......

"....... it was my unique privilege to attend and address the now historic sessions of the Muslim League which met in Lucknow on the 22nd March (1913) to adopt a new Constitution which sounded the keynote of loyal co-operation with the Sister Community in all matters of national welfare and progress........ I found the world famous leader of the Indian National Congress.... 'Oh' he cried with outstretched hands when he saw me, 'have you come to me, to tell that your vision was true "!

Sarojini Naidu writes further on of another episode that left it's mark on her life.

"....... We sat quietly in the gathering twilight till his golden voice stirred by some deep emotion broke the silence with golden words of counsel and admonition, so grand and so solemn and so inspiring that they have never ceased to thrill me. He spoke of the unequalled happiness and privilege of service for India. Stand here with me he said with the stars and hills for witness and in their presence consecrate your life and your talent your song and your speech your thought and your dream to the Motherland".

To the modern young mind such a scene might be considered melodramatic, yet at this clarion call to service her mind reacted with the full force of her idealistic ardour. Here was the altar at which she could give herself body and soul, and the majestic personality whose leadership she could accept. It is little wonder that her life of poetry and dreaming receded and in it's place a new Sarojini began to emerge.

According to her she was only twenty-two when she started making speeches, and by 1905 had plunged into political life denouncing foreign rule and the championing Hindu-Muslim unity. When Lord Curzon decided on Pantion of Bengal a huge public meeting of Calcutta's citizens launched the first organized civil disobedience movement with boycott of foreign goods.

Indian brotherhood was marked by the symbolic tying of rakhis, binding each other to loyal service to the motherland. Students left Schools and Universities with the cry that they were being trained as slaves for British over lordships.

At the Indian National Congress in 1906, Sarojini's oratory coupled with her youthful looks staggered audiences. She seems to have had complete confidence even at that early age, jumping down from the platform after delivering an impassioned speech and joining the women in singing patriotic songs. Her presence at Students Conference which started at this time had a tremendous impact on youth and she spoke at many such meetings in Benaras, Calcutta and Bihar.

From the beginning she addressed these public meetings along with the great leaders of the day.

One of the lesser known speeches she made was in 1906 at the Theistic Conference held in Calcutta in 1906. While she stressed the personal element in spiritual life, she pointed out that, the spirit was India's salvation and because of it India had survived, unlike Greece and Rome whose civilizations had perished. What was perhaps more significant was her emphasis upon unity as demonstrated in all of the great religious heritages of India, a theme which was to be the essence of her contribution as a national leader.

In 1906 at the Indian Social Conference on the Education of Women in Calcutta her amendment substituting "Indian" for 'Hindu' was prompted by the need to establish firmly the unity that did not require caste, creed of religion as difinition.

Sarojini's Talents

Sarojini was nurtured from her earlist years, in this rarefied air and it is not surprising that in her declining years in fact all through her political career, she was to be pained and disheartened by what could only be considered a terrible betrayal of decent human values.

In her ebullience she naturally rode each storm with zest and courage and the kind of soaring confidence, that made her exclaim to, Gokhale that they would see Hindu-Muslim unity in five years. But time and again there would be return to despair and perhaps a repetition of her childhood cry, "what have I done to change the world?" With the stresses and strains of her emergence into active public life and the inevitable inner conflict that faces any woman who dearly loves her family Sarojini's health broke down again in 1913. Sarojini sailed for England. By that time her friendship with Gokhale had ripened into a relationship of greatt depth and meaning.

His missionary zeal which had built up the selfless work of the servants of India Society impressed upon this ardent young woman a sense of national service that made it possible that, the decision to enter public life. Her talents of oratory were so effective in moving audiences that it is not surprising that Gokhale's instant recognition of her powers would affect her profoundly.

He was essentially a spiritual teacher and the logical successor to her father in influencing her life. As her old friend C.P.Ramaswami lyer was to tell the author a month before he died at the age of ninety. Gopal Krishna Gokhale was the guiding spirit of her life from 1902 to his death 1915.

"An acquintance begun on such a happy note of sympathy grew and ripened at last into a close and lovely comradeship which I counted among the crowning honours of my life".

Sarojini wrote. "And though it was not without it's poignant moments of brief and bitter estrangement our friendship was always radiant both with the joy of spiritual refreshment and the quickening challenge of intellectual discussion and dissent"

Through these crowded years, before she sailed for England, Sarojini maintained a tender friendship with Gokhale based upon their common concern for Hindu-Muslim unity and national freedom, but added to this was that rare friendship, sometimes found in India, where a man who is venerated for his high ideals and exemplary life attracts.

Gokhale's Influence On Sarojini Naidu

Gopal Krishna Gokhale was born at Kutluk a small village in Ratnagiri District and came from the line of Chitpawan Brhamins. His early years were shadowed by tragedy and poverty, having lost his father when he was thirteen. But for the generosity of his elder brother, he would have had to give up his studies.

As a student he led a frugal existence cooking his own meals and saving kerosene by reading under the street lamp. He was quiet and industrious and ambitious, but his scholastic record was not particularly distinguished. It was in his college days that his intellectual powers were to unfold. He thought of taking the ICS Examination or joining the Engineeing College in Bombay.

For a year he attended the law classes in Bombay and might have ended up as a lawyer or judge. But then in 1885 he took a step which seemed almost insane to his family; He became a teacher on the paltry sum of Rs.35 per month in Poona's New English School run by a band of young Patriots. His work with Bal Gangadhar Tilak in New English School led in due course to the establishment Deccan Education Society.

In 1890 Gokhale met the patriot Ranade and became the secretary of the Sarvajanik Sabha. Ranade sent Gokhale to London to appear before the Royal Commission where his written evidence with its solid statistical material was a masterly exposition of the Indian case.

In 1899 he entered the Bombay Council and in 1901 the Imperial Council in Delhi. This was the forum where he showed his talent to the best advantage.

His first speech in 1902 on the Budget, marked him out as the most outstanding member of the Imperial Council. Gokhale's emergence as a national leader in 1905 coincided with a crisis in the Indian National Congress. It also coincided with the return to power of the British Liberal Party and the appointement of Morley as secretary of state for India.

During the next three years whenever proposals of constitutional reform were on anvil Gokhale visited England and explained the Indian point of view to the secretary of state. From 1910 onwards Gokhale did his best to make the Morle-Minto Reforms a success and also supported Mahatma Gandhi in the struggle on behalf of the Indian Community in South Africa, the abolition of the indenture system and the extension of elementary education.

Over the years Gokhale had sent Sarojini constant notes of warm aproval of her speeches or actions and often advice and admonition. He had been constantly concerned about her health and like a typical Indian father, felt adulation might go to her head. As so few women in any age adulation and praise was showered on her early poetry, She received recognition all over India, England and Europe. Critics likened her verses to Blake and said that her rich imagery made English poetry look pale. When she began carrer as an orator her fame was instantaneous.

In much 1912 there was an event in which Sarojini played a significant role and one dear to her heart. The Muslim League convened a "historic session" to adopt a new constitution embodying co-operation with Hindus in all matters of national welfare and progress. Sarojini addressed this gathering and gave an impassioned speech.

But it was not so much the speech as the year that must be remembered when she a woman addressed a meeting probably wholly male in which the new proposal were carried unanimously, not only but the young but by the more orthodox elements also.

Though Sarojini's hopes for unity faded over the years at

that time it was said that this meeting of the Muslim League, 'Marked a new era and inaugurated a new standard in the history of modern Indian affairs.

She has recorded Gokhale's reaction to this episode, "He seemed alsomt impatient of my words about the real underlying spirit of the conference. His weary, pain-worn face lighted up with pleasure when I assured him that so far at least as the younger men were concerned it was not an instrict of mere political expediency but one of genuine conviction and growing consciousness of wider and graver national responsibility that had prompted them to stretch out so frankly and fererously, the hand of good fellowship to Hindus and I hoped that the coming Congress would respond to it with equal if not even greater cordiality."

Gokhale told her. "So far as lies in my power it shall be done," And he said later, "You have put new hope in me. I feel strong enough to face life and work again".

In 1915 just before Gokhale's death Sarojini was also ill and in England for treatement. She could never resist the call of youth and that Jinnah had created a centre for Indian students in London fired her imagination so greatly that on an impulse she promised the sttudents who clamoured for Gokhale that, "the incomparable friend and servant of India" would address them.

All this Sarojini decribed in great detail in her "Tribute to Gokhale" published when he died, and mentioned earlier. But her constant concern and identify with the needs of youth come out vividly in the letter to Gokhale in London dated July 29th.

In 1914 Sarojini left for India and Gokhale's last words o her were, "I do not think we shall meet again. If you live, remember your life is dedicated to the service of the country. My work is done."

Sarojini-In Politics

Child of Hyderabad a city in which Hindu and Muslim cultures fused and flowered it is not strange that communal unity was next to her desire of freedom, Sarojini's greatest motivating force. A true integrationist, unlike even her master, Gandhiji, who believed in the closest and most fraternal co-existence, Sarojini was happiest and perhaps as her greatest as harmoniser and unifier.

In 1916 in the historic city of Lucknow which rivalled only Hydrabad in it's harmony of Hindu and Muslim cultures she addressed the conference of the Muslim League in a manner both modest and frank.

"I do not know what claim I have to stand before you today except that I have been for many years a faithful comrade of the young generation of the Mussalmans and champion of the women of the Muslim community and fought with their men folk for the privilege that the Islam gave a long ago but which you denied to your womenfolk."

In 1918, in Jullunder talking to the students of the kanya Maha Vidyalaya, she stressed the need for women's education, saying, "Our Guru gandhi has enjoined us to address meetings in Hindustani. I crave your indulgence for talking in imperfect Urdu. The narrow-minded people say that the education of women is to be condemned because it makes them bold.

Brothers, have you forgotten the heroic stories and scriptures of your mother land ? It was the privilege of India to possess women who were bolder and braver than their brothers.

For the amelioration of a country the co-operation of both sexes is necessary...... You demand political rights pray do not forget that a lame person can-walk but slowly, a one-eyed man sees onoly on one side and that a carriage with one wheel cannot move properly." And turning to the problem of Muslim women, Sarojini said.

"the "Purdah" system did not mean "purdah" on the mind and a "purdah" on the soul," ......and she ended, "Break open the cage of bigotry, the liberty of the soul will be Indias share only when woman is free."

Again and again she reverted to the theme of unity. In Patna on october 13, 1917, it was students she addressed; "President and Brother Hindus and Mussalmans, I feel today a peculiar sense of responsibility such as I have never felt before when dealing with a subject so intimately bound up with my life-strings that I almost hesitate in trying to find words, that might be wise enough to suit the occasion......." Romantically she called upon the Ganges to give her inspiration, and prophetically she hoped that current political developments would not "cause a cleacage between the two communities."

So close was unity to her heart that little was needed for it no find expression. The episode with Gokhale will be recalled, when in reply to his question.

"What is your vision of the immediate future ?"

Her answer was, "Hindu-Muslim unity in less than five years" and he had answered, "You hope too much, It will not come in your life time or in mine."

Undiscouraged she searched for a kindred spirit and crusader; and in 18913 found him in the young and dynamic, M.A.Jinnah, blesse by Gokhale, then the greatest living Indian and united in the noblest of causes.

When Gokhale died in 1915 Sarojini wrote the poem, In Memorium, in which she poured her devotion;

"Heroic Heart ! last hope of all our days !
Need'st thou the homage of our love and praise ?
Lo ! let the mournful millions round the type
Kindle their souls with consecreated fire
Caught from the brave torch fallen from the hand,
To succour and to save our, stricken land,
And in the daily worship taught by thee
Uphold the temple of her unity."

A true Indian Sarojini unlike several of her colleagues never consciously worked for Hindu-Muslim unity. Embodying in herself as she did the finest elements of both faiths she only acted as her natural self.

Sarojini had always made it a point to meet Tagore whenever she was in Bengal. She of course could not read Bengali but she loved to hear his songs and his poems read in that meldious language. As the years passed they came even closer.

It was Sarojini who arranged a Tagore Week in Bombay in 1933 and it was only fitting that, later she was appointed Acharya of Tagore's University Visva Bharati at Shantiniketan.

Devotion to Mahatma Gandhi

Sarojini's devotion to Gandhiji was great. Once she came under his sway as complete and final. Gandhiji little known and regarded as some what of a crank with some newfangled of passive resistance for gaining political ends left Soiuth Africa and arrived in England on August 6, 1914. Accompanied by his wife he had travelled theird class and lived on nuts and fruits dietary concepts Sarojini was to deplore on more than one occasion.

But however strange were his ideas the fact remained that his Satyagraha Struggle had proved largely seccessful.

Gokhale and others wished him to transfer his activities to India. He was therefore warmly welcomed by the Indian Community in England. At another meeting Ganghiji expressed his opinion that, Indians should help in the war effort. He invited volunteers and though objections were raised there was a good response. He had in mind an Indian Volunteer Corps and Sarojini and about other prominent Indians added their signature to a letter he sent to the then under secretary of state for India.

"It was thought by many of us they wrote, that during the crisis that has overtaken the empire and Whilst many Englishmen leaving their ordinary vocations of life are responding to the Imperial call those Indians.

Who are residing in the U.K. and who can to all do so should place themselves unconditionally at the disposal of the authorities" "we would respectfully emphasize" the letter concluded, "the fact that the one dominent idea guiding us is that of rendering such humble assistance as we may be capable of performing as an earnest of our desire to share the responsibility of membership of the great empire if we would share it's privileges.

Sarojini must have been imbued with the spirit of the letter when she wrote her famous poem "The Gift of India."

The New Spirit of Sarojini

When Sarojini was returned to India from her foreign tour, deep tragedy was soon to strike. First in Calcutta her beloved father died and a few days afterwards her "political" father, Gokhale passed away.

Gandhiji had returned to fill the double void. He soon

established his Ashram near Ahmedabad and Mrs. Naidu quickly placed herself at his service. Soon she was lecturing in Andra.

"For years now it has been my great privilege to be more closely identified with what is known as the younger generation. In almost every great city of India I have come into joyful and intimate comradeship with the young men who are going to make the history of tomorrow; In the different cities of India.

I have come closely in touch with what is called the 'new spirit' in India-with what has mostly been called Indian Renaissance was not confined to the intellectual elite. Presenting Medals on another occasion she expressed her happiness in doing so to those who are learning to work with their hands to recognise the dignity of manual labour, as it should stand side by side with the dignity of scholarship.

Sarojini's Great Speeches

Sarojini tried maximum to rouse the people from their apathy and inertia. "All over India today" she said in Guntur" there is a new spirit awakening that thrills the heart of the young generation from end to end, from North and South, East and West the spirit that is called the renaissance not a new spirit but a spirit newborn and revitalized in the past that holds exactly such ideas and dreams that taught by precept and example, such principles as you wish to fulfil in your life for the service of your country, whether you go to Bengal and speak with young men with the passionate spirit of ideals,....... you realise the young spirit is the same, though it speaks in different vernaculars.

By 1916 New winds were blowing in India. By now Sarojini was well launched on a nation-wide campaign of speeches, many of them to youth and women's groups, where she exhorted them to tackle social ills and join hands in the struggle for freedom. It was however at the Lucknow Congress in 1916 that Sarojini gained wide recognition both as speaker and national leader of first rank.

Entrusted with supporting the resolution on self government for India she enthralled and electrified the audiences by declaring;.

"I am merely a spectaror from the watch-tower of dreams; and I watched the swift and troubled. We stand united but united with such strength that nothing from outside not even the tyranny of colonial domination, shall withhold from us our rights and privileges with hold from us the liberties that are due which claim by our united voice........ Centuries have gone by old divisions are healed old wounds, living consciousness that is in united service for the motherland that constitutes the uppermost hope of tomorrow.

There is no one so mean so weak so selfish as not to think that in the service of the motherland lies the joy greater than all personal joys; to die for motherland is no achieve the priceless crown of immortality."

India's March Towards Freedom

It was a momentous session of the Congress in 1930 over which Jawaharlal Nehru presided and infact it may be considered as another milestone along India's march towards freedom. For the first time complete independence was declared as the national goal and in pursuance of this, civil disobedience and non-payment taxes were resolved upon. Gandhiji now returned to Sabarmati to plan the campaign.

All the Congress leaders gathered round him and Sarojini was present when he expressed his anxiety whether his doctrine of non-violence had been fully accepted and understood by those who were likely to take part in the movement.

Much heart-searching and deliberation took place and Gandhiji eventually decided to break the law prohibiting the manufacture of salt except by Government agencies. But characteristically he first informed the Viceroy of his intentions.

Though Sarojini was not among the developed and hardly followers who accompanied Gandhiji when on March 12, he commenced he march to the sea, she was present when on April 6,after a night spent in prayer Gandhiji went down to the beach and broke the salt Law by picking up some dried salt. The Government which had been keeping a close watch now moved into action. On may 5 Gandhiji was arrested.

Later, it has been estimated that 25,000 volunteers had now gathered to break the salt law. Sarojini assumed the leadership inspite of her ill-health. Enjoining them to remain peaceful, whatever the provocation, she led them along the sea shore. The police stopped them.

The volunteers could not proceed they sat down on the sandy road. It was the middle of summer and a scorching hot day. they were cordoned off by the police and the salt field was fenced in by barbed wire. They were trapped there without food or water. The young volunteers suffered from intense thirst and in order to make them suffer more the police it was alleged, drove water carts through the rows of parched volunteers without allowing them a drop to quench their intolerable thirst.

Sarojini Naidu sat in their midst in a deck chair She never stopped smiling or encouraging her army and they were astounded to hear her cheerful remarks and her jokes.

But Sarojini did not sit in her deck-chair for long. Calling for a prayer, she exhorted her followers, "Gandhi's body is in jail but his soul is with you. India's prestige is in your hands, you must not use any violence under any circumstances. You will be beaten but you must not resist; you must not even raise a hand to ward off blows......." Gandhiji, Sarojini and their army of followers were not alone in deying the Government.

Independence and After

In March 1942 the Cripps Mission had come to India to negotiate the formula for an interim Government with the Indian leaders, Sarojini as a member of the working committee meetings in march, April and May, and when the Congress Party members met the Cripps Mission. The talks failed as no formula could be found acceptable to the Congress and Jinnah who was later the nationally acclaimed leader of the Muslim League. Shortly afterwards Sarojini travelled to Labore to see her sister Gunnu, but on arrival in Punjab was served with an order forbidding her to make speeches in public, to take part in processions or meetings or to communicate with newspapers.

On being asked to sign the order she wrote on the back of it that the order served on her was invalid since she was under doctor's orders not to undertake any public work of this nature. From Labore she went to Calcutta and then tragedy struck again in the family with the grave illness of Ranadheera, her beloved younger son "Mina".

On May 6 of that month of sorrow for Sarojini, Gandhiji was released from the Aga Khan's Palace and spent his time resting for some months in Panchgani.

In June 1945 all the leaders were released from jail and the first Simla Conference began, which helped not a little to create a calm atmosphere for the talks, though they did not terminate with any success. By this time Jinnah was quite convinced that the Congress and specifially Hindu leadership would never play fair and there was no hope for Muslims as a minority in this country. Meanwhile political events moved inexorably towards the partition of India which took-place on August 15, 1947. Though the Viceroy and the Labour Government strove to the last to preserve an undivided India. Parts of India went up in flames, Hindu-Muslim relations descended to the lowest point in history and the holocaust known as the "Great Calcutta killing".

Bengal was particularly afflicted and Gandhiji decided to tour areas pof East bengal especially Noakhali where terrible things had taken place.

On August 15, 1947 the two new countries were established and in India the Congress formed a government and also created a Constituent Assembly to prepare the constitution of a free India. An extract of the proceedings of this Assembly on December 11, 1946 displays the remarkable role she played in public life.

At the age of sixtyseven Sarojini was as vigorous as ever capable of making bold and impressive speeches but not capable any more to hope with the blithe confidence of her early years for unity. Life itself had given her bitter insights bitter truths; ther, had been bitter realisations which are now a part of history.

Going on to her own disillusion with her world and the one to which she had given all her life, sacrificing life and family life to do so. She said we have all noted the failure of politicians throughout the world; we have all noted the tragedy of the pledged word broken even as it was given;

Sarojini's beloved doctor Bidhan Roy with his towering figure and personality was suffering from eye trouble and was in America for treatment. Returning to India in November after Independence on August 15, Bidhan Roy found to his delight that, "Sarojini Naidu was quite happy in her new position and performed her duties very well.

Sarojini's Dreams

The India of Sarojini's dreams the strong sheltering comforting Mother had been reborn but the children of this mother continued to be undisciplined unfocussud upon a single concept of nationhood and torn between each other. No one was more aware of this than the Governor of U.P.she often likened herself in that palatial establishment to a bird in a cage, a little, particularly apt in the light of the one given by Mahatma Gandhi of Bharat Kokila.

And if she was the superb hostess of this "gilded cage" making an official establishment into a beautiful home a warm and welcoming official residence into a centre of importance and dignity, at the same time as many speeches and letters attest, her heart was heavy for her people.

None of this was evident to the guests who streamed through that well-ordered house. They would often find her on the wide verandah sitting in the sun reading detective stories or presiding over splanded tease and regaling friends and callers with stories, and ancedotes filled with wit and humour.

Countless friends recall those days speak of her exquisite table and magnificent food, the Indian splendour of the furnishings and the household who loved her so much, yet maintained the residence with the same order and dignity as for the former british masters. For it is well known that the staff who had served the British often became so servile that they had only contempt for an Indian master. But Sarojini could not only command she also generated love. As Governor this side of her nature which loved beaty hospitality and entertaining had ample scoope.

Some say that in her last years she reverted to her Ivory tower, others that she recreated, her father's court and if she could not out do, the Nizam in wealth she certainly succeeded in making the hospitality of her kingdom infinitly more warm and regal what seems much more evident is that she continued to be herself.

When in prison or hut she accommodated to those circumstances and made do with what there was, but when she was given a queen's role, she became a queen. Her talents as a human being were varied and flexible but most important of all as a person, she was never anything but herself.

During meetings of the central Board of Education Maulana Azad Hymayum kabir and army other friends stayed at Raj Bhavan in Lucknow.

Sarojini was greatly concerned over the language issue and well aware of how strong an advocate her own minister of Education was of Hindi replacing both Urdu and English. U.P. was the home of Urdu and there was understandably great uncertainty regarding it's future Language was as personal as one's dress.

In her lifetime, Sarojini had worked with truth in all it's dimensions from the vision of truth through a poet's eyes, to the Karmayogin concept of her beloved leader, Gandhiji that had led her into the heart of the populace and stirred them with her oratory to work for freedom. The life of Sarojini Naidu was a work of art. In death she was alone, but in life she belonged wholly to the living in her life she fulfilled the standard laid down by Tulsidas.

"When you come into the world you cry and the world laughs; so live that when thou departest thou mayest laugh while the world will be in tears."

14

Morarji Desai

Morarji- The Man of Principles

If rigid adherence to principles in which he believed had cost Morarji so much in political terms in personal life also he has been at the receiving end of the slings and arrows of outrageous fortune on account of it.

His father Ranchodji Desai a god-fearing scion of an avil brahmin ancestry and a village school teacher by profession, committed suicide, when Morarjibhai was only 15. He had to bear the burden of maintaining the family consisting of his grand mother, mother, three brothers and two sisters. When he was married a few days later-strangely enough on the third day of his father's death-the number of family members became nine with the addition of his young wife.

Ranchodji Desai was a victim of melancholia and had jumped into a well in a fit of depression. The shock and sorrow were too great for Morarji a sensitive youth; but he did not allow them to overwhelm him. Instead he settled down to the task of rearing his younger brothers and sisters and seeing them through life.

Morarjibhai was in the matriculation class at Bulsar at that time. After passing the examination he moved to Bombay to join Wilson College. He got a seat in the Goculdas Tejpal free boardig house which provided lodging, board, clothes, college fees, and books for its inmates. The college also charged concessional fees from students living in the boarding house.

Morarjibhai was thus able to complete his university education inspite of the extreme poverty of his family circumstances. He lived frugally walking the distance of about three miles from the boarding house to the college morning and evening and avoiding even what present-day students would regard as necessities. He was thus able to send to his family ten rupees whch he received every month as scholarship. After graduation he joined Government service as a deputy collector which in those days was one of the conveted jobs with plenty of influence and power. He could have also enjoyed the creature comforts which went with the position if he were built that way.

Normally persons from deprived sections would plunge into life with a vegeance after they had made good but not Morarjibhai. Until he left the Government service in 1930 in connection with Gandhiji's non co-operation movement he remained true to his obligations to his younger brothers. He had even promised to finance the education in England of one of his brothers who wanted to pursue higher study of medicine there.

Even though married inm 1911 at the age of 15 he started his conjugal life only from 1917 after passing his B.A. Examination. When he joined service he was living with his mother, wife two brothers and a sister. The other sister had died five years earlier from burns. She was firing crackers during Diwali when her clothes caught fire and she was fatally injured.

The Desai's had five children in the eleven years of their

married life, after which in 1928 Morarjibhai took the vow of bramac harya. Of the children the first son born after a daughter, died when he was only 18 months. The youngest also a son, born in 1918, did not survive for more than two years. Of the two daughters the second, who was one year older than Kantibhai put an end to her life at the age of 27. Though Morarjibhai had borne these misfortunes stoically a little probing would reveal the deep wounds in his heart.

Above all he is conscious of the fact that due to his total involvement in the freedom struggle first and the affairs of the state later, he could not bestow on his children, the attention and care, which he would have liked o give them. He had done his duty by his three younger brothers whose education he had financed even when his means were extremely limited. He had promised to see his third brother Nanubhai. Nanubhai had secured admission to the course and also booked his passage to England, when Morarjibhai resigned from Government service and the entire plan had to be given up.

Morarjibhai was sorry that he could not do what he had promised to his brother. In the case of his own children, he could not do even that much. Kantibhai was only four when his father gave up his job. Very soon began the recurring spells of jail going in connection with the series of satyagraha movements. Morarjibhai's wife Gajraben also went to jail one of those occasions. The routine ceased only in 1946 when Kantibhai was 20. One can imagine the sense of neglect which children feel when their parents are so engaged otherwise.

While Morarjibhai had to spend an extra year in the matriculation class because he was too young to sit for the terminal examination. This was because of the repeated interruptions in his studies due to the vicissitudes mentioned earlier.

Morarjibhai wanted him to be an engineer and so made him to take up science at college. Kantibhai who had no aptitude for the subject failed in the inter mediate examination and then gave up his studies altogether. For about two years later he tried his hand at being an aeronautical ground engineer but that too did not hiold his interest

Finally he plumped for insurance business and landed in a job as an insurance agent. It was obviously not a post, which a minister would 'obtin' for his son, and so the critics instead of charging Morarjibhai with Misusing his influence began ato insinuate that Kanti would exploit his father's position for his business interest. Even the most rigid code of conduct would not debar the minister's son from plying his chosen trade as long as there was no nexus between it and the parent's political office. And one of the conditions on which Kantibhai was allowed to take up the business was that he would not insure any Government employee or deal with any Government, department. Still, some critics wanted Kantibhai shift business to some other state. At that rate, after Morarjibhai joined the Central Government his son would have to go abroad if he wanted to be in business.

The irony is, that the more honest a person the greater the tendency to judge him by is absolute standards. This is not to decry public vigilance in matters involving conduct of the business of Government and expenditure of the tax payer's money. But any criticism of the public servants be they ministers, or lesser fry should be in perspective.

Otherwise what is intended as a crusade against corruption will degenerate into a political weapons in the hands of manipulators. Much avoidable pain was caused to Morarjibhai in 1968 by allegations within and outside parliament they were destroying a pillar of the ruling party while the then Prime Minister, and her supporters used it as a lever to buttress themselves further.

Indira gandhi's attitude in that episode was singularly ambivalent. Since some mud will stick even to a saint, Morarjibhai was thrown on the defensive. His conscience was clear as were the facts of the case. But his tactics were too clean to be effective against the forces pitted against him.

To recapitulate the fact of the case Kantilal started his own business through a company called permanent Magnet Limited in 1950-51, and remained with that venture until 1964. By then Morarjibhai had left Central Government in pursuance of the Kamraj plan. When Kantibhai intended to give up his business and join his father as private secretary the latter had no reason to reject the suggestion.

Kantibhai's reason for doing so as stated by him was that he had then earned enough to ensure a monthly income of Rs.2500 and therefore, wanted to enter public life as private secretary to his father. Nobody noticed the switch in Kantibhai's position until Morarjibhai returned to the Government as Deputy Prime minister in Indira Gandhi's second Government.

Kantibhai's story

Madhu Limaye countered the statement with information that Kantibhai was receiving a sum of Rs.2000 per month from one of his former business associates until 1967. Apparently some interested persons were passing bits and pieces of such information to the opposition critics of Morarjibhaii.

As a later statement by Morarjibhai revealed, when Kuntibhai terminated his business conncetions with Dodsals in 1964 it was agreed that he would receive as a kind of retirement benefit a monthly sum of Rs. 2000 for a period of 3 years. It was not suggested that there was anything irregular in that arrangement.

After all, the charge was that the company was trying to

influence Morarjibhai by keeping his son on its pay roll. It was not established. In 1964 when the arrangement was made there was no prospect of Morarjibhai re-entering Government, and he was not a minister until after 1967 general election.

Secondly even if Kantibhai had not been Morarji Desai's private secretary he would have lived with him as a member of the joint family and would have, "influenced" him oif Morarji were a person to be so influenced. Rightly or wrongly, Morarjibhai prides himself in being immune to such influences.

There are also instances when he has been fairly successful in resisting such influences. He says that,'even if he has made a wrong judgement in a case it is not the result of extraneou; factors but of his own volition. The same was the case with Gandhiji who had surrounded himself with persons in business and industry. Some of whom had also taken advantage of their proximity to Gandhiji.

But Gandhiji would never accept that he was instrumental in their receiving such benefits. It was an extremely delicate question. To resume Kantibhai's story despiite the clarification of the issue by Morarjibhai in statements in parliament and private communications to the then Prime Minister allegations continud to be made and mud did not cease to be slung at him.

Morarjibhai's Adherence

Morarjibhai's rigid adherence to principles as he believed in them has also a negative effect on his otherwise noble personality. For instance he has been a firm believer in the maxim that means are ends'. Even unintended violence in a political agitation or industrial strike would throw him off balance. He sometimes regarded all strikes as immoral. His attitude as Home Minister to the long drawn-out strike by the textile workers of Bombay in 1951 was an instance in point. The strike was in pursuance of the workers demand for four months bonus.

The labour tribunal had awarded only two month's bonus. The workers then modified their demand to three months wages as bonus.

The Rashtriya Mill Mazdoor Sangh of the Indian National trade Union Congress was the representative union recognised by the authorities. The obviously more popular Mill Mazdoor Sabha led by the socialists and the communist Girni Kamgar Union launched a strike to press the demand for a larger bonus. The strike was an undoubted success and after it lasted a couple of weeks most of the Mill-Owners also were prepared to concede the demand. But that would have exposed the INTUC Union as lacking in representative capacity.

Guljarilal nanda's manipulations in this respect as Labour Minister in Bombay could not also be unknown to Morarjibhai. But he took the stand that since the tribunal had awarded only two months bonus and since both the employers and the workers as represented by the, INTUC Union had agreed to abide by the award the strike was immoral and would undermine the system of arbitration in industrial disputes. He had no doubt a point that the response to the strike was not an index of the popularity of the different unions.

Members of the INTUC Union were also eager for a larger bonus and did not hesitate to join the strike launched by the Mill Mazdoor Sabha but as the strike continued for several days causing loss to the workers and as there were also repeated instances of arrests and repression against supporters of the strike. it was clear that much more than mere greed for money was the motive behind the workers action. A less inflexible attitude on Morarji's part would have ended the dispute, especially since a larger number of mill owners also prepared to pay the extra bonus. There was obviously no death of resources to meet tne demand.

But Morarjibhai insisted that the claim for higher bonus was un reasonable and actively prevented the management from reaching a settlement with the Mill Mazdoor Sabha. It was a clear case of his partiality for the INTUC Union getting better of his respect for truth. He also would not let Nehru intervene in the dispute because he thought jayaprakash narayan who was in the Socialist Party than had induced nehru to intervene on behalf of the workers.

Principle and Prejudice

Morarjibhai was in the Nasik Central Jail in 1933. When the Congress Socialist group was formed by some other inmates of the prison. Morarji thought that Nehru's Political proximity to the Socialists was a sign of his Moral weakness and lock of clear understanding. Sardar Patel too was close to socialist leaders, like Achyut Patwardhan but not Morarjibhai.

He always believed in keeping them at a distance politically. During the first two decades of independence this had sharpened Morarjibhai's image as an unbending conservative while Nehru whose policies were not different from those of Morarji had shone as a progressive and a friend of the Socialists. This is amply illustar ted by an accountof a discussion Morarji had with Vinoba Bhave in may 1955.

Narayan Desai the only son of Mahadev Desai, had prepared a note on the discussion which was appended to Morarji Desai's autobiography. It would clearly show that Morarjibhai had no confidence in Jayaprakash's conversion to Sarvodaya. Anydody who has been watching Jayaprakash Narayan's search for truth in the social and not metaphysical sense, knows that he has travelled a long way from Marxism, Materialism and Party Politics. Still Morarji Desai complains that, "Those who did not fully believe in truth and non violence when Bapu was in Congress are now talking of non-violence".

At another place Narayan Desai points out that Jayaprakash Narayan believes in both God and the purity of means, Morarji replies perhaps sarcastically;" Yes thai is no. I do believe that he has made progress in this direction, but he has not grsped it fully." His another complaint against Jayaprakash was that he did not subscribe to the theroy of class collaboration but believd in removing classes which according to Morarji Desai was not possible. Finally Morarjibhai syss "I cannot understand why people cannot have faith in God !"

Search For Truth

Intolerance of Dissent is more rampant among believers in god than even among politicians. One can understand atheists trying to make a doctrine of their lack of faith because they are constantly on the defensive against the overwhelming majority who believe in the existence of god. But true believers should be more tolerant towards non-conformists. In fact such tolerance is a sign of enlightment. Though an inveterate believer in god, Morarji Desai has over the years largely shed the prejudices which he initially harboured towards those who differed with him.

The attitude displayed by him in his conversations with Vinobha Bhave has apparently mellowed in the subsequent twenty years; the latest spell of detention from June 26, 1975 to January 19, 1977 had also enabled him to reflect dispassionately on what he was imbibed from the Bhagavad Gita and other books of philosophy and religion. He was also able to gain from the experience of nearly 50 years of public life, tolerance pof diversity if not outright dissent. Solitary confinement which for such a long duration was undoubtedly cruel and was nothing short of mental torture did not unhinge his mental balance. He took it in his philosophical stride and even put it to good use by endless reflection and self-introspection. If he is able to record his life in detention as faithfully and comprehensively as he has written down the story of My Life until 1970 it would be a veritable treasure for posterity.

Even earlier morarjibhai had been relentlessly pursuing his search for truth. Two experiences of his were very important in that connection. The first was a 15-day stay at Sri Aurobindo's ashram in Pondicherry. He found the life there very peaceful and pleasant, enabling him to think deeply on religion and related matters. He was impressed by the self-discipline and devotion to duty of the inmates, especially the permanent ones.

He was also struck by the efficiency and organisational smoothness of the ashram, which was achieved, without any element of coercion. But he came back with the belief that Sri Arobindo had yet to reach the highest stage in his pursuit of yoga. From Pondicherry he went to Tiruvannamalai and spent a day at Sri Ramana Maharshi's abode. The second experience was different from the earlier one, and brought home to Morarjibhai the meaning of real enlightenment.

Morarjibhai writes : "I had the privilege of seeing Ramana Maharshi in the hall in which he usually he sat. He was sitting on a sofa and wore only a loin cloth. I could see an aura on his face which was glowing with peace and joy. I sat opposite to him, but did not ask him anything. He did not stay anything to me. I sat over an hour and just looked at his face. Till today I have not seen that aura, that joy or peace on anybody else's face. While I sat there no question arose in my mind, nor did I fell any desire to ask anything. I was at complete peace with myself It was this experience which convinced me that Ramana Maharshi had realised god or truth."

At a mundane level a relatively trivial incident at lunch at Sh. Ramana Maharshi's Ashram reinforced Morarji's understanding of enlightened behaviour. A few disciples of Sri Raman Maharshi sat apart from the rest because they were believers in untouchability and would not eat with persons belonging to the lower castes.

For Morarjibhai who never practised untouchability and allowed Harijans into his home even at the cost of displeasing his aged grand mother, it was a shock. But Sri Ramana Maharshi sat with the majority and at his lunch without even seeming to notice the behaviour of those disciples who would not mix with others. He did not argue with them, nor did he expect those disciples to change their ways because as Morarjibhai noted, they did not learn from his experience.

Morarjibhai-The Mature Practioner

Morarjibhai has emerged as a more mature practioner of the search for truth after his latest term of incarceration at Sohana rest house in Haryana. This is clear from even glimpses of his conduct at party meetings and private conversations.

Hypothetically speaking he would not have been disappointed or upset if he had not been choosen to head the Janata Party.

Infact after the formation of the Janata Party and it's decision to contest the elections, he was reluctant to be a candidate. But once he was drafted into the leadership of the party and asked to campaign on it's behalf he insisted on disciplined behaviour by all the constituents. That was the reason why he virtually ticked of S.K.Patil when the latter changed his mind about not contesting the election and clamoured for nomination from the South Bombay constituency He was equally resolute that there should be no centralised funding of the campaign and that the different leaders should look after the regions entrusted to their responsibility. This had created difficulties for Janata Party candidates in states like Assam, Andhra Pradesh, Himachal and Madhya Pradesh, where because of paucity of resources.

The posibility of raising money locally was also limited in these areas because traditionally party funds have come from metropolitan centres like Bombay and Calcutta, Mellowed in his attitude of in discriminate to what he regarded as wrong, Morarjibhai retains his penchant for almost brutal frankness in the expression of his opinions.

Sometimes his views are acerbic and evoke unpleasant reaction, but when it is realised that he speaks out his mind without anger or malice the feelings of the victims are soothed. Even towards Mahatma Gandhi whom he revered, Morarjibhai had the same attitude of candour in speech. For instance he did not hesitate to point out to Gandhiji that the latter's habit of resting his hands on the shoulders of his grandnieces, while going for walks involved a great social risk, "When considered in the light of public interest." He did not doubt the fact that Gandhiji had by then completely controlled his passions. But he was afraid that people who were not similarly placed might emulate, Gandhiji's example and justifying their actions by quoting him as an example.

When he conveyed his fears to Gandhiji the Mahatma said he was used to the practice for forty years and pointed out that it had increased his control over himself as well as the confidence of women in this self control. Morarjibhai's answer was that an improper action would not become proper simply because it had been indulged in for forty years.

His intention as he put it down explicitly in his autobiography was not to find fault with Gandhiji but better to understand the latter's philosophy. Gandhiji was not however convinced about the validity of Morarjibhai's apprehensions and the dialogue ended inconclusively but a few days later Gandhiji referred to the conversation in an article in the Harizan and said that the behaviour of a young worker at the Ashram had convinced him about the correctness of Morarjibhai's stand. He frankly admitted that the practice was a source of harm to public interest.

Another incident involving Gandhiji and Morarjibhai's political Guru Sardar Patel throws further light on Morarjibhai's frankness in his dealings with even those whom he normally obeyed unquestioningly. He had sought a private meeting with Gandhiji to discuss with him certain doubts tormenting him at the conduct of the Satyagraha Movement. That was in 1934 and his doubts were about the principles of morality and their practice in life. As he did not raise them in the presence of others he requested Gandhiji to spare him some time for a discussion in private.

Gandhiji asked him to meet him at 2.30 in the morning at his Ashram at Sabarmati. As ill luck would have it, a companion of Morarjibhai who was also a follower of Gandhiji came to know of the rendezvous and wanted to be present on the occassion and Morarjibhai agreed. But when Morarjibhai placed before Gandhiji a general statement about the tendency of some Gandhiji' lieutenants not to observe his moral code, his companion butted in with a direct criticism of Sardar Patel. He alleged that the Sardar's behaviour was sometimes not in accordance with the truth and asked Gandhiji how tolerated it.

Gandhiji did not conceal his dislike of such criticism of Sardar Patel whom loved immensely, and said if Morarjibhai's companion could substantiate his allegations against the Sardar he would enquire into them and would also publish the findings of such an inquiry. Morarjibhai realised that the siuation was taking a turn totally unintended by his and tried to revert to his-original position of seeking general guidance from Gandhiji. Apparently the gist of the conversation was passed on to Sardar Patel who was naturally upset with Morarjibhai who he thought was turning against him.

Sardar patel and Morarji Desai

A more serious point of difference developed between Sardar patel and Morarji Desai in late 1941. The All-India Congress Committee as its meeting in Poona earlier had extended conditional support to the British war effort saying that if India was granted immediate independence, the Congress would co-operate with the British Government against the dictators.

As it mean renunciation of the principle of non-violecne which ruled our co-operation in war in any circumstances Gandhiji Khan Abdul Ghaffar Khan and a few others dissociated themselves from the new Congress policy. Months passed and there was no sign of the British Government responding to the Congress offer of conditional co-operation, So the Congress leaders went back to Gandhiji and requested him to resume the leadership of the Congress and the nation.

Towards that end it was necessary to rescind the Poona resdution and Sardar Patel who was earlier a party to the resdution now set about undoing it.

Morarji Desai did not agree with the tactics. He was not orginally infavour of the Poona resolution, but at the same time he thought it was wrong to rescind it in the way it was being sought to be done. So when the Gujarat Pradesh Congress committee met to carry out Sardar Patel's "advice." Morarji resisted and made his position clear though as a disciplined follower of the Sardar, he ultimately did not oppose formally the resolution rescinding the Poona formulation.

Gandhiji who addressed the meeting of the Gujarat Congress realised the true state of affairs. He said that the minority which stuck to the Poona resolution had voted honestly while he was not sure that was the case with the pro-changers. He there fore abondoned the idea of rescinding the Poona resolution.

Soon after when Gandhiji decided to launch a final struggle for achieving independence, which resulted in the Quit India movement-Sardar Patel had doubts about Morarjibhai's compliance in such a policy and adviced him to meet Gandhiji and clear his doubts with the latter.

Accordingly Morarjibhai had a meeting with Gandhiji, and frankly expressed his doubts about the advisability of launching such a movement. He said some of those who were supporting Gandhi's movement did not believe in non-violence and would not therefore hesitate from violent action after going underground.

Morarji was worried about the growing influence of the Congress socialists in the organisation and because of his extremely rigid adherence to the principle of non-violent action he felt that even if the socialists and other extremists succeeded in dislodging the British from India, the result would not be the same as achieving independence by Gandhian means.

Gandhiji however had a larger outlook and overruled Morarji's doubts. He said that in the context of the situation then prevailing both at home and abroad, the risk of the movement ceasing to be non-violent was worth taking because it was necessary for India to strike for her Independence at that time.

There was another incident of a some what more serious nature between the Sardar and Morarjibhai. Soon after the conclusion of the Gandhi-Irwin pact of March 1931 both sides were on the look out to see how the other was honouring or not honouring the agreement. In that connection, Sardar Patel asked

Morarjibhai to obtain some information from village officers in Gujarat. Morarjibhai knew that such information was confidential and that he would not be able to obtain it unless he used his influence as a former deputy collector he thought that would infringe the principle of purity of means and declined to comply with the Sardar's request. By then it was decided to hold the next session of the Congress at Karachi.

Especially because of the Gandhi-Irwin true it was expected to be a momentous session and for Morarjibhai, who had left Government service and joint the Congress, it would be an experience to attend the session.

Gandhiji opened the conversation with a query whether Morarjibhai wanted to attend the Karachi Congress Session. When Morarjibhai said, "Yes", Gandhiji bluntly advised him to drop the idea saying that he should not leave the work undone which was expected of him in Gujarat and go to Karachi.

Morarjibhai's answer was that there was no work to be left undone by him in Gujarat.

Since it was the first Congress Session after his joing the organisation and also it was expected to be momentous, he desired to attend the session.

But Gandhiji insisted that there after every session of the Congress would be equally momentous and that Morarjibhai could attend said he could forego attending the following session also, if Gandhiji wanted him not to attend. Gandhiji observed that he was not issuing a directive but was only appealing Morarjibhai's heart.

Morarjibhai struck to his saying that though he would abide by the Mahatma's decision his arguments for asking Morarjibhai not to attend the Karachi Session were not convincing.

Morarjibhai's Frankness

Morarjibhai brought to bear a frankness of approach on his dealings with Nehru. Though he knew too well that Nehru was no Gandhiji had that with the passing away of Sardar Patel there was nobody in the Congress who could disagree openly with Nehru he stood by his principles.

Nehru wanted Morarjibhai to join the Central Government but with the states Re-organisation commission at work. Morarjib hai was disinclined to leave Bombay. Nehru then asked Morarji bhai to prevail upon Pandit Pant to give up the chief Ministership of Utterpradesh and more up to the centre.

Morarjibhai had adopted the attitude of frankness and even bluntness of speech. As Chief Minister of Bombay he played host to Bulganin and Khrushchev in 1955 when they were in Bombay in the course of their visit to India.

During a discussion he had with the Soviet leaders, Khrushchev said to him that the policy of the Soviet Union was to keep good relations with those who were good to them and go against those who were antagonistic to them. Morarjibhai's rejoinder was, "There is a difference between your policy and ours. It is natural and easy to be good to those who are good to us and such behaviour is execpted from every human being.

"There is no great merit in being good to those who are good to us, but we can claim goodness truthfully only if we return good for evil. That is the policy wich we try to follow, and that is the difference between our policies." An encounter with Aneurin Bevan during the British Labour Party leader's visit to India in 1958 provides another facet of Morarjibhai's "inflexible" personality.

He was Finance Minister at the Centre at that time and "Nye" Bevan wanted to convince him of the folly of prohibition as an official policy at the cost of enormous revenue. Morarjibhai stood his ground and advanced arguments in favour of prohibition, some of which it must be stated were sound and plausible. It was that since a large Majority of Indians are only vegetarian food because of economic compulsions, they were susceptible to becoming addicts if they took to drinking. It was not so in countries where the staple diet of the people was non-vegetarian.

Charge of Communalism

Morarjibhai entered the provincial civil service as a Deputy Collector in the then Bombay presidency in may 1918. His first posting was at Ahmedabad. Then after two stints as Deputy Collector in Thana and Broach, he was transferred to Panchm ahals district, the head quarters of which was Godhra. That was in December 1924 and his designation was personal assistant to the District Colletor.

There was no love lost between him and the collector and District Magistrate, an English man by the name of Hartshone, who was his immediate superior. A series of incidents both trivial and serious, put Morarjibhai in the position of rubbing his superior the wrong way. Perhaps used to servility by Indian subordinates, Hartshone as soon as he alighted at Godhra railway station, asked Morarji bhai to have his luggage transported to his bungalow.

It was not one of the duties of the personal assistant but still Morarjibhai put up with it. He got the Saheb's luggage sent to his bungalow but gave him the bill for porterage.

The Englishman did not like it. His second request to Morarjibhai was to Procure a she-buffalo. Morarjibhai replied that he could arrange for it if the collector paid the price. Outwitted Hartshone abandoned the idea and made his "own arrange ments" to have a milch buffalo in his compound.

These incidents naturally did not generate bon homie between Hartshone and Morarjibhai. The Collect or realised that his deputy was different from the ordinary run of officials who in-gratiated themselves with their superiors even at the cost of their self-respect. He might have also put down Morarjibhai as a potential rebel influened by Gandhiji and the Congress.

To the average British bureaucrat the Congress then was synonymous with Hindus so that safeguarding Muslim interests became an additional burden of the white man. It was against this background that Morarjibhai found himself in a situation surcharged with Hindu-Muslim tension. Godhra which was his head quarters then had a large Muslim population almost half of the total.

The DSP was a Muslim officer belonging to the Indian Police Service. He was a fair-minded officer. Stray disturbances over slaughter of cows or playing of music before Mosques were common in Godhra. But those which followed a Ganesh Chaturthi procession became seroious.

The Hindu insisted that they should be allowed to play music all along the route of the procession even when it passed by the side of a Mosque. The DSP after some argument gave in and provided police protection for the procession in predominantly Muslim areas.

The DSP. Personally escorted the procession when it passed a Mosque. But when the procession dispersed the participants were attacked individually and some of their leaders were severly beaten. The District Collector entrusted Morarjibhai with the task of investigating the incident, and asked him to record the statements of the injured Hindu leaders, while they were still in shock from the attack.

But what Morarjibhai did was different and it did not suit the District Collector's purpose. He scrupulously noted down the time of each interview with the injured persons and taking it to the District Collector soon after recorded the time when it was submitted to Hartshone.

Morarji In Godhra......!

In Godhra the Hindu leaders started a campaign against the DSP charging him with partiality for his, co-religionists. Morarjibhai knew that it was not true and did not hesitate to rebut the charge when two Hindu Mahasabha members of the Bombay Legislative Council visited Godhra for enquiring into the incident. But the DSP was not aware of Morarjibhai's commitment to truth and wanted to know what he had told the Hindu Sabha leaders.

Morarjibhai declined to oblige him because having taken the statements of the injured persons who were later involved as accused in a criminal case he would have to tender evidence in the court and it would not be proper for him to discuss the matter with the police officer, who was the chief prosecutor. The District Collector also tried to obtain the information form the Morarjibhai, but with no better result. So both the District Collector and the DSP thought that Morarjibhai had confirmed the Hindu leaders charge against the DSP and would not therefore, disclose it to them, The mistrust and misunderstanding grew on each other and made the DSP take sides against the Hindu leaders.

Morarjibhai was also asked to conduct the preliminary hearing of the crminal case launched against the Hindu leaders. As one of the accused was breaved and wanted bail to perform has last rites of his father, Morarjibhai decided to allow all of them bail on proper sureties. That had further enraged the District Collector. The last straw as Morarjibhai's decision after through examination of the pros and cons, that the accused were not guilty of the charge of rioting brought against them by the police. He therefore acquitted them.

A European officer C.A. Milard was then asked to retry the case. Morarjibhai appeared as a witness. In the sessions court also, where the case was taken in appeal the acquittal of the accused was confirmed Further the Sessions Judge ordered the removal of Milard's critical remarks against Morarjibhai though the latter was not a party to the appeal. In other words the highest court which tried the case had placed on record that the aspersions on Morarjibhai's conduct, were unwarranted.

The Government also did not reopen the issue or try to get the sessions court decision reverged by another court. Morarjibhai's initial decision to acquit the accused had also been upheld still the British officers did not hesitate to taint him with the brush of communalism. Morarjibhai had been transferred to Ahmedabad by then and had received notice from the authorities saying that the Collecctor of Panchamahals had aasked for an enquiry into his conduct in the Godhra rioting.

Morarjibhai gave a detailed reply in writing to the charge of Partiality for Hindus in the incident and also met the Commissioner personally to place the facts before him. The commissioner also seemed to have been convinced by Morarjibhai's statements, but he reported to the authorities differently. The result was that the government down graded Morarjibhai. That reinforced Morarjibhai's growing conviction that there was no place for an honest and upright official like him in the British scheme of things for India. So he resigned from Government service on May 21, 1930.

The Political Differences

Long after when political difference put Morarjibhai in the opposite camp some Congress Party leaders unearthed the incident camp some Congress Party leaders unearthed the incident and tried to present him as a communalist. The Pro-Moscow

Communists were especially diligent in that kind of research. But the Muslims of Godhra themselves in their calmer moments, would admit that his conduct as an officer was impartial and that he had never taken sides in Hindu-Muslims quarrels.

There was for instance a Dargah or Muslim place of worship near the Godhra railway station. It had been there long before the railway station was established but suddenly in 1927 the railway authorities decided that the Dargah should be removed. They served a notice to that effect on the Fakir who was in charge of Dargah. When the Fakir approached Morarjibhai he examined the documents and decided that the railway authorities had no right to have the Dargah removed because it. had been there for a longer time than the railway itself. He also asked the railway authorities to construct a fence round the Dargah as protection to it's visitors from moving trains.

Long before he formally quit Government service, Morarjibhai was clear in his mind that been serving the foreign government for 12 years he had committed a mistake. He thought he,......" had done harm to my country. I therefore decided that. I should not spend the rest of my life just earning money and that I should devote myself to the service of the people to alone for my sin."

Subsequently especially after he became a Minister first in Bombay and later at the Centre, people would acclaim Morarji bhai's sacrifice in resigning the Government job. He never liked such praise because he did not regard his action as sacrifice. He would say, "I have not made any sacrifice by resigning my government post. It was no service to help the foreign government to carry on it's work and thus to strengthen it's hold on this country. I was thus betraying my own country which was paying my salary. I only did my duty by resigning from British service. "I cannot be said to have made any sacrifice.:"

Morarjibhai's Career As Congressman

Morarjibhai was a member of the Indian National Congress, as the Congress Party still it self for more than 45 years. Even after the Congress split in 1969 and the assumption of control of one of the factions by Indira Gandhi Morarjibhai remained with what he believed to be the genuine Congress Party though depleted in strength and devoid of power. The history of these four and a half decades of his political life was thus the history of India in microcosm.

The first 15 years were a period of struggle, when Morarjibhai's activities were largely confined to Gujarath and Bombay though he had access to Gandhiji with whom he often candidly discussed general policies and principles.

The Congress being out of power in those days and consisting predominantly of persons who had sacrificed and suffered for the cause inwhich they believed membership of the Congress was a matter of great national honour and psychological satisfaction. That had more than made up for the privations and poverty of power which went with it. He joined the organisation at a fairly high level, with in a couple of years of his becoming a member of the party, he was made one of the secretaries of the Gujarat Pradesh Congress Committee.

Earlier in October 1930 when the Salt Satyagraha was on, he was appointed "dictator" of the Gujarat Pradesh Congress Committee by its president who was expected to be arrested. The Congress had been declared an illegal organisation by the British Government and its normal functioning was not possible, So the system of dictators was introduced to provide for centralised direction of the Satyagraha and to prevent organisation from largescale arrests of party functionaries. The middle two decades of Morarjibhai's career as Congressman were largely spent in office first as Revenue and Home Minister of Bombay and then at the Centre holding different portfolios and rising to be Deputy Prime Minister in 1967. This was a period during which he came to be projected more and more on the national scene.

But for his natural shyness aversion for the limelight and lack of public relations image he would have been a national leader with some charisma. When she started as Prime Minister, Indira Gandhi had nothing to commend herself except being the daughter of Nehru and the reflected glory inwhich she had some times shone due to the surname of Gandhi. She also spread the legend that she was close to Mahatma Gandhi. At the Faridabad Session of the Congress for instance she devoted a good part of her address to tell the people how Gandhiji used to seat her on his lap and teach her politics.

That was when she was a child and had already earned her spurs as a Joan of Arc of Vanarasena. In the case of Morarji the effect of publicity was often negative. The years of his association with the Congress Party were years of intrigue and manipulative politics.

Morarjibhai and Congress

Congress leaders of pre-Independence days were broadly of two categories Organisation men like Sardar Patel who were adept in the nuts-and-bolts aspect of the National Movement and were good at raising funds which largely came from the relativity well to do and those like Nehru who had mass apeal and provided a popular base for the movement.

Gandhiji combined both the categories in his complex personality; he was a theortician too, After 1930 Gandhiji had given up involving himself directly in the day-to-day affairs of the Congress.

Morarjibhai too is a jack of all trades in the sense that he has built the Congress Organisation in Gujrat as general secretary of the Pradesh Congress for about seven years. While also being its image builder among the people. He has been the master where absolute adherence to principles is concerned. Only fund collection had not bee his forte.

As the very first meeting Morarjibhai and Jamnalal Bajaj had with an Ahmedabad millowner there was disagreement and tension uncongenial for money o pass hands.

The millowner tried to be sarcastic towards Morarjibhai by pointing to a news paper report of a speech by him in which he was said to have "warned" the rich to contribute liberally to the quake relief fund. The millowner said that it was strange that which Morarjibhai issued public warnings to the rich, he privately approached them for contributions to relief funds.

Ruffled, Morarjibhai replied "If you read the whole report you will find that I have done no such thing, and that all I have done is to explain to them that they should contribute to the fund as a duty." But the millowner went on rubbing it in Saying that just as persons like Morarjibhai were fond of making speeches from public plat forms, millowners like him were fond of earning and keeping money.

Morarjibhai was quick to report that the millowner might be fond of making money, but he was not fond of making speeches. He also added that he hoped after India became free nobody would speak like that. The millowner took it as a threat and replied in the same vein saying that he also hoped that after independence people would not be have like that towards each other.

Hence the net result of the purpose of fund collection was illserved and Jamnalal Bajaj agreed to leave Morarjibhai alone when he went a round to his fellow industrialists for collecting money.

Morarjibhai's first stint of electioneering was in 1934 when he campaigned for Bhulabhai Desai who was the successful candidate on behalf of the Congress for one of the Gujarat seats in the then central Legislative Assembly a fore-runner in a way of our present parliament.

Electioneering naturally involved compromises especially when the franchise was restricted as it then was and the electrorate consisted only of monied and influential persons. Morarjibhai's first 'encounter' with Nehru was in 1936 at on All-India Congress Committee session in Bombay.

Nehru was Congress president then, and Morarjibhai wanted to move a non-official resolution, Saying that all the A.I.C.C. Work should be conducted in Hindi. When he showed, the resolution to Nehru before asking his permission to move it. Nehru did not conceal his dislike for the substance of the resolution.

Nehru's stand broadly was that the large number of non-Hindi elements in the national movement should not be alienated insisting on the exclusive use of Hindi while Morarjibhai and others thought that the only way to promote Hindi as a future link language was to insist on its use atleast in the Congress organisation. The Non-Hindi speaking Congress members would be initially in convenienced; some of them might also resent it but over time the resistance would be overcome by the larger nationalist sentiment and the cause of Hindi. Instead of going into the merits of the case for Hindi Nehru bluntly told Morarjibhai that the language of the resolution left much to be desired and so it should not be moved.

Sardar Patel and Morarjibhai

By 1937 despite minor differences of opinion, Sardar Patel was Morarji's political Guru and he implicitly the Sardar's directives from time to time especially when they concerned party discipline. Thus he never questioned the propriety of Sardar Patel choosing the leaders of the different Congress legislature parties and even members of the different Congress Ministers.

The Sardar has also acted as a watchdog on the working of the Congress Ministries and was a kind of supreme court for appeals and complaints against individual Congress Ministers. All these are antithetical to the concept of parliamentary democracy. But since the Congress was still mainly an instrument of political independence and the struggle against the British had not ceased such a centralised running of the legislature parties was perhaps unavoidable.

But it had its disadvantages when personal and other factors invaded the realm of political propriety and justice. An instance was the manner inwhich Sardar Patel with Gandhiji's tacit blessings prevented the late K.F.Nariman from heading the Bombay Ministry though he was undoubtedly head and shoulders above the others in the field.

The Sardar instead chose a dark horse like Balgangadhar Kher, an honest and upright person no doubt, but lacking in administrative experience, Morarjibhai was through and through. WIth the Sardar on that issue, though when it came to the formation of the Government, Sardar patel had intially second thoughts about including Morarjibhai in the Kher cabinet. His preference was for Dinkarrao Desai.

In support of his stand on the Nariman issue Morarjibhai recalls Gandhiji's own position than an organisation is more important than an individual, however eminent or important. In other words if the choice is between what one considers to be the needs of the organisation and justice to an individual, the latter will have to suffer. By and large in the circumstances which prevailed in the National Movement at that time the good of the Congress organisation was rarely identified with the personal interests of an individual or group, So cases like that involving Nariman did not cause more than a ripple on the surface.

Morarjibhai's Ideology

Morarjibhai's ideology was Right by principle. His aversion to the formation and functioning of the socialist group in the Congress has been already mentioned. Sometimes he was even one jump ahead of Sardar Patel in opposing the Socialists. He was one of those who were said to have resisted acceptance by Nehru of J.P.'s 14-point programme in 1952 as a means of co-operation between the Congress and Socialist parties. Morarjibhai's antipathy for the Socialists was total, even if more honest. At times he would not even distinguish between the Communists and Socialists, which only helped the communists to project themselves as progressive opponents of Morarji Desai and 'other' Right-wing elements in the Congress and Government.

The differences between Morarjibhai and the progressives" inside the Congress come into the open after he joined Indira Gandhi's Government as Deputy Prime Minister in 1967. That was the year of opportunity for the young Turks, as an amorphous group of radical congressmen headed by Chandrasekhar known.

After Independence the Congress Party always abounded in factions and lobbies, but until 1967 the Congress factions used to manipulate the opposition groups for their factional interests. Notable examples were the rapport between the conservatives within the Congress and then Swatantra Party.

On August 9, 1967 which as the 25th anniversary of the Quit India Struggle was extremely evocative in the history of nationalist India Chandra Sekhar and his colleagues presented a memorandum to the then Congress President Kamaraj demanding faithful and complete implementation of the 10 point programme.

One hundred and eighteen Congress members of parliament including Sucheta Kripalani, Sushila Nayar and Umashankar Dikshit signed the memorandum, while some supporters of Morarji Desai found fault with it and kept away. They said that while the document made a specific mention of social control of banking and demanded that, "let us clearly understand that it definitly does not mean regulated capitalism". Its references to the abolition of privy purses and other princely privileges were general.

They attributed it to the 'Young Turks' for Chavan who was Home Minister at that time. The ground was already being prepared to project Morarji Desai as a right wing opponent of Bank Nationalisation which was the ruse played in 1969, when Indira Gandhi wanted to throw him out of the Central Government. The Pro-Communist group in the Congress which had earlier gone along with the young Turks also changed its tactics.

Throughout 1968 Chandrasekhar on behalf of the Young Turks hammered at two issues Bank Nationalisatiion and curbing monopolies. Both the items were directed against Morarjibhai because, first it would require changing what Morarjibhai described in parliament in December 1971 as a Government decision to have effective social control over banks and secondly reforming basically the official policy on industrial licensing to plug the loopholes. brought to light by the Hazzi report.

It will be necessary here to understand Morarjibhai's stand on the controversy between social control and Nationalisation of Banks. He had repeatedly made it clear that he was not opposed to nationalisation as a principle but the important practical criterion was that it should be in consonance with the national interest. In the assessment of national interest there were wide differences with Morarjibhai insisting that Nationalisation of Banks at that juncture would harm the economy, and the young Turks arguing that nationalisation was very much necessary. Morarjibhai has explained it in his autobiography,

"Our economic condition has deteriorated during the last two or three years. We have had to face many difficulties as a result of the Chinese Aggression in 1962 and have had to incur heavy expenditure as a result. There has been famine for two years consecutively, and the Centre and some States had to spend crores of rupees to meet the situation. The prices of grain and other goods have gone up very high.

Morarjibhai also pointed out that argument for nationalisation rested mainly on the fact that while the industrialists who controlled and manage, the banks had ready access to credit smaller entrepreneurs and the agricultural sector were starved of funds.

Morarjibhai contended that social Control over Commercial Banks through the Reserve Bank would be as effective in getting over this difficulty as formal Nationalisation. As for the rural sector the Co-operative banks were being developed to provide credit to the farmers. That was the reason why the Commercial Banks had not entered field. A credit policy requiring the Commercial banks to give priority to the rural sector would there fore serve the purpose. Finally while nationalisation would only affect the major banks social control would cover the entire banking industry including the foreign banks.

Morarji As the Enemy of Violence

During the campaign for the Loksabha elections, Bal Thakre the Shivsena Leader was vehement in his denunciation of Morarjibhai as, "a murderer of Maharashtrains". The allusion was to the agitation in Bombay and other parts of Maharashtra in 1950's for a separate state of Maharashtra, and the massive violence it had resulted in.

The States Re-otganisation Commission headed by Justice Fazal Ali had in its report rejected the demand for a uni-lingual Marathi speaking state. The Samyukta Maharashtra agitation which was already raging grew in strength after that and assumed a violent form, forcing leaders like S.M.Joshi to risk their lives in curbing the extremist elements, with a wide variety of groups ranging from the Shivsena to the Communists jumping on the Samyukta Maharashtra band wagon it was unavoidable that there would be organised violence on a large scale.

The Maharashtra sentiment also was largely behind the agitation because the Maharashtrians like the Andras always clamoured for a linguistic state. With the former princely state of Hyderabad also proposed to be broken up into, it's three linguistic components the case for a Marathi speaking state was further reinforced. A large number of Congress Party leaders including Y.B.Chavan who was thea a minister in the Morarji Government secretly supported the movement. It was also said that the popular play-back singer Lala Mangeshkar was also financing the agitation.

Morarjibhai had the uneviable task of dealing with such a struggle. His being a Gujarati complicated the matter further through no Maharashtrian who had known him would say that Morarjibhai was moved against Maharashtrians.

His real problem was that he had an almost ideological aversion for violence in public life and when the Samyukta Maharas htra agitation unavoidably became violent. he felt vindicated in his resistance to it. That he was using the police and the home guards against the agitation, and that police firings, Lathi and tear-gas, charges were almost daily occurences did not worry him unduly because unlike Ganmdhiji for whom non-violence was an article of faith, Morarjibhai had a pragmatic approach that, the state could not be run without its coercive apparatus. Reference has already been made to this dichotomy in the earlier chapters. In short Morarjibhai's approach is comparable to the western parliamentary practice avoiding direct action to settle political disputes.

The custodians of law and order can use force to curb violence, but recourse to violence by the public is taboo. Idealistically it was Morarjibhai's dream that India, true to its traditions of Gandhian leadership, would evolve into a democracy in which political and other controversies would be-sorted out by negotiation and argument without recourse to agitations especially of a violent nature. The different agitations for Linguistic States belied such hopes and made Morarjibhai a severe critic of all extra-constitutional action. The repeated shift in Nehru's stand on the future of Bombay also did not help Morarjibhai in handling the situation.

The Toll of Human Life

The toll of human life in the riots in Bombay city in connection with the agitation was as high as 80 according to official estimates. Opposition sources put the number at more than a hundred.

Whether the number of persons killed was 80 or more than a hundred was only a matter of degree, the tragedy which engulfe India's premier city and the fall out from it in the shape of vitiating human relationships was too great too he measured in terms of physical casualties. Some of Morarjibhai's critics thought he was insensitive to the human aspect of the prblem and that his bureaucratic upbringing had rendered him callous to people's suffering.

Nothing could be father from the truth than that. He was all the while conscious of the ordeal he had landed himself in, he was pained beyond description, at the loss of precious human life. But on the other side of the ledger was the duty he had chosen to perform. If he had resigned as Chief Minister and abandoned what he regarded as the duty entrusted to him by popular mandate would he have saved the situation ?

Morarjibhai's successor whoever it might be, would be faced with a similar choice unless the Congress Party and the Central Government decided to reverse their policy on the future of Bombay. If while continuing as Chief Minister he had made the police condone acts of violence and not put an end to mob fury, the reesult would have been for worse it would have amounted to abandoning the city of Bombay virtually to anarchy.

In Morarjibhai's own words. "There is a risk for a person who believes in non-violence and truth that once he accepts office he might have to compromise with his principles in running a government in the public interest. But if he believers that his welfare lies in the welfare of all, he should brave the risk and serve government. When there is a very unpleasant or difficult duty to perform he has to accept it, and must conastantly be vigilant in his actions.

He must not compromise his principles for the sake of easy popularity or wealth or power. He must not waver in doing his duty, in promoting public welfare". Apparently there has been no uniformity in the judgement of others on Morarjibhai's record in his respect.

Morarjibhai and Independent India

If the 1969 split in the Congress Party was a turning point in the history of independent India, it was also a watershed in

Morarjibhai's public life. For about 40 years he had indentified himself with the Congress though not in the sense in which Indira Gandhi had aggravated to herself the attributes of the state and the party. He had believed, as he often said publicly that no person-even Gandhiji was greater than the Congress Party. He also had eseen him rise to eminence in public life and a part of the growth and strengthening of the Congress.

His differences with Congress leadership were sometimes as deep and serious as those which made Acharya J.B.Kripalini and others break away from the parent organisation and launch their separate political parties. At the personal level too he has had a raw deal from Nehru, Kamaraj and the "Syndicate". What would have happened if Morarjibhai had played his cards differently from 1969 onwards and instead of ploughing a lonely furrow which ultimately led to the popular of the "Syndicate" he had joined forces with Indira Gandhi ?

This is one of the "ifs" in history for which any number of possibilities can be visualised . According to Morarjibhai, he himself felt that since it was the Gandhi Birth Centenary Year it would be appropriate to have a Harijan as president of India. In that connection he had discussed with Indira Gandhi the names of Jagjivan Ram and the late Sanjivayya. The later was not considered because he was too young for the post. AT the third formal meeting Morarjibhai and Indira Gandhi had to discuss the matter, Indira Gandhi suddenly announced that she had prevailed upon Jagjivan Ram to be the candidate. It had come as a surprise to Morarjibhai, who had already committed himself Sanjiva Reddy.

Morarjibhai had no objection to it but thought that the observation at the end of the note that they were some stray thoughts jotted down in a hurry should be removed before it was sent to the AICC. The suggestion was accepted and the AICC considered and endorsed the note, with Morarjibhai having the dubious distinction of piloting the resolution on the subject. He had in that capacity prevailed upon movers of amenduments to withdraw them.

One such amendment wanted nationalisation of a few leading banks but Morarjibhai was able to convince the mover that it was implicit in the resolution that if the experiment of social control did not achieve the desired purpose nationalisation would follow. While the economic issues evidently introduced by Indira Gandhi as a red herring failed to throw the party leadership into disarry the political question of choosing the presidential candidate succeeded in doing so to a remarkable degree.

Morarjibhai's Idealism

Morarjibhai's Visits to Australia and New Zealand in November 1975 were as a private citizen and a Senior Member of Parliament. He attended the Commonwealth Parliamentary conference in Wellington in that connection. His last visit abroad before he stepped down as Deputy Prime Minister was to attend General Dwight's funeral in Washington in 1969. On his way back he stopped over in Sydney for the annual meeting of the Asian Development Bank and also had a Sojourn in Singapore.

He had then expressed himself in favour of close relations between Japan, Australia, india and the noncommunist states of South-East-Asia. There was at that time a theory in some American academic circles that, all the non-communists states should come together to constitute a kind to bulwark against China particulary and the spread of Soviet influence in the region generally. Morarjibhai did not subscribe to the theory.

Since Morarjibhai was less ambiguous in his pronouncement he invited on himself the anger of communist at home. Indira Gandhi was too glad to let him face the music because it would reinforce in the public mind his image as a rightist. There was also a statement attributed to him in that connection that India should develop relations with Formosa. That led to heated exchanges in parliament.

Does this mean that because of his ideological aversion for communism, Morarjibhai is anti-Soviet and pro-West in his foreign policy and thinking. His dealings with the Soviet Union though confined at that time to bilateral economic relations and his visits to the U.S.S.R. and poland. His approach was pragmatic. He did not condone the suppression of human rights in the communist states but he did not also made a song of it. He had openly admired the achievements of several Communist States and the sense of discipline and social commitment, which they have inculcated in their citizens.

His quarrel is only with the methods employed for the purpose. His visit to the Soviet Union in 1960 was very significant. He was able to disabuse his hosts of his alleged anti-Communist bias and win from them a commitment to aid the third Five-year plan generously. His perception of the 'danger from China' was shored by many other Indians and was the product of Peking's behaviour in the late 1950's and early 1960's. He thinks if India had not trusted China implicitly but fortified it's northern defences the 1962 experiences could have been avoided. To that extent it was more pragmatic than nationalist.

Morarjibhai was more inward looking. He was not like-any other leaders of India in the pursuit of India. He believed in active cultivation and promotion of mutually beneficial relations. Infact the thrust of his foreign policy thinking was that, India should now pay more attention to the neighbours, than in the past. For the rest he believed in maintaining and argumenting bilateral relations with other countries notably the Soviet Union, the United States the European community and Japan.

15

Indira Gandhi

The Birth

Indira's father, Jawaharlal Nehru, was born in 1889. When he grew up he was sent to England for further studies.

He went to Cambridge University to study law. In 1916. he married Kamala Kaul. A beautiful Kashmiri girl. Indira was their only child.

Indira Priyadarshini was born on November 19, 1917, at Allahabad to an affluent family of Kashmiri Brahmins. Motilal Nehru her grandfather, was one of the most prosperous, respected lawyers of northern India. He was Motilal to his numerous British friends and "Panditji" to his large, Indian clientele. At the height of his legal carrer. Motilal was a liberal and a member of the Indian National Congress but, his total commitment to the cause of India's freedom from foreign yoke, came about only after the horrors of the Jallianwala Bagh massacre. He gave up his legal practice, withdrew his daughter Krishna from the convent school, made a bonfire of all his foreign clothes, including his expensive

London tailored suits and began wearing coarse khadi kurtas and dhotis. His only son.

The Jallianwala Bagh massacre was the greatest of tragedies to have taken place in India, during the British rule. On the day of the spring festival of Baisakhi, over 10,000 people had gathered in a walled garden at Jallianwala Bagh in Amritsar. There was only one entrance to the Bagh, through a narrow lane.

Michael O'Dwyer. callous British general, stationed troops at the only entrance and to teach the natives a lesson issued shooting orders, the troops fired nonstop for 10 minutes, killing and wounding hundreds. Martial Law having been clamped upon at once, the wounded lay for hours without medical attention. What was even more tragic than the massacre, the British were quite indifferent to the violence inflicted upon the "natives" so heartlessly and their rule continued to be as tyrannical as ever.

Jawaharlal-Indira's father had already been inducted into Congress, And, thus from a life of luxury, leisure and affluence, father and son entered years of austerity which were to last a long time. Their decision stretched the Nehru family to the very limits of its endurance making demands on its curage. It-also led them to supreme heights of glory.

In those days, India was an integral part of the British empire. The British who had initially coms as traders, gradually through conquests, became the rulers of the country. The Indians, however, were unhappy with the British rule. They wanted to be independent. And this desire to be independent resulted in the formation of the Indian National Congress in 1885.

Jawaharlal Nehru and Mahatma Gandhi were the most important leaders, and the Congress was the most important force of the independence movement. Gandhiji, a humble and a simple man, was a barrister like Nehru. He was a follower of non-violence. He strongly believed that the people should adopt Non-Violent means in the freedom struggle. He believed that violence only led to death and destruction of cities and towns, and did not solve any problems.

In April 1919, a huge crowd gathered to protest against the British rule at Jallianwala Bagh in Amritsar. This angered the British and just to teach them a lesson, General Dyer ordered his soldiers to fire at the unarmed crowd. Many people were killed and hundreds were wounded in this massacre.

During this period Anand Bhavan became the head quarters for all political activities. Freedom fighters would hold meetings in the Nehru house. It was at this time young Indira met Mahatma Gandhi and many other well-known political leaders.

Kamala's Death

At the time of Indira's birth. entire India had been wide awake to the untold inequities of the British rule. It had been the time of Nationalism. It had been the time of valiant leaders like Bal Gangadhar Tilak, Gopal-krishna Gokhale, Mahatma Gandhi and Sarojini Naidu. Indira's patriotic fervour, in comparison to that of other children of those days, was conspicuous; right in her own home, were a grandfather and a father who both and decided that the country's freedom merited every priority over their own affluence name, fame or wordly comforts.

Kamala Nehru, Indira's mother lived only for 37 years. Having been brought up in traditional Hindu ways of life, Kamala in the early years of her marriage to Jawaharlal, had the up hill task of having to adapt herself to the anglicized Nehru's and, in later life, her husband had become so committed to the cause of India's freedom that he had little or no time for his wife. From her early early childhood, Idira's empathy towards the lonely woman, her mother, had thus become, drew her close to Kamala. Her fondness became even more when, in the last years of her short life, Kamala suffering first from minor aliments and, later, from tuberculosis, had to be confined to one sanatorium after another, in India and abroad.

On Kamala's passing away, Mahatma Gandhi wrote to Indira Kamala possessed qualities rarely found in other women. I am hoping that all these qualities of Kamala will be manifest in you in equal measure. May God give long life and strength to emulate her virtues.

For five years after Kamala's death, Indira had been adrift as a lost soul. At the time of her mother's death in Switzerland the 18-year old Indira had been studying in Europe. After the tragedy of her mother's death. Jawaharlal decided to let her stay on in Europe; perhaps, he had misgivings that, as an only child, she would be petted and spoiled in Anand Bhawan, the family home of the Nehrus in Allahabad also, he must have thought that only the discipline of a European education would give her the strength and the indpendence of mind necessary for Indira to play a role in public life in India; which was Jawaharlal's dream for her.

The Childhood

In spite of being born in a wealthy family, Indira had a lonely and a disturbed childhood. Her father would be away most of the times. Either his work would keep him away or he would be work would be in jail. To add to her loneliness she had an ailing mother. Indira spent most of her lonely hours playing with her dolls. She would arrange her dolls in the way she had seen people demonstrate against the British.

Her father realised her loneliness and often wrote long letters from prison to her. These letters Indira about the political conditions of the country. Later, these letters were also published in the form of a book.

Indira was also fond of reading. She spent hours reading books on various subjects. Her father also sent her books from prison. She was greatly inspired by the stories of Joan of Arc, the French heroine, who fought against the English in the fifteenth century. She often imagined herself to be Joan. fighting for her country's freedom. Indira went to a school in Allahabad. But her education was interrupted. Her mother was a tuberculosis patient, and in 1926 she was taken to Switzerland for treatment. Indira had to leave her school and accompany her parents to Switzerland.

In Switzerland, she went to two schools. She learnt French and Skiing. She also visited the other European cities like Paris and London. Indira enjoyed her visit to Europe in spite of her mother's illness. This was because her parents were together after a long time.

When her mother's condition improved, the family returned to India. Her father continued with his political work and Indira attended a school in Allahabad. As the freedom movement grew stronger the Nehru family gave up their western clothing and adopted Indian clothes. She also burnt her dolls as they were. Made in England.

The Monkey Squad

As Indira grew into a young girl she was greatly influenced by the freedom movement and wished to be a part of it. She decided to form a group. In Allahabad, she gathered some children and she herself headed this group. The group was called the Monkey Squad or the Bajrang Dal. It derived it's name from the epic Ramayana. In the Ramayana an army of monkeys headed by Hanuman helped Lord Rama in the battle with the demon king, Ravana, to rescue Rama's wife, Sita, who had been kidnapped by him. The Monkey Squad used to make flags, posters and banners.

They also cooked and carried the food and water to the demonstrators or freedom fighters who participated in the anti-British demonstrations. Very often these demonstrators were beaten by the English police. Even the dectors refused to treat them because they were forbidden by the British Government to treat the freedom fighters. It was then that the Monkey Squad came to their rescue. They gave them first aid, nursed, and bandged their wounds.

Seeing Indira's enthusiasm, her grand father gave her an old house for her activities. The house called Swaraj Bhawan, Soon turned into a hospital where the wounded soldiers would be brought and nursed. The squad also posted it's volunteers in post offices, Police stations, and near the homes of the British officials.

Their aim was to gather important informations and give it to the Congress activists. The squad soon became popular and it's activities were appreciated by everybody, Thus, Indira exhibited leadership qualities from a very young age. On her thirteenth birthday, Indira's father, Jawaharlal Nehru, was in prison. He wrote another letter to her from there.

He wrote "In India today, we are making history and you and I are fortunate to see this happening before our eyes and to take some part overselves in this great drama.... Good-bye, little one, and may you grow up into a brave soldier in India's service." Jawaharlal's letters greatly influenced young Indira's mind.

In 1930, he wrote a letter from prison to wish her a Happy New Year. He wrote, "And we shall dream of the past and find our way to make the future greater than the past. So on this New Year's Day let us resolve that by the time this year also grows old and dies, we shall have brought this bright future dream of a united and democratic India.

In 1931, her mother was also arrested. The frequent interruptions in her education worried her parents. They decided to send her to a boarding school in Poona run by Nehru's friend. The school had strict rules. But Indira enjoyed her days there. Life at boarding school was a new experience for her. The atmosphere in school was warm and friendly, Indira made many new friends.

The students would sing songs, and perform folk-dances. They also performed plays on the recent events taking place in the country. All these activities brought Indira closer to the Indian art and culture. She herself organised many concerts and art festivals in the school.

However in 1935, Indira had to leave school. Her mother was seriously ill, and had to be taken to a sanatorium in West Germany. Her father was unable to accompany them as he was in jail. Hence, Indira had to accompany her mother. Her mother's health deteriorated day by day and so she had to be shifted from the sanatorium to a clinic in Switzerland. Later, her father also joined them. In spite of the best treatment and medication her mother could not survive, and in 1936 she died at a young age of thirty-eight.

Her mother's untimely death shocked Indira. She lost not only her mother, but also a close friend. As time passed by she came to terms with her mother's death.

After her mother's death, Indira did not return to India with her father, but stayed on in Switzerland. She attended a school there. From Switzerland she went to England where she attended the Badminton school near Bristol.

Feroze Gandhi

In 1937, when Indira was twenty years old she went to the Oxford University. She had the choice between Sorbonne and Oxford but she chose the latter. As an undergraduate student in the Oxford University she studied History, Anthropology, and Administration.

Like her schooling, her university education was also interrupted. Her father was on a long tour of Europe. And Indira accompanied him on this tour. They visited Germany and various other European countries. Indira would always be present at her father's meetings. She would keenly observe these meetings. She met many great statesmen in such gatherings. Listening to these great statesmen made Indira realise that India had to break away from the chains of imperialism. The European tour broadened her outlook, and she returned to England enriched with the experiencee.

The long tour, however, took it's toll on Indira's health and she fell ill. She suffered from pleurisy (chest infection). She was admitted to a hospital in England. Later, she went to Shitzerland to recover. The air of Switzerland could not improve Indira's health. Moreover, she was feeling homesick. She wished to return to India and help her country in it's struggle for independence. So leaving her university course incomplete. Indira left England and set sail for India in 1941. On board the ship Indira travelled with her good friend. Feroze Gandhi.

The home coming was a turning point in her life. From then on she came to play an active role in Indian politics. and also decided to marry the man she loved-Feroze Gandhi.

Feroze Gandhi, a handsome, young journalist, was a friend of the Nehru family. He had graduated from the London School of Economics. He also participated in the freedom struggle. When he was in Germany he used to visit Indira and her mother. He would often meet Indira in the Oxford university.

On her return, Indira told her father that she wished to marry Feroze. He did not approve of the match. He felt that his daughter was too young to get married. Moreover, he wanted her to meet other men before she tied the knot. When her relatives heard the news they too were shocked at her decision.

In India, the bridegroom is generally chosen by the parents and not by the girl. Another obstacle in their path was that both of them belonged to different religions Feroze was a Parsee. The Parsees are followers of Zoroastrianism, and they are a strict and a conservative community. Indira on the other hand was a Hindu. But Indira was a very strong-willed woman. She did not change her mind. Mahatma Gandhi was the only one who supported her decision. Seeing her daughter's determination Jawaharlal Nehru married in Allahabad in March 1942, according to the Hindu rites.

But in September 1942. both Feroze and Indira were arrested for participating in anti-British activities. Indira spent her twenty-fifth birthday in jail. Her health had deteriorated and she had become quite weak. She was released after six months. Feroze and released after six months. Feroze and Indira's first child, Rajiv, was born in 1944. Sanjay was born two years later.

During this time the freedom struggle was at it's peak and the day was not faroff when India would attain Independence. As the second world war came to an end the British decided to free India. On August 15, 1947, India got her independence. Jawaharlal Nehru became the first Prime Minister of "Free India".

But with Independence came the painful oftermath-the partition, India was divided into two, India and Pakistan. Gandhiji was very unhappy as he had dreamt of a free but united India.

The partition of a free but united India. The partition was followed by communal riots between the Hindus and the Muslims. Millions of refugees came to India from Pakistan.

Indira realised Gandhiji's disappointment. She visited him every evening. And Gandhiji always looked for ward to her visits. He urged her to talk to the leaders of the Hindu and Muslims communities. He wanted them to live together in peace and harmony.

Indira was a determined and a fearless woman. She went to the riot-striken areas and met the Hindu and Muslim families. She begged them to maintain peace among themselves. Meanwhile, Gandhiji also went on a hunger strike. The efforts of both Indira and Gandhiji bore fruits. The Hindus and Muslims finally signed a declaration saying that they would maintain peace and order. But Mahatma Gandhi did not enjoy the glory of seeing a free India for very long. He was assassinated on January 30, 1948. The death of Gandhiji was a great loss for Indira, She had lost a friend. and a mentor, Nehru too lost a friend. and a mentor, Nehru too lost a great friend. After his death the nation looked upon Nehru as their leader.

Indira, on her part, bent her will and her intellect, for the next 5 years. to living out her father's dream. Her first steps were towards a good Western education with a view to become free from her narrow self. Around this time, she spent several months in London. sharing a flat with an old friend from Poona. It was at this time that Feroze Gandhi, her future husband, entered her life.

Warm-hearted and friendly, Feroze drew Indira out of her shy and brooding temperament and, gradually, the friendship blossomed into a decision to get married. The first reactions of Indira's father towards this decision were unfavourable. He did not mind that Feroze was a parsee but, that he was someone not connected in any way with some of the distinguished parsees of those days, had been a matter for concern with Jawaharlal. At her father's request, Indira consulted Gandhiji who, as the Nehru's family-friend and well-wisher; seeing that Indira and Feroze were very much fond of each other, gave his consent. With that, Jawaharlal's consent too, followed if a bit, reluctantly. They were married, on march 16, 1942 or Ramnavami day.

While informing Jawaharlal of her desire to marry Feroze, Indira had told her father of her determination to mould her own life, to marry, to have children and to lead a life of anonymity.

The moment Indira and Feroze were back from their honeymoon, however, she was sucked into the freedom struggle by the 'Quit India" Whirlpool ! No sooner had Jawaharlal been released from jail, he was back again in captivity and so was Gandhiji. The Indian flag which Jawaharlal was to unfurl, Aruna Asaf Ali did, Slipping past the police cordon. The arrest of the leaders of the Congress unleashed civil disobedience movements all over India, accompanied by strikes, sabotage and arson. The British rulers, applying brutal force, put the uprising down. Indira, too, was arrested and held captive in Naini jail. It took six months of brutal repression by the British for the rebellion to show signs of ebbing.

Married in March of 1942, byAugust of the same year, Indira developed a sense of Nationalism for her country of birth. From that very moment, it was not for Indira to lead the life of typical Indian bashful brides sheltered by the cloister of marriage.

During the 8 months that she had been in the Naini jail, her determination to serve the country strengthened and the internment helped to harden her physically, mentally and to put up with a lot of hardships. Going to jail having earned her a place in her father's world, it brought a new focus, a new meaning to her life.

Her first son, Rajiv Gandhi, was born on August 20, 1944. Indira and Feroze stayed at the Nehru-family home. Anand Bhawan at Allahabad. once again, the Second world war drawing to an end, Jawaharlal was released from jail since his presence at the talks with the British Cabinet Mission, which had arrived in India by then, was necessary. Negotitations with the Cabinet Mission dragged and dragged and finally, by 1946, the British having consented to leave the Indian soil soon, Jawaharlal was installed as interim Prime Minister Of India would-soon-to-be an Independent Republic.

Indira went to Delhi, From Allahabad, with her little son Rajiv, to act as her father's hostess. Indira, from her childhood, was used to a crowded house, people coming and going, the telephone constantly ringing. But now, as her father's official hostess, she had to take upon herself arduous responsibilities. Jawaharlal was, by now, a legendary figure. Presedents and Prime Ministers lunched and dined at his table; there was a constant stream of scientists, political activitsts, philosophers and poets who visited Nehru. They hardly noticed the daughter She and reserved, she was always seen two steps behind her father.

Indira was the product of many cultures. close association with the freedom struggle and with the stalwarts of Nationalism, had moulded her life. She was, in many ways, a reflection of her father's mind. Her years in England and her association with Feroze Gandhi's left wing friends. journalists and political thinkers had given her a radical conditioning. She was rebel, antitraditional and anti-establishment but, an in born cautiousness kept her far, far away from any major left commitments.

Her early upbringing and her father's influence, through his numerous letters to her, gave her a love of adventure, a fearlessness, an inbuilt sense of the secular, it also awakened a live curiosity and a constant search for new frontiers. From childhood she had an intimate feeling for nature. But, in spite of her early exposure to intellectuals and powerful activists, she had lived within the confines of a society which hemmed her in, gave her little opportunity to teach out, meet people, explore the arts or investigate a life of the mind.

She had her own refuges. her own world of fantasy and an inner sanctuary where, from childhood, she could take shelter; her early years in Allahabad had made her mind rich and potent but, the seeds of that living energy were still dormant. They awaited germination !

Sanjay Gandhi, Indira's second son. was born in December 1946 and, on the midnight of August 14/15, 1947 Independent India came into being ! When the clock struck the magic hour of midight, Indira was present in Parliament House. Pandit Jawaharlal Nehru The first Prime Minister of free India. rose to make a speech-a speech that lingered for decades in the Indian people's ears and minds.

"Long years ago we made a tryst with destiny and now the time comes when we shall redeem our pledge; not wholly or in full measure but very substantially. At the stroke of the midnight hour when the world sleeps, India will awake to life and freedom."

The Asian Conference

In 1955, a conference of Asian and African countries was held in Bandung. Indira accompanied her father to this conference too. The conference focussed on maintaining peaceful and friendly relations among the Afro-Asian countries. Indira learnt a great deal in this conference. She realised that peaceful coexistence was the need of the hour.

After the Bandung conference Nehru went on his first official visit to the Soviet Union. They visited numerous industries, and met engineers, scientists, doctors, etc. They collected informations on issues ranging from setting up industries, to education control Nehru was inspired by the socialist model of the Soviet Union. He wanted to develop the Indian economy along the same lines.

After Independence, Nehru set about to rebuild the nation. Indira was always by her father's side. She got more and more involved with his work. She accompanied him on his foreign visits to Indonesia, China, Egypt, Poland and various other countries. They also attended the coronation of Queen Elizabeth-II

One of the most important task before her was to campaign for the Congress Party during the General Elections. She addressed public meetings, visited villages, towns and cities, and met leaders of other political Parties. At times she used to walk for miles in the scorching heat. The Congress workers seeing her tremendous energy and selfless work for the Party eleccted her as the chairwoman of the Allahabad Congress Committee and a member of the Congress Working Committee. On their return to India, Indira Gandhi plunged herself into politics. In late 1950's, she formed and headed the women's wing of the Congress.

In the 1957 General Elections, she assisted Lal Bahaddur Shastri in the election campaign. In 1959, the Congress held it's annual session in Nagpur. In this session, she was unanimously chosen as the Chairperson of the congress Party.

As the chairperson of one of the largest parties Mrs. Gandhi brought about many changes. She criticised the leaders who visited their constituencies only during elections. She felt that as the representative of the people one should work for the welfare of the nation. She set a good example for other leaders. She went on long tours visiting villages and towns, meeting people and talking to them. However, her political career came to a standstill when her husband died in 1950. She resigned from the post of the chairperson of the Congress Party. The unexpected demise of her husband died in 1960. She resigned from the post of the chair man ship of the Congress party. The unexpected demise of her husband greatly disturbed her.

Later commenting on her relationship with her husband. She said, "It wasn't an ideally happy marriage. We were very happy at times. But also quarrelled tremendously in other times. It was also partly because both of us were so headstrong."

In 1961, she returned to her political work. She was once again elected the member of the Congress Working Committee. She worked for communal harmony in the country.

During her foreign visits with her father, Indira had learnt a great deal about foreign relations. It was now, that she put her knowledge to use. She worked hard to improve India's relationship with other countries. She was appointed as the member of the Executive Board of UNESCO. She also worked to promote friendly relations between Asian and African countries.

In 1962, China attacked India, The Chinese aggression dealt a serve blow to Jawaharlal's dreams of building good indo-China relations. He believed China to be a good neighbour., but the attack on India betrayed his faith. His health also started deteriorating. In 1964, he suffered a heart attack during the Congress Session at Bhubaneshwar, and finally on may 27, 1964 he passed away. The nation was plunged in grief. It had indeed lost a true leader. For Mrs. Gandhi it was a personal loss. She had lost a father, a dear friend, and a mentor.

The First Woman Prime Minister

After her father's death, Mrs. Gandhi set to complete the tasks which had been left incomplete by him. She moved to a smaller house. Every morning she would meet people from all walks of life. For the first time, in 1961. she was elected as the member of the parliament. She was made the minister of information and Broadcasting in the Lal Bahaddur Shastri cabinet.

However, she was not happy with the new government headed by Shastri. She openly attacked the government saying that the interest of the poor and needy were being sacrificed to promote the industrial growth of the country.

She felt that no country could progress if it's people lacked basic amenities. The situation, however, became more complicated when Indo-Pakistan war broke out in 1965. Mrs. Gandhi took a keen interest in the preparations for war. She studied the defence plan and the military power. She even risked her life when she visited the border. Her efforts won her great applause as she was an extremely courageous and an energetic women.

After Lal Bahaddur Shastri's death, in January 1966, Mrs. Gandhi was unanimously chosen as the Prime Minister of India, speaking of herself as the first woman prime minister she said, "I do not regard myself as a woman. I am a person with a job to do."

Mrs. Gandhi's first year in power was full of turmoil. The war with Pakistan had drained the country's resources. Scanty rains coupled with poor harvest caused a shortage of food grains. The people were unhappy with the new Government as it had failed to provide them with the basic amenities. In the same year the elections were held but the Congress won only by a thin margin.

Within the Congress Party itself there were major differences. The older Congressmen were unhappy with her leadership. But Mrs. Gandhi was a fighter, she divided the Party and left her opponents. The Congress headed by her came to be known as the Congress she then drew out programmes for the betterment of the nation. She wanted to build a society based on 'Socialist Ideals'.

As soon as Mrs. Gandhi came to power she took some important measures:

* She ensured that the land was distributed equally among the peasants.
* She abolished feudal Practices.
* She also abolished privileges given to the Indian princes.
* She ensured that minimum wages should be given to agricultural workers.

As a result of these measures the Congress party won a landslide victory in the 1971 General Elections. During her second term as the Prime Minister, Mrs. Gandhi had to face another problem. The problem of refugees.

Millions of refugees came to India from East Pakistan. East Pakistan was ruled by west Pakistan but the people of East Pakistan wanted to be independent. They felt that they had nothing in common with West Pakistan.

They had a different culture and spoke a different language. They demanded an independent status. The soldiers from West Pakistan tried to supress the freedom movement. As a result, a civil war broke out in East Pakistan. Many people fled from there and came to India. They were given shelter, food, and clothing in India.

Mrs. Gandhi also supported their demand for an independent nation. In order to help them she sent the Indian army to East Pakistan. The Pakistani force was defeated by the Indian army within twelve days.

After the war, East Pakistan became Bangladesh. This Victory over Pakistani forces boosted Mrs. Gandhi reputation worldwide. Her Skillful handling of the crisis in West Pakistan strengthened India's Position in the subcontinent, and in the world as well.

The Celebration of Country's Freedom

At the glittering midnight function and the next morning when Jawaharlal first unfurled the flag at the National Memorial at Rajpath and later, from the ramparts of the Red Fort, Indira observing the great day's solemnity, kept the memories of those moments alive within her for the rest of her life. If freedom brought a wild euphoria, unfortunately, it also brought devastation and masacre.

While every bigwig was in Delhi, celebrating the country's freedom, Mahatma Gandhi-the Architect of India's Independence was in remote Noakhali, near Calcutta, in what is now Bangladesh. Totally unconcerned with his own life and security, the fragile 79 year old messiah of peace and non-violence, was busy touring Noakhali; where virtulent massacres, rapes and brulalities by the muslims upon Hindus convulsed the village and it's people. Poor Gandhiji went from house to house preaching of peace and communal harmony and went on a fast.

His devotion to peaceful co-existence moved the Hindu and Muslim leaders, eventually, and a semblance of peace returned to the village. Even after the Naokhali carnage, there were sporadic incidences of violence between Hindus and the Muslims, especially in and around Delhi and at the instance of Gandhiji, Indira who was herself not in good health at the time, worked in refugee camps where Muslims were taking shelter. It was during this time that Indira came to appreciate fully Gandhiji's ways of maintaining rapport with the simple and largely illiterate masses of the country;

A. London- qualified Barrister though he was, Gandhiji's language, free of the complex or the bombastic, carried India's masscs with him. Indira who had known Gandhiji virtually from her very birth understood for the first time the wisdom behind the Mahatma's simple life and language. She always remembered these ways of the wise man when, in her later life, she herself had to be accepted by these very masses as their leader and Prime Minister.

Indira's first encounters with death of people near and dear to her were the demises of her beloved grandfather Motilal in 1930, of mother, her husband Feroze Gandhi in 1960.

Feroze Gandhi's untimely death, due to heart failure, left Indira very desolate. She was deeply indebted to him and, on his sudden death, her words were.... at all times of stress and difficulty, he was by my side even if he had to travel across continents to get there. I feel I am alone in the midst of the unending sandy water.

Jawaharlal had been Prime Minister for 13 years. at the time that Feroze died. The stress and strain of a Prime Minister's office, in the formative years of a free and turbulent India, had left its mark on Nehru and, gradually, he was losing his elan, his energy and his intuitive touch with the people of India.

Indira held her first public office when she was elected unanimously, on February 2,1959, as president of the Indian National Congress and a little while after Feroze Gandhi's death in September 1960, she became transformed totally from the shy young lady walking always two steps behind Nehru, Seemingly seeking his protection.

Her year as president of the Congress and the way she had to face her loneliness after the death of Feroze, had given her a silent, yet assured, confidence. No longer did she hesitate to participate in conversations with her father's friends and her insights were clear and unambiguous.

Indira displayed her courgae for the first time when she travelled, all by herself, to time when she travelled, all by herself., to Tezpur in Assam, towards the end of 1962; there was chaos in Tezpur following severe allack by China over border dispute with India; an instinctive response had awakened in Indira that the Assamese must be assured that they were not left uncared for; refusing to listen to her father, to the Army chief or to her friends, travel to Tezpur she did, gave the Assamese all the solace She was capable of promising them that she would not leave Tezpur till the crisis passed. On the same day as she arrived in Tezpur, China announced a unilateral cease-fire and began withdrawing its troops. !

Jawaharlal's decision to resolve, through aggressive means, India's border dispute with China was truly an impulsive blunder. The humilation he suffered because of it, marked the beginning of a slow decline in his popularity during his last 18 months of life. In the fist months of 1963. When his virulent critics began a campaign "to weaken and, if possible, to dislodge Nehru" an agonized indira noticed that her oncedashing father had neither the energy not the will to confront his adversaries at their level. Instead, on his part, Jawaharlal was turning to his daughter on virtually all the complex issues that people brought to him. Her years as Congress President had convinced him of her shrewd political sense, her passion, energy and determination. So, in the summer of 1963. a move supported by Indira, was started amongst the young ginger group in the Congress party. To revitalize and to bring new blood into the party's working.

Called as the Kamaraj plan, a special slogan "Party before post", was coined, asking resignation of senior leaders from chief and central ministerships with Jawaharlal himself being the very first to offer his own resignation from Prime Ministership. But, Surprisingly, the very critics who had begun to urge him to stay on, declaring that he was indispensable ! Sudeenly, on August 25, 1963, the bomb called as Kamaraj plan burst ! Eleven leaders at the very top were axed and Kamaraj, the twelth, elected as the new Congress president.

Indira's Silent Demeanour

Behind Indira's silent demeanour, there was formidable capacity to assess people and act swiftly and with razor sharp precision. She had tenacity and fierce courage, she had an alert mind, she could listen and learn quickly. Every one of these exemplary qualities came to surface during all the years she had been Prime Minister.

Indira Gandhi had joined the Congress Party in 1938 and, from 1953 onwards. had lead an active political life in her father's home. Her many efforts to escape from politics. to lead the life a wife and mother instead, remained a fantasy.

She recognized. at last, that politics was her heritage which could not be denied, it's goading influence in her life. She had, however, her own definition of what politics was all about; "I was brought up to believe that politics in not a career, it is not a job, politics is certain world trends, where humanity is going, what it is doing. That is what interests me for, politics is centre of everything.

Throughout her life, upto the time of becoming Prime Minister for the first time Indira had maintained a low profile; now the world and all of India, turned to discover the reality of Indira, to see how a woman Prime Minister, with a little known capacity for administrative skills, would tackle the immensity of the problems which awaited her. The politician watched her every move waiting for her to stumble; the bureaucrat was cynical his own position and how best he could take advantage of an inexperienced Prime Minister !

Neither the politician nor the bureaucrat realized, however, that Indira Gandhi, behind her facade of a woman of simple ways, had developed an uncarmy ability to assess schemers around her and to outguess their every move and counter-move.

Towards the end of her father's time, Indira had begun moving away from commitments to any strong ideology. While she was Congress President and as Nehru's confidant, she had quickly grasped that what was wrong with India was not the absence of socialist thought but a rigid administrative structure geared only to maintain a status 9 uo and to monitor law and order but, not at all geared to bring about any creative change.

In one of her early speeches, soon after being elected as Prime Minister, she hinted at administrative revolution. However tentative her approach, she made certain basic issues very clear; the "old order" was over and finished with; the country was changing. WIth a rapidity unknown before; the Congress leaders, dominating state politics, were prisoners of their own narrow beliefs; the fight that lay ahead was between old. entrenched traditionalists and young minds teeming with innovative ideas.

Soon after becoming Prime Minister, she became determined not to lose her nerve while dealing with stalwarts within her own Party and with those in the opposition. She also knew how vital it was to maintain contact with the voice of the people; in this, she had learnt from Gandhiji himself; that the masses do not care for intellectual lectures but, only to a language they understood, they could respond to; towards this end, she started seeing, every morning, before going to her office, a vast number of common people from all over the country; mingling with them, she would listen to their sorrows and troubles, accept petitions, ask her secretary to take notes for follow up action. wherever possible; no letter remained unanswered; on any single day, she would meet 200 to 500 people.

She kept her political life totally apart from her adnministrative one and trusted no one. In between the most stromy meetings, to renew herself, she would find time for artists, painters and dancers. She managed her working hours frugally and was always punctual problems to complex administrative ones, to scientists, to her chiefs of staff, to visitors from abroad, to a poet, to an architect.

One of her first acts as Prime Minister was the carving out of a new state- Haryana much to the delight of the Sikhs; when the Hindi- speaking people of the region rebelled against creation of Haryana. coming down heavily upon them, she quietened the revolt. The next two of priorities were provision of grain for a drought-riven country and harnessing the forces of intellectuals and youth for eradication of poverty. These two tasks occupied her total attention and all of her administrative skills.

The drought-riven country was in dire need of aid from the United States, from world Bank and from the International Monetary Fund. In the interests of her people who were near starvation. Indira set out an a visit abroad to seek help from the affluent West. She stopped in Paris, on her way to Washington. to hold talks with the French President Charles de Gaulle; de Gaulle, who was distrustful of women in politics, had good words, however, to say about Indira; "I don't think they (women) have it in them, but your Prime Minister is a women of amazing strength. She has something-she ill make it." Even later, shortly before his death, de Gaulle's opinion of Indira was : "Those fragile shoulders on which the huge destiny of Indira rests......... don't shrink from the burden."

Her trips to America and Russia's Prime Minister and with the heads of world Bank and International Monetary Fund. Indira exhibited a measure of maturity and political astuteness remarkable for a lady who had been Prime Minister for only a few months. The stalwarts in the Congress were alarmed by her self-assurance and her confidence; they had hoped that she did not have independent judgement could be replaced whenever they choose; attempts by some of them to belittle her when she announced a 35.5% devaluation. did not succeed since even the leading Economists and planners saw that devaluation was invevitable.

Indira's Political Views

Indira was hailed by the common men for her courageous decision to nationalize the banks. The vested interests, however, severely criticized her action and accused her of trying to lead the country towards communism.

These attacks on her and a strong lobdy within the party, openly hostile to her, led to a split in the Congress. After a 100 years, a party which had battled the British which had won freedom, which had surveied innumerable crises, which had held within its ambit members with totally opposed political and economical views, having sadly split, it could never be the same again.

Indira's Congress came to be known as Congress (R) and that of her opponents as Congress (O) with this split Indira having lost her majority in both Houses of parliament, Congress (O)'s attempts to bring a motion of no-confidence against her failed since she had the foresight enough to have wooed and won support from a medly of other parties and from various independent members.

She turned her attention next to abolition of Princes Privy purse; this required a two-third's majority from both the House of parliament and when her bill was introduced in August 1970, it was passed by the Lok Sabha undaunted, she got a Presidential Proclamation issued derecognizing the Princes altogether and, thus, their claim to privy purses ceased to exist !

Determined to remove her as Prime Minister, by hook or by crook, Congress (O) joined hands with a few other parties; the business community, right-wing politicians, disgruntled princes and that part of the media which was controlled by industrial barons made inflammatory speeches condemming her with intentions to turn India into a communist state; the crisis worsened when rumours of an imminent coup began floating around !

Taking a realistic view, Indira understood the weakness of her position; her's was a minority government dependent solely on the support of left parties; she decided on a direct contact with the people knowing, intuitively, that they would support her; with this in mind, she got the president to dissolve the Lok Sabha and to announce fresh elections to be held February 1971.

Both sides knew how crucial the election would be; those who opposed her coined the slogan "Indira Hatao ! (Remove Indira) thus declaring her removal as the central issue; Indira, refusing to demean the election as a personal matter, responded with her own slogan "Garibi Hatao !" (Remove poverty); in the 43 days of her campaign, she travelled over 36,000 miles, addressed about 13 million people in over 300 meetings; at meeting after meeting, Indira was hailed !

Indira's determination, her courage and her sense of responsibility made people feel secure and protected in her presence; they saw that she could fight like a tigress for the people and the country; their eyes lit up when they saw her; it was therefore, a triumphant Indira who returned after her election campaign to await the results.

When the final results were declared Indira had won by a two-thirds majority in the Lok Sabha; the opposition was in a shambles !

Indira's 3rd Term as Prime Minister, between 1971 and 1977, was marked by two momentous events; One was the advent of Bangladesh and the other, declaration of National Emergency.

The thoughtful and extremely successful manner in which Indira engineered India's support to Mukti Bahini, the freedom fighters of Bangladesh, towards liberation. Won for her heartly acclaim not only from her friends and admirers but, also, from her opponents. The war for a free Bangladesh which lasted for an entire year between 1970 and 1971, had posed quite a lot of onerous problems in the way of millions of men, women and children fleeing into India from East Pakistan, unable and helpless to withstand the heartless carnage by the West Pakistan forces. Under Indira's leadership, India braved the situation admiably and, ultimately, a humbled West Pakistan watched East Pakistan being snatched away to be born as Bangladesh.

Declaration of National Emergency was a culmination of a variety of factors inherent only to the dubious "game" called 'Politics'! The inexorable manner in which her opponents had ganged up against Indira left her with no alternative than to clamp an Emergency upon the nation. Indira Gandhi Knew that some' of her actions as Prime Minister were not entirely blameless and, this knowledge of her own shortcomings, made it possible for to see, clearly, how self-seeking her opponents were, wrapped up in themselves, they had little or no thought of the country's welfare when they combined their forces against Indira; theirs was a campaign against her, as personal vendetta, for reasons of jealously at her popularity worldwide amd among the masses, at her courage and at her indomitable spirit. Naturally, Indira judged that an India in their hands would soon be in a shambles. It was in the oberall interests of the country, therefore, that she was compelled to impose the Emergency, Not for her own personal ends.

Immediately after imposition of Emergency, a number of opposition leaders, including Morarji Desai and Jayaprakash Narayan, were arrested; although "arrested", these leaders were not in jail but were under detention, comfortably, in houses but, anti-social elements who had incited anarchy and mass-scale violence ideology or left extremists with a violence ideology who, while not believing in democracy were, however, taking advantage of democratic freedom for their own purposes which were. In the main, programmes of disruption and hartals combined with inciting, Strongly industrial workers, police and the armed forces to disobey orders.

General Public reaction to Emergency proclamation was, however, very favourable; the country had plunged into an abyss of lawlessness that most people felt Indira should have taken this bold step a lot earlier; as a result of such public support, a tranquility quite unknown hitherto, came into being and India was back to normal democratic functioning.

The 20-Point Programme

On July 1, 1975. Indira announced a 20-point programme for the social and economic regeneration of India, since the country's masses had neither understood nor appreciated all implications of the various 5-year plans implemented since India's independence, Indira followed the Mahatma's example and presented her 20-point programme in words familiar to the masses; her's was a comprehensive programme designed for the immediate and future benefits of the middle class, the cnsumers, the landless, the farmers, handloom and other craftsmen, the labourers, the students and the unemployed; severe punitive action against economic offenders, tax evaders, hoarders and smugglers had been provided for; bonded labour was declared illegal.

The 20-Point programme was Indira's economic pledge to the country. Chief Ministers, Cabinet Ministers and state Congress chiefs were directed to follow the programme's provisions, with a view committed to ease the burdens of the poor, since she also initiated action to make her programme operative, India's general economic condition improved noticeably and thus, the first few months of Emergency rule had been truly benevolent to the masses.

Launching of the 20-Point programme was followed by a total ban on all factions comprising religious fanatics and conventing a session of Parliament on July 21, 1975, she obtained Parliament's ratification virtually sailed through since Indira's Congress had enjoyed enormous majority; a few of the opposition expressed, however, a passionate concern about the new laws and their consequences to the nation, Jayaprakash Narayan going a little further to imply Russia's hand behind her actions.

Her censorship of the press and freedom of speech had acute effect on the country; there were no newspapers either to confirm or deny rumours which were becoming rampant fast; the provisions of the emergency rule and press censorship became fertile soil for all kinds of fear to germinate and take root ; added to all these, close friends abroad who were supportive of India's freedom struggle, stunned by the drastic steps taken by Indira branded her a despot and organised meeting aboard protesting against emergency, and the arrests and censorship which followed in its wake. The cumulative result of all these reactions within India and elsewhere in the world, naturally, took its toll on Indira's own peace of mind and her sense of well-being, As a lady who seldom shared her thoughts with others, now, she became even more aloof and withdrawn, virtually friendless.

The Effects of Drought

The war with Pakistan had drained the country's resources. The situation became worse because of poor harvest and delayed monsoon. Many parts of the country were affected by drought. The prices of commodities increased.

Oil and petrol prices also shot up. People were unhappy and the opposition parties blamed the ruling party for the trouble in the country. They even blamed many ministers for being dishonest.

In 1971 she declared a state of emergency. This was the most controversial act of her political career. Many people called her a dictator, but there were others who welcomed her move.

During this state of emergency her younger son, Sanjay Gandhi, rose to prominence. He became the leader of the youth wing of the Congress. He was always at his mother's side. Seeing his enthusiasm and interest in politics., people believed that he would be held in the country. Thus putting an end to the state of emergency. The leaders who were arrested during the emergency were released.

In the 1977 elections, the Congress Party was defeated by the Janata Party, and morarji Desai replaced Mrs. Gandhi as the next Prime Minister of India. Mrs.Gandhi accepted her defeat graciously, she utilised her time by visiting various parts of the country. She met people, talked to them, and listened to their grievances.

Meanwhile, the Janata Party could not rule the country for long. There were mutual differences among the party members and in 1980, elections were announced again.

During these elections Mrs.Gandhi left no stone unturned. She toured the length and breadth of the country. Crowds of people thronged to meet her. Hence Mrs.Gandhi came back to Power with a thumping majority.

Throughout her election campaign Sanjay and his friends were by her side. In fact few of Sanjay's friend were also included in the new Cabinet. His mother always valued his opinion. But Sanjay did not stay long in politics.

One bright sunny morning he along with his friend went to fly an aircraft. He was an adventurous man, and he tried a stunt while flying. Unforrtunately, his plane crashed and he died instantly.

Mrs.Gandhi had lost not only a son, but a person who she felt would go on to play a major role in Indian Politics. At this point she turned to her eldest son, Rajiv. Rajiv was a pilot with the Indian Airlines. He had married an Italian girl. Sonial, whom he met in England. Sonia easily adapted herself to the Indian was of living. She learnt to speak Hindi and wear saris.

Rajiv was an obedient son. He gave up his job and helped his mother in her work. He soon began to learn the ways of politics. He was known for his truthful and candid nature. He was nicknamed "Mr. Clean."

Mrs.Gandhi's day would begin with 'darshan' which was held in her house. She would meet people, and listen to their complaints. After the"darshan" she would go the her office, attend meetings and Parliament Sessions. She spent her free time with her family. She adored her grandchildren. Priyanka, Rahul and Varun.

Like her father she also believed in developing friendly relations with other countries. She visited U.S.A.USSR and Britain. Within the country she continued with her travels. She addressed rallies, and met leaders of various other parties, many people addressed her as "Mother"

The Outstanding Lady

During the early eighties some people began to demand that Punjab be recognised as a separate country. These people had the backing of terrorist groups. They started a reign of terror in order to get their demands fulfilled. Mrs.Gandhi, however, did not wish to make Punjab an independent country. She tried to supress the terrorist movement. So, to protect themselves, the terrorist took shelter in the Golden Temple because the police could not arrest them there.

In June 1981, she took the second controversial decision of her career. She sent thr army to the Golden Temple to arrest the terrorists. A battle was fought between the terrorists and the army. Many were killed and hundreds were wounded. Punjab was put under strict military law. The Sikhs felt that by attacking the Golden Temple she had hurt their honour. Many people wanted to avenge the insult inflicted on the Sikh community.

On the morning of October 31, 1984, Mrs.Gandhi had her breakfast with her family members.Rajiv had gone to West Bengal, Her morning "darshan' had been cancelled as she had to give an interview to a television reporter. As she walked upto the garden path, two of her Sikh bodyguards shot her. She was immediately taken to hospital by her daughter in law, Sonia. The doctor desperately tried to save her; but they failed.

The news of her death was broadcasted on radio and television. Rajiv came to Delhi and was immediately sworn in as the Prime Minister. He appealed to the people to maintain peace and order. However; there were riots in the country. Angry people started killing the Sikhs. Shops were looted, houses were burnt. And thousands were murdered. The atmosphere was tense. Many Sikhs took refuge in the houses of their Hindu friends. This was perhaps the most tragic event in Indian history.

Mrs. Gandhi was cremated with full state honours. He body was covered with flowers and draped in the tricolour. Thousands of people thronged the road to catch a glimpse of her. Rajiv it the funeral pyre.

Once, addressing a rally in Orissa she had said, "I will be proud to die in the service of my country. I believe every drop of my blood will serve my country, helping to make her strong and dynamic." And indeed she died in the service of her country. She was an outstanding dynamic lady, totally dedicated to her country. Like her father, it was her dream to have a advanced united and powerful India.

Mrs. Gandhi was fearless and courageous who accepted challenges in her stride. Her charismatic personally drew people to her wherever she went, whether in India or abroad.

16

Shri Ramakrishna Paramahans

A Brahmin couple called the Chattopadhyayas lived at Kamarpukura, a village in Bengal. They were very poor, pious and devotees of Sri Rama. As the father had refused to bear false witness in a case which would have benefited his neighbour, a powerful land owner, he had been despoiled of all his possessions. When he was sixty years of age, he went to Gaya on a pilgrimage. During the night, the lord appeared to him and said, "I am about to be reborn for the salvation of the world."

At the same time in Kamarapukura, his wife Chandramani also had a dream. There was a temple of Siva opposite her cottage. The idol quickened to life under her eyes and a ray of light penetrated into her being. Chandramani fainted. Later she conceived and was transformed. She heard voices. She carried a God in her womb.

She gave birth to a male child on February 18, 1836. They named him Gadadhar. He was a boy full of fun, Mischievous and charming. He had a feminine grace. One day when he was six years old, he was going to the fields with a meal, which he carried in a fold of his garments. Something strange happened.

He was following a narrow path between the rice fields. As he munched his rice, he raised his eyes to the sky. He saw a great black cloud spreading rapidly. Suddenly at the edge of the cloud a flight of snow white cranes passed over his head.

The contrast was beautiful. His spirit wandered away. he lost consciousness and fell to the ground. The puffed rice was scattered somebody picked him up and carried him home. A feeling of joy overcame him... This was the first time he was seized with ecstacy.

One day, when he was a child of eight years, he was playing the role of Siva in a play. Sudenly he was possessed by Siva Tears of joy rolled down his checks and he was transported. From then on the ecstasies became more frequent.

His father died when Ramakrishna was seven years old, So, it was difficult for the family to make both ends meet. The eldest son Ramkumar went to Calcutta and opened a School there. Though he sent for his brother to join the School, he refused to learn.

At that time a rich woman by name Rani Rasmani, who was regarded as belonging to an inferior caste, built a temple for Goddess Kali. The temple was on the eastern bank of the Ganga at Dakshines hwar. She could not find a Brahmin priest to officiate at the temple. The post was offered to Ramkumar.

At first, Ramkumar hesitated to accept the post of the priest, because the temple had been founded by a lady belonging to a lower caste.

Finally, he agreed. But Ramakrishna could reconcile himself to the idea only with great difficulty. Gradually his repugnance receded and when his brother died, Ramakrishna himself took over the post.

The Temple of Kali

In the temple of Kali, Ramakrishna played with the Goddess for ten long years. He lived in the temple alone with her. A number of pilgrims, Monks and Sadhus and both Hindus and Muslims visited the temple.

The Goddess, the Queen of the world, dwelt there clad in a Varanasi saree. In her two arms on the left, she held the severed head of a demon and a sword, with the right hands she offered boons, throwing an enchanting smile to the devotees.

She was the Universal Mother. The only reality for the young priest was that which he could see, hear and touch. He was associated with all acts of worship during the day. He dressed her and offered her flowers and food. He was one of the attendants. When the queen rose and when she went to bed.

Within the temple she had enveloped him. He wept and used to cry out, "Mother, one more day has been wasted, I have not seen you, I have not understood the truth". He tore off hisclothes, and even the sacred thread which no Brahmin would lay a side. All his actions in this regard became a subject for mockery, even for scandal; but he did not care for the criticisms.

The temple was a vast building with five domes. It was reached by an open terrace above the Ganga between a double row of twelve small domed temples to Siva. On the other side rose another vast temple to Krishna and Radha.

Ramakrishna says, "One day I was torn with intolerable anguish. My heart seemed to be wrung like a wet cloth..... I was racked with pain. A sword was hanging in the sanctuary of Kali.

My eyes fell upon it. An idea flashed through my brain like a flash of lightening. The sword ! It will help me to end my agony ! I rushed up to it and seized it like a mad man..... and lo ! All the things around me vanished.

I saw an ocean of awareness, boundless, dazzling. In whatever direction I turned, great luminous waves were rising. They bore down upon me with a long roar, as if to swallow me. They broke over me and engulfed me. I was suffocated and lost consciousness and I fell..... How I passed that day and the next I do not know; around me rolled an ineffable joy. I was conscious of the presence of the "divine Mother". He saw those around him through a drifting mist. he could no longer control his eyes, body or mind.

He prayed to the Mother to come to his help. Suddenly he understood that he was possessed by the Mother. He did not resist. She filled him. And out of the mists, the maternal from of the Mother emerged, first a hand, then her breath and her voice, finally her whole person.

One evening the rites were over for the day and the Mother was put to sleep. Ramakrishna could not sleep in his room. He listened. He heard her get up. He saw her going to the upper storey of the temple with the joy of a young girl. As she walked, her wrinklets jingled. He wondered whether he was dreaming. He went out into the court and raised his head. There he saw her with unbound hair on the balcony of the first floor, watching the Ganga flow through the beautiful night.

From that day his days and nights were passed in the presence of Goddess Kali. Eventually he was identified with her. Through his body. as through a widnow, appeared the bodies of gods to the devotees.

One day Mothur Babu, the son-in-law of Rani Rasmani, was sitting in his room opposite Ramakrishna's. Unobserved, he watched him pacing up and down upon his balcony.

Suddenly, he uttered a cry, for he saw Ramakrishna alternately in the from of Siva as he walked in one direction and of the Mother as he walked in the opposite direction.

Some people laughed at his ecstasies and criticized him, too. He did not care. But Mathur Babu, his ally and protector, could not tolerate this. He requested Ramakrishna to keep his feelings under control and to follow the conventions of society. He argued with Ramakrishna that even God followed rules of his own. He never made flowers of two different colours bloom on the same stalk.

Ramakrishna was puzzled and asked himself whether he had gone too far. The more he thought over Mathur's words, the more difficult it became to dismiss the doubt from his mind. The following morning, he was gathering hibiscus flowers for his worship of Kali. Suddenly he saw two flowers, one blood red and one white, side by side on the same stem !

Sharada Devi

Ramakrishna was sent back to Kamarpukura, as his well wishers thought he would recoup his health. His Mother thought that marriage would cure him of his divine enchantment. He did not object. He was twenty-three years old. When efforts to find a bride appeared hopeless, he gave a clue to his Mother: "It is useless to search here and there.Go and look in the Family of Ram Mukhopadhyaya of the village of Jayarambati".

Jayarambati is a small village in West Bengal. The family of the Mukherjis was well known in the village as the worshippers of the Holy Mother.

Ramachandra, a worthy descendant of the Mukherjis, was respected for his godliness and compassion for all. He married Shyamasundari Devi, daughter of Haridas Muzumdar of Shihar.

Truly their daughter Sharada Devi had been set-aside for a higher purpose. Ramakrishna's union with Sharada Devi was a mutual offering to God in the person of a spouse.

Ramakrishna was twenty-three years old and his bride Sharada Devi was about five. After the marriage she returned to her father's house and did not see him for eight long years. Ramakrishna returned to his temple after regaining some measure of calm at his mother's house. Goddess Kali was waiting for him in the temple.

As he entered the temple the divine delirium was rekindled. His madness returned tenfold. He could see creatures emerging from him. He remained motionless. Horror paralysed his limbs. He was helpless. He appealed to the Mother. For the vision of Kali was the only hope of survival for him. This mental orgy and despair continued for two years. Help came to Ramakrishna through a woman. One day when he was watching the boats moving on the Ganga, he saw a woman coming up the terrace on which he was standing.

She was tall, beautiful and wore the dress of a Sanyasini. Ramakrishna sent for her. As soon as she came she burst into tears and said, "My son, I have been waiting for you for a long time".

She was a Brahmin, a devotee of Vishnu. She belonged to a noble Bengali family. She was highly educated and learned in the Bhakti scriptures. She said that she was looking for the man inspired by God. She said that she had a message for him. She did not reveal her name but was known as Bhairavi Brahmani.

A relationship of mother and son was established there and then between the woman and Ramakrishna. He told her all his experinces in God and how a few thought him mad, and asked her whether he was really mad.

Bhairavi comforted him with maternal tenderness. She told him that he had reached the highest state of sadhana (spiritual practice). His sufferings were only the measure of his ascent. She took care of him and enlightened his mind. Bhairavi, his Guru, recognized in him the incarnation of Divinity. She held a meeting at Dakshineshwar with the Pandits and insisted that public recognition be given to this new Avatara.

Ramakrishna's fame began to spread and people from all walks of life came to seek instruction. He remained to the end of his life the simplest of men. He was too intoxicated with God to consider himself an Avantara. He disliked even the mention of the word 'Avatara'.

Realization of God

Ramakrishna had achieved the realization of the personal God by 1864. Just then, the messenger of the impersonal God arrived at Dakshineshwar. This man was Totapuri (the naked man), a wandering monk. For a long time Ramakrishna had been haunted by the formless Gid prowling round him. Ramakrishna who remained dissatisfied till he had seen and embraced the living from, wanted to sink body and soul in the Formless. He could not escape it. One who was exploring the continent of the gods could not stop. The formless God lay in wait for Ramakrishna, but Ramakrishna did not go to Him. Totapuri came to fetch Him.

Totapuri saw Ramakrishna sitting on one of the steps of the temple lost in the happiness of the vision. Struck by what he saw Totapuri said, "My son, I see that you have travelled far along the way of the truth. If you wish it. I can help you. I will teach you Vedanta".

Ramakrishna told him that he had first to obtain the permission of the Mother. He got her permission and became an ardent disciple of Totapuri. He had to submit to the test of 'initiation'. He had to renounce his sacred thread, priesthood and other privileges. They were nothing to him.

But he had to renounce his personal God now and for ever. He had to conduct his own funeral rites. Ramakrishna was clothed in the saffron robe of a Sanyasi and Totapuri began to teach him the virtues of Advaitha Vedanta.

The naked man Totapuri taught him to death his mind from all objects and to plunge into the heart of the Atman. Thought he could detach his mind from all objects, the familiar from of the Mother stood before him.

Every time he tried to concentrate on the precepts of Advita Vedanta, the form of the Mother intervened. So he said to Totapuri in despair, "It is no good. I shall never succeed in lifting my spirit to the 'Unconditioned State'.

Totapuri took a piece of glass and struck the point between his eyes and said, "Conecentrate your mind on that point". Ramakrishna says, "Then I began to meditate with all my might and as soon as the gracious form of the Mother appeared, I used my discrimination as a sword and I clove her in two. The last barrier fell and I lost myself in "Samadhi".

Totapuri was amazed; because Ramakrishna had achieved in one day what had taken forty years for him. Totapuri had intended to stay only for three days, but stayed for eleven months to have interaction with his disciple who had outstripped him.

In spite of his vast knowledge Totapuri could not realize that love could be one of the paths leading to God. He scorned Prayers, hymns and religious dances. When Ramakrishna began repeating the names Gods to the accompaniment of clapping of hands, he asked, "Are you making bread ?"

But the charm began to work on Totapuri; for a few hymns sung melodiously brought tears to his. Even his illness played a dominant role in his spirit realizing its limitations. His sickness grew virulent and the ascetic could not concentrate on Brahman. He went down to the Ganga to sacrifice himself But an invisible force prevented him. He came back dismayed. He had experienced the power of Maya. It existed everywhere in life, in death. He admitted to Ramakrishna that Brahman and Shakti are one and the same.

The Divine Mother was pacified and restored his health. He bade goodbye to his pupil who had become his master and went his way, an enlightened man.

Ramakrishna summed up the experience with Totapuri,, "When I think of the Supreme Being as inactive, I call him Brahman and when I think of him as active I call him Maya or Shakti. It is impossible to think of the one without the other. The Divine Mother and Brahman are one".

Ramakrishna recognized that all religions led by different paths to the same God, So he was eager to explore all the paths. Rani Rasmani had desired that rooms should be reserved for passing guests of all religions in her Foundation. From his temple Ramakrishna could see Muslim fakirs passing.

One day Ramakrishna saw a humble Muslim absorbed in payers. He observed, through the outward shell of his body, that through Islam, he had realized God. He asked him to initiate him and for several days he forgot his Gods including Kali. Living outside the temple, he respeated the name of Allah, wearing the robes of a Muslim. He was ready to eat forbidden food.

Mathur Babu was aghast and begged him to desist. He had food prepared for Ramakrishna by a Brahmin. This total surrender resulted in his spiritual voyage and a radiant personage with grave countenance and white beard appeared to him. The river of Islam led him back to the ocean.

Seven years later, an exterience of the same kind led him to realize Christianity. In November 1974, one Mallik, a Hindu of Calcutta, with a garden near Dakshineshwar, read the Bible to him. Ramakrishna heard of Christ for the first time.

The life of Jesus pervaded him. One day when he was sitting in the rom of a rich Hindu, he saw on the wall, a picture representing the Madonna (virgin Mary) and the child (Jesus Christ). Then the figures came to life. The holy visions came close and entered him. he had no room for anything but Christ. He no longer thought of going to the temple.

One afternoon, in the grove of Dakshineshwar, he saw a person coming towards him. He draw near and Ramakrishna heard in the depths of his soul the words, "Behold the Christ. It is He, the maser Yogi. It is Jesus, Love Incarnate".

The son of Man embraced the Seer of India, the son of the Mother, and absorbed him into himself. Ramakrishna was lost in ecstasy. Once again he realized the union with Brahman. The river of Christinity led him back to the ocean. Ramakrishna considered Christ also as an incarnation. Knowledge does not consist in the number of books one has read. Ramakrishna gained his knowledge through interaction with thousands of Monks, Pilgrims and Pandits.

He could say to his disciples, "All religions lead to the same God. A river has several ghats. At one a Hindu draws water and calls it 'jail'; at another a Muslim draws water and calls it 'pani'; at another ghat a Christian calls it water. The substance is the same under different names. A man should follow his own path sincerely and ardently to know God. He will surely realize Him".

Ramakrishna was the loving brother of everything that lives and dies. He would not be satisfied with happiness, which he could not share with others. As the Mother drew him to herself he prayed "O, Mother, let me remain in contact with men. Do not make me a dried up ascetic".

Shri Ramakrishna's Path

In May 1867, after the crises he had passed through, Sri Ramakrishna left for Kamarpukura, After an absence of eight years he was going there to have rest for six or seven months. The good people of the village gave him a warm welcome. They were happy at the sight of their Gadadhar.

He wife Sharada Devi was fourteen years old now. She came to Kamarpukura on learning about his arrival. She had evolved spiritually so far that she could understand her husband's mission. She knew the part she had to play in his life. She recognized him as her guide and put herself at his service.

Though Sri Ramakrishna has been blamed by some people for sacrificing her, she never showed any trace of resentment. "I have learnt," he said to her, 'to look upon every woman as Mother. That is the only way I can think of you. But if you wish to draw me into this world (of illusion) as I have been married to you, I am at your service'. She renounced worldly pleasures and encouraged him in his mission. Touched by her innocence and self-sacrifice, Ramakrishna played the part of her elder brother. He devoted himself to her education as a diligent wife and good manager.

Ramakrishna recognized the Goddess under her veil, One night, when everything had been prepared for worship, he made Sharada Devi sit in the seat of Kali and, as priest, worshipped her. Both of them were in a condition of ecstasy. When he came to himself he called her the Divine Mother. Ramakrishna's worship of womanhood had no limitations. He recognized the Mother even in the most degraded prostitutes. At the end of 1867, Sri Ramakrishna returned to Dakshinesh war and made several Pilgrimages with Mathur Babu, the Patron of the temple.

During these Pilgrimages, he came face to face with poverty and suffering. Till then he had lived in a hypnotic trance. Mother Kali had spread a veil over him and had hidden human suffering from him. When they arrived at Deoghar he saw the ravages made by the terrible famine. He saw the Santhals emaciated and dying of hunger. He told Mathur Babu that they must feed those Santhals. Mathur Babu told him that he was not so rich as to undertake such a task. Ramakrishna sat down among the poor and wept.

During the summer of 1870, Mathur Babu took him to one of his estates. It was the time of payment of dues. The harvest had failed and the tenants could not pay. Ramakrishna asked Mathur Babu to condone their dues but Mathur Babu protested.

Ramakrishna said, "You are only the steward of the Mother. They are the Mother's tenants.You must spend the Mother's money. When they are suffering, how can you refuse to help them ? You must do so." Mathur babu had to give in.

In the temple Ramakrishna had the opportunity of talking to the faithful of all religions and sects. As the Bhairavi Brahmani had announced that Ramakrishna was an incarnation of God, people came from all parts of the country to see him. So, he saw many great personalities.

Among them were Michael Madhusudan Dutt, a Bengali Poet, a convert to Christianity, Narayana Shastri and Padmanabhan, masters of Vedantic learning. Vishwanath Upadhyaya and Maharshi Dayananda Saraswathi, the founder of

Arya Samaj, Maharshi Dabendranath Tagore and Keshab Chunder Sen, head of the Brahmo Samaj.

Ramakrishna's meeting with members of the Brahmo Samaj brought him into contact with the educated middle class of our country. Through them he came to know the pioneers of progress and western ideas about which he knew nothing. He was not a strict and narrow devotee who would pull down the shutters of his cell. He flung them wide open. He was human, curious and eager for the fruits of the tree, of life. In order to understand things better, he identified himself with them. He saw that the God within him could not be satisfied with his personal satisfaction.

He required of him the love and service of mankind. His spiritual struggles, ecstasies and realizations were meant to prepare the way for the development of mankind. It was revealed to Ramakrishna about 1863, that many faithful and pure hearted persons would come to him. The time was ripe. He could wait no longer. Night and day, the thought of the beloved companions possessed him. He cried in His heart. He went to the roof in the fading light and cried out "Come, my children, where are you ? I cannot live without you"....

They arrived one after the other. A write-up in a journal of Brahmo Samaj attracted Ramachandra Dutt and Manmohan Mitra. They came and were conquered. They brought him his two greatest disciples. The one who became the abbot of the Ramakrishna order, Brahmananda, and he whose genius was to enlighten India and the world. Vivekananda.

According to Sharadananda, all the disciples of Ramakrishna arrived before the end of 1884. Ramakrishna did nothing to detach them from the world but captivated them by his charm and his character. People belonging to all classes and castes came to him. He spoke to all with patience. He would spend twenty out of the twenty-four hours of the day answering the disciples. He won their hearts. But he wanted every man to understand, sympathise with, and love the rest of mankind. He wanted every man to identify himself with the life of humanity.

He felt that it was unnecessary to seek God only in temples because he was here, every where, eevery second. We can see him, we can touch him, for he is our brother, our friend; and our enemy. He warned his disciples against any kind of 'Ramakrishnaism' that is, regarding him as an "Avatar' and starting a sect. Above all ther must be no barriers. "a river has no need of barriers. If it dams itself up. it stagnates and becomes foul".

Ramakrishna as a Wonderful Wand

Ramakrishna was a wonderful wand in the hands of the Mother. Towards the end of his life such was his horror of riches that he could not touch gold without being burnt.

Once when Ramakrishna lay down on his bed he felt acute pain, as if a scorpian had stung him. He got up and looked for the scorpian. What he found was not a scorpian but an eight-anna coin ! His body could not bear even the presence of a coin under the covers ! Vivekananda relates, "Even when he was sleeping, if I touched him with a piece of money, his hand would bend and his whole body would seem to be paralysed.

The touch of an impure person gave him physical pain and he compared it to the bite of a cobra. He could read the souls of those who approached him and, if he accepted them as his disciples, it was with full knowledge of their nature.

Ramakrishna did not ask his disciples to forsake everything. To those who had already bound themselves with family ties, he did not say, 'Forsake all to seek salvation'. He could say, "We owe a debt to the gods, we owe a debt to parents, we owe a debt to our wives. No work can be satisfactorily concluded until the debt to the parents at least has been paid. So long as parents remain in want, the practice of devotion avails nothing".

One day in the course of a lecture Keshab said, "O, God, grant that we may be plunged in the river of devotion and attain the ocean of Sachidananda". There were women sitting behind a screen. Sri Ramakrishna pointed to them and said to Keshab, "If you are all plunged at once, what will be their fate? So, you must come out of the water from time to time, then go back; immerse yourself and come out alternately !" Everyone laughed heartily.

Ramakrishna's inner eye penetrated into the problems of his children. He could guide the troubled souls. This becomes clear in the story of the comedian, Girish Chandra Ghosh. At their first meeting Ghosh was drunk and he insulted Ramakrishna. Ramakrishna calmly said to him, "At least you might drink to God. He drinks as well". The drunked, stunned, asked, "How do you know"? Rama krishna answered, "If he did not drink, how could he have created this topsy-turvy world"?

Girish remained in bewildered silence. After he left, Rama krishna told his disciples that Girish was a great devotee of God. Later Girish, became a disciple of Ramakrishna and gave up drinking, though his master did not ask him to.

With his religious sensitiveness, Ramakrishna could identify those who were predestined to a divine sowing, those in whom God was sleeping. He sccrutinized his disciples thoroughly. His true disciples were to be leaders and have charge of other souls. He prefeerrd his disciples to be young and unmarried. He was their companion, brother and guide. The advice he gave was not his own. It came from Mother Kali. He did not hinder their development by putting himself between the pupil and his learning. He was afraid of being loved too dearly. He did not want to be bound by the tenderness of his pupils.

"Let the bees suck your heart, but he careful that the beauty of your heart does not keep one of them captive".

Ramakrishna believed that God is in everything and God is everything. So, if follows that who ever opens his eyes and looks around will end up by meeting Him. Ramakrishna also practiced and preached 'Ahimsa', not only with regard to man but to all living creatures. A parable is given here to drive home the point that God is everywhere and in everything and that at times we should use our discretion in coming to a conclusion.

One day a holy man in a forest taught his disciples that God is in everything. One of the disciples had gone to the forest to collect wood for sacrificial fire. He heard a cry "A tusker is approaching". He did not move a way to save himself, though others fled from the scene.

The man said, "The elephant is God in one from, why should I run away ?" Even when the elephant driver yelled, "Save yourself", he did not move. The elephant lifted him and flung him aside. He was badly bruised. A little later he was asked, "Why did you not run away to save yourself "? He replied, My master has taught me that God is in everything.

So, I thought of God in the elephant and stayed there". They asked him, "Why didn't you think there was God in the elephant driver ? Why didn't you pay attention to his words ?

The Great Disciple

Ramakrishna's life would not have been complete without the association with Narendranath Dutt, who later came to be known as Swami Vivekananda. Narendra relates, "From my youth every night just as I fell asleep, two dreams took shape. In one I saw myself among the great ones of the earth, the possessor of riches, honour, power and glory; and I felt that the capacity to attain all these was in me. But the next instant I saw myself renouncing all worldly things, dressed in a simple loincloth, living on alms, sleeping at the foot of a tree; and I thought I was capable of living thus, like the rishis of old.

Of these two pictures, the second took the upper hand and I felt that only thus could a man attain supreme bliss........ And each night it was renewed". Such was Narendra when he first went to meet the master. Ramakrishna treated Naren in an exceptional way. He had chosen him at the first glance, on account of what he was and what he might become, a spiritual leader of mankind.

At their first meeting Ramakrishna took Naren's hand in his and said. "Promise me that you will come to see me again alone and soon !" Naren promised in order to free himself from the saint, but decided never to return. But the strange vision worked on him and within a month he returned to Dakshineshwar, During his second visit Naren found Ramakrishna sitting on his small bed.

Ramakrishna affectionately called Naren to sit by his side on the bed. Naren thought that he was going to make some eccentric remark. But before he could stop him, Ramakrishna placed his right foot on his body. The contact was terrible.

With his eyes open he saw the walls and everything in the room Vanishing into nothingness. He felt as though the whole universe and his individuality were lost in the nameless void.

He was terrified and feared that he was face to face with death. He cried out, "What are you doing ? I have parents at home". Then Sri Ramakrishna began to laugh, "All right, let us leave it at that for the moment".

As soon as Sri Ramakrishna said these words, the strange phenomenon ended. Naren came to himself again and everything both within and without was as before. At his third visit, Naren was on the defensive, Sri Ramakrishna took him to the garden and after a short stroll they sat in the parlour.

The master fell into a trance and, as Narendra watched, he was suddenly touched by the master. Narendra immediately lost all consciousness of the world outside. When he came himself a little later, he saw Sri Ramakrishna looking at him and stroking his chest. Naren did not want to be a disciple of anyone. His reason would not submit to domination. He wanted to retain his independence and did not want to accept anything from the master. The uncritical faith of other roused his contempt. Naren questioned everything. He alone weighed Sri Ramakrishna's words. He alone doubted.

Sri Ramakrishna loved him the better for it. Naren said to Sri Ramakrishna, "Even if millions of people calld you God, if I had not proved it for myself, I would never do so". Though naren's knowledge gave him intense joy, his severe criticism which had no consideration for others hurt the master. Naren would say, "How do you know that your realizations are not the creations of your sick brain"?

At such times, Sri Ramakrishna would seek comfort of the Mother, who consoled him with the words, "patience, son, Naren's eyes will be opened". It was impossible to satisfy Naren with proof of God's existence. He maintained, "If God is real, it is possible to realize Him".

The master's spirit gradually took possession of the rebel disciple. Naren did not let go even a single opportunity to ridicule his master's beliefs. One day Naren and other disciples and went into side-splitting laughter at the extravagance of Advaitist Vedanta. They said, "This jug is God.... and these flies are God".

Sri Ramakrishna heard the laughter from the adjoining room and came in quietly in a semi-conscious state and touched naren. Again a spiritual tornad to swept through him. All at once everything was changed in Naren's eyes. He saw with amazement that nothing existed but God, He saw went back to his house; all that he saw, touched and was God.

He stopped doing anything, intoxicated by the universal power. He remained in this condition for some days. Then the trance vanished But its remembrance remained with Naren. He repeated 'Shiva, Shiva' like a mad man. In 1884, Naren's prodigal father died. The family was facing ruin. From then on Naren tasted misery. He was facing the realities of life for the first time.

Throughout this tortuous period Naren continued to pray God every morning. One day his mother said, to him, "Fool, be quiet, what has your God done for you "?... He in his turn was filled with anger against God. Why did he not answer his anguished appeals ? Why did he allow so much suffering on the earth ?

He declared war upon God. Now, he openly spoke against God. he told a few disciples of Sri Ramakrishna who remonstrated against his sayings, that only a coward believed in God through fear.

One evening when he had eaten nothing, he sank down, exhausted and wet, in front of a house by the roadside. The delirium of fever raged in his body.

Suddenly it seemed as if he folds enveloping his soul were rent asunder and there was light. All his past doubts were automatically solved. He could say truly, "I see, I know, I believe, I am undeceived".

One that day, Sri Ramakrishna came to Calcutta and begged naren to go with him to Dakshineshwar. Naren tried to escape, but in vain; he was obliged to follow the master. That night, shut up in his room Sri Ramakrishna said to him, "I know that you cannot remain in the world. But for my sake, stay in it as long as I live".

Ramakrishna's Great Path

Shri Ramakrishna lived at Dakshineshwar from 1881 onwards surrounded by his disciples. Pilgrims, worshippers, pandits and religious and curious men thronged the place to overwhelm the master with their questions. He always answered them with patience. He could play both the child and the judge.

He would say, "Too much concentration on ceremonial purity becomes a plague. People affected with his disease have no time to think of man or God".

"It is the sanctity of men that makes the sanctity of places. Otherwise how can places purify a man"? "God is everywhere. God is in us. Life and the universe are his dreams.

"The eyes", he said, "are the windows of the soul". He read through them at the first glance.

The master forgave everything for he believed in infinite kindless. He said, "Do not speak of love for your brother. Realise it. Do not argue about doctrine and religion.

There is only one. All rivers flow to the Ocean. Flow and let others flow too ! The great stream makes a path for itself according to the scope of its journey. But it is all the same water....... Go......... Flow on towards the ocean........."

Ramakrishna's end was approaching. His feeble body was gradually consumed by the fire of ecstasy. It was worn-out by his continuous contact with those who came to seek his advice. In his humorous way he said to Goddess Kali. "Why do you bring hither all these people. who are like milk diluted with five times its own quantity of water ? My eyes are destroyed blowing the fire to get rid the of the water.

My health is gone. Do it yourself, if you want it done. This (pointing to his body) is nothing but a burst drum and if you go on beating it day in and day out, how long do you think it will last? But he never turned away any one. He said, "Let me be condemned to be born over again, even in the form of a dog, if so I can be of help to a single soul". And again, "I will give up twenty thousand such bodies to help one man. It is glorious to help even one man".

In 1884, Ramakrishna's health took a serious turn. The doctors who examined him forbade both speech and ecstasy. But he did not pay attention to them Finally, when the disease was diagnosed as throat cancer, he was put under the care of Dr. Mahendralal Sarkar of calcutta. He was a rationalist, who did not agree with Ramakrishna's religious views. But, gradually he was attracted towards Ramakrishna and treated him free. He said to Shri Ramakrishna, I love you so dearly because of your devotion to truth.

Ramakrishna's condition grew worse. Dr. Sarkar advised that Ramakrishna be removed to the country. In December 1885, he was taken to a house in the midst of the beautiful gardens of cossipore. His disciples begged him to pray with them for his health. A Pandit, who shared their faith, joined them in their entreaties. The Pandit said to Shri Ramakrishna, "The scriptures declare that saints like you can cure, them selves by an effort of the will".

Shri Ramakrishna replied, "My mind has been given to God once and for all. Would you have me ask for it back"? They begged him to pray to Mother Kali. He replied, "I will try what I can do".

They left him alone for a few hours. When they returned the Master said. "I said to her, 'Mother, I cannot eat because of suffering. Make it possible for me to eat a little". She pointed to you all and said, "What Are you not eating through all these mouths ? I was ashamed and could not utter another word".

Shri Ramakrishna ordered his disciples to beg for their food without distinction of caste, to prepare them for a monastic life. Towards the end of March, he gave them saffron robes and some kind of monastic initation. He did not hide the fact that he regarded Naren as his heir. He said to him one day, "I leave these young people in your charge. Busy yourself in developing their spirituality".

One day, while meditating, Nare Had the sensation of a light shining behind his head. Suddenly he lost consciousness and was lost in the Absolute. He had fallen into the depths of 'Nirvikalpa Samadhi', which he had sought for so long and which Ramakrishna had refused to allow him.

When Naren came down to the earth, he approached his Master who said, "Now the Mother has shown you everything. But this revelation will remain under lock and key, and I shall Keep the key. When you have accomplished the mother's work, you will find this treasure again.

Three or four days before his death, he called Naren and asked to be left alone with him. He looked at him and passed into an ecstasy. It enveloped Naren. When he came back from his shadows, he saw Shri Ramakrishna in tears. The master said to him, "Today I have given you my all and am now only a fakir, possessing nothing, By this power you will do immense good in the world". From that moment all his powers were transferred to Naren, the master and the disciple were one. Sunday August 15, 1886...... The last day. In the afternoon, Shri Ramakrishna walked a little and talked with his disciples for two hours. At night fall he became unconscious. But by midnight he revived, leaning against five or six pillows he talked to the last moment with Naren.

Then in ringing tones he cried out the name of his beloved Kali, the Divine Mother, and lay back. After half on hour of this final ecstasy, he died. In his own words of faith, "he had passed from one room to another". His disciples bid farewell with the words, "Victory to Bhagawan Ramakrishna". The holy body was consigned to a sacred fire at the cremation ground on the Ganga. When all was over, the ashes were gathered in a copper vessel and placed on the Master's bed.

In the evening Sharada Devi sat down to remove her ornaments one by one. When she was about to take off her gold bracelets, the Master suddenly appeared as he was before he took ill; and taking hold of her hands he said, "Am I dead that you are removing the signs iof a married woman from your wrists"? She then desisted from doing so.

The Godrealization

Shri Ramakrishna Paramahamsa had virtually no education. But he was one of the great teachers of India. He could express his teachings simply and clearly. He used very apt comparisons. Some one asked him, is sin true or false ? Does it exist in God? Ramakrishna answered, "It exists in God as poison exists in a serpent. It is position, it is harmful to us, not to God".

He taught that religious books, discussion and discourses

are needed only till a man realizes God, but once God-realization is achieved, they fall silent. He gave an analogy. The bee keeps buzzing until it begins to suck honey from the flower; once the sucking begins, the buzz stops. Shri Ramakrishna also narrated memorable Parables. (A parable is a story with a moral.)

Once he was saying that a man living in society should resist evil and defend himself. Goodness does not mean suffering evil silently. He narrated the story of a highly poisonous serpent in a field, where boys grazed their cattle. They were terribly afraid of the serpent.

Once a holy man passed that way. The boys warned him against the serpent. He told them that he would soften it with mantras. When it approached him with its hood raised, he murmured a charm, and it fell as his feet. He asked it not to harm any one and to meditate on god. The serpent became very pious. The boys found it passive, and began to throw stones at it and torment it. On his way back the holy man saw the serpent.

He asked it why it had become so weak. It narrated how it became totally passive, and suffered in consequence. The holy man said, "I forbade you to bite God's creatures. But why did you not raise your hood and hiss, when people harassed you "?

He narrated another story to drive home a point. One day some fishermen were catching fish. An eagle swooped down, caught a fish and flew away. A number of crows were flying about. They chased the eagle for the sake of the fish. The eagle flew to the south, the crows pursued it. It flew to the north, it flew to the west, then to the east, but the crows came in pursuit. Confounded, it flew this way and that and, in its panic, dropped the fish. The crows now ignored the eagle and went after the fish. The eagle sat on a branch and said to itself, "The wretched fish was the cause of my misery. I let it go, and am now happy'.

Shri Ramakrishna explained; Desire is the root cause of all misery. A man wants power, wants money, wants this and that. If he lets go desire, happiness comes of its own accord, Give up desire and be compassionate, taught Shri Ramakrishna. Ramakrishna's story of a doll made of salt is famous. Once somebody asked, "If you have seen God, Why don't you describe him"?

Ramakrishna answered, "Once a doll made of salt set out to measure the depth of the sea. Its object to narrate its experience to people when it returned. But no sooner had it left the shore and stepped into the sea than it melted and disappeared. No one could tell what had happened to it. The attempt of any man to describe his experience of the realization of God is similar to the doll's attempt. He forgets himself in that experience and can say nothing".

Once the image of Radhakrishna fell down because of the carelessness of the priest and the leg was broken. Learned men conversant with the sastras said that, according to the sastras, a flawed image was not to be worshipped but to be thrown away.

But Rasmani did not like the idea of discarding the image which had been worshipped for years. When she requested Ramakrishna to guide her, he said, "If your son-in-law happens to break his leg will you throw him away ? The image can be repaired and used".

Shri Ramakrishna's teaching was simple. A man need not renounce family life and become a sanyasi. Family life is a fortress. It is easier to overcome a foe from within the fortress than from outside.

To attain salvation one has to give up the "I". The object of human life is God realization. 'Bhakti' (devotion) and 'jnana' (knowledge) lead to the same goal. But in our age 'Bhakti' is to be preferred. to realize God, he said, love god. Became the Mother's child. Cry out to her with all sincerity, and she will respond. A mother attends to her household duties, but when the child cries, gives up her work and hastens to the child.

So it is with man, too, If he cries out sincerely to God or the Mother, God or the Mother will hastens to him. The object of human life is to see God. Man need not go in search of God. God is near by. God is every where. But you have to make the necessary effort to see him.

There is butter in milk. But you have to make the necessary effort to get the butter. Surrender everything to him. Pray, pray sincerely. Debates on whether God has form or is formless are not only useless but unnecessary.

He was form, He is also formless. You need the right Guru to reveal your true nature to you, to rescue you from ignorance. So Ramakrishna Paramahamsa taught. And if any one asked, 'Have you seen God '? He could honestly say, "yes, I have seen Him. And I can enable you, too, to see him if you are prepared to make the effort.

Ramakrishna could also honestly say. 'All religions lead to the same goal'. This was not just a matter of belief. He had practised the teachings of every major religion. got them into his blood and bones, and realized God through each of them. He had worshipped Mother Kali; and he had equalled his master Totapuri in the realization of Brahman through Advita.

Ramakrishna Paramahamsa's greatest offering to India was Swami Vivekananda Only a great teacher could would a great disciple. Vivekananda, as Narendranath, began with disbelief and ridicule. But Vivekananda became a fervent disciple of Ramakrishna Paramahamsa, and a light unto generations to come.

17

Aurobindo Ghosh

Aurobindo Ghose

Among the many remarkable men born in the latter half of the 19th century who were to mould India's destiny there is hardly one who has the aura of heroism, romance, mystery and grandeur which surrounds Aurobindo Ghose. A contemporary of Gandhi, an admirer of Vivekananda, a colleague of Tilak, the idol of Rabindranath Tagore and C.R.Das, Aurobindo shot like a meteor through the Indian nationalist firmament in the wake of the partion of Bengal. His passionate and militant patriosim inspired the youth of India. But drove the older nationalist leaders to despair; it gave the British officials many a sleepless night. His abrupt withdrawl from politics seemed something of an ani-climax at the time, but it was the starting point of a great spiritual obyssey, which was perhaps no less important than his brief incursion into the nationalist movement.

Curiously enough, there was little in Aurobindo's ancestry and early environment to suggest that he would shape into a fiery rebel or a great Yogi. He came from a family which's was more anglicised than even most upper class Bengali Bhadralok of that period. His father, Dr. K.D.Ghose, had studied medicine in England and learnt to admire everything British. At the age of five Aurobindo was admitted to an Irish Nuns' school at Darjeeling. Two years later he and his two elder brothers were taken to England and placed in the care of the Rev. Drewitt, an Anglican clergyman of Manchester, with strict instructions that they should not be allowed to make the acquaintance of any Indian or be exposed to any Indian influence.

Aurobindo received a good grounding in French and Latin (English was his mother-tongue) and when he joined St. Paul's School at the age of twelve he struck his teachers as a prodigy. He learnt Greek and German and read Homer, Aristrophanes, Dante, Goethe and the French poets. Indeed, he ranged over the whole field of European thought.

He won a scholarship which enabled him to go to King's College, Cambridge. In his first year he took away all the prizes for Greek and Latin verse, but his interest had already switched on to Joan of ARC, the American Revolution and Mazzini. These were years of deep study and reflection, but also of great hardship, Aurobindo's mother was suffering from a serious mental illness, and his father had run out of funds and was unable to support his sons. Remittances from India ceased, and Aurobindo's Scholarships could hardly support him and his two brothers in England. Luckily, as it seemed at the age of Eighteen, Aurobindo passed the competitive examination for entry into the Indian Civil Service. With it's tangible material rewards and the prestige of belonging to the ruling caste, the I.C.S. was then and for many years later-the El Dorado of brilliant and ambitioous young men.

For Aurobindo, however, the charm of a bureaucratic career wore off even while he was undergoing his probation; he realised that his real interest lay in 'Poetry and literature and study of languages of patriotic action'. He had no desire to become a limb of the alien administration in India, but he knew how much store his family set by his success in the I.C.S; if he resigned it would break his father's heart. Aurobindo sought a way out of his dilemma by a devious route. He failed to appear for the riding test, which was compulsory for the I.C.S. Probationers and was disqualified.

The India office in London was not sorry to see him out of the I.C.S. ; it already had suspicions that he harboured dangerous thoughts which would not easily fit him into the imperial mould. "I should much doubt', the secretary of state for India , Lord Kimberley, wrote, 'whether, Mr.Ghose would be a desirable addition to the service.

Aurobindo's decision to opt out of the Indian civil service showed that he had a mind and a will of his own. The fourteen impressionable years he had spent in England had not turned him into a brown sahib. Indeed, St. Paul's School and King's College did to Aurobindo what harrow and Trinity were to do to young Jawaharlal twenty years later: they sowed the seeds of nostalgic patriotism. Aurobindo imbibed love of English literature, but not of English rule In the privacy of his room at Cambridge, he pored over the pages of the Bengalee and other nationalist papers from India. He eagerly followed the course of Irish politics, read the history of revolutions in Europe and American, and dreamt of the day when Indian would be independent.

Before leaving England, Aurobindo secured a job in Baroda. The salary of two hundred rupees a month was modest, but Maharaja Sayaji Rao was a progressive, and (as faras discretion allowed) a patriotic ruler.. Aurobindo worked in various departments of the State Government; Surveys and settlement, stamp and Revenue, and the secretariat. He prepared memoranda and reports, 'ghosted' speeches for the Maharaja, and occasionally accompanied him on tour. The work could hardly have been exciting for him; with his innate reticence and aloofness from the social life of the court and the city, he did not shine as a civil servant. Fortunately his talents found a more congenial outler when he was asked to take French classes in baroda College of which he became in turn a full-time professor; Vice-Principal and acting Principal. He made good use of his time, learnt not only Bengali (of which he was ignorant of his return to India) but Hindi, Marathi, Gujarati and Sanskrit.

Aurobindo was not destined to end up as a brilliant scholar or even as a great educationist. Academic pursuits and family obligations (he had married in 1901) did not wholly absorb him. Soon after his return to India in 1893, he had anonymously contributed a series of articles to the Indu Prakash, a bilingual paper of Bombay, in which he had made a scathing attack on the aims, methods and leadership of the Indian National Congress'.

"I say 'of the Congress'. Aurobindo wrote, 'that its aims are mistaken, that the spirit in which it proceeds towards their accomplishment is not the spirit of sincerity and whole-heartedness, and that the methods it has chosen are not the right methods, and the leaders in whom it trusts, are not the right sort of men to be the leaders, in brief that we are at present led, if not by the blind, at any rate by the one-eyed'.

Aurobindo ridiculed the declared principles, the well-known jargon and the unstated assumptionsof the Congress leaders :

The bare-faced hypocrisy of our enthusiasm for the Queen-Empress-an old lady so-called by way of courtesy, but about whom few Indians can really know or care anything-could serve no purpose but to expose us to the derision of our ill-wishers. There was too a little too much talk about the blessings of British rule, and the inscrutable providence which has laid us in the maternal, or more property, the step-motherly bosom of a just and benevolent England. Yet, more appalling was the general timidity of the Congress, it's glossing over of hard names, it's disinclination to tell the direct truth, its fear of too deeply displeasing our masters".

Aurobindo agreed that the Indian National Congress was a standard-bearer of liberty', that it had provided a banner under which people of differnt races and creeds could gather. It was however, premature to claim that the Congress had taught the Indian people to act together: at best it had taught them to 'talk together's' .

The Congress seemed to him too unwiedly a body for any sort of "executive' work. It's support almost wholly from 'our new middle class'. consisting of journalists, barristers, doctors, official, graduates and traders with a sprinkling of rich farmers. It was no more National' that the Liberal Party in England would be if it were to hold annual meetings and all itself the English National Congress.

Aurobindo questioned the wisdom of trying to persuade Anglo-India to subordinate it's own interests to 'the sole good of the Indian people'. Such a conduct not reasonably be expected, he wrote.

Save from men of the most exalted and chivalrous character; and the sort of people England sends out to us are not as a rule exalted and chivalrous. They are really very ordinary men and not only ordinary men. but ordinary Englishmen-types of the middle class Philistines, in the graphic English phrase, with the narrow hearts and commercial habit of mind perculiar to that sort of people.

Our appeal, the appeal of every high-souled and self-respecting nation, ought not to be to the opinion of the Anglo-

Indians, no, not yet to the British sense of justice, but to our own reviving sense of manhood, to our sincere fellow-feeling so far as it can be called sincere-with the silent and suffering people of India.

Aurobindo's analysis of the Indian politics in 1893 was ruthless, his logic irrefutable and prose evocative, but he was wholly out of tune with the Indian political elite which composed not only the readership of the Indu Prakash, but the rank and file of the Congress. His view of the future of British imperialism and Indian nationalism was remarkebly incisive and perceptive but it was at least a quarter of a century a head of his time. Indeed, only a young man reared on western political theroy and completely innocent of the facts of political life in his own country could have dared in 1893 to question the very premises of nationalist politics in India, ask embarrassing questions and sugest startling answers.

After the first two articles had been published in the Indu Prakash, Aurobindo, it is alleged, was exhorted by M.G. Ranade to exercise greater discretion. It is doubtful if Aurobindo's articles, despite their literary flavour and patriotic ardour, made many converts. The Indian National Congress had been founded only eight years before; it's votaries had yet no obvious cause for pessimism.

Indeed the passage of the Indian councils Act in 1892 and a resolution passed by the house of Commons in favour of simultaneous examinations for the I.C.S. in India and England in the following year had temporarily boosted the morale of the Congress leaders.

During the next twelve years while Aurobindo was in Baroda State Service, Indian politics remained in a low key and he took little interest in them. During his visits to Bengal, he had noticed the cynicism of the middle classes, whose one aim in life seemed to be the happiness of the relatives and the family', and who were unable to listen to profound subjects, they laugh at and make fun of everything Dharma, philanthropy, high aspiration, great endeavour, liberation of the country : with a grin they want to dismiss anything serious all that is high and noble'. This was hardly a propitious period for struggle against the Raj, but Aurobindo established contacts with the revolutionary underground in Maharashtra and Bengal.

These dangerous forays gave him some satisfaction, but his real chance came in 1905 in the wake of the partition of Bengal. His scene of activity changed from Baroda to Calcutta. He started Bengali paper, Yugantar and joined B.C. Pal in running the Vande Mataram. His articles in the latter expounded the philosophy of Indian Nationalism wiith a sharpness, daring and eloquence Indian journalism had never yet known. He amplified what he had hinted at in his Indu Prakash articles. He ridiculed the ideal of colonial self government for India as a political monstrosity; the only ideal which India could accept was absolute autonomy, 'Unqualified Swaraj'. All talk about expansion of legislative councils, appointement of Indians to executive councils of the Viceroy and the governors struck him as meaningless.

It was foolish to expect reforms from the British Government. Indeed the worse the government, the better it would be for Indian nationalism: disaffection could only hasten the day of liberation.

Aurobindo's prose was like a heady wine to the young radicals of Bengal. He organised Extremists or Nationalists as they called themselves, in the Bengal Congress, and promoted an alliance between them and the Extremists of Maharashtra led by Bal Gangadhar Tilak. He set out to radicalise the policies and programmes of the Congress. He advocated boycott not only of

British goods but of Government aided Schools and indeed of the whole alien administration. A militant ideology and a militant programme were to be supported with a militant strategy.

The result was that the annual Congress Sessions became trials of strength between the Moderates and Extremists. A compromise was patched up at the Banaras Session in 1905 and at Calcutta in 1906, but by the time the Congress met at Surat at the end of 1907, a spilt had become inevitable. Aurobindo was in the thich of the frayat Surat; indeed he precipitated the final tumultuous scenes in which the Congress broke up.

Inevitable Aurobindo's activities earned him the implacable hostility of the British authorities. 'He is the most dangerous man we now have to reckon with'. the Viceroy, Lord Minto, told secretary of state Morley. The Lieutenant Governor of Bengal pleaded with the viceroy to deport Aurobindo; 'He is regarded and spoken of by all as the disciples regard a great master. He has been in the forfront of all...... But he has kept himself, like a careful and valued general, out of sight of "the enemy".

We cannot get evidence against him such as would secure his conviction evidence against him such as would secure his conviction in a court. The Viceroy refused to agree to deportation; he knew how allergic Morley was to deportations without trial after the Lajpat Rai case in 1907. The arm of the law was, however, long enough to reach a fiery journalist and politician.

Aurobindo was prosecuted twice, first in 1907, and again in 1908-9. The latter prosecution in which Aurobindo was one of the thirty-five accused in the Maniktola Bomb conspiracy case, was a serious matter, but he was aquitted after a magnificent defence by Chittaranjan Das. Aurobindo resumed his political activities, started a new weekly, Karmayogin, but after a few months, to the surprise of friends and foes alike, he suddenly withdrew from the Indian political stage. In February 1910 he left for the French settlemet of Chandernagore, and in April next moved on to Pondicherry, where he was to spend the next forty years. The British authorities, who were about to re-arrest him, felt they had been outwitted. Aurobindo's adherents were stunned but continued to cherish the hope that he would return to lead them again. Aurobindo had, however, said a final good-bye to politics.

Aurobindo own mood after renunciation of politics was neither one of elation nor of disappointment. He felt he was in the hands of a higher power which knew what was best for him and for his country. He denied that he had withdrawn from politics in despair. 'I cam away'. he explained 'because I did not want anything to interfere with my Yoga and because I got a very distnict adesh (command) in the matter. I have cut connection entirely with politics, but before I did so, I knew from within that the work I had begun I did so, I knew from within that the work I had begun there was destined to be carried forward, on lines I had foreseen, by others, and that the ultimate triumph of the movement I had initiated was true without my personal action or presence.

Nothing could persuade Aurobindo to leave Pondicherry which he described as 'my place of retreat. my cave of 'Tapasya'. He was not tempted to join the Home Rule movement headed by his friend and hero, Tilak. Nor did he accept the presidency of the Nagpur Congress in December 1920.

In the mid-twenties his admirer and former counsel in the Maniktola case, C.R.Das, headed the Swaraj party, but Aurobindo stood aloof. The iron will with which he had spurned the I.C.S.in 1892, cut professional and domestic ties in 1906, enabled him to turn a deaf ear to the siren calls of politics. In retrospect, it seems at if England, Baroda and Calcutta were only stop-overs in a journey of which the destination was Pondicherry.

To his contemporaries Aurobindo's switch from politics to Pondicherry seemed an anti-climax. There is no doubt that early in 1910 the tide was flowing against his party. The Surat split had proved a disaster for the extremists. They had been expelled from the Congress, and were being persecuted by the Government. Their most important leader Tilak had been locked up in Mandalay fort in Burma; another leader, Bipin Chandra Pal, had slipped away to England.

The anti-partition agitation had lost it's momentum.In 1909 Aurobindo noticed after his release from jail a perceptible lack of enthusiasm among the people; his own meetings in Calcutta, which two years before were thronged by thousands, were attended, as he himself noted, by no more than about a hundred persons, that too mostly passers by. The Extremists were consigned to the political limbo for nearly a decade. To this dismal and some what unexpected denouement Aurobindo had himself contributed in no small measure.

Aurobindo had played an important role in stirring the youth of Bengal, bringing together the radical Congressmen of Bengal and Maharashtra and shaking the complaceney of Anglo-India. The ideal of Indian Nationalism which he expounded in the Vande Mataram was remarkable for it's comprehensivenss. charity and courage. No politician in the warm glow of the Victorian sunset or the Edwardian decade had dispelled more illusions about the British Raj, or attained a clearer vision of India's political destiny than Aurobindo.

It is true that he gave a religious, or rather a spiritual complexion to the struggle for Indian emancipation; his idom was derived from the imagery of the Hindu epics and folklore. There was however, nothing obsecurantist or sectarian about Aurobindo; it would be difficult to find a passage in his writings which smacks of prejudice against other religions. His writing do not, however, indicate that he was aware of other religions or communities in India, and of the problem of communicating with them.

Aurobindo was undoubtedly a brilliant theoretician of Indian nationalism, but if politics are the art of the possible, he was not a skilful or successful politician. His logical mind, missionary ardour and impatience for results drove him to make frontal attacks on political opponents in the Congress and on the British Raj. It is obvious that in a conflict, head-on collission is not always the only or the ideal strategy; indeed calculated patience and compromise may be as important for success as militancy.

Aurobindo's hard-hitting editorials in the Vande-Mataram delighted his young adherents, but they infuriated the Indian political elite and deepend the image of the extremists as irresponsible hot heads, and 'wild young men', especially in provinces other than Bengal and Maharashtra where they were still a tiny minority.. The Banaras and Calcutta Congress Sessions had revealed the growing influence of the Extremists.

If the Extremists had acted with restraint in 1907, they might have retained and even strengthened their foothold in the Congress. But they preferred, largely under Aurobindo's inspiration, the policy of increasing pressure and provocation, which by 1907 drove the Moderate leaders to the conviction that the two factions could not co-exist iin the Congress party.

The moderates position in the Congress party and in the country was not really so weak as the Extremists believed. It was not easy to push men like Dadabhai Naoroji, Pherozeshah Mehta, Surendranath Banerjea and Gopal Krishna Gokhale off the high pedestals they occupied in public imagination. Most Extremist leaders, and Aurobindo in particular failed to see that the middle class which at that time had to bear the brunt of any collision with the Raj-did not have the stamina to stand up to a serious and prolonged assault by the British Government. This was proved in the Punjab by the aftermath of Lajpat Rai's deportation in 1907, and of the arrests of Aurobindo and his colleagues in 1908-9 in Bengal : the result was not a quickening but a paralysis of political activity.

As the war of nerves between the Extremists and the Moderates went on in 1907, Aurobindo made no secret of his preference for an open breach to a patched-up compromise. Indeed, the word compromise did not exist in his dictionary at this time. Were it not for Tillak, the parting of the ways, which occurred at the Surat Congress in December 1907, would have come even earlier.

At Surat, Aurobindo's part (on his own admission) in precipitating the final crisis which led to a break-up of the Congress was much greater than his contemporaries and even colleagues knew. Unfortunately, the real beneficiaries of the Surat split were neither the Moderates nor the Extremists, but the British authorities.

From this it must not be inferred that Aurobindo's contribution to the nationalist movement was not significant in it's own way. His analysis of British imperialism, and the Predicament of nationalist India at the turn of the century was remarkably prescient.

He saw clearly-what was not not obvious to most of his contemporaries-that to wrest power from Britain the nationalist leadership had to be much more objective, that there were definite limits even to the checks which 'British Democracy' could exercise on it's agents in India, that the Indian middle class was too small in size and too vulnerable to official displeasure to pit itself against the alien Government, that only the induction of the urban proletariat and the rural poor into the nationalist struggle could make it irresistible, that the key to success was to be sought in boycott and passive resistance rather than in constitutional agitation for concessions.

All this of course presupposed a complete transformation of the aims, methods and composition of the nationalist movement. This transformation could not be achieved even by Tilak, who had been in politics for twenty-five years before the partition of Bengal much less by young Aurobindo who was still in his late thirties, and a relative late-comer to politics.

It is important to remember that until 1905 Aurobindo had remained in the backwaters of Baroda, and kept himself aloof from overt political agitation, that his active political career lasted no more than four years of which nearly one third was spent as an under-trial prisoner. His famous Uttarpara speech after his release from jail in 1909 showed that he was already under the spell of supernatural forces which were soon to life him out of political affairs. His influence was largely confined to the English knowing Bhadralok in Bengal, and the only other province on which he made some impression was Maharashtra.

Aurobindo thus did not have the aptitude the training or even the time to create a mass movement. Shy, stern, silent and introspective, he was more of an inspirer through the written word, than an organiser of men. He was marx of anti-imperialism, not it's Lenin. It is difficult to say whether his devoted followers were aware of his limitations, but Aurobindo himself came to recognise them clearly at least in retrospect.

In 1920, in the critical years of the non-co-operation movement, when he was invited to preside over the Nagpur Congress, in a remarkably can did piece of self-analysis he described himself as an 'idealist to the marrow', recalled the qualities of Tilak who had 'combined suppleness skill and determination' and confessed: 'I have not the suppleness and skill'. Aurobindo's major contribution was that he gave a coherent and militant ideology to the agitation against the partition of Bengal.

This militant ideology survied the agitation, and indeed the annulment of the partition in 1912. Aurobindo did not have the time, or the 'skill and suppleness', to translate this ideology into practice. But at the very time he was expounding it in the columns of Vande Mataram, another Indian leader only three years older him was actually testing in far-off South Africa.

Gandhi had the advantage of fifteen years of practical work in the small Indian community in South Africa. Ten years after Aurobindo's retirement from politics, Gandhi was to try boycott and passive resistance on a continental scale and to evoke a response which was all the greater because Aurobindo and his valiant band had paved the way for him.

Aurobindo's own spiritual odyssey transformed his way of looking at the world. He was no longer prepared to countenance violence for political, or indeed any ends; his attitude to Britain and the common wealth mellowed with the years. After the fall of France in 1940, he openly blessed the Allied cause. Two years later he favoured the acceptance of the Cripps proposals.

After 1910 his principal interest was in the realm of the spirit. This did not mean that he cut himself off from the problems of suffering humanity. The purpose of the old Yoga, he wrote, had been to get away from life to the Divine; the purpose of the new Yoga was to teach the Divine and bring the fullness of what was gained into life.

At Pondicherry Aurobindo meditated constantly, was seen and heard rarely, but wrote copiously at least during the first decade of his stay there. The synthesis of yoga, the Essays on the Gita, the secret of the Veda. The Ideal of Human unity, the

Human cycle, the epic poem Savitri were eloquent testaments of his profound iinsights into life and reality.

He concerned himself not with religion, but with spiritually, with new visions of divine grace. Inner freedom and joy, and of a society composed of men and women who had realised life at deep levels of consciousness. 'One of the greatest minds of his age', is how jawaharlal Nehru described him. Aurobindo was however, more than a philosopher ; his writings were affirmations of spiritual truths and values which he wanted to make the heritage of mankind. Romain Rolland described him 'as the completest synthesis that has been realised to this day by the geniuses of Asia and geniuses of Europe'.

Sri Aurobindo's Thoughts

Both Indian and Western thought have met in Sri Aurobindo. S.K.Maitra writes : "This meeting is not mere hand shaking, but that there is a real synthesis of these two types of thought in him. There is even something, more, a fulfilment of what each of them aims at but has not been able to realise'. The West aims at a fuller realisation of the evolutionary and comic character of it's thought.But it is hampered by it's intellectualism and it's existential outlook.

What it requires is the acceptance of a spiritual standpoint, leading to the abandonment of it's existential outlook and a modification of it's extreme intellectualism Similarly, Indian thought is spiritual but individualistic and static. It must break its narrow walls of individualism and acquire a dynamic and cosmic character. There lies it's fulfilment.

Sri Aurobindo fulfils this functions by dealing with three main problems of his philosophy : the problem of Evolution, the problem of Yoga and the problem of the nature of Reality.

The idea of Evolution is certainly more prominent in Western Philosophy than in Indian Philosophy. Greek Philosophy is full of it. Although it was not given so much importance in Plato as in Aristotle, it did have a place in the antechamber of his philosophy, when he sopke of creation and dealt with natural Philosophy, as in the Timaeus. In Aristotle evolution was teleogical; it was the gradual transformation of the potential into the actual. The problem of creation has been in fact the stumbling block in Greek Philosophy. 'Anaxagoras solved it by postulating the existence of the soul or nous which, being not of the nature of material objects, could impart motion to them. Parmenides cut the Gordian knot by saying that there is no creation at all, for there is only the one immovable eternal Being.

Unlike Parmenides, however, Plato does not deny creation but assumes the existence of a second principle outside of the ideas but dependent upon them for the plan or scheme of creation. This second principle Plato calls God or the creator. Creation, according to Plato, is not a material process, but is mainly ideal and intellectual. There fore, he speaks of the idea of creation existing prior to creation. We have in Plato, thus a double set of creators-the Ideas which are the ultimate creators, and God. God evidently has not got the power to create without getting the pattern from the Ideas, and the Ideas cannot also create directly because they have no power of generation.

The Greek mind is aways at first directed outward, and it is only at a later stage that it is directed inwards. There fore, the approach from the standpoint of consciouness was never fully established in Greek Philosophy. This is the reason why Plato could not interpret the grades of reality in terms of the grades of consciousness. Indian philosophy from the beginning turned inwards. The highest reality was always conceived as Atman or self.

The interpretation of the universe was, therefore, always from the standpoint of consciousness. The different grades of reality were explained in terms of the different grades of consciousness. Sri Aurobindo looks at the whole universe from the standpoint of the highest consciousness which he calls Sachchidananda.

Sri Aurobindo not only emphasies that all reality is consciousness, but he goes further and says that the measure of reality of anything is determined by the nature of consciousness that is revealed in it.

The higher the position of anything in the scale of reality, the deeper and more unified is the consciousness that is revealed in it. His conclusion, therefore, is just the reverse of that of Plotinus." The Absolute, far from being characterised by the total absence of consciousness, is, on the contrary, the Highest consciousness. And the individual, of he is to attain union with the absolute, must possess the broadest, deepest and most unified consciousness'. Unconsciousness is the characteristic of matter in it's grossest form. Evolution is from unconsciousness or nescien ce to knowledge.

Sri Aurobindo's conception of Divine Descent has an outward similarity with Plotinus' theroy of Emanations. like Plotinus, he also looks upon creation as the emergence from God of a hierarchically graded world, the emergents being of all grades of reality. But the whole conception of creation and the relation of the created world to God are totally different in his philosophy from what they are in the system of Plotinus. In calling creation a descent of God, Sri Aurobindo wants to emphasies it's double significance.

First, that the created world, even in it's lowest levels, exhibits on its face the stamp of its Divine origin. Secondly, that it is a descent for the sake of ascent, so that the lowest order of existence has the promise and potency of reaching the Divine status. The Individual soul in plotinus system no doubt realises God both as the immanent principle working and also as the transcendent source which the individual can reach by a long progression, though a series of stages.

But for the rest of the universe God is only a transcendent Principle, the ultimate source of emanations. In Sri Aurobindo's philosophy both these aspects of Divinity are kept in mind from the very beginning. Even in the lowest forms of matter the absolute is present as an indwelling principle-as the Gita puts it,a dweller within the heart, herddese Arjuna tisthati-pushing it continually forward.

The impulse towards self-improvement, towards fuller and fuller self-expression, comes, therefore, from within. AT the same time the the progress is through a hirearchy of different grades of reality, the products of successive descents iof the absolute, It is not the individual alone who realises this double aspect of Divinity, but the whole universe shares this realisation.

The only limitation which Sri Aurobindo places upon the cosmic realisation of the double aspect of Divinity is the circumstance that it rests with the Divine will to choose the time and occasion for the Divine Descent, without which this realisation is impossible. But this is an inveitable consequence of the Divine transcendence.

For Hegel, Being is thought, and thought is being and the essential feature of the world-view of thought is continuity. He therefore, has banished all absolute contradictions from the real world. For him antitheses exist for the sake of a higher synthesis, negations for the sake of a higher synthesis, negations for the purpose of establishing a higher affirmation. S.K.Maitra writes that Bradley, while trying to play Hegel against Hegel 'has been instrumental in introducing a principle which offers a direct challenge to the Hegelian philosophy. This is the principle of Emergence.

The fight on the philosophical front is no longer between Mechanical Evolution and Teleological Evolution, but between Continuous Evolution and Emergent Evolution'. Bergson's Creative Evolution is also a form of Emergent Evolution, because there lurk in his conception of creativity the ideas of surprise, uncertainty and incalculability.

Evolution for all of them is made possible by the emergence of the new, which must be treated as a fundamental departure from the old and must in no sense be regarded as deduction from, or a continuation of the old. Perennial Philosophy in the West has held fast as its sheet-anchor to the principle of continuity. Its last great champion was Hegel. The phenomenal rise in recent years of the philosophy of values has very much hastened its fall, for the philosophy of values is essentially a champions of emergence. Sri Aurobindo champions a form of Emergent Evolution which constitutes a far greater challenge than any attack it has had so far to face in the West.

According to the Purusa Sukta of the Rigveda, the whole Purusa is not melted into the world. This is the foundation of the emergent view of evolution in India. The evolution of the world can only be through successive emergences of higher and higher consciousness from him. These emergences are really descents of the Divine consciousness. We thus come to the doctrine of Avatar. The Gita speaks of a double current in evolution.

The first, which is the normal current, does not require any Divine intervention, very long. A time comes when it meets with obstacles which are beyond its power to remove. It is then that

Divine intervention steps in, removes the obstacles which blocked the progress of the world, and sets free the current of evolution. Such a crisis in the evolution of the world the Gita calls Dharmasya glani, deterioration of Dharma, because it describes every process in terms of it's spiritual significance.

This direct intervention by God and the resulting emergence of a new consciousness are for the Gita an absolute essential of world-evolution, This does not reject in to the doctrine of continuity, but sets up, along with it, the principle of emergence, without which we cannot obtain a complete picture of evolution. Likewise, it does not mean the elimination of thought from all effective share in the direction of the evolutionary process, but the setting of definite limits to its effectiveness, and the supplementation of it by other types of consciousness which are more at home in a discontinuous world.

For Sri Aurobindo, therefore, the world does not evolve of itself in a continuous process, but it requires at every critical stage of its evolution Divine intervention in the shape of a direct descent of the Divine consciousness. No radical change in the stage of evolution is for him possible without such a Divine Descent. This view of evolution assures man, in addition to his own resources, the Infinite power of God in his aspiration to rise higher and higher in the scale of evolution.

Unlike Bradley's, Sri Aurobindo's conception is based not upon the suicide of the lower principles, but upon their transformation. This transformation we may call a rebirth to indicate the radical nature of the change that will come upon them. The new principle brings about a total change in the character of the world as it existed before its emergence.

In Alexander's scheme of emergent evolution there is no change of the old principles on the emergence of a new one.

The old principles remain as they were before, only a new one joins them. For Sri Aurobindo, however, evolution does not mean merely addition of some new ptinciples to those which are already existent, but it means that the old principles, by reason of the emergence of the new ones, change their character. Life, for instance, as it was before the emergence of mind, is very different from life as we know it ntoday, dominated as it is by mind. So again, Sri Aurobindo believes when the principle of supermind will emerge, all the principles which are existent today, such as matter, life, mind and soul, will undergo a radical change.

Even the physical universe will be very different from what it is at present, for it will cease to offer any resistance to the spirit, but on the contrary will work in perfect co-operation with it.

Professor Whitehead, perhaps, is the most outstanding philosopher of the present day in the West, more evolutionary in his outlook than even Bergson or Alexander. A comparsion of Whitehead's philosophy with that of Sri Aurobindo reveals stricking resemblances as well as fundamental differences.

For both Sri Aurobindo and Whitehead evolution is not merely one principle among many others which explain the world as it is and as it will be in the future, but it is the one principle round which have clustered all the other principles and without which they cannot be understood. They are both equally opposed to all forms of dualism; they are not devotees exclusively either of Being or of becoming and are forward-looking buoyant optimists. As for their fundamental differences, Whitehead's theory of evolution is naturalistic, whereas Sri Aurobindo's is spiritualistic.

The princple of evolution itself is derived from the nature of the highest principle, the ultimate reality. The key to the understanding of the nature of evolution is not to be found in the processes of nature but is to be sought in the ultimate reality.

Evolution therefore, is the ascent of physical nature, life, mind, etc, to the ultimate reality, made possible by the circumstance that these lower principles are themselves expressions in varying degrees of perfection of the same ultimate reality, there is an urge in them to complete and perfect themselves. Like Hegel, Sri Aurobindo therefore, looks at evolution from the standpoint of the end. But the end as conceived by Hegel is a purely rational end, an end conceived by Thought. For Sri Aurobindo, thought is not the ultimate reality, but there are various grades of reality above thought which have to be climbed before the ultimate reality can be reached. No, end, in fact, short of the absolute, is competent to give an adequate acount of the nature of evolution.

Whitehead identifies the principles of creativity with novelty. This creativity or novelty is the inner spring of the process of evolution, both at the lower and the higher stages. It is haunted by a dread, the vanishing of the past. Mere novelty, therefore, has only a negative and hardly any positive value. It is axiologically of natural quality. It can not serve, therefore, as a directive principle of evolution ; it cannot supply the missing element in Whitehead's philosophy, namely, a goal of evolution. In Sri Aurobindo, the dynamic element it not supplied by a mere urge for novelty but by the far more effective teleological idea of a definite goal of the entire process of evolution, a goal which takes it far beyond the limits of the finite-the Infinite.

This goal is again linked up by him with the question of the origin of the world. As the world has originated from Sachchida nanda, so it's goal is to return to him.

Thus we find that both Hegel and Whitehead are committed to the principle of continuity. A true theroy of evolution is an emergent one and treats matter, life and mind as successive and distinct stages in the onward march of the world to it's original spiritual source. Sri Aurobindo's philosophy gives us an assurance that the future will not be a mere repetition of the past but that it will reveal undisclosed possibilities which we cannot dream of.

Evolution, however, is the soul of Sri Aurobindo's philosophy. His theory of evolution is the pivot round which the whole philosophy of Sri Aurobindo moves. Evolution is the movement which is the reverse of the movement of involution or creation. It is because of the descent of the spirit into matter, life and mind, that these can ascend to the higher regions of the spirit. Because the spirit in creation has involved itself in matter, life and mind, therefore matter, life and mind feel an impulse to rise to their source. Evolution thus, "is a sort of home-sickness of spirit'.

The spirit has descended into the lowest particle of matter; therefore, matter seeks to evolve into something higher than, itself-mind, Similarly, there is a descent of the spirit into mind, and consequently mind must ascend to something higher than itself, namely supermind. The highest principle so far evolved is mind.

But evolution cannot stop with mind for mind is not its last word. It, must move further up and come to the next stage, namely supermind. The highest principle so for evolved is mind. But evolution cannot stop with mind for mind is not its last word. It must move further up and come to the next stage, namely supermined. But when it does so, there will be a radical change in the nature of the world for with the emergence of the supermind the process of evolution becomes a process through knowledge, the previous process being through ignorance. Such, in brief is Sri Aurobindo's most optimistic scheme of evolution.

Sri Aurobindo has accepted the cosmic view of evolution of the West but has rejected its mechanical character and replaced it by a spiritual evolution. Likewise he has rejected the cyclical view of the universe of Indian philosophy and the individualistic outlook of its theory of evolution. and substituted for the cosmic and over-personal outlook of the west. The result is an altogether new theory of evolution. It bases itself upon the idea that the source of evolution being Sachchidananda himself, it cannot stop until objective, such as the naturalistic ideal of a perfefct adjustment between the organism and the environment or the realisation of a kingdom of ends, which is Kant's social idea, can be looked upon as the goal of evolution. What the thinkers in India ignored is the great truth that a divinised man can only emerge in a divinised world. The problem of salvation is intimately connected with that of evolution. In fact, evolution many be called a cosmic Yoga.

Sri Aurobindo's Philosophy

Sri Aurobindo's philosophy of evolution is the direct outcome of his integral world-view. In the Life Divine he enunciates four main theories with their corresponding mental attitudes and ideals in accordance with four different conceptions of the truth of existence. These we may call the supracosmic, the cosmic and terrestrial, the supra-terrestrial or other worldly, and the integral or synthetic or composite.

In this last category would fall Sri Aurobindo's view of our existence here as a becoming with the Divine being for it's origin and its object, a progressive manifestation, a spiritual evolution with the supracosmic for its source and support, the other wordly for a condition and connecting link, and the cosmic and terrestrial for it's field, and with human mind and life for it's field, and with human mind and life for it's nodus and turning-point of release towards a higher and a highest perfection.

Our regard then must be on the first three to see where they depart from the integralising view of life and how for the truth they stand on fit into it's structure. In the supra-cosmic view of things the supreme Reality is alone entirely real. A certain illusoriness, a sense of the vanity of cosmic existence and individual being is a characteristic turn of this seeing of things, but it is not essential, not an indispensable adjunct to its main thought-principle.

In the extreme forms of its world-vision human existence has no real meaning; it is a mistake of the soul or a delirium of the will to live, an error or ignorance which somehow over casts the absolute reality. But this idea of the total vanity of life is not altogether an inevitable, consequence of the supra-cosmic theory of existence. In the vedanta of the Upanisha ds, the becoming of Brahman is accepted as a reality.

The cosmic-terrestrial view considers cosmic existence alone as real. Its view is confined, ordinarily, to life in the material universe. God, if God exists, is an eternal becoming ; or if God does not exist, then Nature is a perennial becoming, Earth is the field or it is one of the remporary fields, man is the highest possible form or only one of the temporary forms of the Becoming.

The supra-terrestrial view admits the reality of the material cosmos and it accepts the temporary duration of earth and human life as first fact we have to start from ; but it adds to it a perception of other worlds or planes of existence which have an eternal or at least a more permanent duration; it perceives behind the mortality of the bodily life of man the immortality of the soul within him.

There arises from this view of things the idea that the true home of man is beyond and that the earth life is in some way or other only an episode of his immortality or a deviation from a celestial and spiritual into a material existence.

But, finally, there must open in us, as our mental life deepens and subtler knowledge develops, the perception that the terrestrial and the supraterrestrial are not only terms of being ; there is something which is supra-cosmic and the highest remote origin of our existence. In this integration the supra-cosmic reality stands as the supreme truth of being; to realise it is the highest reach of our consciousness. But it is the highest Reality which is also the cosmic being, the cosmic consciousness, the cosmic will and life; it has put these things forth, not outside itself but in its own self-unfolding and self expression. 'A perfect self-expression of the spirit is the object of our terrestrial existence.

The supra-terrestrial existence is also a truth of being; for the material is not the only plane of our existence; other plane of consciousness there are to which we can attain and which have already their hidden links with us. An integration of this kind would not be possible if a spiritual evolution were not the sense of our birth and terrestrial existence; the evolution of mind, life and spirit in matter is the sign that this integration, this completed manifestation of a secret self contained in it is its significance'.

A complete involution of all that the spirit is and its evolutionary self-unfolding are the double-terms of our material existence. 'An involution of spirit in the inconscience is the beginning; an involution in the Ignorance with its play of the possibilities of a partial developing knowledge is the middle, and the cause of the anomalies of our present nature-our imperfection is the sign of a transitional state, a growth not yet completed, an effort that is finding its way; a consummation in a deployment of the spirit's self-knowledge and the self-power of its divine being and consciousness is the culmination: these are the three stages of this cycle of the spirit's progressive self-expression in life.' It is a perfected and divinised life for which the earth-nature is seeking, and this seeking is a sign of the Divine will in nature.

There are also other seekings and these too find their means of self-fulfilment; a withdrawal into the supreme peace or ecstasy, a withdrawal into the bliss of the Divine presence are open to the soul in earthexistence; for the Infinite in its manifestation has many possibilities and is not confined by itsformulations. 'But neither of these withdrawals can be the fundamental intention in the becoming itsself here; for then an evolutionary progressive would not have been undertaken-such a progression here can only have for its aim a self-fulfilment here, a progressive manifestation of this kind can only have for its soul of significance the revelation of Being in a perfect becoming'.

Sri Aurobindo does not identify Reality either with being or Becoming, but looks upon both of these as poises of Reality. The absolute is beyond the two, it is eternal and infinite, and therefore is in its essence indeterminable and indefinable and inconceivable by the finite mind. It is not describable either by negations-net, net, or by affirmatives-it, it.

Yet this supreme reality manifests itself to our consciousness in the universe by real and fundamental truths of its being which transcend the universe and are the foundation upon which the universe rests, These truths present themselves to our intellectual knowledge as the fundamental aspects in which we see and experience the Infinite Reality.

This Supreme Reality or Brahman, as it manifests itself to our consciousness, is an eternal and absolute self-existence, self-awareness and self-power and self-delight of being. It is Sachchid ananda. Its self-existence appears in three forms : self, conscious being or spirit, and God or the Divine being, or to use the more expressive terms of Indian philosophy, it manifests itself as Atman, Purusha and Ishwara. Similarly its self-awareness or force of consciousness, Consciousness-Force, appears in three forms : Maya, Prakriti and Shakti.

Maya is the force of the absolute consciousness, conceptually creative all things. Prakriti is Nature of Force as dynamically executive, working out all things under the supervision of the supreme spirit. Shakti is the conscious power of the Divine

Being which is both conceptually creative and dynamically executive. And the fundamental determinates of Bliss are Love, Joy and Beauty. These three aspects and these three powers embrance the whole of existence and all nature and, if viewed as a whole, reconcile all apparent contradictions, all apparent disparateness and incompatibility between the supra-cosmic transcendence, the cosmic university and the separativeness of our individual existence. Brahman is omnipresent in all relativities; it is the absolute governing, pervading, constituting all relativities.

'There is the difficulty of understanding how the indeterminable determines itself as both Infinite and finite, how the One becomes an infinitely diversified multitude, how the impersonal creates or supports an infinite of persons, and is itself also a person. In despair, our logical reason gives up the chase and proclaims the universe to be an unmeaning jumble of phenomena'.

But what is magic to our finite reason, observes Sri Aurobindo, is the logic of the lifinite. The reason behind the seemingly meaningless processes is a greater reason, a greater logic, because it is more vast, subtle, complex in its operations.

The difficulties of failure to understand the logic of the Maya of Brahman. 'Its logic is magic to them, because it refuses to come under their narrow logical categories'. Its logic is the logic of the universal being of Brahman and the infinite intelligence of Maya. In order to understand it, we have to grasp certain fundamental powers or potentialities oof the Infinite Reality: these being the powers of infinite self-variation, of self-limitation and of self-absorption.

This logic of all the Infinite Consciousness shows the weakness of the sankhya position. The fundamental mistake of the Sankhya lies in its dualism. Prakriti must be the Prakriti of Purusha. Force must be the force of the conscious- Being;

otherwise force loses all its dynamism. An unconscious force developing into life and consciousness force developing into life and consciouness is a contradiction in terms. It can only develop that which is already in it.

Bliss is the most important of all the components of the triune reality. It gives the reason for the world-process; it is the 'why' of creation. So also declared our ancient sages: 'for from bliss alone, it appears are these creatures born and being born they live by Bliss and no Bliss they go hence and return'.

The Parabrahman, thus, is at once eternally self-realised and eternally self-realising. It is at once indeterminable and infinitely determinable. It is the indeterminable source of infinite determinations. Its indetermina bility is the natural, the necessary condition both of its infinity of being and its infinity of power of being, it can be infinitely all things because it is nothing in particular and exceeds any definable totality.

The absolute is also indeteminable in the sense that it transcends all conceptual formulations of verbal characterisation, whether positive or negative. The formlessness of the absolute is the condition for its power of assuming infinite forms.

Again, the Intergralist conception of the absolute provides a synthetic reconciliation of Advaitavada, Visishtadvaitavada and Dvaitavada Integralism holds that Ultimate Reality has such inseparable aspects as plurality, totality and essentiality, or compromises such eternal poses of being of the spirit as supra-cosmic transcendence, cosmic universality and unique individuality.

The absolute is both saktijukta and also saktimukta. That is why the Intergal Non-Dualism of Sri Aurobindo maintains that supra-cosmic transcendence, cosmic university and unique individuality are three equally real non-temporal poses of being of the same supreme spirit.

Sri Aurobindo's philosophy is neither an abstraction of the mere intellect nor a metaphysical justification of the ignorant human nature. There is in his teachings an integral spiritual vision, a synthetic comprehensive world view, the rate and sublime fusion of the ideals and approaches of the East and the West. There is above all 'the authentic divine dynamism, capable of transforming human nature and creating a new world order'.

This transformation is made possible first through an ascent of onsciousness towards the Infinite and next the descent of Infinite into the finite. Man is wrapped up in manifold ignorance of which he has first to become conscious. Ignorance according to Sri Aurobindo is seven fold in its nature.

We are ignorant of the absolute which is the source of all being and becoming; we take partial facts of being, temporal relations of the becoming for the whole truth of existence this is the first, the original ignorance. We are ignorant of the spaceless, timeless, immobile and mutation of the cosmic becoming in the second, the cosmic ignorance.

We are, ignorant of our universal self , the cosmic existence, the cosmic consciousness, our infinite unity with all being and becoming; we take our limited egoistic mentality, vitality, corpora lity for or true self and regard-every thing other than that as not self-that is the third, the egoistic ignorance. We are ignorant of our eternal becoming in time; we take this little life in a small span of Time, in a petty field of space, for our beginning, our middle and our end that is the fourth, the temporal ignorance. Even within this brief temporal becoming, we are ignorant of our large and complex being, of that in us which is superconscient, subconscient, intractconscient, circumstanceient to our surface becoming, we take that surface becoming with it's small selection of overtly meantalised experiences for our whole existence-that is the fifth, the Psychological ignorance.

We are ignorant of the true constitution of our becoming; we take the mind or life or body or any two of these or all three for our true principle or the whole account of what we are, losing sight of that which constitutes them and determines by it's occult presence and is meant to determine soverignly by it's emergence their operations-that is the sixth, the constitutional ignorance.

As a result of all these ignorances, we miss the true knowledge, government and enjoyment of our life in the world; we are ignorant in our thought, will, sensations, actions, return wrong or imperfect responses at every point to the questionings of the world, wander in a maze of errors and desires, strivings and failures, pain and pleasures, sin and stumbling, follow a crooked road, grope blindly for a changing goal-that is the seventh, the practical ignorance.

Integral Yoga

Integral yoga, aims at the plenatry perfection of the embodied soul in it's triple term of existence individuality, universality and transcendence. It's union with the supreme is complete only 'when it is a union with him in his universal immanence as well as in his featureless transcendence'.

Individual liberation is not end of man's striving after perfection for liberation is not 'an ultimate retreat from all individual and universal play of God's delighting creation into his immutable transcendence', but a perfect manifestation of his Love, Light, Power and Bliss in and through the mental, vital and physical. Also, Sri Aurobindo's integral Yoga effects a sublime synthesis between the visions and experiences of Advaita, Visishtadvaita and Dvaita.

It is a spiritual, rather a supramental synthesis and certainly not a philosophical synthesis for it fusesthem all and transcends them. According to Sri Aurobindo there are three poses of the creative supermind : 'The first founds the inalienable unity of things, the second modifies that unity so as to support the manifestation of the many in the one and the one in the evolution of a divesified individuality which, by the action of ignorance, becomes in us, at a lower level, the illusion of the separate ego'.

The truth and rationale of Advaita has it's basis in the first poise of the supramental, for, in this poise there is no individua lisation, and all is held and developed in the unitarian consciousness as one, and not a many. In the second poise of the supermind 'the Divine consciousness stands back in the idea from the movement which it contains, realising it by a sort of apprehending consciousness, following it, occupying and inhabiting it's works, seeming to distribute itself in it's forms'.

It is in this that there 'is a multiple concentration and a creation of countless soul-forms but all within the fundamental unity and harmony of the One'. The original unity is here modified but there is yet no division or essential difference.

It is this poise that supplies the truth and justification for the experience of Visishtadvaita. It is only in the third poise of the supermind that the stress of the consciousness falls on multiplicity, but well within the play of unity. This is 'a sort of fundamental blissful dualism in unity-no longer unity qualified by a subordinate dualism-between the individual Divine and its universal source'. This is the basis of Dvaita.

An integral supramental realisation would regard them all 'as indispensable strains of its developing harmonies' and there fore genuine and perfectly valid. It is only the human mind with it's separative perception that cuts up the unity of existence. A aupramental truth-consciousness is at once the self-warness of the Infinite and Eternal and a power of self determination inherent in that self-awareness; the first is it's foundation and status, the second is it's power of being, the dynamics of it's self-existence. The Infinite of being must also be an Infinite of power; containing in itself a eternal repose and quiescence, it must also be capable of an eternal action and creation.

Creation would then be a self-manifestation. It would be an ordered deploying of the infinite possibilities of the Infinite. But every possibility implies a truth of being behind it, a reality in the existent; for without that supporting truth there could not be any possibles.

But in our mind we do not see the complete process, we see only possibilities that determine themselves into actualities and though we infer or conjecture, we are not sure of a necessity, a predetermining truth, an imperative behind them which capacitates the possibilities, decides the actuaities. 'Our mind is an observer of actuals, an inventor or discoverer of possibilities, but not a seer of the occult imperatives that necessitate the movements and forms of creation. But to the supramental truth-consciousness these imperatives would be apparent, would be the very stuff of it's seeing and experience.'

The supermind, therefore, is a principle of active will and knowledge superior to mind and creatrix of the worlds. It is the intermediary power and state of being between that self-possession of the one and this flux of the many. It is the vast self-extension of the Brahman that contains and develops.

By the idea it develops the triune principle of existence, consciousness and bliss out of their indivisible unity. It differentiates them but it does not divide.'In a sense', says Sri Aurobindo, 'the whole of creation may be said to be a movement between two involutions, Spirit in which all is involved and our of which all evolves downwards to the other pole of matter; in which also all is involved and out of which all evolves upwards to the other pole of spirit'. Supermind is Real-Idea. It is the vast; it starts from unity, not division, it is primarily comprehensive; differentiation is only it's secondary act.

Thus the indivisibility of the comprehensive supermind which contains all multiplicity without derogating from its own unity, is a truth upon which we have always to insist, if we are to understand the cosmos and get rid of the initial error of our analytic mentality. In this comprehensive knowledge there is no independent centre of existence, no individual separated ego such as we see ourselves' the whole of existence is to it's self-awareness an equable extension, one in oneness, one in multiplicity, one in all conditions and everywhere'.

The Psychic Entity

The Psychic entity is the representative within the evolving nature of the unchanging self above. It is, therefore, essential that the psychic movement inward to the inmost psychic entity should be supplemented by an opening upward to a supreme spiritual status or a higher existence. This is the beginning of what Sri Aurobindo has called spiritualisation. Thus the second transformation we require is the transformation by the spiritual consciousness.

The initial requirement of spiritual transformation is an upward movement of the mind to the higher ranges of super conscience. But this spiritual change will not lead to man's attaining the highest spiritual level of which he is capable, unless there supervenes the third and final transformation.

This is the transformation by the supermind which completes the passage of the soul through ignorance and for the first time places it's consciousness, its life and power upon a completely effective basis of self-knowledge. Psychic change was found to be a change circumscribed within the limits of the natural instrumentation and consequently it was found to effectuate only a reflected and modified manifestation of the supernal riches such as peace, light, bliss etc., above us. Spiritual change gives an unfettered vision of the truth of things above, and succeeds in bringing down into play in our terrestrial embodied existence the selfuminous instrumentation of the transcendent self.

But both this vision and this dynamisation which spiritualisation implies are after all inadequate. We know that most integral, inclusive and harmonious vision, or rather, identify-knowledge of the Real in all its rich diversity of aspects can be obtained by the supermind the supermind alone. So nothing short of Supramental realisation can satisfy the spiritual aspiration of the Integral Yogi.

The transition to supermind is really a passage from Nature to supernature. This being so, it is not in the power of mind to effect this transition. All the previous stage of evolution that we have described are stages in ignorance, but the supramental change is a stage in knowledge. The emergence of the supermind is not possible unless there is a direct descent of it.

The descent of the supermind into our earthly nature is the only way in which the ascent of the evolutionary process to the supermind can take place. The acion of the supermind, representing as it does the perfect identify of knowledge and will, is always and under all conditions intrinsic, automatic and irresistably self-achieving. It can descend to any depth of obs curity without losing it's full power of action; and if it limits itself or it's working, it is by choice and intention, not by compulsion; in the limits it chooses it's action and the results of it's action are harmonious and inevitable. This self-limit ation of self-imposed restriction is for the fulfilment of a specific purpose.

Sri Aurobindo points out that 'for a real transformation there must : be a direct and unveiled intervention from above; there would be necessary too a total submission and surrender of the lower consciousness, a cessatior of its insistence, a will in it for it's separate law of action to be completely annulled by transformation and lose all rights over our being'.

This does not mean that we can by our efforts force the supermind to descend. In fact, the whole of the process, the gradual Psychicisation of our being and the slow spiritualisation of our nature by the light of the higher reaches of the mind and the over mind are preliminary conditions for the descent of the supermind.

As a result of the descent of the supermind there will be a real participation by the individual in the working of the universal consciousness-Force; the individual 'Purusha' would be the master of his own creative energy, and at the same time a conscious partner, agent, instrument of the cosmic spirit in the working of the universal energy; the universal energy would work through him, but he also would work through her, and the double working a single action.

It is this crowning phase of supramentalisation that alone can usher iinto existence a new era of the unveiled manifestation of the spirit in the material universe; Nature becomes transformed in to supernature and human beings in to Gnostic beings. The blossoming forth of human evolution in to super-manhood is the goal particularly stressed by the Integral Yoga of Sri Aurobindo.

He refues to believe that man is the last world about the process of universal evolution. he is firm in his conviction that the final fruition of all human progress would consist in a unique form of self-exceeding and self-transcending. "Just as the animal has been the living laboratory in which Nature has worked out man, so also man himself is a thinking and living laboratory in whom and with whose conscious co-operation she is striving to work out the Divine Man or Superman.'

Man is essentially a mental being, manomaya purusha, with mind as the dominant power of his consciousness and as the guilding principle of his life. But mind is in essence only an inferior mode of operation of the true power of knowledge, self-luminous and self-realilsing, which are have called the supermind, Supermanhood implies the bringing into play of the supermind in man, it's overt operation in all the parts of his existence, and its success in tansforming his throughly into an image of the Divine.

The superman is thus man transfigured in all the members of his being by the sovereign dynamism of the spirit. The vision of supermanhood sums and brings to a focus the loftiest ideals which have been inspiring mankind throughout the ages. It is the supreme vision of the rich out-flowering of the Divine in man.

The ideal of supermanhood steers clear of two opposite extremes. It neither accepts the path of negation that leads to the silence of Nirvana or Kaivalya, nor encourages the path of egoistic self-affirmation which leads to spiritual death. Haridas Chaudhury writes; "Having struck a middle course between asceticism and materialism it directs man's attention to the goal of dynamic self-identification with the Divine will in the world".

To be a superman is not simply to rise above the binding limitations of humanity and to get absorbed in the transcendent Divine. It is immensely more than that. The superman is essentially the playmate of the Divine in his cosmic self-expressions and creative adventures. Superman-hood implies not only the realisation of God on the lofty summits of spiritual experience. but also the dynamic manifestation of God in the material circumstances of our human living.

Supermanhood as envisaged by Sir Aurobindo in quite in keeping with an integral view of ultimate reality and with a coherent account of the process of terrestrial evolution. When we speak of the superman we refer to a new race, almost a new species, that will appear on earth as the inevitable result of Nature's evolution. The new race will be developed out of the present humanity, but it does not mean, however, that the whole of humanity will be so changed of a sudden.

Supermanhood means, of course, a very radical change; it means giving up altogether many and some very basic human qualities and attributes. Again, 'the superman is not a purified and moralised man, even as he is not a matgnified glorified animal man; he is man of a different type, qualitatively different'.

The superman or the Divine man, as envisaged by Sri Aurobindo, on the contrary, has for his distinguishing mark a through divine transformation of all the parts of his embodied existence including even the grossest physical.

He will have the infinite power of God, but he would be loath to make my personal or egoistic use there of. As a playmate of the Divine, he would unreservedly offer his body, life and mind as plastic instruments in the hands of God so that life on earth may be turned into a sacred poem of divine ecstasy.

Again the superman is not, as Nietzsche thinks him to be, the highest embodiment of the biological force of Nature, not even as modified and tefined by the aestghetic and aristocratic Virtues of which the higher reaches of humanity seem capable . For that is after all humanity only accentuated in certain other fundamentally human modes of existence. Instead of the ethical and intellectual man, we get the vital and aestheric man. It may be a change but not a transfiguration. Again a full grasp of the distinction between the extraordinary great man and the superman, mahamanava and atimanava, is vital to a proper appreciation of the message of Sri Aurobindo and the ideal of Bernard Shaw.

The superman will differ from the greatest among men as profoundly as a normal human being differs from the mightiest or the most intelligent animal. Again, the superman would not be simply a great man or a human hero; he would rather be the embodiment of some unique emergent quality.

Sri Aurobindo is firm in his conviction that the birth of the Divine in man is the supreme consummation towards which the march of human civilisation has been proceeding through the ages. The advent of superman and gnostic beings would, therefore, be the crowning consummation of the increasing process of self-manifestation of the spirit in material conditions'.

Finally, a word about Jivanmukta and the superman: while the superman of Sri Aurobindo must needs be a Jivanmukta purusha, not all Jivanmukta are superman-superman hood is a far richer concept and a greater achievement that Jivanmukti. There have indeed been numerous instances of Jivanmukti in the past; but supermanhood is yet to blossom forth in the course of further evolution. Thus we find that it is Sri Aurobindo who is par excellent the philosopher of the superman, the thinker who has proclaimed more strongly than they other, the absolute necessity of the emergence of race of Divine man.

Sri Aurobindo-Poet as Seer

Sri Aurobindo once said that he had been first and foremost a poet and a politician and only later had he become a Yogi. But outside a small if growing circle, he is but little known as a poet. This is unfortunate but a fact. As it is, the response has swayed between enthusiasm and denigration. In the process few have seen the object as it is. remains a controversial, even as enigmatic figure.

The reasons for controversy and misunderstanding are not one but many. To begin with, Sri Aurobindo is a distinguished person. a culture, hero. Romain Rolland described him as the greatest synthesis between the genius of the East and the genius of the West. A leader in more fields than one his successive roles as a nationalist, a metaphysical thinker and latterly a Yogi, has tended to throw his work as a poet in to the back ground.

Even devotees have been known to shy at it, many look upon it as ancillary, a by-product rather that what it, in fact is, essential to his mode of expression. Another difficulty is that there exist in certain quarters the fixed idea that no Indian can write worthwhile poetry in English. His own indifference to publicity is another factor. The collected poems and plays (1942) has long been out of print. But the real difficulty would seem to lie in the fact that in his maturer verse, his more intimate utterances Sri Aurobindo deals almost exclusively with states of being, subtle ranges of experience that are never easy to grasp, much less to judge. In the contemporary crowd he appears to be of somewhat antique cast.

The poet seems so much like his own Shiva :

A face on the cold dire mountain peaks
Grand and still, it's lines white and austere
Match with the unmeasured snowy streaks
Cutting heaven, implacable and sheer.
A moon-ray on his forehead blue and pale,
Stretched after it's finger of still light
Illumining emptiness. Stern and male
Mask of peace, indifferent in might !

The modern consciousness, everyone is agreed, has lost it's centre. In fact, the loss is it's very raison d'etre. Poetry today is mostly the poetry of crisisnow and then the crisis of poetry no less ! It is at the same time an age of eager, unconventional experiments in form, and formlessness-all of which may be a cover for a tortured and confused seeking for integration.

But integration is ever from within and depends upon a change of consciousness. This is where a good many of our poets and thinkers fail. Placed by their side Sri Aurobindo speaks almost a new tongue, an Orphic voice of such sanity and serenity, of imcontestable inwordness and maturity as almost mocks at our agonies, real or pretended. To many he would seem to belong to a tradition which is hard to admit or to continue, passe. (This of course is a convenient error.)

He seems so stand outside the main-stream of Modern poetry or what has imposed itself as the mainstream. Perhaps we are in for a revolution of the word, and poetry such Sri Aurobindo's might help in that emergence and revalution. You have the word, Tagore had said to him. Only a poet can recognise another. The degree of vision that dwells in a man is a correct measure of a person and the poetry in him.

To presume that visionary writers have a weak hold on life is part of the order of ideas has to be left aside if we are to enter the world of Aurobindo an poetry. For it deals with as it depends upon experiences 'not very much frequented by common readers of poetry'.

An openness to these experiences and some knowledge of the conditions of their fit expression would seem to be part of the reader's minimum equipment if he is to make sense of and profit from this poetry, largely, of inner life. In this case "The wisdom of the East' did not make for any loss of poetic potency. In fact, it gave a new tone and range, an intensity characteristic of the author. Perhaps to appreciate this poetry we need a hierarchy of the imagiinative life, a renewal of symbolic modes of correspondence which have all but also, a loss to which the proliferating interest in myths and symbols is an oblique reminder. Before we can hope to earn this poetry, 'too far from our surface nature's postal routes' the doors of perception have to be cleansed.

For some that many not be easy. The way out, for such people, is no dismiss this poetry as philosophic, obscure or occult. But, as stephen spender had once said, art is a Hindu temple in which many gods can co-exist. Here is poetry such as the Rishis wrote, or might write. Not to recognise it is to declare oneself insensitive. The failure of the spirit is a failure from which poetry alone can deliver us.

Sri Aurobindo's 'Savitri'.

Many readers of Sri Aurobindo's Savitri are baffled by the metaphysical Subtlety, the mystical depth and the Spiritual radiance of this epic. But we forget that there are other facets to this epic which appeal as much to the common man as to the initiated reader. Some day the metaphysics, the mysticism and the spirituality will have to be the concern of the common man too. Culture may be said to have come of age when the individual is interested in all facets of life.

Nature, Love and Contemporary Thought Kindle a general interest even in the uninitiated reader of poetry. They present a subject-matter which is of common human interest. They arouse what Mathew Arnold called the perimary human motions. It is true that Nature and love can also be treated in a manner which brings in metaphysical subtlety, mystical depth and spiritual radiance.

But this is linked up with common human experience, and the reader feels than he is at home with the poetry. This human interest in Savitri is evident in the descriptions of Nature in Book IV (cantos I and U) and Bood v (canto I). I do not mention Book I canto I as the description of dawn is highly symbolic ; in the treatment of love in Book v (cantos 2 and 3); and in the poetic commentary on science in Book VII (canto 4); "The Triple Soul-Forces' (the books concerned with the debate between Savitri and Death) have also to be reckoned with in this context. These passages brings the epic much nearer to the common reader and throw a bridge by which the passage into the other realms of the epic is some what faciliatated.

In Book VII Canto 4, Savitri, who is out to find her soul comes across three soul-forces each one of which claims to be her soul. One of them is the Goddess of pity or the Mother of the seven sorrows, The voice of wrath that, like an echo from below, takes up the refrain is the unchastened vital or desireself in man that expresses itself in cynical of pessimistic terms. Another goddess who meets Savitri is the Mother of Might, Durga.

She also claims to be the secret soul of Savitri. The burden of her speech is taken up by a warped echo, the voice of a dwarf-Titan, the ego of this great world of desire, the human will. The Mother of Might maintains that she is the secret soul of Savitri. The Ego maintains that he is a claimant to the throne of heaven. The third goddess that claims to be the secret soul of Savitri is the Madonna of Light, who is also the Mother of joy and peace, for light makes for joy and peace. The burden of her speech is taken up by the warped echo of her voice-the sense-shackled mind or intellect of man.

Savitri tells each one of these three goddesses that she is only a portion of her soul put forth to help mankind and help the travail of time. One day, when she has found her soul, Savitri will return, a bringer not merely of strength but light which gives the mirror of God, and love which will make man see the face of the absolute, for all these are but faculties of the soul. Modern philosophies are glanced at passingly in all these situations. Scientific socialism is a noble doctrine because it is pity that man feels towards his fellow men that is it's basic inspiration.

But this pity is not aided by warped indignation that proceeds from cynicism, which is not a constructive attitude to life. That is how pity-gets mixed up with hatred. This is what we understand from the discussion that Savitri has with the Goddess of pity and her echo. Then there is the situation that brings in the Madonna of Light and the sense-shackled mind. It is true that the human intellect has unravelled many of the secrets of the universe :

I have detected plasm and cell and gene,

The protozoa traced, man's ancestors,

The humble originals from whom he rose

As Savitri says :

But not by showering heaven's golden rain upon the intellect's hard and rocky soil can tree of paradise flower on earthly ground.

These two 'interviews' make it clear how Sri Aurobindo has been able to bring in contemporary knowledge into an epic which sums up the legendary past and looks forward to the future prefigured in symbols We may deal here with the colloquy between Savitri and the mother of might in some detail. The situation brings out the value as well as the futility of applied science technology.

The Goddess of might sat on a boulder carved like a huge throne. Dressed in gold and Purple Sheen, She was armed with the trident and the thunderbolt. Her feet rested on a couchant lion's back. A formidable smile curved round her lips, heaven fire laughed in the corners of her eyes.

A halo of lightning flamed around her head, and majesty and victory, which sat with her, guarded Truth, Ideal wisdom, Love and Bliss against the flat equality of death and the all levelling night in the cosmic battle-field. Her speech was a charm restoring hope in failing hearts.

In the battle that goes on between the bright and sombre powers on earth, Durga has her own part to play.

To the strong I bring the guerdon of their strength.

To the weak I bring the armour of my force. She gives fortune to the great and wise and then tramples them down with the armed heel of Fate.

My ear is leaned to the cry of the oppressed,
I topple down the thrones of tyrant kings;
I smite the Titan who bestrides the world
And slay the tiger in his blood stained den.
I am Durga, Goddess of the proud and strong.
And Lakshmi, Queen of the fair and fortunate;
I wear the face of kali when I kill.
I trample the corpses of the demon-hordes.
I am charged by God to do his mighty work.
I reason not of virtue and sin
But do the deed he has put into my heart.
I fear not for the angry frown of Heaven,
I flinch not from the red assault of Hell,
I crush the opposition of the gods,
Thread down a million goblin obstacles.

I guide man to the path of the Divine
And guard him from the red wolf and the snake.
I set in his mortal hand my heavenly sword.
And put on him breastplate of the Gods.

The goddess also breaks the ignorant pride of human mind and tears to pieces man's narrow and successful life so that he may die to earth and live in the soul.

But the great sorrow of the mother of might lies in the fact that mass falls back unsaved.

I know the goal, I know the secret route ;
I have studied the map of the invisible worlds.
I am the battle's head, the journey's star.
But the great obstinate world resists my word,
And the crookedness and evil in man's heart is
stronger than reason, profounder than the pit,
And the malignancy of houstile powers
puts craftily back the clock of destiny
and mightier seems than the eternal will.

Her only consolation is that she guides. a few who pass towards the Light. She was also the conviction that the world is going to be saved in the end.

Slowly the light grows greater in the East,
Slowly the world progress on Gods road.
His seal is on my task, it cnnot fail.

The burden of her speech is then taken up by the

unregenerate vital or the desire-self from the lower human world. This dwarf-Titan always strives to make the universe his instrument. He claims to be himself vessel of the Godhead that must be. Struggling to be a lord of Nature, this thinking animal has made of Nature his nurish and total and slave.

But actually he himself is a tool and slave of Nature who is supposed to be his slave and tool. The heart's grief and body's pain are Nature's means to make man grow, see and feel; and his death assists the immortality of Nature by perpetuating the type. Man thinks that he is endowed with free will and a master mind. But it is Nature that pushes him on her own chosen paths. He claims to be the possessor and ruler. But he is in truth ruled and possessor and ruler. But he is in truth ruled and possessed by Nature. He is her conscious automation and dupe of her desire. His soul is her guest-a mute and inert sovereign. His body is her robot and his life is her way to live. It is only his conscious mind that revolts now and then against Nature. But even the mind is nothing more than her, 'strong revolted serf'.

Man's claim is that though he is the last born of the earth, he stands the first. He has progressed so fast that now the earth is his floor and the sky his living's roof. The conquest of Nature by man through his intellect is a thrilling saga of great daring and achievement.

Sri Aurobindo and Gita

To Explane Aurobindo's approach to and interpretation of the Gita, to bring out the differences between him and other commentators, and to fit in Aurobindo's Essays on the Gita with the main pattern of his philosophy is a forbidding task. It is not possible to do full justice to the subject in this paper. What is attempted here is a summary of it's main aspects as discussed by Sri Aurobindo in his Essays on the Gita.

Before the main subject is discussed, it is necessary to say a few words about the position of the Gita as a religio-philosophical text. Hindus believe that the Gita is the record of the dialogue that took place between Krishna and Arjuna on the battlefield of Kurukshetra. All the manuscripts of the Mahabharata discovered so far have been placed at about 8th century A.D.However, we learn from the kuvdlayamala, completed by Uddyotanasuri in A.D.779, that people in those days used to recite the Gita. But more important than the antiquity of the Gita is the problem of its influence on Hindu religious thought.

More reliable commentary on the Gita is by Shankaracharya who was probably biorn in A.D.788 and died in 820. Shankara in his introduction to the Gita states that he was induced to write his commentary because the existing ones were full of errors. Shankar's criticism is at least partially sustained by the Yoga. Vasistha-Ramayana written within a century of Shankar's birth, which contains a bow-dlerized version of the Gita.

Apparently, by, Shankara's time, the text of the Gita needed revision, and Shankara fixed the number of the verses at 700 which was accepted by all. Some years ago, the Kashmir recension of the Gita was discovered which contains about 45 extra verses. But all the Acharyas who followed Shankara, including those who opposed him, have commented on the text approved by Shankara. Some-times, one verse is added at the beginning of chapter 13, and Aurobindo has accepted this verse.

The methodology of writing a commentary demands that each were should be explained separately, if indeed any explanation is needed. All the commentators from Shankara's time have followed this method, including Lokamanya Tilak, whose commentary on the Gita is one of the most important written in the modern age. Here Aurobindo differs from others; he has written essays on the Gita, which work is divided into two parts and contains, forty-eight essays. However, in the second part, the last five chapters of the Gita have been treated in as many chapters, while the last essay, called the 'message of the Gita', gives a summary of the text. In their totality the essays bring out the central theme of the Gita, but each essay is complete in itself.

This method is not without its advantages and disadvantages. One cannot obtain the meaning of each verse of the Gita from the essays, but as an introduction to the study of the Gita, there can hardly be a better method. Moreover, Aurobindo's Essays on the Gita is not only for beginners, even those who have read the text thoroughly will find his observations revealing in a flash, some meaning of the text which no other commentator has noticed or said. For example, Aurobindo's statement that the most vital part of the Gita is not its philosophical system, but that its suggestive ideas are not only 'eternally valuable and valid' but are 'enduring truths of spiritual experience, verifiable facts of our highest psychological possibilities.

This indeed is the main dfference between the approach of Sri Aurobindo and former Acharyas. But in order to understand the stand point of the Acharayas, it is necessary to take into account that the Gita, since Shankara wrote his commentary, has been accepted as one of the three principal sources of the vedanta doctrine, the other two being the ten or eleven principal Upanishads, and the Brahma-Sutra.

Shankara accepted as mahavakya or fundamental principle the Upanishadic statements, namely, tattvam-asi (that thou art) and aham Brahm-asmi (I am Brahman) and his commentaries were written with a view to prove that all these texts yield this meaning, or at least that they are capable of bearing this interpretation, though even he is not very sure of his position in his commentary on the Gita, which is probably his most nature work.

However, the Acharayas who came after Shankara took up his challenge, and interpreted the Gita in a manner which favoured their schools of philosophy. and as a result, the Gita has always been studies as a work of systematic philosophy. Even Tilak interpreted it to prove the superiority of karmayoga as he understood it, and wrote an in-troduction which incidentally is probably the best introduction to traditional Indian philosophy. But Aurobindo differs from all of them when he says.

The Gita stars from this vedantic synthesis and upon the basis of its essential ideas builds another harmony of the three great means and powers. Love, knowledge and works, through which the soul of man can directly approach and cast himself into the Eternal. He then declares :

We of the coming day stand at the head of a new age of development which must lead to such a new and larger synthesis. We are not called upon to be orthodox vedantins.......or to entrench ourselves within the four corners of the teaching of the Gita. That would be to limit ourselves and to attempt to create our spiritual life out of the being, knowledge and nature of others, of the men of the past, instead of building it our of our own being and potentialities. We do not belong to the past dawns, but to the noons of the future. Hence, he says that our study of the Gita must not be scholastic or academic, but we should seek 'for help and light in the Gita and our aim must be to distinguish it's essential and living message, that in it on which humanity has to seize for it's perfection and it's highest spiritual welfare.

This practical approach is different from the traditional view But Aurobindo does not accept the assumption of modern critics that the Gita is a later composition inserted in to the Mahabharata to invest it with the epic's authority. On the other hand he emphasise's that the battle of Kurukshetra and it's effect on Arjuna have to be understood in order to realise the central drift of the idea of the Gita. Indeed he says that three things in the Gita are spiritually significant; 'they are the divine personality of the Teaccher, his characteristic relations with his desciple and the occasion of his teaching. The teacher, Aurobindo says, 'is god himself descended into humanity.

Aurobindo believes in Avatarhood, that is, incarnation of God as mortal, and in support of his view he quotes the Gita (iv.7-8) which includes the famous utterance of Krishna: 'For whensoever there is the fadling of the Dharma and the uprising of unrighteousness, then I loose myself forth into birth. For the deliverance of the good, for the destruction of the evil-doers, for the enthroning of the Right I am born from age to age.

But Aurobindo points out, the upholding of Dharma in the world is not only object of the descent of Avatar, as it is not an all-sufficient object in itself', and adds, that 'there are two aspects of the divine birth ; one is a descent, the birth of God in humanity, the Godhead manifesting itself in the human from and nature, the eternal Avatar; the other is an ascent, the birth of man into the Godhead, man rising into the divine nature and consciousness.

Here Aurobindo realise on the Gita (IV.10) where Krishna says : 'Delivered from' liking and fear and wrath, full of me, taking refuge in me, many purified by austerity of knowldge have arrived at my nature of being; and he explains madbhavam of this verse, as 'the divine nature of purushottama. Aurobindo's view seems to be supported by the last verse of chapter XI in which Krishna declares : 'Whoever works for me alone, makes me his only goal and is devoted to me, free from attachment, and without hatred toward any creature-that man '0 Pandava, shall enter into me'. Here it may be noted that even shankara has said that this verse represents the central idea of the Gita. Hence, it can be said that the final destiny of man is to enter into godhead or as Aurobindo says:

If there were not this rising of man into the Godhead to be helped by the descent of God into humanity, Avatarhood for the sake of the Dharma would be an otiose phenomenon, since mere Right, mere justice or standards of virtue can always be upheld by the divine omnipotence through its ordinary means, by great men or great movements, by the life and work of sages and Kings and religious teachers, without ant actual incarnation.

The Avatar comes as the manifestation of the divine nature in the human nature......... in order that the human nature man by moulding its principle, thought, feeling action......... transfigure itself into the divine the Gita contains as its kernel this second and real object of the Avatarhood.

Aurobindo, however, does not minimise the aspect of re-establishment of dharma by the Avatar, but for him 'dharma' has a very wide connotation and embraces 'the relations of man with other beings, with Nature, with God, considered from the point of view of an active divine principle. Fundamentally 'dharma' is eternal and unchanging but in its formal manifestation. it is continually changing and evolving because man does not already live in it by struggle towards perfection in knowledge and practice, overcoming 'adharma', which strives to overcome dharma. This struggle has been typified in the vedas as between the Divine and Titanic powers, in Zoroastrianism by Ahuramazda and Ahirman, and in Christinity and Islam as the contest between God and his angels and Satan ior Iblis.

'It is things,' says Aurobindo, 'that condition and determine the work of the Avatar. Hence,' in Buddhism, the aspirant takes refuge in Dharma, 'sangha' and the Buddha, and in Christianity there is the law of Christian living, the Church and the christ. Similarly in Vaishnavism we have the Bhagavat, Bhakta and Bhagavan, the Bhagavat being the law of the Vaishnava dispensation of adoration and love, the Bhakta representing the fellowship of those in whom the law is manifest, while Bhagavan is the divine Lover and Beloved in whose being and nature the divine law of love is founded and fulfils itself.

Sri Ramakrishna Paramahamsa also used to emphasise their triune aspect by saying that 'Bhagavat, Bhakta and Bhagavan are three in one and one in three', but Aurobindo develops the significance of this cryptic sentence, and states that' these three are always the necessary elements of the work of the Avatar.

On the basis of this principle, the Gita may be said to have three elements, Krishna the Avatar, Arjuna the bhakta, and the text itself, the Bhagavat. The importance of Krishna in the Gita is of course too obvious and the only question to be determined is whether he is an Avatar or not. As we have seen, Aurobindo accepts him as an Avatar and here he may be said to have been following the traditional view, but for his re-interpretion of the purpose of Avatarhood, Aurobindo has also brought ourt the Significance of Arjuna in the Gita.

The Gita, Aurobindo says, 'can only be understood-as a

developing argument. This argument takes place between an Avatar and a typical Aryan Prince who has ben trained in warfare and a typical Aryan Prince who has been trained in warfare from early boyhood. For the moment he is assailed by doubts. Which indeed have overcome him, hence he has turned to his friend for advice and guidance as to the proper conduct of a Kshatriya Prince under such circumstances.

He does nt ask for the secret of life or of the world, or their meaning and purpose, but for clear rule of action. But the divine Teacher, as Aurobindo calls Krishna, wants to impart precisely these teaching to his favourite disciple.

In the process Arjuna is fustered. Hence after Krishna has explained Yoga and samadhi as fixed anchoring of the intelligence in a state of desireless equity, Arjuna asks impatiently: 'O Janard ana, if thou holdest the intelligence to be greater than action, why then does thou appoint me to an action terrible in nature ? Thou bewilderest my understanding with mingled word.

Speak one thing decisively by which I can attain to what is the best.' Krishna tries to remove these doubts, and in due course tells him at the beginning of chapter IV that it was he (Krishna) who in ancient times revealed this Yoga to Vivasvat. Since vivasvat was a very ancient sage, Arjuna frankly expresses his doubt about the veracity of this statement by pointing out that Krishna was born long after Vivasvat, and it is then that Krishna declares that he is an Avatar in the most well-known verse of the Gita.

18

Gautama Buddha

The Birth

It was the middle of the sixth century before Christ. Queen Maya Devi was fast asleep in her silken bed. All of a sudden she sat up; her body was trembling. King Shuddhodhana asked her "What Happened"?

She said, "What a dream ! My lord ! I watched the radiant Elephant entered my womb". Next morning the king sent for the royal astrologer Veggala. He narrated the Queen's dream.

He said, "Your Majesty, in a short while a son will be born to you. He will be the embodiment of compassion and will win world-wide fame. The radiance that entered the queen's womb will be the deliverer of mankind, he will be the light unto the world". The King bestowed priceless jewels on Veggala and took respectful leave of him.

Maya Devi was nine months pregnant. She desired that the child should be born in her father's palace. The King sent her in a golden chariot with a retinue, But Maya Devi was delivered on the way in a grove called Lumbinivana. This was in 623 B.C. The King was delighted to hear the news of the birth of his Son. The entire city joyously welcomed the Queen and the child. The family belonged to the Gautama Gothra and so he came to be known as Gautama.

But the King's joy was short lived on the seventh day Maya Devi died. The King asked his second wife Prajapathi to take care of the child. She loved it more than she would have loved her own child and took affectionate care.

A sage Asitha Rishi who lived near the Himalayas and could perceive the past, came to know of the birth of the child. Full of curiosity he came to the Palace. The royal priest welcomed with all respect. The sight of the child glowing like gold. thrilled the sage and he touched the feet of the infant with reverence. He was thrilled to find that the child had not only the thirty-two auspicious signs but also eighty two care signs. He touched the feel of the child with his head and said.

"King this is no ordinary child. Any one who has these thirty-two auspicious signs will have only two paths before him, if he accepts the material would he becomes the mightiest of monarchs; he becomes the sublimest of sanyasis, an enlightened soul and the prince of Philosophers. The King choose the best Masters in every branch of knowledge to educate his son. The boy was given the name siddhartha. The boy was exceptionally intelligent, and soon mastered the scriptures.

Childhood

A master of martial arts called Sulabha made siddhartha a superb warrior. One day Siddhartha and his cousin Devadatta were engaged in the practice of archery. At that time a line of lovely Swans appeared in the sky.

Devadatta at once aimed an arrow and let it fly. It pierceds swan, which fell to the ground. It was bleeding. The poor bird was in great pain. Siddhartha was deeply moved; he ran to it and taking it in his hands, and gently stroked it. He wiped the blood with his loose upper garment. He applied the juice of a herb to its wound. Devadatta was proud of his bowmanship. Siddhartha said, "Violence is a sin".

Siddhartha was a pleasant child to whom wealth was not important. Though he lived in Palace and was given whatever he desired, he spent more time thinking and asking serious questions than enjoying his riches. The young prince had the most wonderful toys, the best things to eat and the most beautiful clothes but he preferred to be alone, so that he could think or play with his animal friends. He was very spiritual and was continuously worrying about birth disease, old age and death. He could not bear anyone to suffer and was always trying to improve the lives of the few people he saw.

King Shuddhodhana wanted his son to be a true Kshatriya-a warrior ! After a lot of thought and advice from his trusted Ministers the King decided to give the young Prince, something else to think about. So he made up his mind to find a wife for Gautama. Messengers were sent to all the Kingdoms that the King wanted a bride for his son.

King Shuddhodana was a very brave and popular King. He made Kapilavastu as his Kingdom. The city of Kapilavastu is said to be in the Tarai region, of the Indo-Nepal border.

The Swayamvara

Siddhartha grew up into a handsome youngman. His father was very happy. In the meanwhile A King of the Shakya race,

Dandapani arranged a Swayamvara for his daughter. He announced that his lovely daughter Yashodhara would marry the youth who could lift and string a heavy bow he had in his palace. Siddhartha a hero won the hand of the Princess.

He was blessed with a lovely and virtuous wife who was exceedingly devoted. Husband and wife were happy together. And yet king Shuddhodhana recalled at times the words of sage Asistha and was troubled.

He did everything that say Siddhartha's mind was immersed in a life of luxury and never turned towards renunciation. He had three palaces the homes of luxury, built for his son. One was for summer a second for the rainy season and the third for winter. Each Palace was splendidly furnished and every luxury invited the inhabitants at every step. Enchanting maidens were appointed to delight the prince with music and dance.

Yashodhara gave birth to a son. But already Siddhartha was growing indifferent to worldly life. The son was named Rahul. The child was captivating and his wife, beautiful, so Gautama turned his attention to his family.

He spent many happy hours with them, but neither his love for his wife nor his affection for his child could hold him for long. He continued to think about the world outside tha palace gates about the common people and their lives.

With the passage of time Gautama grew restless. He began to go for long rides outside the Palace in his chariot. When he saw the way people lived the suffering they had to bear and the trials and tribulations that they had to face Gautama was saddened.

The Renunciation

One day Gautama rode out in his chariot accompained by

his charioteer Channa. As they went along they came across an old man. He was and tired and sat beneath a tree all allone. Gautama stopped the chariot and stepped down. He asked the question to the old man.

"Who are you"? The old man started crying. He answered as follows.

"Your highness, I am old and of no use to anybody, my relatives have thrown me out of the house".

The prince was saddened he could do nothing. He returned to his chariot and continued his way. After some time he heard a man moaning and groaning as if in great pain. The prince asked his charioteer, "Why is than man groaning Channa"?

Channa answered as follows - "O Prince, he is sick; he is in deep pain, so he is crying out loud".

Gautama became silent. He had never seen old age and a trouble of a sick person. In his comfortable life at the palace there had been no place for sickness and disease. The harsh realities of life life had been hidden from him all his life and now seeing the old man and then the sick man made him asd.

After sometime the prince heard a wailing and beating of chests. The prince looked up and was puzzled at want he saw. A man lay still on a plank. He had been convered with a white cloth and flowergarlands had been thrown over the body, all around the man people cried.

The prince asked his charioteer, "Why is that man sleeping peacefully ? why are they crying"?

Channa answered. "Your highness he is dead, and his family weep, for they can have him no more". "But why does a man have to die why can we not live forever"? asked the prince.

Channa replied "When a man is born he has to die. That is life. It is a law of Nature. Whatever is born must pass through the various stages of life and then die. None can change that; it is God's will". After some time, as they drove on they came across an ascetic-a Sadhu.

The Sadhu walked along in his orange robes and wooden slippers with a begging bowl in his hands.

The Prince asked, "Who is he Channa"?

"Why has he worn those clothes ?" The charioteer answered as follows.

"That man has renounced the world your highness. He has left his family and given up his family responsibilities to escape from the misery of life. He wishes to search for truth, to find the way to salvation". By this time they had reached the palace.

The Prince was deep in thought. He had been shocked by all that he saw. His mind was restless. He decided that he would not rest until he had found out why there was sorrow in the world, and how men could be free of it. The old man forsaken by his relatives, the sick man crying with pain and the dead man surrounded by his wailing relatives, had convinced him that, life involve's aging, sickness and death.

The luxuries of his royal life an the attraction of a happy marriage life failed to provide prince a with any peace of mind and finally the fourth sight that he had seen of the ascetic who had renounced the world in search of truth made him decide to leave his wife and new born son.

One night, when Gautama was twenty-nine years old, he

left the palace without telling anyone, where he was going. He broke all the worldly ties leaving even his wife and child behind. What he was doing was not so easy, but it had to be done. As long as he stayed among the people he loved enjoying the good things of the palace, he would never find answers to the questions that would trouble him.

And after one long, last look at his sleeping wife and son Gautama left the palace for ever. It was the full moon night, of the month of vaishaka. The entire city of Kapilavastu was immersed in sleep. The prince felt he could not stay in the palace even for a moment.

At mid night he went to the royal stables. He stroked lovingly the back of his beloved horse. Perhaps the horse felt the agony of the master: he seemed ; to look at the master lovingly.

Siddhartha asked his charioteer Channa to have the horse ready and silently stepped into the bed room, where his wife and son slept and untroubled sleep. He touched them gently and them left in the chariot. Siddhartha asked Channa to halt when they reached the banks of the river Anoma. Channa was in anguish.

Heart-broken, Channa returned and gave the shattering news to the King and others. It was as if lightening had struck the palace. The King and the Queen were beside themselves with grief. Yashodhara felt that the world had grown dark for ever. Her parents-in-law and others comforted her as best they could.

Shuddhodhana could not bear this shock. He put Dedvadatta the son of his second wife on the throne and spent his days in the forlorn hope that Siddhartha would return. Gautama not only left his family, his friends and the Palace but he also gave up all the luxuries that he had been used to.

After the Renunciation

After the great Renunciation Gautama spebnt a few years in the caves of Rajagriha the capital city of Magadha. He practised very severe penance.

Gautama believed thant an austere life was the only way to salvation. As a result he was very harsh on himself. He bore all kinds of pain and at the end of six years he had become a mere skeleton. But all that he inflicted upon himself brought him only pain and hardship. He was no closer to finding the answers that he sought.

No divine light shone upon him and he was finally forced to admit that such penance alone could not lead him to his desired goal. Gautama acknowledged the need to concentrate and to meditate.

At last Gautama sat down to meditate under a peepul tree at Gaya. He sat crosslegged and straight backed. His eyes were closed and his mind blocked out all other sounds. For days on end, he sat in this manner concentrating completely.

One day in 537 B.C., a divine light dawned on him. All his doubts left him. He felt as if he knew all the secrets of the world. Gautama had become the Buddha.

The Vedic Age

In ancient India in the vedic age people followed their inherited profession and lived in peace. But later a number of republics appeared on the map. There were frequent clashes for land and water.

In the meanwhile many holy texts also appeared and

differences of opinion cropped up. In course of time the rulers came to depend on the priest class. The holy texts were in Sanskrit and when other languages like Pali and Magadha appeared the sacred texts became the monopoly of a few who had learnt Sanskrit. Magadha was then a prosperous state. The capital was Rajagriha.Bimbisara was the ruler. He had a great faith in religious rituals.

King Bimbisara treated Gautama with great respect. He was won over by the dignified and wise words of the youth. He did not want such a gifted youth to beg for his food and said,

"Young man this life of a wandering Sanyasi is not for you. I shall give you half my Kingdom live happily".

Gautama replied. "King you are very generous. The wealth and luxury of a worldly life mean nothing to me. I seek peace and wisdom".

The King said, "When you receive enlightenment come and guide me, I beg of you". Gautama agreed and continued his wanderings.

The Divine Knowledge

Buddha decided to preach the divine knowledge that he had attained. He wanted to share all that he had acquired with the people of his country. So he set off for the deer park at Saranath near Benares.

Gautama reached Saranath. After his first sermon he earned a lot of respect and reknown. Five holy men became his first disciples in a park near Varnasi. They absorbed his knowledge and learned all that he had to teach. Eventhough the beginning was small, the incident took most fame and reknown.

Gautama continued to preach in Magadha and the neighbo uring Kingdoms. His followers went from place to place preaching their message. At first only a few people came to listen.

When they heard the Buddha's message they were amazed. It was all so simple ! They could understand his teachings and more important they could use it in their daily life. Buddha taught that all men should learn to control themselves. If someone was angry, one should not be angry in return, but he kind instead. If someone did a bad thing, one should try to do god in return. One should not kill or hurt anybody not even animals. One should tell the truth, keep one's thoughts pure and show loving kindness to all.

In those time Hinduism had become so rigid and complex that the common man had lost faith in it. The ordinary householder needed something which he could understand and accept. The common man was crying for reform in traditional Hindusim. In the meanwhile Buddha's simple teachings appeared as a readymade answer.

Nehru said, "Buddha's whole approach comes like the breath of the fresh wind from the mountains after the stale sir of Metaphysical speculation".

The Uruvelavana

Once Buddha entered a thick forest. On its edge lay Uruvelav ana. As he approached it he heard an animal groaning in pain. He bent his steps towards the spot whence came the sound. He saw an elephant caught in a pond. It could not come out ; it must have been there for days. It was crying out in pain. All four legs were caught up in the mire.

Gautama went up to the elephant; his heart melted. He managed to collect dry branches of trees and piled them one on top of another near the Elephant. He brought bamboo poles and tied them up with strong creepers and made a platform. He gave the animal leaves to eat and sat by its side as it ate them. The starved creatures slowly regained strength. It struggled and struggled and at last was free It came up to Gautama and sat near his feet.

The hours of the night slide by. At dawn the Elephant once again looked at Gautama as a saviour. It went to a river nearly and bathed. Having cleaned its body it drank water. And then it carried water in its trunk and poured it over Gautama and the mud clinging to him was washed away.

Gautama once again looked into the eyes of the Elephant which were full of greatitude and stroked it gently, and continued his sojourn.

Siddhartha halted on the banks of the Narianejana near the Uruvelavana. Nearby were villagers and the villagers were simple and kind folk. He could seek alms in the village. He stayed there and began his tapas. His practice grew dusterer as days went by. He gradually reduced the quantity of food he used to take..

Finally he learnt to be content with just a morsel. He practically cut off all contact with the rest of the world controlled rigorously his breath and concentrated on meditation. He delved deep into his mind and meditated with the total concentration on the transience of life.

The True Spirituality.

Gautama rooted out all thoughts of earthly life and filled his mind with auspicious spirituality. As he held his breath with severe determination his body sweated. Harsh noises filled his ears. His head ached as if it would break into a thousand pieces.

But he suffered everything, and continued his tapas single-minded. He had been starving himself. One day he lost consciousness and fell down. A shephered lad near by saw him and came to his rescue.

Without touching him he managed to put a few drops of milk into his mouth. Gradually the ascetic regained consciousness. He looked at the boy with weak eyes and asked for a cup of milk.

The boy stepped back nervously and said "No master. I belong to a low caste. It would be wrong for me to give you milk". Gautama said,

"My child, where there is compassion there men become kinsmen". He got some milk and drank it and it restored his energy.

Five seekers of knowledge, Kaundinya, Vashpa, Bhadrika, Ashwajit and Mahanama had come to Gautama, hoping that, when he attained enlightenment, he would be their guru.

Gautama reflected, "For six years I have been engaged in the severest austerities and mortified my flesh. If the body falls what would I have gained ?

Mortification of the flesh if futile". So he once again bent his steps towards the villages to seek alms. The disciples felt let down. They left him and went away.

On the way to a village stood an ancient and mighty banyan tree. Lost in thought, Gautama was sitting under its kind branches. The sum was scorching and there were few passers by. A young woman of the village came up with an infant with a bowl containing 'Payasa' in her hand.

She saw the radiant sage with his eyes shut, meditating under tree. She was filled with wonder. She placed the bowl before him and bowed to him. She stood for a while, but the sage was lost to the world.

She said, "Venerable Sire".

He opened his eyes and looked at her. What a serene light dwelt in his eyes ! She reverently gave him the bowl and said, "Be pleased to accept this. He drank it; then he said, "Who are you sister"?

She told, I am the daughter of the elder of the village Senani. I am called Sujatha" "do you desire nothing else in life Sister"?

She said, "What more do I need, Master, I am content and happy".

When the woman left Gautama sat on the grass in the Padmasana Posture facing the east. He said to himself with iron determination, "I shall not budge from here, even if my bones crumble and my blood evaporates until I attain enlightenment".

Buddha's Great Personality

Buddha's great personality influenced the people to a great extent. They were comforted by his solemn dignity and outward calm. He seemed to be at peace with himself and with the world.

Buddha always had time for his disciples. He comforted the bereaved and consoled the afficted. All this led to the popularity of Buddhism as a religion.

All his life Gautama went from place to place teaching people the truths he had found. One day Buddha return to his palace at Kapilavastu. The people were over-joyed. They eagerly accepted his philosophy. Gautama's wife and his son Rahul became his followers and joined the group that accompanied the

Buddha on his wanderings.

Buddha's teachings were very simple. He spoke and preached in the languages of the people of Magadha, that is Prakrit and Pali. The language used by the chaste Brahmins was sanskrit. This was not easily understood by the common man, so when they heard Buddha explaining beliefs in their language they embraced his religion whole heartedly.

Buddha's first sermon at saranath consisted of the seeds of his Philosophy. It was the nucleus of his religious doctrines. Everywhere he went, he would repeat these ideals explaining to people convincing them that a simple life was the best life.

Of his many belief's Buddha felt strongly about the four Noble Truths, the Eight-Fold path. He had no faith in the caste system and in sacrifices, and rituals and was generally silent about the existence of God.

Buddha's transformation from prince Gautama was brought about after he had seen the four Great sights. The four noble truths were based on this. Buddha believed that the world is full of suffering. This was the first Noble truth.. Secondly he believed that, suffering is caused by human desires.

According to Buddha the desires were not necessarily physical. Man's unsatiable taste for pleasures is the root cause of all our suffering. Man's greed for Money, for Love, for Food, for Comfort and for Power has been responsible for much of the suffering and sorrow, that exists in the world. This was the second Noble truth. Thirdly Buddha preached that the renunciation of desires is the path to salvation. If man has no desire no craving to be the best, to have the most, he will be able to live in peace with himself and with the world. There is no place for selfishness and greed in his life and he is happy.

Lastly Buddha believed that this salvation can be achieved by following the Eight-Fold path. When a man lays down guide lines for himself and live his life according to these, he is able to live happily. There will be discipline in his life. All this Buddha explained to the common man in his language Pali.It was something so simple and so logical that everyone could accept it. Not only did Buddha stress the four noble truths, but he also gave the people the golden path, which would guide them to salvation.

The Enlightenment

As Gautama slipped into deep meditation worldly bonds assailed him. Recollection of his earlier life came in waves. He seemed to hear his old father's calling. But Gautama was unmoved. Then Yashodhara seemed to stand before him and weep and weep. Then came the picture of Rahul weeping for his father. Pictures of other friends pining for him crowded his mind.

But Gautama knew that this was the work of Mar the enemy of Enlightnment, and brushed aside all these illusive pictures. He steeled his mind and endeavoured to teach the very foundations of true knowledge.

So he meditated for four weeks. Gautama's mind was lost in Meditation. It was the full moon night of the month of vaishaka. Old memories assailed him in the first quarter. In the second quarter they vanished and a divine power dawned with in him. In the third quarter the last shreds of darkness with in disappeared.

In the fourth quarter a light of Enlightenment blazed within him. He was in meditation and yet conscious and a serene joy beyond words filled his being. He saw the pure perfect and radiant path of Nirvana before him.

Two questions had assailed him. Sorrow is a grim reality in life. The first question was ; 'what is the origin of the inherent sorrow ? The second question was; 'How can this sorrow be overcome ?' He now had the answers to both. This knowledge is called Sammabodhi in Pali and Samyakbodha in Sanskrit. The banyan tree under which he had attained Enlightenment came to be known as 'Bodhivriksha'. and the holy Gaya came to be known as 'Buddha Gaya'.

Gautama was thirty-five, when he attained Enlightenment. In families this would been a subject of mirtth for Sarojini discoveredGautama now Bhagavan Buddha sat under the tree for four weeks, savouring the joy of the Nirvana path. His mind was an ocean of serenity and joy; but at the same time he felt the urge to share with others the knowledge he had attained.

He wished to share if first with his earliest gurus. Later he learnt that they were dead. But Buddha's life of luminous light had started. Gautama's majesty his compassion, his magnanimity with no thought of high or low, his transparent conduct and speech all won the spontaneous reverence of one and all. He who came of a great dynasty now lovingly welcomed into the fold now disciples, the lowest and the least.

Kisagautami's Grief

A woman called Kisagautami lost her only child. Her grief was heart rending. Some priests went to her and said, "Go to Shakyamuni : he can bring back your child". Kisagautami ran to Budha with the child's body. The priests thought that, when Buddha failed to restore the child to life, people would lose respect for him.

Kisagautami placed the child's body at his feel and said

"Mahatma this is my only child, Bring him back to life". Buddha was surprised. He saw through the game of the priests. He was unhappy. However he said to the woman; "Get up daughter will you do what I ask you to do"?

She said, "of course my father". "Daughter go and bring little mustard seed from a house which death has not visited".

Then Kisagautami went to the nearest house and begged for mustard seed, explaining what Buddha had said. The mistress of the house said" I would willingly gave you mustard seed, daughter but my parent in-laws are dead". It was the same story everywhere.

Realization dawned on Kisagautami now she saw what every one must die. She went back to Buddha now soothed bowed to Buddha and left with the child's body. The preists who were watching unseer disappeared.

The Elephant

Once Buddha was lost in Meditation in the Harinavana in Shravasti. Elsewhere Kootadanta and Devadatta were plotting to kill Buddha. After meditation Buddha and his disciples went around seeking alms. When they neared the city they split into three groups.

All of a sudden people saw an intoxicated Elephant charging down the road. The conspirators had chosen a powerful elephant, given it liquor and applied to its skin the juice leave which would create a burning sensation and let it loose. The mahout would pierce it with his hook every now and then. The enraged Elephant charged down the road. Buddha's disciples ran away in terror.

Buddha stood where he was, his face serene. The Elephant trumpeted. The Mahout again stabbed the animal. If came up to

Buddha and raised its front legs to crush Buddha the Master only smiled.

The animal dropped to its feet as if in obeisance, its eyes full of tears. Buddha now recognized the elephant-the very animal he had saved from the pond !. The Mahout was ashamed and revealed the conspiracy hatched by Buddha's enemies and begged for forgiveness.

The Middle Path

Buddha discovered from his own life eat the palace that too much of pleasure and comfort did not lead to happiness.

Having spent the first six years after leaving the palace performing austere penance he realized that extreme behaviour too does not help. He began to preach, the Middle path. He explained to his followers that whatever they did however they led their life, they Should do things in Moderation. He warned them against practicing severe penance and against indulging in material comforts.

The middle path was what Gautama advocated. Once again it was so simple and easy to follow, that the people began to model their lives around it. Buddha preached

* Right Thought
* Right Belief
* Right Speech
* Right Action
* Right Means of Livelihood
* Right Meditation

* Right Effort
* Right Remembrance of Memory.

Gautama Buddha asked the people to think good thoughts. He told them that if you think well of other and yourself, then speak only what is good and true, help others at all times, then the path to salvation is much easier. Gautama Buddha wanted his followers to believe in what was right and to spend at least some time every day in Medtation.

Buddha urged them to cultivate their memories and to put in their best efforts in order to accomplish any-thing. No goal can be achieved without a person doing his best with complete concentration and total dedication.

Buddha In Rajagriha

Buddha had promised Bimbisara that he would return to Rajagriha to enlighten him.

True to his word he visited Rajagriha. The King received Buddha with reverence and himself became his disciple. He gifted the spacious gardens known as Venuvana to the Master. The news reached Kapilavastu that Buddha had reached Rajagriha. He had been away from Kapilavastu for seven years. The old King and Queen and Yashodhara had been immersed in grief. From the day of Siddhartha's departure Yashodhara had given up wearing splendid dressed and jewels. Clad in simple wear she lived the life of a nun in the Palace.

Shuddhodana sent his Ministers to invite the Master and somehow prevail on him to visit Kapilavastu. Buddha agreed. The city rejoiced at the news. Thousands gathered joyfully to welcome him. Shuddhodana and his wife Prajapathi and every one in the Palace came to have his darshan. But Ya^hodhara did not come. Till that moment she was grief-stricken.

Buddha himself went to see her. She touched his feet tears streaming down her cheeks: His soothed her and shared with her the enlightenment he had recived. He stayed for a week in the gardens on the outskirts of the city. Yashodhara sent Rahula to receive his father's blessings.

During Buddha's stay in Kapilavastu large numbers became converts to Buddhism. Among them was Ananda, a cousin of Buddha. He followed the Master like his shadow to the end. After Shuddhodana's death Prajapathi and some other women desired to become sanyasins. Thrice they requested Buddha to permit them but he declined. But Ananda prevailed on the master to charge his mind. Five hundred women took to sanyasa with the Queen. They were the first nuns of Buddhism.

Buddha's glory soared day after day. This was a torment to Devadatta consumed by revenous envy. That those who belonged to the lowest castes were being absorbed into Buddhism added to his fury.

One day he heard that Buddha would be taking a particular route to Venuvana from Shravasti. He hid behind a boulder on top of a hill, and -pushed it down to Buddha, and his disciples appeared. But the boulder did not harm Buddha, but a cobra hiding under the bouldr bit Devadatta.

Devadatta who lost consciousness landed at the feet of Buddha. The compassionate lord himself sucked the poison from the wound and saved him. Devadatta was contrite and surrendered to Buddha.

Bimbisara's son Ajathashatru had joined hands with

Devadatta in his evil deeds. He had imprisoned his father and usurped the throne. He had starved Bimbisara to death. Buddha visited rajagriha and Ajatashatru became his disciple.

The Types of Salvation

Nirvana is salvation. It is a state of being. where the mind is at peace. The individual becomes tranquil and has no cravings. When a man attains nirvana he has no greed. He does not crave for money and power. He does not desire love and material possessions. He is happy with what he is and what he has.

Gautama Buddha preached the attainment of Nitrvana through the Middle Path. He believed that if a man lived by the guiding principles of the Eight-Fold Path, he would get salvation.

Buddha also preached that when a man attains salvation he is released from the chain of births and deaths, and hence Nirvana was an important goal to strive for. A man's life is governed by his actions. If a person does good, he will get the benefits of his good deeds.

In the same way if a person lives by evil actions, he will bear the consequences of his deeds at some time or he other. No man can escape the consequences of his actions-his Karma. Buddha believed very strongly in a man's Karma, both in this life as well as in future births.

In the Eight-Fold Path that Buddha preached he advised his followers to always do what was right. He helped them believe that their 'right behaviour' would directly or indirectly affect their karma. 'All life is sacred' said Gautama Buddha. 'It is cruel and consequently impious, to deprive a creature of life'. He was against the Killikng of animals and spoke strongly in favour of protecting all kinds of life.

Buddha criticized animal sacrifice. In fact he even carried a broomstick of sweep the ground before he walked so that he did not tread on any harmless creatures.

Gautama Buddha believed that a man must be compassionate. This compassion must be not only towatrds fellow human beings, but also to animals whether they are big or small-this is the path to the realization of God. Buddha held strong views on morality, believing that a benevolent religion included the right ideas in any individual. He wanted his followers to lead honest lives.

"Blessed the solitude of the man who
Knows truth
Blessed he who does evil
To no living creature,
And lives in compliance with the law !
Blessed he for whom all passion,
All desire have come to an end !
Vanquish one's self,
Such is the supreme bliss !"

In fact, it is on the side of morality that Buddhism is best known in the West. Buddha himself lived a highly moral life and excepted not only the ascetics, but also the layman to follow the five moral rulers :

i) to refrain from killing.

ii) to refrain from taking what is not given.

iii) to refrain from wrongful indulgence in the passions.

iv) ro refrain from lying, and

v) to refrain from intoxicants.

Conclusively, it can be said that the religion that Buddha preached had a deep seated tolerance which encouraged the moral behaviour of its believers.

According to Buddha, there is a basic equality among man. Man was born to live to harmony with his fellow-beings. He denounced caste and class systems of all Kinds. This was another aspect of Buddha's Philosophy which appealed to the people of ancient India. The poor and the lowly were attracted towards his religion. Because Hindusim ahd become too stepped in casteism.

Buddha did not see any difference between the castes. According to him, All castes met in his religion, as rivers run into the sea. He loved all men, whether they were Kings or show-makers, Brahmins or Shudras (untouchables).

Many times he refused invitations to the houses of rich people of high caste in order to visit the poor or those needed him more. When Buddha was questioned about the existence of God, he was silent. He did not denly the fact that there is a God, nor did he give any importance to a single, all important. Being.

Instead Buddha believed in 'Dharma'. He held that the whole universe was controlled by a universal law i.e .Dharma. Infact, these questions of God had troubled even the young Gautama. Before he renounced the palace, he said "I feel there is some power that governs everything, the world, the universe and all sorts of actions and ideas.

I understand that it is the soure of all thoughts that turn everything into thing into physical or occult entities. It is a great mystery and instead of working for the Kingdom, I shall prefer to understand the original source of light. If I succeed, I shall offer it for the service of mankind".

Gautama Buddha had no faith whatsoever in Yajna, sacrifice and ritualism. Since he believed in 'Ahimsa'. Buddha was against the sacrifice of animals, and he repeated again and again, the importance of life in any form. But, he did not believe that a life force existed even in inanimate objects like trees and plants. Though Gautama was a contemporary of Mahavira, he did not agree with Mahavira's belief in 'plants being alive'.

Buddha with Angulimala

There was a notorious brigand in Kosala Angulimala by name. He was a brutal robber; he would kill way. farers and cut of their thumbs, make a garland and wear them. The entire state trembled at the mention of this terrible monster. The King Prasenajit felt helpless and turned to Buddha for help.

Buddha decided to go to the forest in search of Angulimala. People warned him again and again that Angulimala was heartless and a monster, but Buddha bent his steps towards the forest.

Angulimala saw Buddha from a distance. He was happy that a victim was courting death. Sword in hand he came towards Buddha. The lord only looked at him; like one under a spell Angulimala suddenly halted in his track.

Before him was a majestic figure of serene of effulgence. The raised arm slowly descended. His mind was now in utter turmoil, he stood with bent head, his eyes fixed on the ground. He felt abashed. He threw aside his sword bent down and touched the feet of the Master. He begged him to accept him as his disciple.

Buddha's Philosophy

According to Hindu Mythology Gautama Buddha was the ninth incarnation of Lord Vishnu (who, it is said had ten incarnations or 'avatars'). He was also known as 'Sakya Singha' which meant 'the lion of the Sakya dynasty'. Born to the royal family of Kapilavastu, the young Gautama was a source of worry to his father.At an early age, the court astronomer had warned King Shuddhodana that his son would teach the world the path of peace and love.

Unlike other children of his age, the Prince had no interest in games. Even when he was married to Gopa, the beautiful daughter of Dandapani, the Prince would not accept his responsibilities.

Instead of paying attention to matters of the court, Siddhartha was pre-occupied with the problems of the world and the miseries of man-kind. He told his father and the Ministers, "Nothing is real in the world. And there is nothing that one should assume stable in any sense. Life is terribly momentary and is like the spark produced by the friction of stones. The light of life is extinguished very soon and no one can answer-where it came from or where it goes. It is like the sound of a lyre and even the wisest men of the world failed to understand the mystery of it".

According to the puranas* Vishnu's main aim in coming to this world as Buddha was to stop the sacrifices and unnecessary rituals that had been prescribed in the Vedas, and to destory the evil that had raised its head among men.

Legend has it that the demons wished to rule the world. When they approached Indira for help, He asked them to make sacrifices and to transform the soul with putrity. At once, they began to make arrangements for the sacrifice and for mass purification.

In the meanwhile the deities went to Lord Vishnu to ask for His help to control the situation. Moved by their please, Lord Vishnu went to the demons dressed as a Sanyasi named Buddha.

Vishnu's hair wasbraided in a knot on the top of his head. He wore flowing robes and held a broom in his hand. When the demons questioned him on his untidiness and the broom in his hand, Vishnu (in Buddha's form) told them that he has against ablutions (ceremonial washing. rituals), and that he carried the broom to sweep the ground before he walked. In this way he avoided stepping on harmless reptiles and other creatures.

When their questions had been answered, Buddha began to denounce animal sacrifice. He spoke strongly about the sanctity of life and told them that no living being had the right to take the life of another living creature-no individual could assume that he was superior and hence permitted to sacrifice another whom he considered inferior. All creatures were equal in the eyes of the Buddha. Lord Vishnu, in the avatar of Buddha was so passionate in his appeal against animal sacrifice that the demons were soon reduced to tears. They begged forgiveness for their actions and gave up the idea of performing sarifices and purification acts, to achieve material wealth. They accepted him as a compassionate Lord, who would lead them to higher glory with his infinite knowledge.

Buddha's philosophy, his beliefs and his doctrines grew into the religion we know today as Buddhism. This religion has given the world many famous structures.

The first great stone monuments were built at Sanchi in central India, almost three hundred years after Buddha's death. in about 220 BC.These were the Stupas put up by the Kings of the Maurya Dynasty. The stupas are dome-like constructions. They were mainly built of sandstone and contained relics of Gautama Buddha-the Great Teacher.

Besides their simplicity, the tonranas or gateways of the stupas have many small carvings which show aspects of the day-to day life of the Buddha and his followers. In fact the Sanchi stupa even shows a procession which was supposed to portray Gautama's departure from the palace.

One unique feature of this early Buddhist architecture was that the Buddha was never represented as a man. The Wheel or Chakra, his Footprints or Padukas and the Bodhi tree generally symbolized Buddha's presence.

Later however, artists in the far, Northern region of India began to give Buddha a human form almost 500 years after his death, the sculptors of Taxila and Gandhara began to portray the Enlightened one in their carvings. Artists in Mathura began to improve on the form given by those in Gandhara and Taxila. In fact it was they who gave the statues the finishing touch.

At last, the Buddha image Symbolized the very essence of the man ; they conveyed his true nature to all who saw them the compassion that Buddha had for his fellow-men was brought out completely. The inward-gazing eyes seemed to bring out his meditative powers. In fact the statues themselves are as Serene, Calm, and Tranquil as Gautama Buddha had always been.

Besides the stupas and the statues, the Buddhists contributed Monasteries or Viharas and Temples or Chaitya halls at many places. Amongst these, the most famous are at Ajanta and Ellora. It is said that "the Buddha has bequeathed to Indian are a rich tradition and a set of forms which provide the basis for the aesthetics of coming centuries".

The Moving Lamp of Supreme Knowledge

Buddha had been constantly on the move for forty-five

years, walking from village to village or city to city a moving Lamp of supreme knowledge, and serenity, the hope of Millions. He had shown his followmen the path of virtue and liberation from sufferings. He had brought hope into the lives of those who had lost all hope he had purified the lives of the worst sinners, and had returned love for hatred.

Age and strain had begun to tell on the physical frame the senses were no longer as keen as they used to be; Gradually his health failed. The Lord travelled from Vaishali to Rajagriha. For the first time in eight decades his health was causing concern. His disciples summoned the best physicians.

The chief physician was Jivakumara Brithya. He was the best of doctors, and also a devoted disciple of Buddha. He treated Buddha for four months but his health did not improve. Buddha preached to his disciples for the last time. Ananda realized that the master would soon be departing from the earth and could not bear the thought. He sat near the master nursing him with love and reverence. Buddha said to him.

"Ananda now I am assured you must be the Tathagatha, when the present Tatagatha departs. It deolves upon you to ensure that Buddhism does not decline and fade away but spread. Some people may denigrate our Sangha. Pay no held to such persons.

I am hopeful that you will guide the disciples on the right path. All of you be a light unto yourselves a refuge unto yourselves. Let the Dharma be your light your refuge naught else". He then fell silent.

The Five Precepts

1) I Voluntarily undertake the precept to abstain from killing.
2) I voluntarily undertake the precept to abstain from stealing

3) I Voluntarily undertake the precept to abstain from sexual misconduct.

4) I Voluntarily undertake the precept to abstain from lying.

5) I Voluntarily undertake the precept to abstain from intoxicating drinks.

To understand the way that Buddha pointed to, we have to understand his life. We have to look at his life and his teaching as one. His life is his message. As yet an young man, Siddhartha gave up a beautiful and loving wife, a darling child, loving parents, the throne, power, luxury and wealth; he did this in order to understand the Truth about life.

A wounded bird, a lamb about to be sacrificed-these seemingly insignificant creatures were important to him; he gave them his time, his concern and his effort. He accepted the invitation of a prostitute. Undaunted and unflinching, he faced an intoxicated Elephant and a heartless monstrous brigand,. His was a life of spotless purity, a life of active compassion.

Buddha made man responsible for the fruit fulness or futility of life. His teachings imply, You are yourself responsible for what you become, for what your life amounts to". No one is great or worthless by birth; birth means nothing. A man need not perform rituals and sacrifies and try to please the gods. No help of priests is needed. Introspection and self-realization are important.

A man cannot make his life meaningful and fruitful by sacrificing sheep or horse. He has to keep the light within bright. He must eschew Violence desire, Anger, Covetousness, Arrogance, Attachment and Envy. He must cultivate fearlessness. Above all he must be compassionate. He must help others. Life is full of sorrow. A man can overcome this sorrow by right thought right conduct and right living.

In Buddha's one day his message spread far and wide. Thousands became converts to the new faith. This naturally displeased and incensed the priest class.

Buddhism soon crossed the borders of India. Simhala (Sri Lanka of today), China, Tibet, Burma (Mayanmar). Indonesia, Sayam, Japan and several other countries welcomed the new faith. The life and the teachings of Buddha can be a light unto our times; they can be a light unto all times. In his own day he guided thousands of men and women to the path of peace.

King Ashoka, whose soul was tortured and tormented by the massacre in the Kalinga war and the agony of the living, found peace in the teachings of Buddha.

The Last Days

A man called Chanda begged him to have dinner at his house. When the Master returned from his house he became afflicted with diarrhoea. Yet he blessed Chanda, crossed the river Hiranya and entered a grove on the other bank. There was a marbie platform there between two Simshupa trees. The platform was strewn with flowers that the surrounding trees had shed.

The Tathagatha walked with slow steps. His Principle disciples walked with him. Ananda, Nanda, Angulimala, Upali, Moggala and others lifted Buddha and laid him on the marble platform, on a bed of flowers.

The villagers of Khushinara were all there for the last darshan. Now it was the full moon day of Vaishakha. Buddha was about to depart from this world between two Shimshupa trees ina grove. His face was serene, and his body radiant.

He called his beloved disciple Ananda and said. "Ananda, if any disciple has a doubt let him seek guidance for the last time". Those standing near and around Buddha were overwhelmed by grief. There was profound calm everywhere. In that silent serenity Buddha departed from this world.

Buddha expounded the Four Truths. The First Truth is suffering. Birth is suffering, decay is suffering, disease is suffering, death is suffering, contact with those we do not like and separation from those we like are suffering.

The Second Truth is the cause of suffering. The desire to live and to survive is the cause of suffering. The Third Truth is the Surcease of suffering. Suffering ends only when the deisre to live or survive, the craving for pleasure and the craving for rebirth are annihilated. The Fourth Truth is the Noble Eight Fold Path, which is explained below.

Buddha delivered his first sermon after attaining enlightenments at Saranath. This was the beginning of the dissemination of Buddha's message to mankind, and is, therefore, known as the Dharma Pravarthana Chakra. Desire is the root of all suffering. But man can find the path to Nirvana by developing his intellect through a life of utter purity and by overcoming desires unworthy of a man. A man's existence in this life is determined by his actions in an earlier birth.

Man's life is full of Suffering. But man can put an end to the sorrows of life. Men and women suffer and keep groping in the dark because they have not seen the light of Truth. This darkness has first to be dispelled. Desire which is the root of sorrow has to be relentlessly rooted out.

A Physician who has to treat a patient first of all makes an accurate diagnosis and then determines the method of treatment. Similarly first of all a man has to determine accurately the source of his disease, namely, Suffering. The path of Nirvana is the treatment. The man who finds this path transcends sorrow, disease and death. The bonds of earthly life can no longer bind him. There is an Eight-Fold Path to Nirvana.

The First of these is Samyak Drishti, that is, Right Understanding. A man has to understand correctly the Truths about man, the nature of human life and the goal of life. He has to realize that man's life on earth is full of sorrow, and that the goal of life is liberation from the cycle of births. This enables him to overcome obstacles and find and purse the path of True Happiness. A man has to understand the Four Noble Truths.

The Second of these Truths is Samyak Sankalpa, that is, Right Thought. The mind has to be disciplined so that it tends towards renunciation rather than acquisition, towards good will rather than friction, and towards friendliness rather than violnece. The mind has to be trained to be compassionate rather than cruel.

The Third of these Truths is Samyak Vacha, that is, Right Speech. One has to eschew falsehood and harsh speech. One has to learn to refrain from idle talk and slandering others. This is impossible without the cultivation of Right Thought.

The Fourth is Samyak Aajeeva, that is, Right Living, One should eschew evil habits, drinking, stealing, gambling and violence and all that is evil. One should lead an honest life. harming no one, and without indulging in bad habits. 'Samyak Aajeeva' is a good and clean life.